THE GENERAL

KENNETH BILBY

THE

GENERAL

DAVID SARNOFF

and the rise of the
communications industry

1817

HARPER & ROW, PUBLISHERS, New York

Cambridge, Philadelphia, San Francisco, Washington
London, Mexico City, São Paulo, Singapore, Sydney

TO JOANNE

FIRST EDITION

Designed by Ruth Bornschlegel
Copyedited by Mary Jane Alexander
Index by Maro Riofrancos

Library of Congress Cataloging-in-Publication Data

Bilby, Kenneth.
  The general: David Sarnoff and the rise of the
communications industry.

  Bibliography: p.
  Includes index.
  1. Sarnoff, David, 1891–1971. 2. Broadcasters—
United States—Biography. 3. Industrialists—United
States—Biography. 4. Radio Corporation of America—
History. I. Title.
HE8689.8.B55   1985   384.54'092'4 [B]   85-45621
ISBN 0-06-015568-X

86 87 88 89 90 RRD 10 9 8 7 6 5 4 3 2 1

Contents

Author's Note

I am indebted to the Harvard Business School for the stimulus that led me to write this book. Soon after David Sarnoff's death in 1971, the RCA Board of Directors voted to endow two interlocking professorships in his memory for studies in the management of technology, one at Harvard, the other at the adjoining Massachusetts Institute of Technology. As an associate of Sarnoff in RCA's management, I became involved with faculty members of both institutions in the planning of the new program, and particularly with Professor Richard Rosenbloom, who occupied the new David Sarnoff chair at the Harvard Business School.

In 1980, with the program well advanced, Dick Rosenbloom, who had also served as an associate dean and head of research at HBS, visited me in New York to inquire whether I would be interested in becoming an executive in residence at the school. My primary mission would be to research and write about Sarnoff's career and the industry he led, drawing upon the vast repository of business documents in the school's Baker Library.

I suspect Dick was motivated by perplexity. Little more than a decade had elapsed since illness had removed Sarnoff from RCA's affairs. Yet, Rosenbloom said, he was often confronted by students at the beginning of the school year with the question: "Who was David Sarnoff?" How could these bright young minds, he asked himself, be ignorant of the man's transforming impact on society? How could they flick on a color television set without realizing that Sarnoff was the shaper of the technology that made it possible? Why had his name not become the eponymic symbol of the early wireless age? I was puzzled too. Nearing retirement at RCA, I accepted the offer. Perhaps I could shed a little light.

My association with Sarnoff reached back nearly twenty years, first as an officer of NBC and later when I became an executive vice-president overseeing corporate affairs at the parent RCA. I was a member of his management council. In the 1960s, his final active years, we were together on an almost daily basis, usually beginning the day in his private barbershop and often lunching in his executive dining room. Together, we traveled all points of the compass, both in America and abroad. On the last of his many European tours, in 1967, we were with our wives, half vacationing, half inspecting RCA offices and manufacturing and research facilities in England, France, Germany, and Switzerland. Many of his reminiscences on the great industry battles attending the introduction of radio and television in America emerged from this month-long trip, which began and ended with shipboard crossings of the Atlantic. In his last major undertaking before becoming terminally ill, the preparation of the David Sarnoff Library, I was his associate. Together, through many days and nights in Princeton, New Jersey, we assembled and collated the visual and printed records of his long career, some of it personal detritus but much of enduring value for scholars of the era.

Arriving on February 1, 1981, at the campus on the banks of the Charles River in Boston, I was proffered all the assistance any aspiring writer could hope for—a comfortable office in Cotting and later in Morgan Hall, an expert secretary in Pauline Henault, two capable and energetic research assistants who were seniors at Harvard College, Mark Dean and Gaye Lister, a generous research budget for documentary probes in Baker Library and in adjoining libraries of the Boston-Cambridge educational complex. Perhaps the greatest assistance for one unschooled in the arts of biographical and historical composition came from faculty members who were trained business historians and who gave generously of their time and advice as I sought to construct a business profile of Sarnoff and early wireless communications. I feel particular gratitude to Professor Rosenbloom; to Professor Alfred D. Chandler, Jr., a Pulitzer Prize–winning historian; to Assistant Professor Margaret Graham; and to David Ewing, managing editor of the *Harvard Business Review*. Also, I owe special thanks to Mary Chatfield, Librarian, and her staff at Baker Library, for placing the resources of that remarkable institution at my disposal. It never ceased to astonish me that, after a thirty-year career at NBC and RCA, I first learned of the existence of the NBC Advisory Council and its significant role in early network broadcasting through minutes of its annual meetings that were on file deep in the bowels of Baker.

By 1983, with a year out to return to RCA at the request of its new chief executive officer, Thornton Bradshaw, I had completed my research and written a 250-page study of Sarnoff and the development of wireless communications for use at the Business School. It was then that Harriet Rubin, an editor at Harper & Row, approached me with the suggestion that I broaden this study into a book on Sarnoff and his industry for general publication.

In writing the book during the ensuing two years, I drew upon material in the Sarnoff Library in Princeton and upon the extensive Department of Information files in RCA's headquarters at 30 Rockefeller Plaza, New York City. I also drew upon the recollection of some of my senior colleagues at RCA who had shared part of the Sarnoff years with me. Yet I never sought permission from the company's management to write about RCA and its longtime leader. This, therefore, is not, as so many books about American business institutions are, an "authorized" volume, sanctioned, edited, and financially underwritten by management. Indeed, it is quite possible, even likely, that some of the conclusions I have drawn concerning Sarnoff's managerial style, and the causes of the chaotic upheaval that followed several years after his death, might not win the unanimous endorsement of current and prior RCA managers. The responsibility for everything set forth in the pages that follow is solely mine.

As a final personal note, I must acknowledge the help of my wife, Joanne. Herself a university teacher and trustee of many years' experience, the possessor of a Ph.D. degree in psychology and literature, a contributor to scholarly journals and books, she understood better than I the difficult dimensions of the writing assignment I undertook. Without her support and prodding encouragement, plus that of the gifted Ms. Rubin, the assignment probably would not have been completed.

Introduction

The electronics industry is a product of the twentieth century, with ante-cedents in the late nineteenth, when scientists of many nations began ex-ploring that minute particle of electrical energy known as the electron, one of the basic components of all matter. Over many fertile years of discovery and conceptualization, a new body of communications technology, based on the wireless transmission of electromagnetic waves, would emerge and would profoundly alter the patterns of civilized life, socially, economically, and politically. Its catalyst would be the electron.

Many companies and many individuals contributed to this vast trans-formation, which accelerated rapidly after the conclusion of World War I. But in America one company and one individual were at the forefront, pro-jected there by unique happenstance, and this book is devoted to the story of their rise, together with that of the industry they led through its crucial formative years.

Together, the company and the man shaped new concepts of commu-nications usage, pioneered new entrepreneurial patterns linking business and science, and provided an early role model for the high technology culture that followed. In two manifestations alone—radio and television—they, more than any others, induced the most basic reorientation of living patterns since the Industrial Revolution. They achieved their goals through years of bitter competitive struggles, at times risking dismemberment by the government and their competitors but seldom deviating from the Dionysian dictate that "those who have greater power and strength shall rule over those who have less." They seemed born for leadership.

Yet after the man had gone, the company dissipated its power, sometimes surrendering leadership to others more nimble in the marketplace, diffusing its technological strengths in a search for alien product lines, falling into a series of unseemly management squabbles that earned it, little more than sixty years after its founding, *Fortune* magazine's designation as one of America's worst managed companies. It was a company of paradoxes, as was the man who guided it to luminous heights and ruled it with iron purpose for thirty-five years. He did not live to witness its decline and subsequent brief revival—or its final envelopment, in one of the most stunning reversals of corporate history, into its own parental womb. Its long corporate journey, like the wanderings of Odysseus, would end where it began.

The company was the Radio Corporation of America, founded in 1919 at the instigation of the United States Navy to give the nation what it had lacked in World War I—an American-owned, international communications arm. Even though thus draped in a flag of patriotic purpose, RCA, as it soon became known, was in a sense conceived in sin—the sin of monopoly— since all the major patents of the emergent art of wireless communications were placed in a patent pool under its hegemony, which it shared with the companies who initially controlled most of its common and preferred stock— General Electric, Westinghouse, American Telephone and Telegraph, and United Fruit. This configured centralization of control over a new industry, unprecedented in that it was initiated and sanctioned by an arm of the American government, flouted the provisions of the Sherman Act and later forced RCA into years of unrelenting antitrust warfare against that same government. Yet its early patent strength provided the essential means for bringing order and rationalization to a wildcatting, patent-infringing radio industry that burst on the American scene with galvanic force in the early twenties. For RCA, patents underpinned leadership, first in radio, later in monochrome television and then, its crowning achievement, color television. From the fees of patents licensed to its competitors, it obtained the financial sinews to build the first great research laboratory dedicated solely to the electron, providing much of the inventive thrust that gave America a dominant position in consumer electronics until the mid-sixties, when the Japanese, having learned well from the RCA experience, began their successful invasion of world markets.

From the early thirties, when with government help it freed itself from the stock control of other companies, RCA was emblazoned on the industrial landscape, as well-known as any company in America. Not until IBM's dominance of the data processing world in the sixties did any major enterprise so exemplify the superiority of America's electronic technology. RCA was the vanguard company, the daring risk taker, operating always on the cutting edge, binding the nation through its creation of radio and television networks, building the transmitters and vacuum tubes and receivers that carried the desperately needed escapism of comedy and entertainment and information to a depression-scarred populace in the thirties and forties. For many years, it would boast in its slogans that it was a world leader in electronics, first in radio, first in television, and this was more than advertising hyperbole. For beyond leadership, RCA pioneered a new concept in the management of technology that to this day influences the nurturing and marketing of the proliferating offshoots of the electron, from Silicon Valley to Tokyo.

Even more improbable than the company was the man. David Sarnoff was a Russian Jewish immigrant, a product of New York's turn-of-the-century Lower East Side ghetto, a newspaper peddler and messenger boy, a grade school dropout, a skinny, pinched-face youth who never played games, who sang in synagogue choirs to support his impoverished family, who started at the bottom, a friendless Jew, in an industry, communications, known for its exclusionary anti-Semitic practices. Within three decades of his arrival in New York, when he spoke not a word of English, he had driven with remorseless purpose up through the executive ranks to the presidency of RCA, the bellwether company of the nation's fastest-growing industry. Within another ten years, he had become the dominant voice of that industry, its prophet of new products and services, its most listened-to voice in the councils of government, a friend of presidents and world statesmen, an internationally known baron of technology. Unlike virtually all his chief executive contemporaries, he consolidated his power without the leverage of stock control. He was neither the founder nor the possessor of a significant ownership interest in the company, never as much as a half of one percent. But he ruled longer, and without challenge, than most other industrialists who were. In the view of Owen D. Young, an early head of General Electric, his career provided the "most amazing romance" in business history.

America, of course, was a land built by immigrants, but none spanned the antipodes of culture, geography, language, and profession more swiftly and thoroughly than he. Apparently destined at birth to be a rabbi, he shed any spiritual aspirations when he first set foot in America at age nine. Almost immediately his family's main source of support, he developed a work ethic of total commitment that made his life in a sense narrow gauge, with no room for sports or recreation, the camaraderie of the country club, or for the theater or art museums or literature. Lacking formal education ("the world is my alma mater"), he taught himself the rudiments of the complex new electronic technology, mastered its jargon so that he could converse with and inspire its inventors and engineers. Almost alone among the corporate leaders of electronics, he knew what made the electron tick. He became as much at home in the laboratory as in the boardroom.

His personal transformation was as swift and complete as his professional. From the skinny boy who seldom laughed, he metamorphosed into a corpulent, immaculately dressed, manicured, barbered, massaged, chauffeur-driven, cigar-smoking corporate prince, poised and assured, a dominating presence whose steely blue eyes fixed on subordinates could bead their brows and moisten their palms. Some felt his ascent had been so rapid that he suffered a form of personality bends, his ego bursting to the surface before he could properly contain it. Like young Siegfried in *The Ring of the Nibelung*, he insisted that he never knew fear. He fancied himself the captain on the bridge, his guidance sure, his orders unassailable. In the view of one of his oldest and closest RCA associates, Elmer Engstrom, "he always had about him the air of a person who sensed that he was destined for greatness." To another associate, he fit Clare Boothe Luce's famous description of General Douglas MacArthur: "His egotism was of a magnitude that demanded obedience not only to his orders, but to his ideas and his person as well." Among the leaders of American history, Abraham Lincoln was the one he most identified with, not only because they shared humble origins but because they both possessed a monumental will to win.

Sarnoff believed his leadership qualities stemmed from his mother, Leah, who was descended from a long line of chief rabbis. In the Russia of his youth, the chief rabbi of a village was far more than a spiritual leader. His will was supreme in every aspect of living—from social customs, family responsibilities, schooling, and economics to dealing with external forces and arbitrating disputes between families and individuals. His early years were thus spent in an environment of absolutism, shaped by the spiritual dictates of an ancient orthodoxy and the external threat of a czarist Russia that despised and maligned his people. Survival depended on unity of purpose and obedience to authority. The wagons of his early years were constantly circled against the threat from alien ethnic strains. Thus he grew to equate security and well-being with strong leadership. And when he achieved leadership, he could never shake the childhood-imbued conviction that those who opposed him were his enemies, and that, whatever the surface reasons, the core of their enmity was his racial origin.

Much of his latter renown was shaped on his ability to foretell new trends in technology. He felt he was born with a percipient sense of the future, perhaps stimulated by his childhood immersion in the prophetic utterances of Hebraic literature. His birth coincided with the discovery of the electron, and as he matured he speculated endlessly on what new uses it could be put to. Through good fortune and his own resourcefulness, he became a youthful crony of the inventor of wireless communications, the Italian Guglielmo Marconi, and it was Marconi who, over many years, inspired and excited his desire to conceive of new careers for his "twin"— the electron—in home radio, black-and-white and color television, and in broadcasting networks that linked nations and continents. He boasted that he always looked only ahead. He quickly put the defeats he suffered in life behind him, seldom complaining and seldom explaining, and refocusing his sights on the electronic horizons. When Henry Luce, founder of the *Time* publishing empire, once described him as "David, our man of the future," he preened himself on the title.

Few people really knew Sarnoff well because he was never, in the popular jargon, one of the boys. And among those who did, or professed to, few were neutral. They either admired him extravagantly or disliked him. Perhaps this was because he was a nonneutral himself, quick to make judgments of whether people were "on his wavelength," as he described it. He seldom turned against those he liked, but once he did, whether a subordinate or a boyhood chum, it was almost impossible to revise his judgment. "Once you don't love the girl anymore, nothing she does can please you," he would explain. Loyalty, and particularly loyalty to him, was the cardinal virtue.

His feuds were numerous, often protracted and flamboyant. Eugene

McDonald, founder and head of Zenith Radio, a principal RCA competitor in consumer electronics, detested him. For years they hurled verbal slingshots at one another. To McDonald, Sarnoff was a monopolistic predator who played scheming "Russian tricks" to enforce RCA's illegal clutch on the industry. To Sarnoff, McDonald was a bloated "parasite" who feasted on the products of RCA research to build a huge consumer business and a personal fortune. Out of differences over the allocation of channels for broadcast services, he broke with one of his oldest friends, Edwin Howard Armstrong, one of radio's premier inventors. The issue was space in the ultrahigh frequency portion of the spectrum. Armstrong wanted it for the FM (frequency modulation) radio system he had invented, Sarnoff wanted it for television. A deadly personal feud developed, which was fought for years through the courts and was terminated only when the frustrated, embittered Armstrong hurled himself to his death from a courtyard window of his apartment in Manhattan's River House.

In reality, Sarnoff needed his enemies to keep him stimulated. Although physically sedentary, he possessed formidable reserves of nervous and intellectual energy, which were unleashed whenever a crisis loomed. In Engstrom's recollection, he was "never more alive" than during periods of intense industry conflict. In the rare interludes of peace during a long and combative career, he was sometimes bored. These were the times when he turned from more constructive pursuits to building an image of himself that was larger than life, even to reconstructing events of his early years in order to surround them with a purplish nimbus of heroism. His yearning was to be overwhelmingly visible in his adopted land, to belong to the establishment elite, to be accepted as an American of viceregal stature. As his successes mounted, he reached insatiably for publicity, for honorary degrees and parchment scrolls and medals. His psyche seemed to require certification of his greatness, an almost narcissistic need. In his waning years, he was on the glory road to a degree that discomfited some of his intimates. His associate and old friend David Lilienthal, once head of the Tennessee Valley Authority, found him more publicity-avid than anyone he had known.

Sarnoff played life in the Cyrano tradition, his finger always on the pulse of his audience. Whether speaking to a congressional committee, an RCA executive gathering, or a Waldorf grand ballroom banquet, he sensed what his audience would respond to, and he provided it, sometimes in humorous anecdotes, often through soaring rhetorical phrases that would move to cheers or tears. He early mastered his adopted English tongue, and he trained himself to speak it in the sonorous, reverberating tones of the orator. While there were sometimes fustian overtones in his rhetoric, he was capable of delivering alliterative metaphors that brought his subject matter to life. ("Radio, which made the world a whispering gallery, will turn it into a world of mirrors through television.") In his view, his speeches were the stuff of history, and he crafted them with infinite care, often devoting hours to chiseling a single phrase.

During most of his life he was onstage. The role he espoused was that of the farsighted and fearless leader of a new technology, and he surrounded himself with the plumage of his trade. His Manhattan town house was filled with the latest electronic gadgetry from RCA's laboratories, which he would explain to visiting statesmen or even Catholic cardinals. He loved to entertain guests in his skyscraper executive dining room by dialing a number on his telephone that would cause a wall painting to slide aside, revealing a mural television screen. He could also dial into the live channels of his broadcasting network, NBC, and monitor conversations between producers and correspondents. His limousine was one of the first in New York equipped with a wireless telephone. These were the toys he never had as a child.

In a curious sense, he was puritanical. He abhorred alcohol and those who imbibed it too freely. Given a choice between nesting with scorpions or participating in the aimless chitchat of a cocktail party, he probably would have agonized over the decision. Had he lived in Puritan times, he would never have been in the stocks for indulging in such frivolous pursuits as sporting contests on the Sabbath. Of the seven deadly sins, he considered sloth the worst. In Engstrom's understated view, "he pushed himself hard and expected others to do the same. He was not tolerant of poor performance." He was always slightly suspicious of those associates who devoted their weekends to golf and tennis and nineteenth-hole frivolities. Why would they waste life's precious hours in such aimless endeavors? In his moralistic approach to the work ethic, he possessed the zealotry of a Cotton Mather.

To many in the vast company he built who knew him only slightly, he became a remote, legendary, and somewhat fearsome figure. But to those who worked closely with him over the years, other facets of his character emerged. To them, he could be warm and earthily humorous, and he was solicitous of their well-being. When a young associate was caught in a stock option bind, Sarnoff offered to bail him out with his own money. He was tireless in helping scores of his relatives, many like himself immigrants, to find jobs, often within the RCA sphere, and in offering financial assistance. Giulio, son of his friend Marconi, found an immediate job haven at RCA on his arrival in America, and Sarnoff monitored his progress, took him on trips with his own family, and reported to his parents in Italy on how he was faring. He was married more than fifty years to one woman, French-born Lizette Hermant. The vital importance of family ties in a sometimes hostile and racially biased world was bred into him, and it never waned.

Of the seven deadly sins, he was most guilty of pride—a pride that in his later years became a form of extreme hubris, leading him into sometimes wasteful and fruitless ancillary pursuits. Out of World War II, in which he served in uniform briefly, he emerged with the one star of a brigadier general, and he soldered the title of General to his name as a permanent prefix. Even his family often referred to him as such. But the one star was not enough to satisfy his compulsive ego, and for over five years he pursued a relentless, but ultimately unsuccessful, search for the second star of a reserve major general. His sensitivity to criticism increased in direct proportion to his growth in renown. His irritation at the press, which on occasion seemed to enjoy pricking his pride, was often intense. His public relations staff became adept at writing letters of protest to errant editors.

But beneath the layers of plumage, the bravura poses, was a complex human being of infinite substance. His mind was sharp and penetrating, capable of cutting through layers of obfuscation and plunging to the core of a technical labyrinth. His memory was awesome. He was blessed, in Engstrom's words, with "a strong intuitive sense of what was right in business." Some called him a genius, but that, although he never denied it, is debatable. What is not debatable is that, to a unique degree among industrial leaders, he was attuned to the tumultuous era in which he lived, shrewd, farsighted, resolute, fearless, willing to bet his company and his career, as he occasionally did, on the dictates of his judgment. For thirteen years, against the unyielding opposition of government agencies, the courts, his industrial and broadcasting competitors, and the doubts of even some of his own colleagues, he battled to sell his color television technology to America. And he prevailed.

To most who followed his career, color television represented his supreme triumph. But, measured against the reach of history, that, too, is debatable. More than any other, he sensed the long-range implications of his new technology, the need to bridge the gulf between corporate management and science, the need to accompany the electron wherever it led. No longer, after him, would the old truism be applicable: build a better mousetrap and the world will beat a path to your door. He wouldn't wait for the world. He forced his mousetrap on it. In the informed opinion of his contemporary, Dr. Jerome Weisner, president of the Massachusetts Institute of Technology and scientific adviser to President Kennedy, he combined to a unique degree the qualities of "visionary, determined builder and hardheaded industrial leader." He was, in Weisner's words, among the first to recognize the role of science in modern industry "and to stake his future entirely on that promise." That was perhaps his most enduring contribution, and it is relevant today in any study of the communications industry, its growth and maturation.

Luck, Sarnoff often said, was an important factor in his career, and that was true. He was lucky to be born in tandem with the electron. He was lucky to arrive in America at the beginning of its greatest era of growth, which was made possible only by the unifying technology that absorbed his life. The America of his boyhood was little more than a decade removed from the bows and arrows of the western frontier. From Morse code telegraphy, laboriously hand-tapped by operators of whom he was one of the most expert, to ponderous transmitters hurling wireless signals across the Atlantic, to space communications of incredible sophistication that blanketed the globe via synchronous satellites, the new art that emerged during his lifetime was of enduring and transforming import. And more than any other man, he was the leader of its formative years.

To the contemporary business reader, Sarnoff's career offers various constructive insights into the evolution of American business management. He was perhaps the last of that remarkable strain of individualistic entrepreneurs—Rockefeller, Ford, Carnegie, Frick, Harriman were among them—whose autocratic governance of industrial oligarchies bruised the precepts of free competitive enterprise but spurred the tumultuous growth of the late nineteenth and early twentieth centuries in America.

A question that might be examined in graduate business schools today is whether electronic color television—the last major electronic consumer product to bear a made-in-America brand—would have responded to the quickened rhythms of invention and technical development that Sarnoff induced without his dominating, imperious management style.

A corollary question might be whether the much discussed decline in the nation's technological leadership in the latter twentieth century bears a relationship to the phase-out of Sarnoff-style management. Is the current crop of MBA-trained managers less inclined to risk taking, more concerned with financial controls, with acquisitions, mergers, and takeovers, than with the creation of new wealth through new technologies? Has absorption with quarter-by-quarter results on the bottom line replaced the desire to lead, shape, and inspire, as the sine qua non of American business?

Viewed from an international perspective, the question becomes whether foreign industrial leaders, most notably the Japanese, have preempted the Sarnoff approach to managing technology. Are they his true heirs in understanding the difficult cycle of technological gestation, in their willingness to accept setbacks, to return to the drawing board, to gamble capital and sacrifice quick profits, in order to achieve long-term goals? Japan's march to world dominance of the video recorder and cassette industry, a thirteen-year effort marred by repeated failures, bears remarkable resemblance to Sarnoff's lonely struggle to implant color television in America.

In accepting the Goethe Prize in 1930, Sigmund Freud said: "It is unavoidable that if we learn more about a great man's life, we shall also hear of occasions on which he has done no better than we, has in fact come nearer to us as a human being." It is in that spirit that this book has been written.

1 / *The Early Years*

Predawn on November 20, 1953, at the beginning of a tranquil Indian summer day in the New York metropolitan area, a twin-engine aircraft owned by the Radio Corporation of America touched down at its home base in Teterboro, New Jersey, returning David Sarnoff and a young associate from the state of Washington and signaling completion of one of the most satisfying missions of Sarnoff's long career. Two days earlier, he had joined Admiral Robert B. Carney, chief of United States Naval Operations, at Jim Creek Valley in the remote and rugged Cascade Mountains, fifty-five miles northeast of Seattle, twenty miles inland from Puget Sound. There they had jointly and triumphantly dedicated a radio station vastly more powerful than any ever built, a station that promised to provide the navy with a long-dreamed-of secure global wireless communications network.

The station had gestated slowly. Since early 1947, scores of RCA and naval engineers and technicians had labored on its design and construction at the RCA Victor Manufacturing Division in Camden, New Jersey. Its revolutionary centerpiece was a 1.2-million-watt transmitter whose VLF (very low frequency) signals were expected to reach naval land installations around the globe, and aircraft, submarines, and surface vessels on, below, and above the seven seas. More than twenty-two times as powerful as any American commercial radio station, the largest piece of electronic equipment ever built, the transmitter represented a new frontier in the emerging art of wireless transmission, capable of cracking through magnetic storms, virtually jamproof, capable even of defying the northern lights and other meteorological phenomena that had teased and frustrated early wireless operators, among them a youthful David Sarnoff.

To achieve this awesome capability, sufficient power had to be generated to meet the needs of a city of twenty-five thousand population. And the coded signals to be sent and received had to pass through a vast antenna array that consisted of fifty thousand yards of steel and copperweld cable stretched across six thousand acres of Jim Creek wilderness and coupled to twelve giant steel towers erected on its neighboring peaks in joint defiance of snowstorms, icestorms, and sweltering summer heat. Twenty-seven freight cars had been required to ship all the equipment from Camden to the northwest. In the view of RCA's engineers, Jim Creek represented one of the great macroengineering feats of the twentieth century.

But to Sarnoff, the meaning of the station extended beyond its size and power. First, it assured him that his company—and he—continued at the crest of the new technology of electronics. Beyond that, it possessed a deep personal significance. Viewing the vast complex for the first time, the day prior to handing it over to the navy on behalf of RCA, he told his associate: "This is my way of saying thanks." He meant to his adopted land, to America.

The flag-drenched dedication ceremony took place in a massive concrete transmitter building, with a naval band playing martial airs outside. Admirals abounded, as well as congressmen, Washington State leaders, and a large contingent of the nation's press flown in from major population centers by naval aircraft. The ceremony was structured as a blend of the old and the new—in effect a report on wireless communications' progress since the first transmission of electromagnetic signals by Sarnoff's old friend Guglielmo Marconi from his father's farm in Bologna, Italy, little more than a half century earlier. The bulging press kits distributed at the ceremony forged a spiritual kinship between Bologna and Jim Creek—and between the inventor Marconi and the industrialist Sarnoff.

In the first message from Jim Creek to fleet units around the globe, Admiral Carney described the installation as "a new security channel from America to the naval units which form its outer ramparts of defense." As he spoke, his words were tapped out in measured cadence by Sarnoff in Morse code at the modest rate of twenty words per minute. The telegraph key was the same one he had used forty-six years earlier when he was employed by the Marconi Wireless Company of America as a junior telegraph operator. This juxtaposition of the old and new, as naval and RCA publicists had hoped, commanded the interest of the visiting press. The *New York Times* reported on page one that Sarnoff, then sixty-two years of age, a familiar national figure as head of the Radio Corporation of America, and the widely acknowledged leader of the newly emerging television industry, still possessed the skilled telegrapher's "fist" of his youth. Acknowledgments of Carney's encoded message were received within minutes from a world apart—from the flagships of the Far Eastern and Mediterranean fleets, from the submarine *Sablewish* sheltered by polar ice caps in the northern Arctic, and from the cruiser *Pittsburgh* rounding Tierra del Fuego at the southern tip of Argentina. The *Times* also reported that many old-time ham operators, Sarnoff's contemporaries, picked up the dedicatory message and claimed they recognized at once his transmission style, still distinctive after four decades. After the ceremony, at a naval reception, the atmosphere of nostalgia heightened when Admiral Carney's wife recalled to Sarnoff that as a small girl in Italy, the daughter of a career American naval officer, she had been introduced to Marconi by her father and the great inventor had promptly perched her on his knee. To which Sarnoff swiftly replied that since Marconi had been his mentor and intimate friend, he would be happy to serve as the inventor's surrogate at a repeat of the ceremony.

Returning to New York after an eighteen-hour cross-country flight—including a stopover in Chicago for refueling and for a successful perusal of the newsstands in search of more Jim Creek stories—Sarnoff developed a heavy head cold, complete with running nose. For one of the few times in his life, at the urging of his companion, he gulped a tumbler of medicinal whiskey, grimacing as it went down, saying it reminded him of the foul-tasting cough syrup his mother used to force down his throat. But he was still buoyed by the depth and warmth of the press coverage and he was in a reminiscent mood, probably induced by the touch of his old telegraph key. So he suggested to his young associate, as they approached Manhattan from Teterboro, that they make a brief tour of the Lower East Side where much of his boyhood was spent.

In the fading early morning darkness, Sarnoff's chauffeured limousine bore them beneath the Hudson River by tunnel and thence downtown through winding and silent streets, passing under the dilapidated tracks of an elevated train and finally into a run-down low-rent apartment area, its streets potholed and congested with debris. This, Sarnoff said with a sweep of his hand, had been the heart of New York's teeming Jewish ghetto in the early twentieth century. With a sure sense of direction, as though a half century were only a pause in the calendar, he coached his chauffeur to an apartment site on Monroe Street. The cramped, wooden tenement home of his youth had been razed and replaced by a rather seedy low-income apartment dwelling, but it was here that he had begun his life in America.

The year was 1900, and David Sarnoff was nine years old.

His birthplace was Uzlian, a shtetl in Russia, in the province of Minsk, an area he later remembered as bleak beyond redemption. It was a pinpoint in the central fastness of the Russian pale in which the czars had sequestered their second-class Jewish subjects since the rule of Catherine the Great. Except for climatic differences and the presence of a dominating synagogue, Uzlian could have emerged in America's pioneering west. Its few hundred inhabitants lived in a cluster of ramshackle wooden houses facing on rutted and unpaved roads, lacking electricity, gaslight, interior plumbing, and any form of mechanized transport. Theirs was an isolated, theocratic enclave, remote from the political winds of change then gusting about the Romanoffs, ruled with doctrinal rigidity by a chief rabbi, linked to Russia only by occasional, and unwelcome, Cossack-accompanied visits of the regional tax authorities, or by the more frequent drunken incursions of bands of roving peasants.

In this remote environment, David was born on February 27, 1891, the eldest of five children, four boys and a girl, of Abraham and Leah Privin Sarnoff. The father, tall, bearded, and slender, possessed the high forehead and abstract gaze of a philosopher or poet. But he was neither, eking out a subsistence living for the family as a house painter and paperhanger. His frail physique was not designed to withstand the rigors of the long Uzlian winters, with temperatures reaching forty degrees below zero, and soon after his first son's birth he showed the initial symptoms of consumption. David's first memories of his father were of a withdrawn, gentle, but rather morose man with a hacking cough.

David always felt he drew the qualities of character and intellect that produced his extraordinary success in life from the genes of his mother. Leah Privin was descended from a long rabbinical line and was clearly the dominant influence in the upbringing of her family. Early photographs show a rather small, stout, brown-haired woman whose most arresting feature was a pair of widely spaced and penetrating eyes. Her expression seemed more resolute than intellectual, that of a woman determined to face and conquer whatever challenges life brought.

The Sarnoffs lived in one of Uzlian's indistinguishable frame houses, which Abraham had helped build. David's first memory was of building blocks, a gift from his mother and the only childhood toy he recalled ever receiving. Mainly, his early recollections were of books—theological and liturgical tomes, their covers scuffed and faded from generations of handling— that became the companions of his boyhood. He was small-boned and slender as a child, but possessed of an abundance of energy and an intellectual precocity that soon captured the attention of Uzlian's elders. By his fourth year, as he later recollected, he was comfortable with his mother tongue of Yiddish and was absorbing passages of the Old Testament in Hebrew. David was quickly assessed by his maternal grandfather, Rabbi Privkin, as prime rabbinical material, and all his reading assignments were directed toward that goal.

There was the Talmud to be mastered and other learned studies of the prophets. As the oldest of the scores of grandchildren of Rabbi Privkin and his indomitable wife, Rivke (Rebecca), David seemed fated by the dictates of primogeniture as well as his own early unfolding learning capacities to devote his life to the service of the God of his ancestors. Life was serious, life was a disciplined regimen imposed by the patriarch. "I guess I was hermetically sealed off from childhood," he commented in a rueful remembrance that morning in 1953. He never participated in organized games or childhood escapades in the village, or certainly none that left any lasting impression on his memory.

The sense of aloneness that stamped his boyhood was enhanced when David's father decided to emigrate to America to seek a better life for his increasing family. Abraham gambled that he could earn sufficient dollars as a paperhanger and painter to send for Leah and the children. He thus became part of the Jewish tide—nearly two million people within four decades— that flowed from Russia and eastern Europe to the fabled Golconda of the West, seeking escape from pogroms, enforced czarist military service of four years, and a standard of living little superior to that of Russia's peasant masses, only recently freed from generations of serfdom.

After a tearful farewell from his father, David moved with Leah and two younger brothers, Lew and Morris, into the larger frame house of the Privkins, already cramped by the presence of seven other Privkin daughters and a son, David's aunts and uncle. To relieve the congestion, David was soon farmed out for further intensive religious schooling in the home of a granduncle, a leading rabbi in the village of Korme, hundreds of miles from Uzlian in the region of Barisov. There he was the lone child in a household of religious elders who, while treating him kindly, were more concerned with questions of pilpulistic logic than with the balanced upbringing of a five-year-old.

For four years, from sunup to sundown, six days a week, David's life was devoted to study. The Talmud in Aramaic and the prophets in Hebrew consumed his waking hours. It was Uzlian compounded. Each day, he later contended, he was compelled to memorize an assigned two thousand words and repeat them to his granduncle before dinner, which was not forthcoming if he fell short. Only the Sabbath allowed him respite, and that was devoted primarily to religious services. During those four years he never saw a member of his immediate family, never knew a playmate of either sex, and never participated in any form of sport or other recreational activity.

In his 1953 view, reflecting on the sidewalk in front of his first New York home, the results of this extraordinary regimen were mixed. The retentive capacity he developed and the ability to combat fatigue over prolonged periods of intense mental exertion were, in his judgment, central to his professional achievements and particularly to his ability to analyze complex problems of technology and arrive at rational solutions. But those years also cheated him of the ability to enjoy many of life's amenities in adulthood, even when he could well afford them. He never developed an interest in sports, either as a participant or spectator. He never acquired a taste for classical literature, the graphic arts, or popular entertainment, whether on the Broadway stage, in motion pictures, or on the television sets he was so instrumental in bringing into the American home. Life to him was always a serious affair, not to be frittered away.

Perhaps even more significant, the years in Korme persuaded him that the rabbinate was not his calling. "Four years of the prophets was enough," he recalled that morning. "Maybe I was too young to take it in such massive doses, maybe there was a pragmatic streak in me, but I remember telling myself there had to be some better way to pay for my supper." Even the extreme orthodoxy of his upbringing was too much, and he converted to lukewarm Reform Judaism as an adult. Religion indeed became secondary to his other interests in life.

It took Abraham Sarnoff five long years, working at a variety of menial jobs on New York's Lower East Side, sharing a single room with three others in a slatternly boardinghouse, to acquire sufficient cash to underwrite the passage ($36 per person) of his family to America. David was nine, in 1900, when he was joyfully reunited with his mother in Uzlian and informed that the great trek west was about to begin.

Laden with hampers of prepared kosher food for the long sea voyage, plus linen, bedding, and household supplies, Leah and her three sons traveled by horse-drawn cart to the provincial capital of Minsk, where for the first time a wide-eyed David saw paved streets, multistoried buildings, and streetcars. He also witnessed something that repelled him—a Cossack charge against a large group of Russian citizens demonstrating for greater political freedom under Czar Nicholas. "I saw them lashing out with their whips, trampling women and children with their horse's hooves," he recalled. "It also trampled out of me any lingering feeling I might have had for Russia as my homeland."

In his latter years, when he read of himself as Russian-born, he involuntarily flinched at the term. Not that he attempted to conceal his origin, but he possessed no feeling for Russia as a nation, no understanding of its long, stressful history nor sympathy with its nationalistic aspirations, whether under the czars or the Communists. He had only passing acquaintance with its language and customs. Had the civic microcosm of Uzlian been dropped into the fastness of Outer Mongolia, Sarnoff's circumscribed boyhood would have been little changed.

This deeply ingrained distaste for Russia, which surfaced most conspicuously in the 1950s when Sarnoff became one of America's foremost cold warriors, a staunch adherent of John Foster Dulles' brinkmanship, led him in adult years to draw contrasts between his life and those of contemporaries in Russia who grew up to convulse their country in revolution. There was, for example, Vladimir Ilyich Ulyanov, later to be known as Lenin, who came from a secure and affluent family in Simbirsk; his father was a state councilor loyal to the czar and with the status of a minor noble, his mother of upper-middle-class parentage, her father a doctor and prosperous landholder. While the Sarnoffs struggled in Uzlian for bare subsistence, the Ulyanovs enjoyed a seemingly idyllic existence, a close-knit family of six children whose summers were spent at their grandparents' thousand-acre manor estate picking mushrooms and splashing in the river. The parents were devoted and benevolent, mediating childish quarrels. They also participated in games with their children, which would have bewildered Sarnoff. In his study of the physiological matrix of leadership, the historian James MacGregor Burns points out that there was nothing in the early life of Vladimir Ulyanov, whose first name meant "ruler of the world," to support the fashionable theory that great revolutionaries suffered from mother or father fixation, maladjusted childhood, youthful rebellion, or other signs of queerness or abnormality. Compared to Lenin, Sarnoff started far lower on life's rungs, and it gave him a perverse satisfaction in later years to limn the contrast.

From Minsk, Leah Sarnoff and her boys progressed to the port city of Libau on the Baltic Sea, where they boarded a small freighter for Liverpool, England, and thence transferred to a large steamship for the Atlantic crossing. Somehow, the family's hamper of kosher food got mixed up with the luggage, and David, who was standing on the deck, saw it disappearing into the hold. Reflexively, he plunged in after it and was fortunate enough to land, many feet below, on a soft bundle. A seaman threw a rope in after him and he was pulled out of the hold, dazed but clutching his hamper of food. "I still remember that seaman telling me, 'Boy, you're going to do alright in America,'" Sarnoff recalled.

Endless days in the fetid bowels of the storm-tossed vessel left David with another lasting memory—of "sweaty bodies close-packed and the stench of vomit." In his adult years, when he often crossed the Atlantic for diplomatic or business purposes, Sarnoff preferred travel by sea rather than air because he loved the contrast with that first voyage. He engaged first-class quarters on the upper deck, preferably the largest cabin suite. He measured his life's progress in that span between decks from steerage to the captain's table.

More than a month after their departure from Uzlian, the Sarnoffs landed in Montreal. They proceeded by coach train to Albany, and then by Hudson River steamboat to New York City, where, because of a garbled message, they spent an agonizing day searching for Abraham, who awaited them at a different pier. By nightfall, the steamship company had united them, but David, despite the joyousness of the occasion, was startled by his first sight of the stooped, gaunt, and graying man whom he scarcely recognized as his father.

An even greater shock awaited him when Abraham led them to their first American home. As the family entered Monroe Street, the stench of rotting garbage in a July heat wave almost overpowered him. The $10-a-month flat Abraham had rented was on the fourth floor of the dilapidated tenement structure, accessible only by a dark, grease-stained staircase. The apartment was known as a railroad flat because its three narrow rooms were in line like railroad cars. A single befouled toilet at the end of the stairwell hall served all the tenants on the floor. The flimsy building shook periodically from the rumble of passing elevated trains. The dispirited newcomers' tenement was in the heart of a ghetto neighborhood whose population density was greater than that of the worst London slums chronicled by Charles Dickens.

Fifty-three years later, returning from his Jim Creek triumph, Sarnoff stood in front of the site of his first American home in the November dawn. His eyes swept the neighborhood which, while improved by more modern apartment buildings and the addition of electric lights, still bore the unmistakable stamp of its menial heritage. Sarnoff was dressed in an immaculately tailored three-piece business suit, with suede gloves and a gray fedora hat. Puffing reflectively on a fresh cigar, he sought to recapture for his associate his feelings during his first few days in America. Initially he was overcome by despair. His ailing father was obviously incapable of supporting his family (which still had one son and one daughter to come). Beyond that, the sheer volume of compressed humanity depressed and overpowered the nine-year-old boy. He was conditioned to the solitude of small village life, and the strange mixture of tongues and cultures bordering and sometimes overlapping the Jewish ghetto—Irish and Italian and Slavic—left him with a sense of total alienness. "It was like being tossed into a whirlpool—a slum whirlpool—and left to sink or swim," he recalled.

But Sarnoff said that beyond the culture shock he was soon gripped by the vitality of his new environment. The brashness and freedom of children his own age was far removed from the studied discipline of his life in Korme. These young Americans played stickball games in the streets, brawled with one another in ethnic gang fights, stole rides on the backs of newly introduced electric streetcars, swam from piers on the Hudson and East rivers, and generally comported themselves with a degree of confidence and independence that Sarnoff envied. "Even the police were somewhat understanding," Sarnoff recalled. "We had no Cossacks to fear."

The turn-of-the-century America that became Sarnoff's home was in a period of turbulent transition, from gaslight to electricity, from horse-drawn carriages to combustion engines, from telegraphic communications to wireless, from the passionate isolation of its early years to an incipient imperialism in foreign affairs. Spurred on by the jingoism of its penny press, America savored its victory in the Spanish-American War. Only a year before Sarnoff's arrival, New York had welcomed the hero of Manila Bay, Admiral Dewey, with a ticker-tape parade up Broadway. In the White House, President William McKinley and his Rough Rider vice president, Theodore Roosevelt, spoke confidently of America's expansionist destiny. Great fortunes were being amassed in mining, fuels, automobiles and railroads, banking and merchandising. The Carnegies, Rockefellers, Harrimans, Fricks, Astors, and Goulds were creating a new aristocracy based on wealth. The seventy years spanning Sarnoff's career would see more change and innovation in America than in any country in any period of recorded history.

But in the immediate area of Monroe Street, not even a trickle of the new wealth had come down. Although sweatshops and child labor were theoretically curbed by new legislation, they still existed within the loosely defined boundaries of the East Side ghetto and in the Hell's Kitchen area, where his family later moved. Pennies, nickels, and dimes were the currency of exchange in a grinding atmosphere of poverty that Sarnoff said he never completely shed.

To the immigrant youth, life presented two immediate challenges: first, to earn some money so his family could survive and, second, to learn the language of America so he could more quickly be absorbed into its society. Within days of his arrival, he was hawking Yiddish-language newspapers in a competitive race with other boys. When bundles of the afternoon *Tageblatt* were delivered to an East Broadway station, David would vie with the others to get one of the first bundles and then run to his ghetto neighborhood to hawk them at a penny a copy. For every fifty sold, twenty-five cents went into the family coffers. He remembered himself then as thin and wiry and rather fleet of foot—"I got more exercise in two years as a newsboy than I got in the rest of my life." He also developed a routine for delivering the morning edition of the paper. The bundle was dropped off from the elevated train at 4 A.M.—"I schooled myself to awaken at the first sound of the approaching train. I'd throw on my pants and shirt and shoes and get to the street about the same time the bundle landed. Then I'd deliver them by running up and down the stairs of the various tenement buildings. It was great for the appetite."

In September, two months after his arrival, David was enrolled in an English language class for immigrants, regardless of age or grade. The intellectual discipline that he acquired in mastering Talmudic Hebrew stood him in good stead. At a far faster pace than his fellow students, he solved the spoken and written intricacies of his new tongue. By the end of the year 1900, he said he had a fairly passable English vocabulary. To supplement his class work, he searched waste bins for discarded English-language newspapers and read them in bed at night by gaslight. Throughout his life, he sought to prove the validity of the Hungarian phoneticist's comment in Shaw's *Pygmalion:* "Only foreigners who have been taught to speak English speak it well." Sarnoff soon came to feel an almost Churchillian reverence for his adopted tongue, and in his adult years he spoke it clearly and eloquently—occasionally a bit sententious and prolix, but always with unaccented fluidity.

From newsboy Sarnoff graduated to his own newsstand, employing other newsboys, including his younger brothers, to run his routes. He also supplemented his income by singing a boyish soprano for $1.50 a week at a neighboring synagogue. His father worked when his health permitted and when painting jobs were available, and the determined Leah augmented the family income by stitching and sewing. But it was David who to an even greater degree became the family provider while attending grade school during the day. At night he enrolled in classes at the Educational Alliance, an East Side settlement house that provided specialized instruction for young and old of all faiths, although its attendees were predominantly Jewish. Here he had his first exposure to platform speaking, which became an underpinning of his professional career. By the age of fourteen, he was confident enough to participate in his first debate on the topic: "Resolved: The United States should grant independence to the Philippines." His team took the affirmative and it won.

Sarnoff later valued the insights that the Educational Alliance, even more than the public schools, gave him into the melting pot that was then America. Many other immigrant enrollees achieved renown, including Governor Alfred E. Smith of New York, who became the Democratic presidential nominee in 1928; the celebrated comedian Eddie Cantor; and a nationally syndicated political columnist, George Sokolsky. In the last decade of his life, Sarnoff and members of his family endowed a building at the Alliance which was named after him and to which he bequeathed a bronzed head of himself sculpted by Jo Davidson. "It was at the Alliance that I first felt a sense of belonging," he recalled. He drew on its library for studies of America's heritage and its leaders, particularly Abraham Lincoln, whose log cabin heritage he linked to his own. He participated in seminars in its classrooms and meeting rooms, and witnessed dramatic presentations and speeches by political leaders in its auditorium, which seated seven hundred. Only its gymnasium and roof garden were bypassed; he didn't, he said, have time for such nonessentials of life.

At age fifteen, David had completed the eighth grade of elementary school, achieving consistently high marks and easily qualifying for a college preparatory school such as the nearby Townsend Harris High School. But coincidentally his father's health took a drastic turn for the worse, confining him to bed and requiring Leah's almost constant attendance to his needs. Upon David fell the principal responsibility for supporting a family that had grown to seven, and further schooling was out of the question. He concluded that what he needed was a regular job with a weekly paycheck of a known amount, so the family could budget its level of expenditures. And a job in a business that promised some hope of advancement and ultimate escape from the ghetto.

Sarnoff's first thought was journalism. There had been scarcely a day during his six years in America that he had not read a newspaper, first in Yiddish and soon in English. Writing and English had been his favorite subjects in school. The prospect of witnessing and describing great events, whether in America or distant lands, excited a youthful mind whose level of learning, ranging from the Old Testament prophets to the charge up San Juan Hill, was already exceptional in breadth of subject matter. Ultimately he envisaged himself as an editor or publisher, a successor to William Randolph Hearst or the flamboyant James Gordon Bennett, whose New York *Herald* was then a dominant force in metropolitan journalism. He would craft editorials that influenced or even shaped the course of national policy. Heady dreams for a fifteen-year-old, but total self-confidence and an unbridled imagination, two key qualities of character in his adult years, already were beginning to manifest themselves.

It was to Bennett's *Herald* that Sarnoff went by foot on a Saturday morning early in 1906, and it was to the same location that Sarnoff ordered his limousine forty-seven years later after completing the inspection of his ghetto home site. He said he could still recall his feelings as he trudged up to Herald Square, at 35th Street and Broadway, to the landmark brown-orange stucco building, then New York's tallest skyscraper, that housed the *Herald*. Any job would satisfy him, even the most menial, as long as it got his foot in the journalistic door. He felt little regret at the end of his formal education, in part because there was no practical way for him to continue but even more because of his growing desire to be a thoroughly assimilated American. Journalism seemed the best way to telescope that transition. Reporters had access to the great and powerful of the nation and to the inner workings of government. By being one, Sarnoff could learn more about the speech, the mannerisms, the personal qualities, even the dress, of America's leaders than a classroom could ever teach him. "More than anything in the world," he reminisced, "I wanted to rise above that ghetto background."

Dressed in his only suit and tie, the youthful Sarnoff entered the *Herald*'s lobby and approached the first man he saw, standing behind a wired screen window. He announced in a firm voice that he was interested in a job, any that the *Herald* had open. "Well," said the man, "you're in the wrong place. This is the Commercial Cable Company, not the *Herald*. But we are looking for a messenger boy. Do you think you can handle it?" The pay was five dollars weekly, with ten cents per hour for overtime. Without a second's pause, Sarnoff accepted. It was a regular job and it was in the environs of a newspaper.

The Commercial Cable Company, a tenant on the ground floor of the *Herald* building, was the American arm of a British firm that controlled the world's underseas cable traffic, linking New York with such capitals of the Western world as London, Paris, and Rome. And it handled the incoming dispatches of the *Herald*'s far-flung staff of foreign correspondents.

By the following Monday morning Sarnoff had donned a messenger's uniform and begun delivering cablegrams by bicycle to Manhattan customers. In addition, he hand-carried carbon copy "flimsies" of incoming news reports to the *Herald*'s bustling city room upstairs. Soon he became casually acquainted with some of the newspaper's staff. Yet he made no effort to shift jobs and become a newspaper copyboy, the accepted launching platform for future journalists. Why?

Over the gulf of years, Sarnoff recalled that the clacking of telegraph sounders lured him more than the staccato pounding of typewriters. He found something almost hypnotically appealing in the small telegraph keys transmitting living intelligence over vast distance, linking continents by code. One of his duties was cleaning up at night, filing copies of the day's incoming traffic in the proper bins, and often he found himself staying beyond closing, fascinated by the reports of great news events and commercial developments. He also began toying with the telegraph keys, the little "bugs" that sparked information electrically across vast oceans. Out of one of his first paychecks, which he normally turned over to his mother for household expenses, he sequestered two dollars to purchase his own key. Within weeks, he had mastered the Morse code and was tapping out messages in short bursts. Soon, some of the operators allowed him to sit in when they took short siestas, and he became sufficiently proficient to read incoming coded traffic at normal speeds. "It really wasn't that hard," the adult reflected. "I'd sometimes practice at night in bed. Or wake up a half hour before the El train delivered my morning papers. It was more fun than work."

But the fun lasted only a few months. While working as a messenger, Sarnoff also moonlighted at his newspaper jobs and on the Sabbath by singing in the synagogue choir. His still boyish soprano was in particular demand for services during the high holy days of Yom Kippur and Rosh Hashanah, and he asked Commercial Cable's office manager for a three-day leave of absence without pay. He was refused, and when he insisted he was peremptorily fired—for the first and only time in his career.

From the vantage point of 1953, it wasn't that much of a blow. With the limousine parked in Herald Square, and with dawn glowing faintly over the city, the tycoon said he shed no tears because he now had the crutch of a professional capability to lean on. He considered himself a qualified junior telegraph operator, and the older cable operators with whom he had worked would, he was sure, guide him to other openings. The cable field had recently been augmented by the development of wireless telegraphy, which embraced both transatlantic and ship-to-shore communications. Only five years had elapsed since Marconi had constructed a wireless transmitter on the English coast at Cornwall and then traveled to Newfoundland, where an antenna borne aloft by kites had picked up the letter s transmitted from Cornwall. Two years later President Theodore Roosevelt and King Edward VII of England were exchanging greetings via a Marconi station in England and another at South Wellfleet on Cape Cod, Massachusetts. A small American Marconi branch, offshoot of the parent English company, was soliciting commercial wireless messages from an office at 27 William Street in Manhattan's financial district. It was here that Sarnoff, on the advice of his former cable associates, appeared on September 30, 1906, to seek work as a junior operator, his telegraph key in hand, again garbed in his only suit and tie, hair severely brushed back to simulate maturity.

George De Sousa, traffic manager at the Marconi office, seemed more amused than annoyed by the bravado of the short, skinny fifteen-year-old with the piercing blue eyes and the determined chin. "Could you use a man as a junior operator?" the youth asked, and the man parked at Herald Square still remembered the benign smile of response. "We don't need a man," De

Sousa said, "but we could use an office boy." The pay was $5.50 weekly, with no overtime. Again, without pause, Sarnoff accepted, thus shifting allegiance from cable telegraphy to the newer and more rapidly growing wireless field, although at the same low entry level. Even more strongly now, he responded to the lure and the mystery of this empyrean art, which seemed to his youthful mind as awesome as the firmaments themselves. Like most avid newspaper readers, he was generally familiar with the exploits of Marconi, who had become somewhat of a cult hero to the penny press, often compared with Thomas Alva Edison and Alexander Graham Bell for his inventive genius. And although Marconi was not aware of it, he soon became the subject of an intense scrutiny by his newest employee, who pursued him in newspaper morgues and library files. After all, Sarnoff reasoned, they were now associates.

Marconi, in fact, was not far removed from Sarnoff's generation, only seventeen years his senior. He was reared on his family's small estate, Villa Grifone, on the outskirts of Bologna, where his father earned a comfortable living cultivating silkworms. Like Sarnoff's, his parental alliance was strongest with his Irish-born mother, Annie. He was indifferent to his father's business, refused his entreaties to enter a university or the naval academy, and devoted endless hours to reclusive study in the family's well-stocked library, which contained numerous reports of experiments in electricity by European scientists in the 1880s. He had just turned twenty when he read, in 1894, a newspaper obituary of the German scientist Heinrich Hertz, who had demonstrated seven years earlier the existence of electromagnetic waves in the atmosphere. His imagination fired, Marconi determined to demonstrate that intelligence could be borne over those airwaves. In the family attic, amid trays of silkworms, he built a crude spark transmitter, a telegraph key, and a wire antenna. Working far into the night, ignoring the entreaties of his fretful father to come to dinner, Marconi sought to ring a bell at the other end of the room. One night he called his mother to the attic in a high state of excitement to witness a spontaneous demonstration. As he tapped the Morse key, the bell sounded. There was nothing between them but air.

As he related Marconi's triumph, the man in the limousine said he had found the first true hero of his life. He sought parallels between them: they were neither college educated, both were intuitive self-starters, both indifferent to obstacles. A statement by Marconi, in particular, captured his imagination. "My chief trouble," Marconi wrote, "was that the idea was so elementary, so simple in logic, that it seemed difficult for me to believe that no one else had thought of putting it into practice." Sarnoff repeated it by rote that morning in 1953, almost reverentially. As the great battles of his life unfolded, the challenges to the types of technology he espoused, Sarnoff loved to play back those words.

From his attic, Marconi commandeered his backyard for further experiments, employing longer antenna strands to achieve greater distances. By 1895, his wireless signals were reaching beyond a mile; a year later, with the encouragement of his mother's English friends, he was in London demonstrating wireless to the British government. England was the nerve center of the world's cable communications, and Marconi applied there for the first wireless patent, which was granted in 1896, when the five-year-old Sarnoff was immersed in the prophets at Korme. A year later, when Marconi was twenty-four, he founded, with British capital, the Marconi company, of which the inventor was a principal shareholder and chief research scientist. It evolved as an international wireless concern after the success of the transatlantic experiment, and a new era in communications began.

By 1906, when Sarnoff entered his employ, Marconi was an international figure of high renown, soon to be awarded the Nobel Prize for physics and soon to receive the Knight Grand Cross of the Royal Victorian Order from King George V of England. As the new office boy began his duties—sweeping floors, dusting wireless equipment, emptying wastebaskets, running errands, filing correspondence, and announcing callers—Marconi had replaced Hearst and Bennett as the figure he would emulate. Sarnoff, of course, had never met the inventor, but from his first day at Marconi he said he planned and schemed to do so.

Three hours after it began in the lower Manhattan ghetto, the 1953 limousine tour ended at the seventeen-room Sarnoff town house on East 71st Street in the residential epicenter of the city's rich and powerful. Despite the hours without sleep and the nagging head cold, Sarnoff seemed refreshed and content, and almost reluctant to see the journey conclude. He stood on the sidewalk, his glance sweeping over the imposing facade of his five-story home. "I'll enjoy it more because of our little trip," he said by way of good-bye.

2 / The Sorcerer's Apprentice

The fifteen-year-old office boy who reported for work at the Manhattan headquarters of American Marconi on September 30, 1906, was only eight years older than the company itself, and both were of impoverished stock. The American branch had struggled since its inception to create an awareness of its nascent wireless service. It had installed equipment on four ships— the *New York,* the *Philadelphia,* the *St. Paul,* and the *St. Louis*—and it operated a network of four coastal wireless stations—at Sea Gate and Sagaponack in New York, and at Siasconset and South Wellfleet in Massachusetts. But it had yet to win serious acceptance in America's maritime industry, and it was profitless.

The problem in part was the unsettled state of the wireless art. Scientists from many nations were engaged in a race to improve on Marconi's basic discovery. Since 1901, not only the dots and dashes of the Morse code but the human voice itself had been transmitted without wires. A Canadian-born scientist, Dr. Reginald Fessenden, was responsible for this continuous wave transmission, which he first achieved in his Pittsburgh laboratory. Four years later, on Christmas Eve, wireless operators on vessels in the middle of the Atlantic were startled to hear, between the dots and dashes, a man reading poetry and a woman singing Christmas carols. The transmissions originated from Fessenden's experimental wireless station at Brant Rock, Massachusetts. Another American inventor, Dr. Lee De Forest, had applied for a patent on an Audion tube, which enormously increased wireless signal amplification and which later became one of the key building blocks in the development of home radio reception. At the conclusion of the Russo-Japanese war in 1905, seven different wireless systems were in use at the front to transmit the dispatches of foreign correspondents. New wireless enterprises were spreading through Europe and America, and often they were undercapitalized, poorly structured, and in violation of patent rights. Infringement litigation, commercial bribery, and bankruptcies became commonplace. Even the English Marconi company, possessor of more basic patents than any of its twenty competitors, and the most prestigious because of the inventor's personal fame, had yet to reward its stockholders with a dividend.

The parlous balance sheet of its American offshoot was quickly brought home to young Sarnoff. One of his first jobs was to call on friends of his new boss and general manager, an Irishman named James Bottomley, to pick up cash loans that were occasionally required to meet the weekly Saturday payroll. The entire staff of the American company—telegraph operators, traffic administrators, and salesmen—numbered fewer than a dozen. Any task that was unassigned or unbudgeted fell to the newcomer, who quickly became the office factotum. When Marconi-equipped ships visited the port of New York, Sarnoff would board them with spare parts and assist their wireless operators in repair work. He became the custodian of the company's technical library and when not occupied sweeping floors or running out for sandwiches, or during off hours, he would browse in it. He soon became adept at the jargon of the trade, and he probed for opportunities to display his new skill as a telegrapher. Whenever operators at Sea Gate or Sagaponack reported in ill, he volunteered to replace them, and occasionally he was permitted to. Within months of his arrival, Sarnoff's two principals, Bottomley and commercial manager George De Sousa, were conceding to themselves that this youngster with the insatiable curiosity and the inexhaustible energy possessed capabilities that dwarfed his years and his paycheck.

The encounter that Sarnoff had fantasized since his first day at Marconi became a reality in December of 1906, when he was studying technical papers one night at the William Street office. He noticed the unheralded arrival of a slender and immaculately dressed man who looked vaguely familiar to him. Sarnoff asked an operator if he knew the stranger, and the response electrified him: "He's the man who makes the lightning." It was Marconi himself, the fabled inventor, the sorcerer of the airwaves as the penny press had dubbed him, making one of those frequent visits to America that had begun soon after the success of his first transatlantic wireless test and the founding of his American wireless subsidiary. The youngster watched with awed fixation as Marconi, dressed in a tailored gray suit with matching fedora, spats, and a walking cane, moved easily from one operator's post to the next, inquiring in fluent English about the quality and volume of transmissions and receptions, exchanging technical comments, asking after the health of wives and children. Then Sarnoff overheard his idol mention to Bottomley that he was en route to his Manhattan office on Front Street, and the office boy determined to trail him. He would see for himself the fount of Marconi's technical work in America and, somehow, he would introduce himself.

When Marconi unlocked the Front Street office, he was startled by the sudden emergence out of the shadows of a youth with right hand outstretched. It was Sarnoff, announcing himself as Signore Marconi's newest American employee. Despite the suddenness and the brashness of the confrontation, the inventor accepted the proffered hand. Something in the boy's respectful and gravely forthright demeanor apparently struck a responsive chord, and he was invited to accompany Marconi inside the office. There the story of the exodus from Russia, the ghetto upbringing, the determination to become a wireless telegraph operator poured out of the youngster, and Marconi listened attentively. A brief tour of the office followed, coupled with an invitation to Sarnoff to avail himself of Marconi's technical files in his spare time.

In later years, when Sarnoff recounted the story of the first meeting, his friends often expressed incredulity that immediate rapport could have been established between two individuals across a generational, cultural, and professional chasm of such vast proportions. To which Sarnoff invariably responded, "We were on the same wavelength." By that he meant they were transmitting and receiving human wireless impulses to which each was attuned. He could not explain it technically, but he was persuaded that such transmissions existed. Throughout his life, Sarnoff explained his affinity for certain people and his distaste for others through the wavelength metaphor.

Having at last established a link with his hero, Sarnoff was determined to nurture it. Before leaving the Front Street office, he volunteered to run messages for Marconi during his American visit—and his timing happened to be fortuitous. The inventor was, in fact, then in acute need of a messenger service, and it was a service of even greater scope than Sarnoff had envisaged. The combination of his newly acquired fame, his aquiline good looks, and his rather shy aristocratic bearing had made Marconi an irresistible target for the opposite sex, and he was not unresponsive. During his frequent New York visits, he had cut a wide swath among American ladies perhaps unmatched by any foreigner except England's Prince of Wales. So Sarnoff found himself during the next few days, and on subsequent Marconi visits, busily occupied in bicycling between flower shops and East Side apartments and town houses, convoying large bouquets and boxes of candy to which were attached handwritten notes from the inventor.

Sarnoff reveled in this new responsibility, assuming quite shrewdly that the inventor would never have entrusted him with such delicate missions unless he was confident of the messenger's discretion and judgment. And it enabled him quickly to become much more than just another youthful face to Marconi. On later visits, Sarnoff was invited to join the inventor when he was in residence at Front Street, and even when Marconi was not there Sarnoff felt free to accept the invitation to study the technical files. His youthful curiosity seemed to remind the inventor of his own childhood, and perplexed older Marconi employees began overhearing conversations between the man and the boy on the mystery of static or the propagation characteristics of electromagnetic waves. Sarnoff became known as Marconi's American apprentice, carrying his dispatch case, arranging his appointments, even hailing transportation for him. Nothing was too menial. In later remembrance, Sarnoff said those months of early exposure to Marconi implanted in him an awareness of the potential of technology and, even more, a respect for the mystery of science. "David, we know how things work, but we don't know why they work," the inventor once told him, and he never forgot it.

Within a year of his employment at American Marconi, and a few months after his sixteenth birthday, Sarnoff was graduated to the position he had originally sought. With the inventor's personal endorsement, he was promoted to junior wireless telegraph operator, and his salary vaulted to $7.50 weekly. At a time when a nickel bought a beer and a sandwich, he considered it substantial. But more than the money, his ascension into professional ranks made the transition a milestone in his life. It was a step further away from the ghetto, and as if to solidify this break with the past, he sold his newsstand, which he had been overseeing in the evenings, and turned over his remaining newspaper routes to his younger brothers. And within a few months, he made the transition more complete by moving his family out of Hell's Kitchen to a walk-up apartment in a five-story building on Thatford Avenue in the Brownsville section of Brooklyn.

Sarnoff's career satisfaction was soon tempered by the death of his father. During the year that David became an operator, Abraham lost his long struggle with consumption and slipped from life as quietly and unobtrusively as he had lived it. It was not unexpected, and his eldest son's principal emotion was sadness—sadness at a pain-strewn and unfulfilled life, sadness that at age sixteen he had been unable to provide the amenities of life that were beyond his father's reach. But David also realized pragmatically that it was a burden removed, and he experienced no aching void at the departure of a man he had never really been close to. Besides, he now had, in Marconi, the father figure that Abraham had never been—someone he could look up to and revere.

One of the junior telegrapher's first assignments was to serve as a substitute operator for an Atlantic crossing of the steamship *New York*. For fifteen days, wearing the uniform of a ship's officer, living in his own cabin, Sarnoff maintained wireless contact with other ships and with Marconi stations in America and England. It was just seven years since his crossing in steerage, and the contrast made the man-boy euphoric. Soon after his return he had a chance encounter with some schoolmates from his ghetto years. They were then in high school, laden with textbooks, and he felt infinitely their superior, at least a generation advanced.

Nevertheless, Sarnoff recognized the serious gap in his own formal education, and in 1908, when he was seventeen, he volunteered for wireless duty at the remote Marconi station at Siasconset on the offshore Massachusetts island of Nantucket. His primary reason was the station's excellent technical library, which he felt could serve as a substitute for high school. And the salary, because of the isolated nature of the duty, was seventy dollars per month, more than double his current wage. There were three other operators on duty at Siasconset, all men at least twice his age, and aloof in their response to his arrival. In a sense, it was a reversion to his four years in Korme; he was surrounded by people of another generation in a remote area, with only work and study to occupy him. Apart from the technical library, he took a correspondence course in algebra, geometry, and trigonometry. On his off days, he bicycled seven miles to the Nantucket village library for supplemental reading on American history and culture. A picture on a bicycle taken at the time shows a scrawny young man, brown hair close cropped, the thin and determined face looking severely ahead, without the hint of a smile.

Besides education, Siasconset provided Sarnoff the opportunity to hone his increasingly formidable telegraphic skills. The station was the principal gateway for traffic between Europe and America and a vital wireless link to ships beyond the range of the New York stations. Speed and accuracy were essential to cope with an expanding volume of transmitted and received messages, and Sarnoff's quick fist, the cadenced flow of dots and dashes from his telegraphic key, made his style distinctive and his reputation equal to the most senior operators' on the Atlantic network. His progress was monitored closely in New York by Bottomley and in London by Marconi and was rewarded after eighteen months at Siasconset by his recall to New York to become manager, or chief operator, of the Sea Gate station. Ironically, because it was not considered hardship duty, Sarnoff's promotion cost him a ten-dollar cut in salary. But now he was in charge of other operators, all his senior in years, and at the age of eighteen the youngest chief operator in the worldwide organization. At Sea Gate he experienced his first taste of giving orders and issuing directives to others. Until then, his interest had centered on the technical aspects of the business—the theory of wireless, and how the equipment functioned and how to repair it—and the prospect of pushing papers at a desk had seemed distasteful to him. But as a manager he soon found his ego responding to the seductive call of authority, and his thoughts of the future began focusing on broader horizons.

After a year of managing Sea Gate, Sarnoff felt he had crossed the executive threshold and was securely wedded to the Marconi hierarchy. His relationship with the inventor was refreshed and strengthened on each of Marconi's American visits. The Sea Gate station's ship-to-shore wireless traffic had increased 30 percent during his tenure, and American Marconi itself was emerging from the fiscal wilderness because of a burst of orders from the U.S. Navy for wireless equipment for its fleet. The path to growing executive responsibility in a growth industry seemed clearly delineated to the ambitious young man. Yet he deviated from it in uncharacteristic fashion, and for reasons that were never quite clear even to himself. One night, on a visit to the William Street office, he noticed on the bulletin board an appeal for a volunteer Marconi wireless operator on a seal-hunting expedition to the Arctic. Sarnoff still retained a boyish ardor for adventure, the sense of exploring something new that had attracted him to wireless initially, and he was stirred by the prospect. Impulsively, he volunteered and simultaneously resigned as manager of the Sea Gate station but not as a Marconi employee.

This time there was not the rationale of undisturbed study in a technical library to lure him. Perhaps it was the prospect of recognition as a pioneer wireless operator in the Arctic ice fields; perhaps the opportunity to impress a young lady from his Brooklyn neighborhood whom he had been dating, although not seriously. Whatever, he journeyed to St. John's, Newfoundland, to board the *Beothic,* the same vessel on which Dr. Frederick Cook had made his dramatic dash for the North Pole, and promptly installed and tested its wireless equipment. He was accorded the rank of a ship's officer, and a picture of him taken by his own camera as the *Beothic* entered Arctic waters showed an anything but heroic figure—a thin youngster perched on a pile of tarpaulins, his oversize officer's cap nearly eclipsing the determined look on the boyish face. He seemed nearer sixteen than twenty, which was the birthday he celebrated on February 27, when the seal hunt was in progress.

The Arctic trip assumed special significance to later chroniclers of the Sarnoff career because, for the first and only time in his life, he kept a diary. Written in pencil because ink froze in the subzero temperatures, in the same bold, free-flowing, and highly legible hand of his mature years, the diary provided the first indication of the high sense of drama that Sarnoff would later attach to every aspect of his life. It also revealed an attention to sentence structure and to graphic and alliterative phrasing quite remarkable for one of his age whose exposure to English scarcely exceeded ten years. And it was replete with tales of peril in which Sarnoff prominently figured. He wrote, for example, of a Sunday, when the killing of seals was forbidden and the crew rested out of respect for the Sabbath. He and other crew members were watching a family of seals disport themselves on the ice floes below, and he was seized by the desire for close-up pictures. So he disembarked and moved over the densely packed floes to within a few feet of the seals. Suddenly the father seal, his huge bulk moving with surprisingly alacrity, charged the intruder.

"I took to my heels and ran," Sarnoff wrote, "but I had sufficient presence of mind to follow a zigzag course. This gave me a slight advantage because it was difficult for my pursuer to twist his big body at every turn. I had progressed only a few feet and the seal, with murder in his eyes, was gaining on me. But the strongest man could not hold out long on the jagged, slippery ice. I was near exhaustion. My breath came in gasps and my knees shook.

"Suddenly a shot rang clear in the Arctic air. While the crew had watched my plight with awful fascination, one of the sailors had dared break the Sabbath law and shoot the seal. I think the captain believed privately that it would have been better if I died a martyr to the law, but the man was never punished and all the men aboard heartily approved his action, none more heartily than I."

Other tales of Bunyanesque youthful daring cropped up in the diary. The wireless equipment on a nearby sister ship broke down and Sarnoff volunteered to cross the treacherous ice floes, accompanied by the ship's doctor, on a repair mission. Dusk was falling, with gale winds whipping up, as they prepared to return after Sarnoff had restored the wireless to working condition. "At every step of the way," he wrote, "we fell in the water, grabbing the ice en route which, after we had again mounted it, promptly broke in half and gave us another thorough ducking." Finally, members of the *Beothic*'s crew experienced in navigating ice floes were dispatched to rescue them, and the two men, half drowned and frozen, were carried back to the mother ship.

As the *Beothic* returned after six weeks in the Arctic, more dramatics were captured in the diary. Sarnoff picked up a wireless message from a ship one hundred miles away reporting that a sailor had suffered serious internal injuries and there was no doctor aboard. He promptly asked for details of the injuries and then relayed, over several days, instructions from the *Beothic*'s doctor on appropriate treatment. The sailor recovered.

In his report of the voyage to his Marconi superiors, Sarnoff compiled an impressive dossier of wireless accomplishments. The scattered ships of the sealing fleet had maintained continuous contact in the Arctic, advising one another where the hunting was best or where the seal herds had been depleted. The *Beothic*'s cargo holds were jammed with a record thirty-six thousand seals, and the impressed fleet owners negotiated with Sarnoff a deal for the permanent installation and servicing of Marconi equipment on all their ships. It was his first commercial contract.

Flushed with this achievement, Sarnoff was determined to recapture a position at least equal to Sea Gate in organizational prominence. The opportunity arose when the John Wanamaker department stores installed Marconi wireless stations atop their Philadelphia and downtown New York branches. The wireless link between them was intended to provide information on inventories, pricing, and sales, but its primary purpose was promotional—to lure customers to the stores by appealing to public curiosity over wireless. Sarnoff grasped at the opportunity to manage the New York station, not only because of its high public visibility but because the station kept the same daytime hours as the stores. This freed his nights for further study, and he promptly enrolled in an evening course in electrical engineering at the Pratt Institute. Since life in a sense was a cram course to him, he did not find it difficult. Of sixty entering students, Sarnoff was one of eleven to complete the program; the ten others were all high school or college graduates.

By his twenty-first birthday, in 1912, Sarnoff was becoming a recogniz-able figure within the still arcane world of wireless. Besides his telegraphic skills, his knowledge of wireless equipment and how to install and service it was probably exceeded by no one in Marconi's employ. Yet he was, of course, still an unknown to the general public. Only those at the crest of the wireless boom, beginning with Marconi, had achieved significant public rec-ognition. Indeed many inventors became showmen in the P. T. Barnum tra-dition in order to win financial support. Lee De Forest, for example, rented the top of the Eiffel Tower to broadcast music with his Audion tube trans-mitter to Paris wireless receivers within a twenty-five-mile radius. In 1910, De Forest insinuated his transmitter onto the stage of the Metropolitan Opera, and nearby shipboard wireless operators, plus a handful of reporters in De Forest's office, listened to the rather garbled strains of an aria sung by Enrico Caruso.

Sarnoff had followed all these developments attentively. From his prox-imity to Marconi, he observed how the inventor, despite his innate reserve, was quick to arrange public demonstrations of new developments and per-suasive in exploiting his fame to enlist figures of world renown in support of his enterprises. To Sarnoff, it became clear that it was not enough just to achieve; it was essential to develop skills in exploiting those achievements. Before the phrase "public relations" was commonplace, Sarnoff was a student of the persuasive art, and he attributed greater importance to it throughout his career than perhaps any of his contemporaries in American industry, most of whom had been schooled to avoid the prying eyes of journalists. In later constructions of his life, a single incident during his tenure as manager of the Wanamaker wireless station became the public relations vehicle for explaining his swift transition from an unknown youngster, only months into his majority, into a figure of national stature.

On the night of April 14, 1912, the newly christened British luxury liner S.S. *Titanic,* en route to New York on her maiden voyage across the North Atlantic, struck an iceberg and sank, with a loss of 1,517 lives. This epic sea disaster, involving the largest, fastest, and theoretically most secure ship afloat, cost hundreds of American lives and riveted the attention of the world as few accidents before or since have. According to Sarnoff's official biog-raphy, written in 1966 by his cousin, *Reader's Digest* contributing editor Eugene Lyons, the role of the young manager at Wanamaker's in the *Titanic* disaster was of heroic scope:

"On April 14, 1912, David Sarnoff was listening casually to the routine flood of dots and dashes. Suddenly he was stung to startled attention. The message was dim and faraway and choked by static, but he deciphered it notwithstanding. It was coming from the S.S. *Olympic,* 1,400 miles away.

" 'S.S. *Titanic* ran into iceberg. Sinking fast.' "

According to Lyons, Sarnoff signaled receipt of the message and then alerted the press. Soon extras began appearing on the streets, and "the eyes of the world, it seemed, along with its hopes and fears, were fixed on young Sarnoff and his earphones." Reporters and crowds of friends and relatives of those aboard the stricken ship converged on the department store. Police were summoned to control them, so that Sarnoff could have the privacy he needed.

Other wireless stations began jamming the airwaves, trying to help. So President Taft, the biographer said, ordered all of them closed down in order that Sarnoff not be impeded in his continuing attempts to maintain wireless contact with the *Olympic,* which was a sister ship of the *Titanic.* "This was to be a one man job," as Lyons explained.

For three days and three nights, according to the biographer, Sarnoff maintained his lonely vigil, without sleep and virtually without food, and "a horrified world hung on his every word." The reports from the *Olympic* were primarily names of survivors hauled from the ocean by wireless-equipped vessels that had rushed to the scene. Not until he had forwarded to the press the names of the last survivors, seventy-two hours after his receipt of the first distress signal, did the exhausted young operator relinquish his post and collapse into sleep.

"The stark drama of the scene—a young man in Manhattan as the sole contact with a great catastrophe in mid-ocean—made a terrific impression on the public mind," Lyons wrote. What had been a scientific curiosity was raised in a few tragic days to the status of a necessity. Hundreds more could have been saved if ships in the area, several of them closer to the *Titanic* than those that did hurry to the rescue, had been wireless-equipped to hear the distress call. This sad fact was too obvious and too devastating not to register.

"The *Titanic* disaster, Sarnoff once summed it up, 'brought radio to the front,' adding quietly, 'and incidentally me.' The limelight that played for three harrowing days on the twenty-one-year-old operator would rarely dim for him in the crowded decades that followed."

The Lyons account, printed forty-four years after the event, repeated in precise dimensions a story that had already been woven into the fabric of American history. Daniel Boorstin had reported it similarly in his Pulitzer Prize–winning volume *The American Experience.* Erik Barnouw's *Tower of Babel,* widely considered the most authoritative history of early radio in the United States, offered the same picture of the young operator's heroics and wound up with the assertion, "The name Sarnoff was known all over the country." In subsequent years, as his reputation as an industrialist and an electronics prophet grew, the picture of the wireless boy at the dike was recounted in *Fortune, Forbes, Time,* the *Saturday Evening Post,* and the

Reader's Digest. This then, if history texts and responsible journals were to be believed, was the spectacular launching pad for the Sarnoff career, his overnight baptism in public waters.

Yet there are gaps in the story, and contradictions difficult to resolve. The *New York Times,* for example, provided the most voluminous coverage of the *Titanic* tragedy of any American newspaper, but nowhere during the days that its columns overflowed with *Titanic* reports does the name Sarnoff emerge. The *Times* reported on April 15 in an eight-column-headline story that the first distress signal was picked up at 10:25 P.M. on April 14 by the Marconi station on Cape Race on the eastern shore of Newfoundland. The following day, April 16, the *Times* ran a partial list of survivors, which it said had been received by Cape Race, the nearest wireless station to the disaster. Another story reported additional names of survivors picked up by a Boston wireless station. The *Times* described the Cape Race station as "the storm center of the great battle for news of the missing passengers." No reference to the Wanamaker station—or Sarnoff.

On its fourth day of coverage, April 18, the *Times* reported that the American Marconi company had formally requested all government wireless stations to cease sending messages so there would be no interference with the attempts of its shore installations in Massachusetts and at Sagaponack and Sea Gate to maintain communications with the rescue ship *Carpathia*. In a prompt response, Secretary of the Navy Meyer, according to the *Times,* said orders had been issued to all ships at sea and at the navy yards not to attempt to call the *Carpathia*. But again no indication of intervention by President Taft to effect a wholesale closedown of all wireless stations except Sarnoff's. And where historians later talked of crowds storming the Wanamaker station, the *Times* reported only that "excited crowds" of relatives and friends of the passengers were gathering at the New York offices of the White Star Lines, which owned the rescue ship *Carpathia*.

Similarly, the *Wall Street Journal*'s voluminous coverage of the tragedy mentioned wireless intelligence received from various eastern and northeastern stations, including principally Cape Race, but nowhere were there references to Wanamaker's or its manager. On April 16, the international edition of the *Herald Tribune* in Paris devoted its entire front page to capsule dispatches on the tragedy from around the world, but not a single verification that, as Sarnoff's biographer had it, "a horrified world hung on his every word."

Was the Sarnoff-*Titanic* story therefore merely the concoction of a biographer's agile imagination, prodded by his subject? Not entirely, for the fact that Sarnoff had a role is established by an article in the Hearst-owned New York *American* of April 16, 1912. Apparently, after the initial reports from Cape Race, the *American* had made a promotional deal with the Wanamaker store whereby any information on the *Titanic* disaster picked up by its Marconi station would be turned over exclusively to that paper. A two-column headline on page six read: N.Y. AMERICAN TURNED WIRELESS STATION INTO A BRANCH OFFICE: JACK BINNS WAS IN COMMAND. The ensuing story clarified the rather confusing implications of the headline:

"The wireless office of the Wanamaker stores [sic] at Broadway and Eighth street, conducted jointly by John Wanamaker and the Marconi Wireless Telegraph Company, were converted into a branch office of the *New York American* last night.

"Jack Binns, the hero of the Republic, the Florida disaster [sic], when he shot to the world the wireless CQD and saved the lives of more than 2,000 passengers and crew, took charge for the *American*." (Binns was the shipboard wireless operator on the *Republic* in the first passenger-ship sinking in which wireless distress signals brought rescue ships to the scene in time to avert a tragedy. This was in 1908.)

"The office was directed by David Sarnoff, manager of this station, assisted by J. H. Hughes, an expert Marconi operator, who was placed at the services of the *American* by the Wanamaker stores. Incidentally, it was Mr. Sarnoff who was at the Siasconset life saving wireless station when Jack Binns' message was picked up.

"With every bit of energy at their command these men stood by their posts all night and fired scores of messages and captured scores concerning the wreck.

"From all over the coast line and far into the interior, even to Chicago, appeals for news of the disaster were heaped upon the *American*'s temporary office.

"The Wanamaker station is located on the roof of the famous department store, and is one of the most powerful along the Atlantic seaboard. Last night through all the pandemonium of wireless controversy and confusion that prevailed this station managed to pick up direct communication with Siasconset, Sagaponack, Cape Cod, Hatteras, Sable Island and many other stations along the coast.

"Faint signals were heard from the Olympic, but owing to the terrible confusion and disruption of static conditions Mr. Hughes, the operator, was unable to pick up the strands of direct communications: no other New York office was able to report any communication at all with the Olympic."

The *American*'s story concluded by listing bulletins picked up by the Wanamaker station from other Marconi listening posts, such as Cape Race. On the following day, with other newspapers still ignoring Wanamaker's— perhaps because of its tie-in with a competitor—the *American* sought to exploit its station's role in the disaster. In an April 17 story on page five, it insisted that the first direct message picked up from the *Olympic,* corroborating the earlier Cape Race bulletins of the sinking and reporting that the rescue ship *Carpathia* was returning to New York with 866 women and children survivors, was at the Wanamaker outlet:

"David Sarnoff, manager of the wireless station, and Mr. Hughes, an expert Marconi man, assisted by the hero of the Republic disaster, Jack Binns, have waited over the wireless instruments for the faint tick of the instruments that will bear to the world what news is available concerning the passengers," the *American* reported. "A faint signal from the Olympic sounded on the apparatus over which those atop the Wanamaker building bent with strained ears. Then came the astounding news verifying the report that the Titanic had floundered." When the *American* published this news, according to its account, "eager thousands" descended on the Wanamaker station clamoring for more information, among them Vincent Astor, son of the merchant prince John Jacob Astor, a doomed passenger on the ship.

But the *American,* intent as it obviously was on dramatizing the Wanamaker role, made no effort to portray Sarnoff as the solitary hero of the occasion. He was part of a wireless triumvirate called into action after the nation has been informed, via Cape Race, of the disaster and even the extent of his station's contribution does not emerge clearly. If it were as central to the rescue mission as the *American* suggested, why was Wanamaker's among the stations closed down by the Marconi company to prevent interference with its four coastal stations? The fact that it did close at some point in the rescue proceedings is established by an announcement in a full-page Wanamaker's ad of April 19 that the station was preparing to resume service. Out of the flood of reportage engulfing the most famous of sea disasters, the inescapable conclusion to be drawn is that no individual wireless operator and no single station monopolized the gathering and transmission of wireless intelligence concerning it.

How then did David Sarnoff emerge in the pages of history as the lonely, indefatigable link between the *Titanic* and the waiting world? Why did subsequent generations of journalists join with historians of national repute in accepting as fact a story with which their own files were at variance?

The answer, quite probably, is that the later real accomplishments of Sarnoff's life were so profuse and so remarkable that any myth or legend seemed plausible. As his achievements reached heroic proportions, those who wrote about him began to recast all of his life in heroic terms. It had to fit in the same shining mold. Yet, this was hardly unique. As with the returning war hero, the passage of time added luster to his feats.

Sarnoff's first known print recounting of his *Titanic* role was in March 1923, eleven years after the disaster. He told an interviewer for the *American* magazine (not the newspaper) that he had maintained a seventy-two-hour vigil at Wanamaker's after picking up the first faint signal from the *Olympic*. There was no reference to others manning the wireless station with him, nor any indication of the involvement of other wireless stations. At the time Sarnoff was a well-known figure in the radio world, moving rapidly up the executive ladder at RCA, and presumably no one challenged his description.

Thus the snowball of legend began to roll. By 1930, when he became president of RCA at age thirty-nine, *Fortune* devoted a major story to his unprecedented rise in industry, including a separate sidebar feature on his lonely *Titanic* heroics. But this time the retelling was not attributed to Sarnoff, it was simply presented as fact. *Fortune*'s reputation for careful research perhaps influenced other publications to repeat it without attribution, and the snowball gathered speed and dimension. In Sarnoff's own mind, undoubtedly the equation between fact and legend blurred as he continued reading in reputable publications of his singular feat. When he told the story in later years, he told it with the ring of truth, which it had undoubtedly become in his inner conviction.

Only one writer ever swam against the historical and journalistic tide. He was Carl Dreher, an early RCA engineer and an associate of Sarnoff's during the company's formative years. In an unauthorized Sarnoff biography published after the RCA leader's death, and largely ignored by the press, Dreher scoffed at the idea that the young operator could have picked up the first distress signal. The Wanamaker station, he pointed out, kept store hours and was closed at night when the initial flash was received. Without mentioning the *American*-Wanamaker promotional tie, of which he was apparently unaware, Dreher speculated that Sarnoff might have read or heard of a news bulletin on the sinking, rushed to the Wanamaker station, and joined, with great intensity, in a sleepless hunt for wireless intelligence. But the construction that ultimately emerged of a lonely "tryst with the sea," as Lyons came to describe it, was in Dreher's judgment—and he was an admirer of Sarnoff—a significant exaggeration.

Indisputably, however, the *Titanic* disaster projected wireless communications, if not Sarnoff, into national and worldwide prominence. Legislation swept through the United States Congress mandating wireless transmitting and receiving equipment and wireless operators on oceangoing vessels with fifty or more passengers. An immediate result was that ship and shore installations of the American Marconi company, and the volume of traffic between them, began to grow exponentially. Stock of the parent company in London more than doubled in price. In the flush of new prosperity, a staff buildup at the New York office was ordered, and Sarnoff became one of its first beneficiaries. Within the company, his cool and credible managerial performance at Wanamaker's station during the *Titanic* convulsion had been favorably noticed, although not because of the modest publicity it generated in the *American*. As 1912 neared its end, Sarnoff—still short of his twenty-second birthday—became inspector of Marconi-equipped ships in the New York harbor, responsible for maintenance and repair work and with a staff to support him. At the same time, he became an instructor at the Marconi Institute, which had been organized to meet the burgeoning demand for trained wireless operators. And he organized and taught a course in the techniques of selling Marconi equipment, with new members of the New York staff as his students. Without any particular blueprint for progress, he had gained exposure to, and proficiency in, every area in which Marconi functioned. In 1913, seven years after his office boy start, he was made chief inspector for all ships equipped and serviced by American Marconi and was given the additional title of assistant chief engineer.

These were stimulating days for the expatriate from Uzlian. His salary had more than tripled since his operator years, and he had begun accumulating a business wardrobe, searching the racks of cut-rate department stores for suits that would approximate the flanneled elegance of Signore Marconi's Bond Street tailors. And cigars, big cigars, although not of the premium Havana quality of his later years, became a favored accoutrement, his personal symbol of maturity and rising affluence. Most important of all, he was able to make a final break with his ghetto past—and to carry his family with him. Soon after becoming chief inspector, he appeared at the family's apartment in the Brownsville slum and ordered his mother to pack up their personal belongings and follow him. The trail led to a new apartment building in the Bronx, north of Manhattan and as far removed from the ghetto as was possible within the municipal confines of New York City. With a flourish, Sarnoff turned the latchkey on a freshly painted five-room apartment that had electric lights, modern kitchen facilities, hot water and steam heat and indoor plumbing—and it was completely furnished. Sarnoff instructed the bewildered Leah to sell or give away all the Brownsville household furnishings. He wanted every reminder of the lean and grubby early American years expunged, and he had exhausted his savings and risked a low-interest loan in order to make complete the transition to a comfortable, middle-class environment.

With the American company in a new growth cycle, Godfrey Isaacs, head of the parent English Marconi, decided to install an experienced cable executive of American citizenship as general manager in New York, and his choice was Edward J. Nally, fifty-four, vice-president and general manager of the domestic Postal Telegraph Company. In part Isaacs' decision was dictated by rumblings of concern in Washington, and particularly from the United States Navy, that America's principal wireless communications link to an unsettled and rapidly rearming world was in the control of a foreign power, albeit a friendly one. Nally's appointment was intended to give American Marconi more of a domestic character.

Perhaps more important, Isaacs sensed that war was approaching in Europe, and that the entire energies of the British firm would be absorbed in meeting the communications needs of its government. As 1914 dawned, Kaiser Wilhelm II of Germany was overseeing war games by his massive ground forces, Europe's largest, and reinvigorating his naval arm under Grand Admiral Alfred von Tirpitz, with particular emphasis on the construction of

U-boats. In London, First Lord of the Admiralty Winston Churchill was pressing a reluctant Parliament to approve the largest naval appropriations bill in the history of the island empire, with the construction of more dreadnoughts high on his preparedness agenda. A chain reaction of military alliances had enmeshed all the great European powers, and the spark needed to touch off a world conflagration was provided on June 28, 1914, by the assassination of Austrian Archduke Franz Ferdinand and his morganatic wife, Sophie, in the Bosnian capital of Sarajevo. Britain, including British Marconi, mobilized for a war that would cost it one million of its young men and presage the decline of its empire.

At American Marconi, the war meant greater autonomy under the experienced Nally, who had devoted thirty-five years to wired telegraphy but was somewhat of a neophyte in wireless. To the ambitious Sarnoff, this spelled fresh opportunity as a tutor for his new boss, and he exploited it. The same material he taught at the Marconi Institute to other staffers, he supplied to Nally at private night sessions. Within months the older man was looking upon Sarnoff as his technical rudder. He found in his youthful chief inspector a broader grasp than anyone else in the organization possessed of the full inventory of Marconi equipment and services, plus an acute perception of competitive wares. For months during weekends and at night, Sarnoff had roamed the New York waterfront, visiting not only ships equipped by American Marconi, but those of other nations with other wireless brands. He peppered Nally with memoranda on new competitive devices, such as the quenched spark transmitter introduced by Germany's Telefunken. Occasionally he was improvident enough to direct his memos on technical developments to Marconi himself with carbon copy to Nally, an oblique reminder to his new boss that he still considered himself the great sorcerer's apprentice. Within a year of Nally's arrival, Sarnoff received the additional title of contract manager, responsible with a staff for negotiating all sales and service contracts and thus involving him full force in the commercial as well as the technical end of the business.

World War I provided enormous impetus to the further development of wireless, not only in the warring nations of Europe but in the technical laboratories of American industry. The electrical giants, Westinghouse and General Electric, and the American Telephone and Telegraph Company were deeply involved in the exploration of radiated wireless signals—radiotelegraphy or radiotelephony as they were then called, but soon to be shortened in the popular vernacular to radio. The Alexanderson alternator, a 20,000-cycle high frequency transmitter sufficiently powerful to hurl the human voice with great clarity across the Atlantic, came to fruition at GE in the war years. AT&T's laboratories constructed a giant transmitter at the naval wireless station at Arlington, Virginia, and on occasions in 1915 its voice transmissions were picked up as far east as Paris and as far west as San

Francisco. And a young Columbia University physicist unveiled a regenerative feedback circuit, to become known as the oscillating audion, that magnified enormously the ability of a wireless receiver to pick up distant transmissions. He was Edwin Howard Armstrong, the same age as Sarnoff, soon to become one of his best friends and later one of his most bitter enemies because of differing perceptions of the future of wireless.

Within the same time frame, General H. C. Dunwoody of the United States Army developed a carborundum detector that provided an inexpensive means of picking up wireless signals. It was soon followed by even less expensive silicon detectors, and thus was born the homemade crystal set that soon engrossed hundreds of thousands of American men and boys. Attic inventors patched together cheap amateur sets, with the silicon crystal replacing more expensive vacuum tube detectors; wire antennas began sprouting on America's rooftops, and countless enthusiasts sacrificed their sleep for the thrill of intercepting remote dots and dashes, and occasionally even the human voice.

Sarnoff sought to keep his Marconi colleagues abreast of each development. At his old Wanamaker station, an arc-type transmitter was installed, permitting the transmission of phonograph music. And Sarnoff personally manned the telegraph key when the first successful experiment of wireless transmission from a moving train was achieved in 1914. He was aboard a fast-moving Lackawanna express whose passengers were five hundred members of the Society of Civil Engineers, plus members of the press, and the publicity this time centered mainly on him.

In the fusillade of memoranda that he continued firing at his Marconi superiors during this period, Sarnoff later singled out one he composed on September 30, 1915, when he was twenty-four, as the most important of his career. Indeed, he was often known to describe it, without any concern for undue modesty, as the most significant conceptualization in the annals of radio, and he was later supported in this belief by leading industry historians such as Gleason Archer. It became known as the radio music box memorandum, as important in its way to the Sarnoff legend as the *Titanic* disaster and more substantive in character.

In the formative years, the prevalent conception of the role of wireless communications was message transmission from one point to another. Even when voice was added to the flow of dots and dashes, it was assumed that an overarching desire for privacy would confine message traffic to two individuals or two stations. It had always been thus—with cable, with telegraph, with telephone. Indeed, the lack of security of wireless messages, the ease with which they could be plucked out of the air, was seen by many observers of the new art as its greatest weakness. But as Sarnoff continued to probe developments such as the crystal set and the high-powered transmitter he began asking himself why wireless had to be confined to this one-on-one straitjacket. Perhaps, he reasoned, the ease of interception could be turned to advantage. Why not advance wireless from point-to-point transmissions to point-to-mass, from an audience of one for the message to an audience of thousands?

"I have in mind," he wrote to Nally, "a plan of development that would make radio a household utility in the same sense as the piano or phonograph. The idea is to bring music into the house by wireless.

"While this has been tried in the past by wires, it has been a failure because wires do not lend themselves to this scheme. With radio, however, it would seem to be entirely feasible. For example, a radiotelephone transmitter having a range of, say, 25 to 50 miles can be installed at a fixed point where instrumental or vocal music or both are produced. The problem of transmitting music has already been solved in principle, and therefore all the receivers attuned to the transmitting wave length should be capable of receiving such music. The receiver can be designed in the form of a simple 'Radio Music Box' and arranged for several different wave lengths, which should be changeable with the throwing of a single switch or pressing of a single button.

"The 'Radio Music Box' can be supplied with amplifying tubes and a loudspeaking telephone, all of which can be neatly mounted in one box. The box can be placed on a table in the parlor or living room, the switch set accordingly, and the transmitted music received. There should be no difficulty in receiving music perfectly when transmitted within a radius of 25 to 50 miles. Within such a radius, there reside hundreds of thousands of families; and as all can simultaneously receive from a single transmitter, there would be no question of obtaining sufficiently loud signals to make the performance enjoyable. The power of the transmitter can be made 5 kilowatts, if necessary, thereby giving extra loud signals in the home if desired. The use of head telephones would be obviated by this method. The development of a small loop antenna to go with each 'Radio Music Box' would likewise solve the antenna problem."

In the throes of composing his landmark memo, Sarnoff later recalled, he became carried away by possibilities far beyond mere music. "Events of national importance can be simultaneously announced and received," he continued to Nally. "Baseball scores can be transmitted in the air by the use of one set installed at the Polo Grounds. The same would be true of other cities . . . to farmers and others living in outlying districts . . . they could enjoy concerts, lectures, music, recitals, etc."

Sarnoff knew that if he were to enlist the support of the pragmatic Nally, he would have to construct sound commercial underpinnings for his scheme. Large quantity production of the radios, he estimated, would make possible their profitable sale at $75 per unit. And a secondary source of revenue would be the sale of transmitters.

"The company [Marconi] would have to undertake the arrangements," he continued, "for music recitals, lectures, etc." Then, as though he sensed that would startle an old-line telegrapher like Nally, he quickly reverted to commercial prospects. "There are about 15 million families in the United States alone and if only 1 million, or 7 percent of the total families, thought well of the idea, it would mean a gross business of about $75 million, which should yield considerable revenue [i.e., profit]." And then he drove home his concluding—and what he hoped would be conclusive—argument: "The possibilities for advertising for the company are tremendous, for its name would ultimately be brought into the household, and wireless would receive national and universal attention."

Like many young conceptualizers throughout history, Sarnoff proved to be ahead of his time. At that moment, Nally and his small management cadre were overwhelmed by orders from the United States Navy. The administration of Woodrow Wilson was veering day by day toward increased moral and logistical support of a Britain and France hard pressed by their Teutonic foe. Transatlantic wireless links became vital because the growing German submarine flotilla posed the threat of Britain's underseas cables being sundered. In this atmosphere of tense uncertainty, the Sarnoff radio box proposal was too fanciful and visionary, too all-encompassing in its requirements, to move the overburdened Nally to action. But he didn't want to argue it out and he didn't want to offend Sarnoff, to whom he was entrusting increasingly vital naval contract negotiations in Washington. So he simply pigeonholed the memo. The original gathered dust and then apparently disappeared into the waste bin of history.

But Sarnoff did not forget it. Originally, he toyed with the idea of sending a copy to Marconi in Italy, but the inventor's nation, too, was at war and the apprentice reluctantly concluded that the sorcerer could not reasonably be expected to wax enthusiastic over the prospect of creating musical concerts and music boxes for Iowa farmers. So he bided his time, five years to be exact, before he renewed his proposal in a different environment—and to a different company and a different boss.

At Marconi, his responsibilities continued to enlarge. A new commercial department was formed in early 1917, combining all contract and business operations with the government and private customers, and Sarnoff, approaching his twenty-sixth birthday, was placed in charge, his salary $11,000 annually. The staff under him had grown to 725 employees, and he supervised the installation and servicing of wireless on 582 vessels. His reputation was spreading in the industry and he was elected secretary of the newly formed Institute of Radio Engineers. On occasion he represented it in Washington, testifying before congressional committees on various legislative proposals for control of wireless in periods of both war and peace.

As his career flourished, Sarnoff's personal life also added new dimensions. His attraction to women was intense, and in this he needed no coaching from Marconi. One of his first attachments was to Nan Malkind, a secretary at the Institute of Radio Engineers, and they went together for four years. She came from a large Jewish immigrant family of modest circumstances, and Sarnoff frequently made the long trek to the Malkind home in Brooklyn during the post-*Titanic* years. The relationship finally foundered, perhaps because of diminished interest on Sarnoff's part or perhaps because, as Miss Malkind later told a friend, she found the clinging aroma of cigar smoke not to her taste.

The romance in Sarnoff's life that endured resulted from a prearranged meeting in the Bronx. His mother, Leah, became acquainted at a neighborhood synagogue with the mother of a French immigrant family recently settled in the Bronx. In the ancient Jewish tradition of matrimonial matchmaking, the mothers conspired to bring son and daughter together. It was love at first sight, David later wrote, when he met Paris-born Lizette Hermant. She was fair-skinned and blond, several years his junior, and the little English she spoke was laced with a French accent he found charming. Her warmth and quick Gallic wit offered a relaxed counterpoint to the rather formidable professional mien that he was then cultivating. Her ignorance of the wireless art was total, as was his command of the French tongue, so "What could we do?" as David later asked. They got married, following an extended family-supervised courtship, at a modest ceremony in the Bronx synagogue on July 4, 1917. In the fifty-four years of their marriage, which produced three sons, Independence Day was always celebrated in the Sarnoff household as the day David "lost my independence." Through the storms and the triumphs of his life, Lizette was his fiercely loyal companion. Occasionally they quarreled, for both were hot tempered. Occasionally he wounded her deeply because of the philanderings that accompanied his march to fame and power. But the marriage proved the bedrock of his life.

In February 1917, the Wilson administration culminated three years of increasing support for the Allies by severing diplomatic relations with Germany and then, in April, declaring war. Despite his impending marriage, Sarnoff promptly applied for a commission in naval communications. He was shocked and angered when the navy turned him down on the ground that his civilian services were essential to the war effort. Like everyone his age, he had registered for the military draft and now he refused, despite the urgings of his Marconi associates, to seek an exemption. He suspected anti-Semitism had blocked his naval commission, but he was determined to wear a uniform—to prove the totality of his Americanization—even if it meant starting as a buck private in the army. Only the urgent intercession of Admiral R. S. Griffen, the navy's top engineer, with Sarnoff's local draft broad kept him out of khaki. "Exemption is considered absolutely necessary," Griffen wired the board, "in order that the fleet will not suffer delays due to unsat-

isfactory deliveries in existing contracts." This confirmation of his indispensability was sufficient to soothe Sarnoff's ire, and he raised no further
objections.

In reality, the Marconi commercial manager, then twenty-eight, did serve
the navy in mufti. At the outset of war, President Wilson ordered a government takeover of all wireless facilities in the United States and its possessions.
The navy, with the greatest stake in maintaining communications with its
far-flung fleet units and ground support depots, became the instrument to
accomplish it. All Marconi installations, facilities, and personnel fell under
naval authority, and Sarnoff soon became almost a Washington commuter,
spending more than half his time in the capital negotiating contracts at naval
headquarters and providing expert advice on communications to congressional committees and government bureaus.

The business of Marconi boomed. In 1917, its gross volume exceeded
$5 million, nearly double the prior year's. Even more than the *Titanic* episode,
the war confirmed the vital role of wireless. For what had been feared had
in fact happened. German U-boats had succeeded in cutting Britain's underseas cables, and wireless became America's lifeline to the allied governments and to its own military forces abroad. At the Marconi installation at
New Brunswick, New Jersey, the navy installed a 200-kilowatt Alexanderson
alternator, the most powerful transmitter then built, which provided reliable
and clear voice transmission across the ocean. When President Wilson in
January 1918 enumerated his Fourteen Points as the basis for a peace settlement, the New Brunswick transmitter relayed the text, and within hours
nearly the entire population of Europe was aware through crystal sets and
word-of-mouth relay of the American president's initiative. Never before
had a message of such depth and complexity been disseminated so swiftly
to so many. It was a forerunner of the point-to-mass application of wireless,
and to Sarnoff, who was present at the New Brunswick transmission, it
provided further validation of his radio music box concept. Over two years
had elapsed since Nally cubbyholed his memo, but the author still clung to
his copies.

The navy's wartime role in communications profoundly influenced
Sarnoff's views on the future of the wireless industry. A naval communications monopoly was in effect, which included a moratorium on patent
rights, and the Marconi executive saw how easy it suddenly became to build
apparatus that heretofore had led to court challenges for infringement. No
longer were the patents of Armstrong or De Forest or Alexanderson in contention, because the navy controlled them. Sarnoff marveled at how quickly
order and purpose gripped the previously chaotic wireless industry. He
emerged from the war an ardent devotee of industry rationalization, and
many of the great battles of his career would focus on his determined attempts
to impose and maintain it.

In the flush of wartime patriotism, Sarnoff also came to share the belief of the navy's communications hierarchy that America must never again face a national emergency depending upon communications owned by others. His love and respect for Marconi, despite a wartime hiatus in their relationship, never wavered, but the communications of his adopted country, he was persuaded, were too vital to entrust to foreign owners. When the navy, immediately after the cessation of hostilities, began moving toward implementation of that goal, Sarnoff was an energetic behind-the-scenes supporter, both in Washington and among his industry associates.

His wartime experiences had, he felt, matured and benefited him. He had become acquainted with men of power, and he revered power. He had been a dinner guest in the Washington homes and apartments of senators and congressman, he had lunched with leaders of the armed services and listened to them strategize over the battles of Meuse-Argonne and Château-Thierry. Even his hunger to don a uniform had been assuaged by a letter of commendation for his wartime services from the head of the Radio Bureau of the U.S. Navy. "Our constant association throughout this trying time," Commander Sanford C. Hooper wrote Sarnoff, "led me to admire your work and your organization tremendously, and I came to realize that I could depend upon you above all others."

By now Sarnoff was a settled family man. With the aid of a $5,000 interest-bearing loan from his longtime friend Dr. Alfred Goldsmith (an eminent electronics inventor who later became RCA's chief engineer), he had purchased a home in suburban Mount Vernon, north of the city. In July of 1918 Lizette gave birth to their first son, whose name, Robert William Sarnoff, was as American as his father could make it. Two other sons, Edward and Thomas, would soon follow. Physically, David was as far removed from the skinny youth in the ghetto world of Monroe Street as he was spiritually and emotionally. He had grown to five feet eight inches in height and his posture was ramrod straight, which he believed lent credence to his executive presence. His girth, under the stimulus of the bread, potatoes, and meat he loved to ingest—in time of stress voraciously—was beginning to expand, although not to the tumescent proportions of his later years, and his hairline to recede. The pinched, almost hungry, face of the boy had fleshed out, becoming full-jowled and ruddily healthy. Only the eyes, blue, steely, and piercing in their intensity, remained the same.

Perhaps the greatest change was in his psyche, for now he literally brimmed with self-assurance. The fact that he was the only Jewish executive in his company—and, so far as he was aware, in his industry—had persuaded him that if he could overcome that obstacle he could overcome any other. He had encountered his peers in competitive enterprises and had become totally convinced that none possessed his combination of leadership qualities. He had upgraded his business dress with a walking stick and a homburg.

He had trained his voice to a deeply resonant pitch and had become a forceful, at at times eloquent, public speaker, skilled in apothegms. He had stored his childhood knowledge of Yiddish and Hebrew in a remote memory bin. As the war to end all wars ended, the Americanization of David Sarnoff was complete.

3 / A Company Is Born

To the United States Navy the virtues of monopoly in international communications had become incontestable. Through its wartime powers, the navy had coalesced a bickering and fragmented wireless industry into an instrument of national utility. The temporary abolition of patent restrictions unfettered development of the technology, and the nation emerged from the conflict with an international communications voice that seemed commensurate with its emergence as a world power. The navy wanted to freeze the status quo, and, a month after the armistice in November 1918, Secretary Josephus Daniels appeared before Congress to urge enactment of a bill "that will secure for all time to the Navy Department the control of radio in the United States, and will enable the Navy to continue the splendid work it has carried on during the war." To Daniels it was unthinkable that the prewar dissonance be permitted to resume. "It is my profound conviction," he testified, "as is the conviction of every person I have talked with in this country and abroad who has studied the question that it [radio] must be a monopoly." Every other nation with a wireless capability, he argued, was nurturing it through a government monopoly.

Because of Daniels' intimacy with President Wilson, it was assumed the administration stood squarely behind him. The State Department, indeed, expressed its "entire approval of the bill as drawn." But the mood of the nation was at variance, and Congressman William S. Greene of Massachusetts more accurately reflected it. "Having just won a fight against autocracy," he testified—meaning, of course, Kaiser Wilhelm—"we would start an autocratic movement with this bill." Then he pronounced: "I have never heard before that it was necessary for one person to own all the air in order to breathe." The country wanted back to normalcy with private enterprise, and the bill died in committee before a major controversy could build.

Denied its own monopoly, the navy preferred a private monopoly to a restoration of the prewar free-for-all. Radio, Commander Hooper of the Naval Radio Bureau argued, was a "natural monopoly; either the government must exercise that monopoly or it must place the ownership . . . in the hands of some one commercial concern and let the government keep out of it." And because of a chain of events that originated before the war in the research laboratories of the General Electric Company in Schenectady, New York, the Navy targeted GE, then as now America's preeminent electrical equipment manufacturer, as its choice to effectuate that natural monopoly rather than a communications company such as AT&T, which already possessed a wired voice monopoly.

The key was GE engineer E. F. W. Alexanderson's high frequency alternator, which had passed its laboratory tests in 1914. Originally operating at a frequency of 20 kilocycles, the 200-kilowatt generator bulled through atmospheric disturbances and other sources of signal interference with a dimension of reliability that dwarfed competitive voice transmitters. Among the first to recognize the quantum leap was the inventor Marconi, who came to Schenectady in 1915 to inspect Alexanderson's invention. His unqualified endorsement led British Marconi to initiate discussions with GE on the sale of worldwide exclusive rights. However, America's entrance into the conflict postponed agreement, and the navy preempted the alternator as its principal wartime vehicle for international communications, culminating in the transmission of Wilson's Fourteen Points. In 1919, with America racing to free itself of wartime controls, British Marconi reopened negotiations and submitted a $5-million order for the purchase of twenty-four Alexanderson alternators, plus worldwide exclusive rights to their use. In the United States the rights would be vested solely in the subsidiary American Marconi.

To GE, seeking to recoup a heavy research investment and to fill manufacturing capacity idled since the war, it was an enticing order—and from its most logical customer, since Marconi controlled many of the world's wireless links and was a heavy purchaser of new communications apparatus. The man entrusted to consummate the deal was Owen D. Young, GE's forty-five-year-old general counsel, a lawyer from the small upstate New York farm community of Van Hornesville, who later achieved international renown for war reparations work and for his skill in resolving industry-labor conflicts. Young had moved seemingly effortlessly through the apprentice ranks into a partnership in a private law firm that specialized in utilities litigation and handled much GE business. His ability to untangle complex legal issues had captured GE management's attention and led to an invitation to him to join the company's upper executive echelon.

Perhaps out of courtesy to an important wartime client of GE, but more likely because he sensed the far-ranging implications of the order, Young notified the Navy Department by letter of GE's intention to sell the alternators to a foreign company. In Washington, the response was consternation. Word was quickly dispatched to Paris, where Secretary Daniels was assisting Wilson in peace negotiations that were in part deadlocked by the punitive demands of Britain's prime minister, David Lloyd George. In Young's later recollection, corroborated by the statements of various naval officials, Wilson himself, already irate at the British, made the decision that the order must be blocked. The head of naval communications, Rear Admiral W. H. G. Bullard, was directed by Daniels to lead the "fight against British monopoly." On April 4, 1919, a letter to Young from Acting Secretary of the Navy Franklin D.

Roosevelt asked Young to confer with naval officials before consummating the Marconi order. Four days later, Admiral Bullard, Commander Hooper, and Young appeared before the GE Board of Directors with the outline of a proposal that would alter the structure of American communications.

In essence GE was asked to reject the order from British Marconi and place the alternator in a new company that would operate the United States end of international wireless circuits for both government and commercial traffic. As an inducement, the navy offered to place its own valuable wireless patents, derived from intensive wartime research, on a royalty-free basis in a patent pool, together with those controlled by GE and American Marconi. The pool would be operated by a new subsidiary of GE, to be created through a buyout of American Marconi stock. Since earlier competitors of American Marconi had mostly disappeared, either through acquisition or bankruptcy, the result would be, the navy suggested, a private monopoly initiated and supported by the navy and inferentially by the United States government.

To GE's board, the proposal was compelling in every aspect. It would appeal to patriotism because it promised America its own international wireless voice and the end of a foreign monopoly; it would appeal to the military forces, because of the increased message security it promised in event of future wars; it would appeal to the business community as a competitive form of traffic that could undercut the price of British cablegrams; and, finally, ·it would appeal to GE's shareholders as a new profit center of great potential. Sensing support from all these constituencies, the board authorized Young to execute the project as promptly as possible. Within days he was in Washington to secure the formal endorsement of Secretary Daniels, just returned from Paris. Daniels not only anointed the plan but recommended that Young seek bipartisan support by outlining it to Henry Cabot Lodge, the powerful Republican leader of the Senate. Lodge, too, was supportive, although he persuaded Young not to attempt to obtain a congressional charter because of political crosscurrents that might impede quick implementation. Perhaps Lodge's assumption was correct, but failure to win congressional sanction would plague the new enterprise for decades to come.

The name that Young and GE decided upon for their subsidiary was the Radio Corporation of America, which made explicit its national origin. A team of negotiators, including the president of the Marconi subsidiary, Edward J. Nally, was dispatched to London to arrange the transfer of ownership, and it was not as difficult as GE had anticipated. The navy still retained Marconi's American coastal wireless stations and gave no indication of an early surrender of control. Implicit in the negotiations—as the head of British Marconi, Godfrey Isaacs, quickly recognized—was the threat that, if the British firm balked, the navy would not only block the Alexander alternator sale but would encourage the development of a competitive American entity to which all government wireless contracts would be awarded, and American Marconi would presumably atrophy. Within three months the negotiators had hammered out a sales agreement that transferred British Marconi's controlling block of American Marconi stock to GE for $3.5 million.

On October 17, 1919, the Radio Corporation of America, soon to be known as RCA or simply Radio, was incorporated as the successor company, with an authorized five million shares of common stock and three million of preferred. Stock still held by individuals in American Marconi was to be exchanged for RCA common. To ensure the domestic sanctity of the new enterprise, the bylaws prohibited more than 20 percent stock ownership by foreigners, and its executives had to be American citizens, although not native born. To give it legitimacy as an instrument of national policy, a Navy Department representative was empowered to attend board of directors' meetings as an official observer, and Admiral Bullard was so designated. As chairman of the board of its new subsidiary, GE nominated the dominant individual in its creation, Owen Young.

The staff of American Marconi was transferred intact to RCA, and headquarters remained in a single wing on the eighteenth floor of the Woolworth Building at 233 Broadway. A three-paragraph story buried inside the *New York Times* told of RCA's formation. Its first president was Nally and twenty-eight-year-old David Sarnoff came along as commercial manager. At first, the young man felt a sense of personal ambivalence about the change. It meant severing his organizational link to Marconi, the most important figure of his early career. But as he reflected, Sarnoff became persuaded that it would be a good thing for him as well as for his adopted country. The war had convinced him America must have its own instrument of international communications, and he was now an American. Even if a corporate entity other than American Marconi had been selected for that purpose, he probably would have sought to join it in whatever executive niche was open. The idea of the radio music box still obsessed him, and he reasoned that the opportunities for consummating it were far better in an American-owned concern than with foreigners, even Marconi.

As the first order of business, wireless links were forged with England, France, Japan, and defeated Germany, and wireless equipment was leased to the merchant marine. In the first year of operations, RCA transmitted seven million words across the seas, undercutting British cable rates by more than 30 percent. While revenues reached $2 million, there was no profit because of start-up costs. From the navy, RCA inherited all the ship installations and land stations owned by Marconi, and its future, by virtue of its baptismal monopoly, seemed assured despite the profitless beginning.

Young, the legal tactician, the shaper of policy, was not a technical man, but he soon sensed the existence of powerful technological crosscurrents swirling around his new company. During the war, the armed services had conscripted 100,000 young Americans who had been crystal set enthusiasts and ham radio operators. In the service many had been exposed to the latest radiotelephonic apparatus, and when they returned home the dots and dashes transmitted by their prewar ham sets no longer interested them. Transmission by voice became the newest fad. In attics and garages, in hamlets and urban centers, the veterans hand-tooled simple transmitters that would permit them to talk with fellow amateurs within a twenty-five to forty mile radius. In Washington, the Department of Commerce, which had been designated as the licensing authority for new international wireless stations that would further couple America with the world, suddenly found itself deluged with license applications from clamorous amateurs who wanted to talk by wireless with their friends just as much as the navy did with its ships—or RCA did with its foreign correspondents.

Within a year of the new company's founding, Young was caught up in domestic wireless developments. Engrossed in forging further foreign links and building powerful new transmitters for a "Radio Central" on eastern Long Island, RCA found unsolicited orders for wireless components suddenly pouring in over the transom. The amateurs were hunting everywhere for apparatus, and RCA, as the successor company to Marconi, was becoming familiar to wireless buffs. Should the company respond to this domestic demand of uncharted dimension, or should it adhere to its original mandate to establish an international network that would free the nation of foreign communications domination? This was the crossroads decision facing RCA, and it created deep divisions within the company. To the veteran wireless contingent headed by Nally, the answer was clear: hold the line to the original mission and thus fulfill the patriotic founding concept. But arrayed against the traditionalists—the international wireless messenger boys, as *Fortune* magazine later rather deprecatingly called them—was the insistent voice of RCA's twenty-nine-year-old commercial manager. To Sarnoff, the domestic opportunity spelled the beginning of the fulfillment of his radio music box memorandum. To Young, he argued that RCA could respond to the new pulsations of the American market without abandoning its original charge. But to confine the company simply to the international field, he warned, would be to foreclose its future in a growth industry of limitless opportunity. Project RCA into American radiotelephony, he implored—and Young was caught up by the vision of a vast new market to be seized.

Among the stories of Sarnoff's career most deeply rooted in apocrypha, as insistent in a sense as the *Titanic* legend, was that RCA was founded by him. As recently as 1981, in a cover story on the company, *Business Week* wrote of him as RCA's founding father, the dominant force in its creation, and the magazine was simply echoing what countless other publications had written over the decades of Sarnoff's rise to the summit of electronics. Perhaps the length and visibility of his company and industry leadership encouraged the misconception, but the fact is that the youthful executive urging on

Young a change in RCA's course in 1920 was not then even in its policy-making councils. At the time he was neither an officer of the corporation nor a member of its board of directors. His first meeting with Young, in fact, had occurred only weeks before the formation of RCA, when the founder asked for a full accounting of American Marconi's fiscal condition and Sarnoff, as commercial manager, presented it to him at the request of Nally. But again, as with Marconi and Bottomley and Nally before him, Young found himself drawn to the younger man's personality, the breadth of his knowledge, the clarity and forcefulness of his presentation, and the enthusiasm with which he interpolated projections on the future.

Young's decision to move RCA into domestic radiotelephony won the approval of GE management, but it soon became apparent to him that its successful implementation would require far greater resources than RCA, even with GE support, possessed. The patent pool had been configured to international wireless needs, not to domestic radiotelephony, where inventions were emerging like spring shoots. And other major corporations, suddenly intrigued by the vast potential of this new business, were reaching to possess them. The radio patents of De Forest, Armstrong, and Michael Pupin came under the control, through licensing and acquisition, of Westinghouse and AT&T. Radio's individual inventors, the heirs of Franklin, Bell, and Edison, were being absorbed into corporate research laboratories, with their vastly greater resources, and the era of the lonely workshop, so much a part of American history, was nearing its end.

With the reimposition of peacetime patent restraints, Young realized that RCA, unlike the navy in wartime, could not impose its will upon the industry unilaterally. But without some form of rationalization he saw nothing but conflict ahead. "Half a dozen concerns all had patents," Young would recall in a *Saturday Evening Post* interview a decade later, "but not one concern had enough to operate . . . the whole problem was one of releasing an art."

Young's solution was to eliminate the patent conflict by enlarging the RCA pool to include competitors' patents. In exchange for patent rights, he would offer stock ownership in RCA and membership on its board. Thus, as the navy had brought stability to the international wireless field, he would bring it to the domestic market by the creation of a radio combine in which competitors would join together to manufacture and market both transmitting and receiving equipment under a protective patent umbrella. The fact that such an arrangement might transgress the nation's antitrust laws, either or both the Clayton and Sherman acts, was apparently subordinated in Young's judgment to the need for order and stability in the emerging industry.

To Sarnoff, Young deputized the principal negotiating role in the creation of the combine, and their first approach was to the giant of the communications industry, AT&T. Their timing was fortuitous, for the telephone company was then involved in intensive internal evaluation of its role in radio-telephony. Should it attempt to duplicate its wired voice monopoly, which already reached to every village crossroads in the nation? It possessed some patent strength in radio, for it had acquired the rights to De Forest's Audion tube and its Bell Laboratories were heavily involved in the development of radio circuitry. But AT&T's management, as Young correctly perceived, concluded in its initial studies that, while it might have the power to block others from domestic radiotelephony, it did not possess a broad enough range of patents to permit its domination of the industry. Within weeks, Young and Sarnoff worked out a cross-licensing agreement that gave the telephone company ownership of 10.3 percent of the outstanding common and preferred stock of RCA in exchange for the inclusion of its patents in the radio pool.

Next the RCA executives approached Westinghouse, the principal but junior competitor of GE in the manufacture of electrical equipment. For months, Westinghouse had watched with alarm as GE maneuvered with the navy, using the leverage of its Alexanderson alternator, to secure a potential monopoly in international wireless. Fearful of being foreclosed also from the domestic field, Westinghouse had acquired the vital radio patents of Armstrong, including the regenerative feedback device, the oscillating Audion, which gave it a strong position in the receiver field. It had also begun an ambitious program of acquiring smaller domestic wireless concerns, and it had begun experimenting with radio transmission at its Pittsburgh headquarters. So the price it exacted from Young and Sarnoff for placing its radio resources within the combine was 20.6 percent of RCA's stock.

To complete the rationalization process, the RCA negotiators brought aboard as a junior partner the United Fruit Company, which had pioneered in wireless as a means of linking its banana boats with its Latin American plantations. For 4.1 percent of RCA's stock, United Fruit's patents on crystal detectors and a loop antenna were cross-licensed to the pool, which now numbered nearly two thousand patents covering all the key elements of an integrated radiotelephone system—transmitters, receivers, circuitry, and components, including the vacuum tube that would soon outmode the Alexanderson alternator on which RCA was built.

The price of the Young-Sarnoff coup was diluted ownership of RCA, but it was a price they felt essential to the creation of a stable industry. GE still retained the largest block of RCA stock—30.1 percent of the common and preferred—with the remaining 34.9 percent scattered among individual holders and brokerage firms. There seemed no competitors on the horizon in 1921 who could challenge the might of the new combine. Yet within two years it would begin to unravel under the impact of events far different than Young had envisaged. The concept of the usage of radio would be dramatically altered, the partners in the combine would quarrel over their allotted roles, and the charge of monopoly would be unleashed against the combine—by the Federal Trade Commission, the Justice Department, the Congress, competitors, and the press—with a ferocity and a durability perhaps unmatched in the nation's legal annals.

Initially, the structuring of the new cartel proceeded smoothly. Membership on the board of directors of RCA was apportioned among the partners according to ownership percentiles, with Young, who was also a GE vice-president, continuing as chairman and Nally as president. The functions to be performed by the different owners were also neatly compartmentalized. AT&T would manufacture wireless transmitters, and GE and Westinghouse would manufacture receiving sets, with incoming orders to be apportioned 60 percent to GE factories and 40 percent to Westinghouse. To RCA, which would continue to operate its international wireless business, was left the rather subordinate role of sales agency for the receiving apparatus built by the electrical companies. Coordination between functions was to be achieved through a group of interlocking committees on which each of the owners was represented.

The radiotelephonic equipment to be manufactured was still contemplated to be for communications between individuals—from one operator to other operators within his transmitting radius—or from one station to another station, as it had evolved in international wireless. But experiments that had begun even before the radio combine was born would soon alter the fundamental character of the new service, would transform its role from that of narrowcasting to that of broadcasting—as Sarnoff had prophesied in his radio music box memorandum.

Yet it was to be another American—of Scottish descent, not the immigrant from Russia—who first accomplished the historic transition. Frank Conrad grew up in Pittsburgh and started his career working on a production line at Westinghouse. Like Sarnoff, he was a grade-school dropout and an early devotee of wireless. Before the war, he was a ham operator, transmitting dots and dashes from his Pittsburgh garage. Unlike Sarnoff, he was an inventor foremost, and he spent the war years developing radio devices for the armed forces, such as a wind-driven generator to power wireless transmitters in aircraft. More than two hundred patentable radio devices sprang from his fertile brain, but as he grew into engineering status at Westinghouse he was confined to electrical projects. So he continued to tinker with radio at home, building a small voice transmitter to replace his telegraph key.

Purely as an avocation on Sunday afternoons, Conrad began transmitting recorded music, both operatic and popular, after announcing where the music originated from. To his great surprise, scores of letters began to arrive from amateur set owners in the greater Pittsburgh area. Word of the broadcast reached the local Joseph Horne department store, and it got Conrad's agreement on what it considered a novel merchandising scheme. He would continue the recorded music transmissions at fixed times on Sunday, and the department store would advertise them in advance in Pittsburgh newspapers and would offer for sale amateur wireless sets, priced at $10, capable of receiving the music. Within days of the first advertisement, Horne was sold out of sets.

More significant, the advertisements captured the attention of a senior Westinghouse executive, Harry P. Davis. Although he was not aware of the Sarnoff memorandum, the same concept of vast audiences tuned to a single transmission came to his mind. As he later told the Harvard Business School, he was gripped by a possibility of "limitless opportunity." Westinghouse could manufacture home receivers for Conrad's broadcasts in the same factories that were turning out other electrical apparatus. And it could also advertise in advance to attract set sales and increasing audiences. He encouraged Conrad, with Westinghouse financial support, to build a new and more powerful transmitter on the roof of a company plant and to develop a more extensive broadcast schedule, including announcements on the weather and other news items of local interest. Next Davis went to Washington and applied to the Department of Commerce for a station license, which was granted on October 27, 1920, with the call letters KDKA and with an assigned frequency removed from the standard amateur band.

So at precisely the time that Young and Sarnoff were negotiating their patent concord with the telephone company, Westinghouse was germinating a new wireless service that would soon capture America. A glimpse of what it portended came in the Harding-Cox presidential election of that year when Westinghouse arranged to receive voting returns by wire at its headquarters and then broadcast them over station KDKA. The event was heavily promoted in newspaper stories and advertisements, and thousands of Pittsburghers clustered around newly purchased receiving devices to become the first audience to receive national election returns via radio.

By the time the patent consortium was completed in 1921, others were testing the mass audience theory. The Detroit *Daily News* installed a transmitter adjacent to its news room and began broadcasting news bulletins to amateur set owners in its circulation area. Later the *News* would claim that it, and not Westinghouse, was the first in radio. On the West Coast, an electrical engineer named Fred Couples began entertaining his neighbors in Hollywood with recorded music broadcast from his 5-watt bedroom transmitter. As the idea of reaching broad audiences spread, the thousands of small voice transmitters built by war veterans became incipient broadcast stations.

Absorbed as he was in patent negotiations, Sarnoff nevertheless was aware that the developments he had portended were occurring without his, and RCA's, direct involvement. To associates, he applauded the Westinghouse action but privately he was crestfallen, and he determined to regain the initiative. With Young's concurrence, he submitted a refurbished version of his music box memo to E. M. Rice, Jr., president of the parent GE. He laid heavy emphasis on the sales potential of home radios that would far exceed in sophistication of circuitry and cabinetry the simple amateur sets then being pieced together in parts shops. He estimated sales of 100,000 units in the introductory year, increasing to 600,000 units in the third year, and with dollar volume growing from $7.5 million to $45 million. This time, his memo was not pigeonholed, although the response was lukewarm, perhaps because wireless seemed remote from GE's white goods production. Rice forwarded it to the RCA board, which granted Sarnoff $2,500 for developmental work. It was a dollop, and it told him that home radio was low on the agenda of the electrical company. Nevertheless, he persuaded his friend Dr. Alfred Goldsmith, RCA's first director of research, to put together a breadboard model of his music box. Goldsmith christened it the Radiola, and the name adhered when the company later made a delayed entry into the home radio market.

As he pushed for greater RCA involvement, realization began dawning on Sarnoff that life would not be the same in the more structured empire of GE as it was in the familial environment of American Marconi. While his ties to Young were strong, he was far removed from Marconi's beneficent oversight. And he was, for the first time, encountering open resentment at his forays across organizational lines, such as the memo dispatched directly to Rice. Among second- and third-tier GE executives, his reputation for intrusiveness soon translated into brashness. Worse yet, he was a brash Jew. In a number of subtle ways a process of hazing Sarnoff began. Unwanted visitors to GE's headquarters, such as inventors with utopian schemes and irate individuals bearing malfunctioning toasters, began appearing outside Sarnoff's office demanding an immediate audience. Invitations to company social functions, to which his position entitled him, were mislaid or misaddressed. Make-work reports of insignificant developments at RCA were demanded of him, often with overnight deadlines. Years later he remembered how "all the stray cat and dog problems of management were being dumped on my desk."

The only person who could stop the harassment, Sarnoff concluded, was the man who bridged the worlds of GE and RCA and who had been with him in the patent negotiations. He gambled that Young's dependence upon him in business matters was sufficiently strong that a discussion of personal problems would not turn the older man against him. When Young accepted his invitation for dinner one night in early 1921, Sarnoff rented a small private dining room at Delmonico's restaurant. There the two of them spent four hours together over a leisurely meal and there, as he had with Marconi fifteen years earlier, he poured out the story of his life—from Uzlian to the East Side ghetto, from news peddler to office boy, the struggle to hold his family together, the years of self-education, the rise through the Marconi ranks, and finally the problems he was encountering at GE, which he attributed bluntly to anti-Semitism. Young listened intently and sympathetically, occasionally asking a question but never foreclosing any conversational route the younger man chose to explore. Finally, past midnight, the talk bridged over into the future, with Sarnoff blueprinting the role he hoped RCA would play in radio.

The dinner became, in Sarnoff's memory, a milestone of his career, cementing the relationship between the two and stimulating Young to place a mantle of executive protectionism around his commercial manager. Within days, according to Sarnoff, word seeped through the organization that when he spoke on RCA matters, he spoke with Young's voice. Any further barbs and slurs aimed at Sarnoff would be considered an affront to Young himself. Henceforth he would be known as the protégé of the chairman, and he now considered himself immune to the envy of the less talented.

The dinner also encouraged Sarnoff to move more aggressively to counter Westinghouse, which appeared determined to preempt radio broadcasting following the national attention it gained from the Harding-Cox election returns. Nothing in the agreement between members of the radio combine anticipated the emergence of broadcasting stations, and Westinghouse quickly secured licenses for KYW in Chicago, WJZ in New York, and WBZ in Springfield, Massachusetts. A broadcast division was created under Vice-president Davis, who sooner than anyone but Sarnoff had grasped the potential for mass appeal, and he became radio's first showman. At the premiere of KYW he placed Westinghouse microphones in the Chicago Opera House, and the glamorous diva Mary Garden sang to an audience estimated at twenty thousand in homes, social clubs, and restaurants. This was soon followed by the broadcast arias of Madame Schumann-Heink and Tito Schipa. At WJZ, Vincent Lopez enthralled a New York metropolitan area audience with popular melodies from his dance band, and the concept of live broadcasting, rather than recorded fare, began to take hold.

Sarnoff reasoned that only through a live broadcast that captured the nation's attention could RCA hope to arrest the Westinghouse momentum and could he fortify the position he sought for himself as radio's prophetic voice. His ability to plan such a coup was vastly enhanced when Young, as an aftermath of the Delmonico dinner, made him general manager of RCA and a corporate officer on April 29, 1921, two months after his thirtieth birthday. He now felt secure enough to make a major broadcasting gamble, even at the risk of abrading one or more of RCA's multiple owners.

Although not a sports fan, the new general manager knew that the eyes of the nation were riveted to an extraordinary degree on an impending world heavyweight championship fight between Jack Dempsey, the famed Manassa Mauler, and the challenging champion of France, Georges Carpentier. If he could arrange to broadcast the fight, Sarnoff reasoned, RCA would be as well known in radio as Westinghouse. All the elements of high drama were present—the international rivalry, the contrast between the two combatants: Carpentier, the gracefully stylish Orchid Man, the war hero severely wounded in the service of France, versus Dempsey, the ruthless and scowling defending champion who had been accused of slackerism for failing to don American khaki in the war.

The fight was scheduled for July 2, 1921, at Boyle's Thirty Acres in Jersey City, across the Hudson River from Manhattan. Sarnoff knew he would have to move quickly, too quickly in fact to secure the formal approval of the radio combine. First, he secured the permission of the promoter, Tex Rickard, to broadcast the fight from a microphone placed at ringside. Next, with a subtle assist from Young, he borrowed a powerful GE radiotelephone transmitter that was destined for the Navy Department in Washington, and detoured it to a Lackawanna Railroad shed at a siding near Boyle's Thirty Acres. RCA engineers created an antenna by stringing wires between railroad towers at the siding, and a telephone line coupled the ringside microphone with the transmitter shed. All this was accomplished without a budget, and Sarnoff later admitted, "I plucked what I needed from whatever departments had a little cash in the till." All told, the bill came to about $1,500.

To widen the audience and to give the fight a patriotic cachet, Sarnoff enlisted the support of Miss Anne Morgan, daughter of financier J. P. Morgan. As the head of an American charity raising funds for the rehabilitation of war-devastated France, Miss Morgan seized on the broadcast as a lure for charity gatherings whose proceeds would go to French relief. Wherever the broadcast signal promised to reach, the charity affairs were scheduled, more than one hundred in all across the eastern United States, from northern Florida to southern Maine. Heading up the sponsoring committee was Franklin D. Roosevelt, only weeks away from his near fatal polio attack. And the promoter Rickard, the first major sports figure to sense the revolutionary significance for sports of broadcasting, worked enthusiastically with Sarnoff to widen the audience further by placing sets with amplifying speakers in Rotary and Elks clubs, school auditoriums, town halls, movie theaters, and dance emporiums. To handle the ringside blow-by-blow account, Sarnoff selected one of his employees, a glib boxing buff named Andrew J. White, who edited RCA's internal magazine, *Wireless Age*. As deputy at ringside, ready to take over if laryngitis or excitement felled his announcer, Sarnoff selected himself.

In the searing heat of July 2, with Boyle's Thirty Acres' wooden grandstands packed with more than ninety thousand raucous fight fans, White gave the first live accounting for an unseen audience of a major sports event. Ironically, his excited description of the savage demolition of the French champion by Dempsey's iron fists went no farther than the Lackawanna transmitter shed. There an RCA technician, J. O. Smith, reported White's story from his headset into another microphone attached to the transmitter. It was Smith's flat twang and prosaic description that the audience heard, but that did nothing to vitiate the drama of the match, which ended with a Dempsey knockout of his smaller foe in the fourth round. To Sarnoff, the quality of the broadcast was more important than the fight's outcome, and he learned within minutes of the referee's final toll that he had narrowly averted a fate worse than Carpentier's. The furnacelike heat in the railroad shed, plus an electrical overload, blew out the transmitter, and when Sarnoff inspected it with Dr. Goldsmith, his chief technician, it was (according to the later wording of Goldsmith's official report) a "molten mass." Another round would have been one too many, and Sarnoff later professed enduring gratitude for Dempsey's quick and workmanlike job.

Despite the loss of the transmitter, the impact of the broadcast on GE and RCA was profound. It had produced national headlines before and after the fight, and RCA was deluged with laudatory telegrams and letters. More than 300,000 Americans listened to the broadcast and Miss Morgan's charity reaped its greatest single windfall. In Europe, where a detailed account had been arranged through the use of RCA's international wireless links, the response was similarly enthusiastic. From London, where he was attending a wireless conference, Nally telegraphed Sarnoff: YOU HAVE MADE HISTORY. And the corporate hierarchy, led by Young, echoed the praise. But the most important aftermath to the general manager was the permission he received for RCA to operate its own broadcast transmitter in New York. He was on the way in radio.

The nation, too, was on the way. By the end of 1921, the Department of Commerce had issued thirty-two broadcast licenses, and a year later the number of applicants had passed six hundred. Voice transmitters were simply too easy to construct, and too accessible for purchase by those of limited means, for large corporations to control their distribution and usage. Small radio parts stores were proliferating, offering both transmitting and receiving equipment. Local program schedules began appearing in newspapers, and their staples were anything that was available without cost, from aspiring local singers and thespians to ministers and real estate promoters. Transmitting studios were stitched together in hotels and department stores, their walls insulated against external sounds by mattresses or straw stuffed in burlap, and soon long lines of aspiring performers were forming outside them. In 1922, if you could trill a note, finger a piano octave, or recite with minimal clarity a verse by Edgar Allan Poe, you probably responded to the lure of the radiotelephonic art. Even if you were Rudolph Valentino, the essence of romance and mystery to the nation's female populace, you would risk the passions of the mob to appear before the microphone of Westinghouse's Chicago outlet.

In many ways radio began to mirror the buoyant decade in which it was born. From the deprivations and restraints of the war years, America burst into the free-wheeling decade of the Roaring Twenties, with its speakeasies and bathtub gin, its gangster folk heroes like Al Capone and Owney Madden, and its flappers dancing the Charleston until dawn. Before its apocalyptic end, the decade produced vast stock bonanzas and blue-sky market riggings, created overnight millionaires and a new pantheon of sports heroes to whom radio gave voice—Dempsey and Babe Ruth, Bobby Jones and Bill Tilden. It was an era of unprecedented mobility and change, at its heart a search for escape, and nothing could reflect it like the ubiquitous microphone, moving with equal facility between convention hall and sports arena and dance ballroom.

The broadcasting boom was paralleled by the introduction of brand-name radio sets powered by vacuum tubes and enclosed in cabinetry of sometimes ornate design. Soon the crystal receiver would become a wireless dinosaur, and the names Philco, Atwater Kent, Grebe, Stromberg-Carlson, and Zenith would become part of the American lexicon. Their sets sold for up to $400, but the torrential rush of buyers quickly backed up production lines. Unlike the electric light or the automobile, where product introduction was relatively orderly and spaced out over years, radio's entrée to the marketplace more closely resembled Sutter's Creek or the Klondike when gold was struck. Demand developed with an intensity that industrial America had never before experienced—and not according to the blueprint of the giants of the radio combine.

To Sarnoff's chagrin, RCA was months behind competitive brands in getting the Radiola into dealer stores. He blamed the delay on the tedious process of securing design approval from technical committees dominated by GE and Westinghouse engineers. Then there was the further complication of sandwiching set production between the output of light bulbs and refrigerators, which were still the bread and butter business of the electrical companies. But Sarnoff fretted more over the direction the industry was taking. A wildcatting mentality born of early wireless still prevailed. By 1923 an incredible total of two hundred set manufacturers and five thousand component makers had surfaced in every section of the country. Most operated in the bucket shop tradition, purchasing brand-name sets, cannibalizing the parts, and replicating without concern for patent infringement. Even the major brand names, Sarnoff began to suspect, were purchasing RCA tubes on a flourishing black market and incorporating them in their product, with patent rights ignored. The situation, as he then saw it, was later summed up by radio historian Lawrence Lessing: "A raggle-taggle mob of free enterprisers was running away with the business." And it was a mob that for a brief period had a certain aura of respectability. Beyond the wildcatters, community groups were banding together to assemble components into finished receivers—women's clubs and Rotarians, even high school classes in the manual crafts.

In this chaotic environment, Sarnoff determined that he had to act decisively, not only for RCA but on behalf of all its owners. Otherwise, the game would be lost in the first inning. He was chairman of the patent committee of the radio combine, and he won the committee's approval to begin patent litigation against infringers in the federal courts. Since it was impractical to strike at all, target companies were carefully selected, among them one of the largest brand names, A. H. Grebe. At the same time, Sarnoff decided to clamp down on the distribution process for RCA's patented products. As later recounted by historian Erik Barnouw, RCA began "to put increasing pressure on its distributors. It dropped distributors who ordered only tubes and favored those who pushed 'the entire Radio Corporation line.' " Increasingly, tubes were allocated in proportion to the number of complete sets ordered. And distributors were required to return, with their orders for certain critical tubes, an equal supply of burned-out tubes. They were also warned by a message on shipping cartons that tubes were not authorized for use with non-RCA components, assembled or partly assembled.

In the vernacular of a later generation, Sarnoff began playing hardball. He was assuming the role of the industry's policeman and it was an unpopular one, leading to enmities that would later scourge his career. Since the formation of the radio combine, the fear of competing enterprises had centered on the prospect of punitive action by RCA to protect its patent monopoly. Now they saw it happening, and they were outraged. An Association of Independent Radio Manufacturers was formed, with Commander Eugene McDonald, president of Zenith, at its head, and a vigorous lobbying effort was mounted in Washington against the allegedly anticompetitive thrust of the combine. The independents also began warning publishers of newspapers, in which they were substantial advertisers, that unless the press was vigilant another great monopoly would suddenly blot out competition, in the pattern of oil and telephony. In Chicago, home of Zenith, editorials in the daily press questioned whether the radio combine intended to drive its competitors to the wall. And the *New York Times* suggested bluntly that the chief function of the patent pool was "to intimidate the trade and to make the evasion of the anti-trust laws possible."

The sense of anxiety within the industry heightened as the partners of the combine also moved vigorously into broadcasting, following the lead of Westinghouse. GE erected a station in its headquarters city of Schenectady, and AT&T, already involved in the manufacture and sale of broadcast transmitters, built and began operating a New York station. And Sarnoff, capitalizing on the approval his fight broadcast had won, placed RCA's first transmitter on the roof of the Aeolian Hall in midtown Manhattan, opposite the New York Public Library. He followed this with the construction of an

RCA station in Washington, with the presumed intention of giving the combine a voice that the Congress could hear. Each of the stations owned by the partners was in the superpower category, meaning that it covered a broader area with a stronger signal than most of the independents could generate. The specter of a few strategically placed superpower stations, in the hands of the combine, blanketing the nation was raised in Congress with increasing frequency.

As criticism of the radio "trust," as it was becoming known, mounted in volume and intensity, Young concluded that he needed a new president of RCA, a man of national stature whose integrity was beyond challenge and who could project an effective image for the company before the various tribunals that molded public opinion. He would let Nally continue as director of international wireless until his impending retirement and Sarnoff would remain as operating chief with the additional title of vice-president. Much as he admired and trusted his thirty-one-year-old general manager, Young concluded that a person of greater maturity, one better known to the general public, was needed. The search for a replacement, which required several months, led Young to a man he had known only by reputation, a professional soldier named James G. Harbord, who was serving in the War Department in Washington. The intermediary was Secretary of War Newton D. Baker, and several secret meetings ensued before Harbord agreed to swap his uniform for the mufti and the vastly enhanced financial emoluments of the RCA presidency.

While totally without experience in commercial radio, Harbord fulfilled Young's essential qualifications. He was a man of impeccable reputation whose mere presence would tend to cloak the company in a patriotic mantle. He had won national fame as chief of staff for General Pershing with the American Expeditionary Force in France. And he was the apotheosis of the career soldier: a young Rough Rider under Teddy Roosevelt who was commissioned in the field; a much decorated veteran of Pershing's Mexican border campaign who rose to the final rank of lieutenant general. He was a soldier of such pure flame that he once described war as "a permanent factor in human life and a very noble one . . . the school of heroism from which a nation's noblest sons graduated into highest manhood."

The arrival of Harbord on January 1, 1923, coincided with a mounting crescendo of complaints that even his reputation could not mute. Sarnoff's campaign to crack down on patent violators and foreclose the use of RCA components by others was producing angry stirrings in the Congress. Competitors complained that RCA's refusal to license its vast storehouse of patents left them in an untenable position—either infringe the patents or go out of business. The fact that the Navy Department, and implicitly the Wilson administration, had fathered the patent pool only four years earlier bore little weight with congressmen besieged by local manufacturers, department stores, and newspapers with radio interests. These were their moneyed constituents who feared being pinched off just as the bonanza of radio was materializing. On March 3, 1923, the Congress responded by passing a resolution that empowered the Federal Trade Commission to launch an investigation of the patent structure of the radio industry and thus help the legislators determine whether antitrust laws were being violated.

The initial consternation at RCA was quickly replaced by a determination to fight back, which Sarnoff embodied more than any other executive. The patent litigation would be pursued unrelentingly, and the top management of Young, Harbord, and Sarnoff would form a battle triumvirate appearing jointly or individually as required before the trade commissioners, committees of Congress, at industry conventions, and on major speaking platforms. They decided to appeal for public support, and their defense would be the rectitude of the patent laws and the compelling need to harmonize an industry in disarray.

Much of the opposing fire centered on Sarnoff and his role as industry policeman. This was the first of many industry struggles in which he would be center stage, and he found that he relished the spotlight of controversy, the give-and-take of internecine struggle. His quick mind, crammed with radio facts and supported by a personality that vouchsafed deep inner certitude, made him a commanding witness at hearings that soon would consume much of his business life.

Despite the job pressures, Sarnoff's personal life flourished. His salary had increased to $15,000, and he had surprised Lizette with a new Lincoln, their first car. Also he had moved the family back into a comfortable Manhattan apartment. With his distaste for exercise and leisure activities, he felt circumscribed by the bucolic life of Mount Vernon and he resented the time spent in commuting. On weekends, when not traveling to Washington for hearings, he was often at his Woolworth Building office, catching up on the reading and mail that his twelve-hour days often could not accommodate. And he was generous with time given the press. Major New York newspapers, among them the *Times, Globe,* and *Sun,* were adding radio sections and he was often called upon for advice on industry developments and to forecast future trends. His music box memorandum had been extracted in the press, and he was rapidly becoming a public figure, in demand as a speaker and always concentrating his perorations on the future. The image he was carefully cultivating was that of the prophet of the radio age.

Initially, Sarnoff's attitude toward RCA's new president was ambivalent. He admired the military, with its aura of panoply and power, and General Harbord seemed to him its quintessential symbol. Nevertheless he was temporarily distressed that his chairman had considered him too young to be Nally's successor, because he considered himself fully qualified. Yet he soon discerned that Harbord, thirty years his senior, represented no long-range threat to his corporate aspirations. The famous soldier seemed almost schoolboy eager to learn the rudiments of radio from his general manager, and Sarnoff was flattered. He found Harbord, unlike some military types he had known, particularly in the navy, free of the slightest taint of anti-Semitism. And the new president remained aloof from operational matters, thus persuading Sarnoff that his organizational stature had not diminished. The fealty between the two men soon approached that of Young and Sarnoff.

In 1922, its first full year of radio sales, RCA's gross income from sets and components totaled $11,286,489.41, more than $3 million in excess of Sarnoff's original music box projection. So his vision of radio's growth prospects had been vindicated. Yet the RCA annual report for that year was strangely silent on the veraciousness of the general manager's prophecy. In their remarks to RCA shareholders, the chairman and president said:

"At the time your Corporation was formed in 1919, for the purpose of building up a worldwide international wireless communications system, wireless telephony had not passed out of the experimental stage, and it was not at that time foreseen that the broadcasting art would ever reach the high point of popularity that it has in the past year. The engineers and scientists had anticipated the development of wireless telephony for communications purposes, but no one had visualized the phenomenal expression of wireless telephony as used today for broadcasting."

Had Young consciously omitted any reference to his general manager's prescience for fear of irritating RCA's other owners? Or was the music box memo accorded less significance at the time than broadcast historians, and Sarnoff's biographer, later bestowed upon it? Even in his own later recollection, Sarnoff derived little personal satisfaction from the relative accuracy of his forecast, because RCA's sales were dwarfed by those of the industry, which reached $60 million in 1922. The fact was that, while the FTC investigation and the patent litigation inched forward, others were running off with the market. The leading independents, like Philco and Atwater Kent, were simply more nimble than RCA in incorporating new selling features, such as a set without batteries that could be plugged into an electrical socket in the home.

To Sarnoff the primary reason for RCA's position was the committee structure imposed by the radio combine. There were technical, legal, and administrative committees on which he served, in addition to the patent committee he chaired. Most of the endless hours he spent in committee deliberations in his opinion were wasted. He chafed under what he considered to be the elephantine slowness of the decision-making process, and he agreed with a *Fortune* magazine evaluation several years later of why RCA lagged in early radio.

"The sorry truth of the matter," the magazine wrote, "was that when it got right down to radio sets the public often was not convinced that the

Radio Corporation offered the best bargain ... the radio industry, during the years of its evolution, was just not the kind of business in which a great industrial organization, with its huge overhead, its complicated bureaucracy, could thrive. Any ingenious young man with a cellar to work in might hit upon a way of putting together a better radio, get a backer, and have his set in the stores before the same idea, had it originated in RCA's laboratories, had the okay of a department head. RCA just could not turn around fast enough."

Sarnoff's frustrations were compounded by what he felt was the lethargy of the courts in dealing with patent infringements. Many of the most vital patents were the subject of litigation, and the courts would give no injunctive relief against infringers until the certitude of the patent had been established up through the final appellate process. How could you proceed against five thousand infringers, many of whom were so undercapitalized that they might be out of business before you could collect on a final decree? In *Fortune*'s judgment, "A wholesale disrespect for the sanctity of patent rights nurtured an independent radio industry," and Sarnoff did not dispute that.

At the heart of the controversy was the vacuum tube, where the radio combine's patent rights were clearly controlling but were being almost totally ignored. More than 75 percent of the home radios sold in 1922 and 1923 were competitive brands, but they possessed vacuum tubes that, in RCA's view, were illegally obtained. Nevertheless, this did not restrain the Federal Trade Commission from reporting to Congress in 1923 that an incipient monopoly threatened the new industry and that RCA "has practically no competition in the radio communications field." It arrived at this curious conclusion by assuming that RCA had the potential for monopoly even if de facto the monopoly didn't exist.

"There is no question," the FTC reported, "that the pooling of all patents pertaining to vacuum tubes has resulted in giving the Radio Corporation and its affiliated companies a monopoly in the manufacture, sale and use thereof. With such a monopoly, the Radio Corporation apparently has the power to stifle competition in the manufacture and sale of receiving sets, and prevent all radio apparatus from being used for commercial radio communications purposes."

Within months, the FTC would follow up with a formal complaint against GE, Westinghouse, AT&T, United Fruit, and RCA, charging them with "having conspired for the purpose of, and with the effect of, restraining competition and creating a monopoly in the manufacture, purchase and sale in interstate commerce of radio devices." Although the FTC charge would ultimately be dropped, the groundwork had been laid for a series of antitrust attacks that would consume much of RCA's, and Sarnoff's, time over four decades. Although failing in their ultimate purpose, the dismantling of RCA, the attacks would result, through a series of consent decrees, in the emasculation of the patent pool and in the dissolution of the original radio combine. And they would also, at a far later date, raise at the highest levels of the Justice Department the grim possibility of criminal prosecution of Sarnoff himself.

At times Sarnoff felt he was viewing the world through the distorted prism of Alice's looking glass. On the one hand he was hammered by the anvil chorus of monopoly, on the other he saw that radio had become more intensely competitive than any industry in American history, with a growth rate far faster than he, the prophet of growth, had envisaged. And, despite the turbulence of the times, he saw the affairs of his own company prospering, with even international wireless making good progress. The number of message words increased to 18 million in 1921 and 23 million in 1922. Gross income from wireless traffic went from $2,138,635 in 1921 to $2,914,283 a year later, and radio marine service, the other original business, went from $553,000 to $630,000. But it was radio that propelled RCA. Sales more than doubled in 1923, with gross income reaching $26,400,000, which produced a net profit of $4,737,774.

Despite its lagging competitive position in radio set sales, RCA was riding the industry tidal wave. Within two years, the public's investment in all aspects of the new service had grown to $358,000,000. Nothing had ever mushroomed that fast that soon, and radio was soon being accorded unique and wondrous qualities. GOD IS ALWAYS BROADCASTING read the sign in front of a Lexington, Kentucky, church. To William Jennings Bryan, perennial Democratic presidential candidate of an earlier day, it was "a gift of Providence." And the nation was now immune from surprise attack, according to no less an authority than former Navy Secretary Josephus Daniels. "Nobody now fears that a Japanese fleet could deal an unexpected blow on our Pacific possessions," he told a North Carolina student audience on October 16, 1922. "Radio makes surprises impossible." Yet radio caught its share of blame too. A Kentucky farmer complained to station WHAS in Lexington that a radio wave had struck a flock of blackbirds, and one of them dropped dead at his feet. "What if the wave had struck me?" he asked.

No one was more fulsome than RCA's general manager in projecting the scope and meaning of radio. As part of his defense of the patent structure, but also to conceptualize the role radio would play in the nation's life, he had taken to the hustings. Years later, Henry Luce, founder of the magazine empire, would describe Sarnoff as "our man of the future," and it was a title accorded him in part because of his visionary talks to service clubs, industry organizations, and business schools, beginning in the early twenties. In one typical address, before the electrical jobbers convention at Hot Springs, Virginia, on May 26, 1922, he was in full rhetorical flower:

"In radio broadcasting we have a force, an instrumentality greater than any that has yet come to mankind. Back of it is a philosophy, something more than a mere merchandising situation. When you transmit the human voice into the home, when you can make the home attuned to what is going on in the rest of the world, you have tapped a new source of influence, a new source of pleasure and entertainment and culture that the world thus far has not been able to provide with any other known means of communications . . . certain it is, in my mind, that the day is coming, and perhaps not so far distant, when a man will be ashamed to admit that his home is not equipped with a radio broadcasting device, just as a man today would be ashamed to admit that his home is not equipped with a bathtub. I regard radio broadcasting as a sort of cleansing instrument for the mind, just as the bathtub is for the body. Now the broadcasting station makes possible, for the first time in the history of civilization, communications with hundreds and thousands and, perhaps, millions of people, simultaneously."

Between speeches and Washington testimony, Sarnoff was also engrossed in a major organizational buildup at RCA, to cope with a business that was doubling its volume annually and that emitted no hints of slackening. He was hiring engineers and auditors, creating a publicity and advertising department, and enlarging his legal staff for the tests ahead. In the chaotic environment of the industry, he was determined that RCA would be a disciplined organization, with authority concentrated in his office. Those guilty of slovenly practices quickly felt the lash of his tongue or pen. Once, when two of his calls to Pierre Boucheron, the new head of publicity and advertising, went unanswered, he strode into Boucheron's office and found it empty, but the desk strewn with papers. A memo awaited the chastened newcomer on his return: This was not the way RCA functioned, it was a company of clean desks, orderly files, and prompt return of telephone calls, particularly those of the general manager. Implicit was a shape-up or ship-out warning. To some, those who did not remain, Sarnoff's demands smacked of the martinet, but the majority of his employees soon ascertained that he asked nothing of them that he did not of himself. None worked longer hours, and his work was always in an atmosphere of total control. Only one paper at a time crossed his desk. When a subordinate sent him an action memo, the response normally came within hours. He warred against the pigeonhole tactic of delay, perhaps remembering the original fate of his music box proposal. To a unique degree, he won the respect and loyalty of his organization, and it was reflected by years of stable and long-tenured management.

Sarnoff often remained at the office long after his staff had departed because it was then, free of the press of operational matters, that he could reflect and conceptualize. Late in 1923, mulling over the problems facing his company during a solitary night, Sarnoff came to the conclusion that he had to break new ground in the patent situation. The independent manufacturers were increasingly adroit in their propaganda. They were the little fellows battling the "trust," and RCA was being coupled in the public's mind with earlier predators in oil and steel. "It seemed the whole industry would soon be moving from the research laboratories to the courts," he later reflected, and to ward off that unpalatable prospect he developed a plan that would make the radio combine's principal patents legally available to its competitors.

The primary complaint of the independents was that RCA's refusal to license patents left them with two alternatives—either infringe or go out of business. Now Sarnoff proposed to cloak their solvency in legality. A package of RCA's key patents would be made available to the leading independents for a fee on each set they manufactured. Initially it would be 7½ percent, so that for every set retailed at $100 RCA would collect $7.50.

The plan won Young and Harbord's concurrence, along with that of the board of directors, and soon after Sarnoff's announcement most of the major independents signed licensing agreements, with archrival Zenith among the first. Later the offer was extended to smaller producers, particularly if they atoned for past infringements by paying up a portion of what RCA felt was owed it. Royalties were soon reduced to about 5 percent per set, and more than 90 percent of the radios manufactured in America, beginning in the mid-twenties, were under RCA license. The pool had grown to nearly four thousand patents, and it provided RCA with millions of dollars in additional income, giving it a degree of industry influence that it had yet to win in the marketplace. As the company grew, patent licensing income fueled it, underwriting research activities that in turn led to further patentable inventions and new products. During the depression years, license income would sometimes spell the difference between profit and loss in the annual balance sheet.

While Sarnoff was widely applauded within the combine for his adroit maneuver, he did not, as he had hoped, completely blunt the monopoly thrust. He had bought some time for his company and perhaps lessened temporarily some of the political pressures on it, but a new form of resentment began welling up. The independents had agreed to the licensing arrangement to free themselves of onerous and protracted legal proceedings, but they soon began chafing at paying "tribute" to an entrenched rival they considered increasingly demanding. In their view the essential elements of monopoly remained unchanged. They considered the patent pool intrinsically illegal, regardless of the new licensing policy. The vast combined resources of the electrical companies behind RCA, they felt, gave it an unfair competitive advantage, and the sharing of functions between competitors did violence to the very concept of free enterprise. Zenith and Philco, in particular, continued stoking antitrust fires in the Justice Department and the Congress, and their target was Sarnoff as much as his company.

For wholly different reasons, RCA's general manager was also beginning to question in his own mind whether the linkage with the electrical companies should endure. "The system was just too sluggish," he reminisced years later to one of his associates. "We were submerged under too many layers of electrical company management. Somewhere down the road, in some manner I couldn't then foresee, I felt that RCA was going to have to break loose, and I assumed I'd play a central role in accomplishing it. The thought didn't particularly bother me, despite my affection for Owen Young. I was pretty much persuaded early on that if RCA was ever to become a great company, it would have to do it on its own."

Over a period of many months, usually in solitary reveries at night in his office, he began crystallizing in his mind what could make RCA merit the criterion of greatness. Not only must it be independent but it must acquire a proficiency in every element of its emerging technology, manufacturing its own receiving sets and components and transmitters, owning its own broadcasting stations and creating what was transmitted over them, building its own centralized research laboratories and fueling them with proceeds from the patent pool. Wherever research in communications and electronics led, whatever new wireless products the future ordained, RCA must be in the vanguard, always the industry's creative force, always the leader, never the follower. The more Sarnoff gave free reign to his imagination, the more he became persuaded that such an integrated monolith would give America a new dimension of technological leadership, unique in its creative capabilities and dramatically different from other enterprises then on the national scene. Only to his wife, Lizette, did he occasionally let his dream unfold, and, as she later reported, "I never interrupted him."

All of Sarnoff's formative years had conditioned him to think in terms of bigness. In his apprenticeship at American Marconi, he was part of an organization that aspired to global monopoly in wireless. He had seen foreign communications monopolies emerge. He had observed at intimate proximity the navy's effort to impose a unified structure on America's international wireless arm through a patent monopoly. While he believed in competition in his industry, except in international wireless, it was competition in the oligarchical sense—among a few great enterprises and with one usually leading the way, just as it was occurring in automobiles and as it had occurred in oil and steel. He was confident a great shakeout would come in the domestic communications business, with one company emerging from the cauldron of competition as its leader. That was the role he envisaged for RCA, and he was soon to pursue it with singular intensity.

4 / The First Network

The years between 1922 and 1926 were the most crucial in the development of American broadcasting. The service matrix that exists today, for television as well as radio, was configured then. A decisive battle for leadership was waged between paladins of the business world. The unity of the original radio combine was shattered. Bitter personal animosities developed, tinctured by charges of anti-Semitism. Yet despite the outsize dimensions of the struggle for control of the broadcast service, the public was oblivious to it, for the press failed to unearth it. In security-sealed corporate board rooms and Manhattan legal offices, and at secret arbitration hearings, the penumbral drama unfolded.

By 1923, with over six hundred transmitters operating, radio's dispersion was nationwide. Yet the broadcast service remained essentially local in character. Even with highly visible broadcasts, such as the Dempsey-Carpentier fight, the live account went over a single transmitter whose signals accommodated only a region of the nation, not all of it. Among leaders of the new art, realization was dawning that a more cohesive and universal broadcast service was the essential next step. But how to achieve it? Through a few superpower stations, strategically sited to blanket the nation? Or could other technical means be developed for linking up existing transmitters in a broadcast chain capable of relaying programs simultaneously from a central originating source?

Even Sarnoff, in his original music box memorandum, had viewed broadcasting from a local perspective. He posited a station that would cover its neighborhood with a signal radius of twenty-five to forty miles, and create its own local programs. But after observing radio's inchoate spread for three years, its signals often ululating with static and colliding with one another in the unregulated spectrum, he became concerned that radio might smother in its own dissonance. Some form of disciplined superstructure had to be imposed on this increscent local service, and the solution he arrived at was the creation of a national broadcasting company that would become the central program repository for the nation. He became the first industry leader, in the consensus of broadcast historians, to translate the idea into a specific plan of action.

On June 22, 1922, again short-circuiting organizational lines but again with Owen Young's approval, Sarnoff addressed a lengthy letter to GE's president Rice which contained both an analysis of radio's problems and a recommended solution to them. He suggested that the novelty of radio would soon wear off, with the public "no longer interested" in the means by which it was able to receive but, rather, "in the substance and quality of the material received." Then, he said, "the task of reasonably meeting the public's expectations and desires will be greater than any so far tackled by any newspaper, theater, opera, or other public information or entertainment agency . . . the broadcasting station will ultimately be required to entertain a nation."

But the accomplishment of that goal, Sarnoff continued, could not be realized within the existing framework of manufacturing and communications companies interested in radio. They simply didn't have the talent or experience for it. "This kind of job calls for specialists in . . . entertaining, informing and educating . . . it requires expert knowledge of the public's taste and the manner in which to cater to the public's taste." His solution: "Let us organize a separate and distinct company, to be known as the Public Service Broadcasting Company or National Radio Broadcasting Company or American Radio Broadcasting Company, or some similar name. This company to be controlled by the Radio Corporation of America, but its board of directors and officers to include members of the General Electric Company and the Westinghouse Electric Company and possibly a few from the outside, prominent in national and civic affairs. The administrative and operating staff of this company to be composed of those considered best qualified to do the broadcasting job. Such company to acquire the existing broadcasting stations (of the radio group); to operate such stations and build such additional broadcasting stations as may be determined in the future . . ."

This would be the nucleus of Sarnoff's national network. To "defray its expenses"—for he did not visualize his broadcasting company as a profit-making enterprise—he offered the novel suggestion that RCA, GE, and Westinghouse contribute 2 percent of their gross radio sales, and that "our licensees," i.e., competing set manufacturers, be asked to do the same. If that were insufficient, the tithe might be extended to others in the distribution chain, down to the dealer level. They were, he reasoned, the ones who stood to profit from the network, since it would stimulate set sales. Outside the industry, Sarnoff speculated that "there may even appear on the horizon a public benefactor who will be willing to contribute a large sum in the form of an endowment.

"Once the broadcasting company is established as a public service . . . I feel that with suitable publicity activities, such a company will ultimately be regarded as a public institution of great value, in the same sense that a library, for example, is regarded today."

This vein of altruism coursed through the letter to Rice. Sarnoff rejected the idea of the public's being required to subsidize broadcasting through payment of a monthly rental or fee on receiving sets, an idea soon to be adopted in various European countries. The airwaves belonged to the public, the broadcasters were simply custodians, the executors of a public trust. Nowhere in his letter did he consider an advertising base for radio, such as underpinned newspapers and magazines. Later, when advertising became an issue of national contention, he would oppose it, fearing it would "debase" the new medium just as it would a library or an art gallery.

Sarnoff's network proposal, like his music box memorandum, created no sudden bonfire of enthusiasm at GE, although Young, who was still only a vice-president, endorsed it. Rice sent it to one of the interlocking committees of the radio combine for evaluation and recommendation. Only pressures from the outside, principally generated by the American Telephone and Telegraph Company, ultimately brought the plan, as well as Sarnoff personally, into the dispute that emerged over control of a national service.

When AT&T joined the wireless patent pool, it did so with the aim of securing a dominant position in international voice transmission. But then radio erupted domestically in a manner totally unforeseen by the phone company's planners. "We had quite unconsciously cleared the way," Young would explain years later, referring to the patent pool, "of the greatest impediment in the development of domestic broadcasting and reception . . . and as a result the radio broadcasting art blossomed into being almost overnight." However, it blossomed in a way not to the phone company's liking. While the sales of radio sets, the province of the electrical companies and RCA, were doubling annually, AT&T was receiving a mere pittance from the sale of transmitters, its province under the cartel arrangement. By 1922, it had sold only thirty-five of the six hundred broadcast transmitters then operating, and it placed the blame on patent infringements by local broadcasters. So it initiated police action similar to RCA's against set infringers, first threatening legal steps and then demanding that the infringers pay license fees for the right to continue operating. When they balked, target stations were selected for a court challenge, beginning with independent station WHN in New York. Predictably, an outburst of monopoly charges descended on AT&T, and it found itself operating in the cacophonous worst of worlds— on the one hand, pilloried for squeezing the little independents; on the other, trapped in a narrow interstice of the total radio market, with the profitable core business enjoyed by others.

No one recognized the dilemma more keenly than Walter S. Gifford, AT&T's rising young vice-president of finance. In his judgment, the original agreement intended to harmonize patent relationships in point-to-point wireless telegraphy had been outmoded by the new circumstances of mass broadcasting, in which the financial stakes were far greater than originally envisaged. Why should AT&T, a communications company by birth, subordinate itself to electrical manufacturers and their small RCA wireless subsidiary? He urged a new course of action on the phone management, geared to a vastly greater role in radio, a course that would soon collide with the ambitions of the radio group and its now principal planner, Sarnoff.

No two men could have been more opposite in background and personality. Six years older than Sarnoff, a native-born New Englander, Gifford was reared by affluent parents in Salem, Massachusetts, with generations of American in his pedigree. In 1905, when the Russian immigrant was abandoning public school to support his family, Gifford was graduating from Harvard College, having completed his undergraduate work in three years with distinction. His academic specialty was finance, and he was recruited off campus by AT&T, with the entry level position of payroll clerk. Within ten years, he was the phone company's chief statistician, and by 1919, when he was thirty-four, vice-president in charge of finance—a rise almost as rapid as Sarnoff's subsequent one through the RCA-Marconi ranks, and in a company of vastly greater resources and stature. In manner and dress, Gifford embodied the business establishment. He favored pin-striped double-breasted suits, with wing-collared shirts and somber bow ties, and his closely clipped lip mustache was groomed to suggest maturity. His voice and manners were Yankee patrician, in concert with the Lodges, Saltonstalls, and Cabots of his New England background, and he was financially independent through marriage.

But despite his conservative orthodoxy, there were elements of daring in Gifford's character, and he was innovative in corporate finance. In 1919, when utility bond issues were not in great favor in Wall Street, he persuaded his management to go directly to market with a $90-million offering of its own securities. It was a gargantuan sum at the time, larger than any ever raised without the underwriting support of investment bankers. But the over-the-counter offer was quickly subscribed, and AT&T received the full amount without payment of large brokerage commissions. Gifford was later rewarded with promotion to executive vice-president, the heir apparent to AT&T president Harry B. Thayer, whom he succeeded in 1925 at the age of forty— only one year older than Sarnoff when he became president of RCA. Gifford would later cap his career by serving as United States Ambassador to the United Kingdom.

When Young persuaded the telephone company to become an RCA owner, Gifford joined its board of directors. He meshed easily with the other board members, senior electrical company executives, and his relationship with Young, in particular, quickly became cordial. At first his contacts with Sarnoff, who was not a board member, were only casual, but as the young general manager began pushing his radio goals, Gifford seemed discomfited by him. Perhaps the cultural gap was too great; in any event, a cool reserve developed between them. In Sarnoff's remembrance, Gifford described him to other board members as more interested in enhancing RCA's stature than in respecting the sensitive constituencies of the owners. Soon the suspicion grew in Sarnoff's mind that Gifford was not a true partner in the new enterprise, but more the condescending emissary of a powerful potential enemy, one that secretly aspired to the same goal as he, which was leadership of American radio.

Sarnoff's misgivings were not without foundation, for, within two years of joining the patent pool, AT&T announced that it had sold its RCA stock. Gifford withdrew from the board. The innocuous public explanation was that the phone company had decided, as a policy matter, to hold only the securities of its associated companies in the Bell System. The press did no probing, the *Times* devoting only a paragraph to the announcement, so the first hint of a fissure in the combine attracted little attention, either in Congress or in the industry. Privately, AT&T's management had decided to reappraise its role in radio, as Gifford had urged, and the RCA tie was seen as an encumbrance. The central question to be answered: Should AT&T seek a wireless monopoly in radio to parallel its wired monopoly in telephony?

There were compelling reasons to support the creation of such a service duopoly. With its sixteen million phone network, its capitalization in excess of $2 billion, AT&T was one of America's two major industries, rivaled only by the automobile. It was the world's largest public utility and the world's largest communications company, with nearly 350,000 employees and an equal number of shareholders, and had not missed paying a quarterly dividend for more than thirty years. No one else could bring comparable resources to bear in achieving radio's swift maturation, not the combined electrical companies and certainly not four-year-old RCA, with less than a thirtieth of the Bell System's capital resources, and yet to pay its first dividend. The emerging management view was summed up in 1923 by A. H. Griswold, an AT&T vice-president, in a confidential bulletin to the associated telephone companies, which surfaced years later in the antitrust files of the Federal Trade Commission:

"We have been very careful, up to the present time," Griswold wrote, "not to state to the public in any way, through the press or in any of our talks, that the Bell System desires to monopolize broadcasting; but the fact remains that it is a telephone job, that we can do it better than anyone else, and it seems to me the clear, logical conclusion that must be reached is that sooner or later in one form or another, we have got to do the job.

"I may state to you that I have talked this idea over with Messrs. Thayer, Gifford and Bloom [a vice-president] and each of them think [*sic*] it is a proper idea."

While Sarnoff's broadcasting proposals languished in committee, an AT&T planning group, stimulated by Gifford, began conceptualizing how to "do the job," and a dual approach was soon recommended: first, intensify radio receiver research in the Bell Laboratories, with the goal of designing a home set that eluded entanglement with RCA's patent pool; second, initiate a broadcast service that would have financial underpinnings comparable to those of the telephone service and that would ultimately be as comprehensive in its national reach.

The key to the latter service was already in place. AT&T had been quick in following Westinghouse's lead by constructing and operating its own broadcasting station in New York City, its call letters WEAF. Even before it withdrew from RCA, it was thus involved in broadcasting, with a high-power station available to test any financial support ideas developed by Gifford's planners, and they were soon forthcoming. Against Sarnoff's advocacy of a public service network, shored by tithes or endowments, they proposed a commercial toll structure. Just as the telephone was supported by tolls levied on subscribers, so should radio be. Chunks of air time would be sold to individuals or organizations, and they would be permitted to broadcast messages of "interest to the listening audience." No direct advertising, no hard sell of products, would be permitted, but the message to be delivered would be at the discretion of the purchaser, subject to the restraints of good taste. Just as you picked up your telephone, now you would pick up a microphone at an AT&T station. And you'd pay the same way. Fixed time at fixed rates.

Sarnoff became aware of this radically different approach when the first toll test was made over WEAF on August 28, 1922, only months after he had written Rice and the phone company had severed its RCA ties. Ten minutes was sold for $50 to a local realty concern, the Queensboro Corporation, to stimulate the sale of new apartment dwellings in Jackson Heights, Long Island. The historic first commercial message of American broadcasting was lyrical in its phrasing, far removed from the clangorous Crazy Eddies of later generations, but graphic nonetheless in its depiction of how to achieve the good life. The program opened at 5 P.M. with the subdued voice of an announcer saying the Queensboro Corporation would offer "a few words concerning Nathaniel Hawthorne and the desirability of fostering the helpful community spirit and the healthful, unconfined home life that were Hawthorne ideals."

Then followed the nation's first broadcast salesman, a Queensboro executive introduced only as Mr. Blackwell, who began by observing that fifty-eight years had elapsed since the death of the illustrious novelist, and that Queensboro was commemorating his passing by naming its new "high grade" cluster of apartment dwellings Hawthorne Court.

"I wish to thank those within the sound of my voice," Mr. Blackwell said, "for the broadcasting opportunity afforded me to urge this vast radio audience to seek the recreation and daily comfort of the home removed from the congested part of the city, right at the boundaries of God's great outdoors, and within a few minutes by subway from the business section of Manhattan. This sort of residential environment strongly influenced Hawthorne . . . He analyzed with charming keenness the social spirit of those who had thus happily selected their homes and he painted the people inhabiting those homes with charming relish."

More such Hawthorne vignettes, Mr. Blackwell continued, were needed to portray "the utter inadequacy and the general hopelessness of the congested city home. The cry of the heart is for more living room, more chance to unfold, more opportunity to get near Mother Earth, to play, to romp, to plant, and to dig.

"Let me enjoin you as you value your health and your hopes and your home happiness, get away from the solid masses of brick, where the meager opening admitting a slant of sunlight is mockingly called a light shaft, and where children grow up starved for a run over a patch of grass and the sight of a tree."

And so on. The only escape from the villainous clutches of the city, as the listener by then might well have surmised, was an apartment home on the tenant-ownership plan fostered by Queensboro. The response to the first message was less than galvanic. New York City did not rise in wrath, and only a few inquiries were elicited concerning the cost of apartments. But they were sufficient to encourage Queensboro to continue its sales messages over WEAF in two subsequent $50 afternoon broadcasts and one at night, which cost $100. The cumulative impact led to sales of several apartment units, and interest began stirring within New York's advertising community. In September, Tidewater Oil and American Express purchased parcels of WEAF time, to be followed soon by the Gimbel, Macy, and Wanamaker department stores.

Even though revenue for the first two months of tollcasting amounted to only $550, that was sufficient for Gifford's planners to decide they were onto something. With management approval, a new broadcast studio was constructed at AT&T's headquarters building at 195 Broadway to give the toll venture maximum visibility within the company and before the New York business community. An anteroom adjacent to the studio was adorned with elegant tapestries, so that waiting toll customers would sense the high quality of commercial radio. To flesh out the time between toll messages, more and more programs were needed. So Ma Bell became a radio producer, offering live programs of dance music, piano recitals, choral offerings by musical conservatories, lectures by educational authorities, Walter Damrosch symphonies, and news reports and commentary by H. V. Kaltenborn of the Brooklyn *Eagle,* who soon became the first well-known broadcast journalist. Showmanship had not been the forte of the utility giant, but once the decision had been made to test tollcasting, nothing was held back in manpower or resources. As Gifford put it to the organization, "There's no reason to do anything about broadcasting at all unless we do it right." New salesmen were added to the WEAF staff, and radio set manufacturers, like A. H. Grebe and Atwater Kent, soon joined a mounting list of toll sponsors, which within a year numbered sixteen.

Sarnoff was appalled by the sudden outcropping of commercialism and worried about its effect on his public service concept. He sent warning memoranda to Harbord and Young, and he urged speeded-up examination of his network plans. Outside the radio combine, he found a considerable constituency opposed to radio commercialism, although not necessarily for the same reasons as his. The Newspaper Publishers Association began issuing warning bulletins to its members of a potential competitive threat for advertising dollars and suggesting they withhold from their news columns any mention of toll-sponsored programs. In Washington, in particular, the cry began to be heard that radio was different from the print media—the public owned the airwaves, and therefore they must not be sullied by commercialism. In the Congress, Representative Sol Bloom of New York introduced legislation to ban advertising from radio. And Sarnoff found another powerful champion of his viewpoint in Secretary of Commerce Herbert Hoover.

The Commerce Department had inherited an oversight responsibility for American radio almost by default. It had been designated by executive decree as the licensing authority for the country's international wireless and maritime stations. When domestic radio burst on the scene, ham operators turned to Commerce for licenses for their transmitters because there was no place else to turn. An independent federal agency with full regulatory authority over the spectrum would not be authorized by Congress until late in the decade. So Hoover found himself the government's principal arbiter of radio problems, but with little authority to deal with them. In 1922, he called a radio industry conference in Washington in the rather forlorn hope that the industry's leaders could recommend solutions to such major problems as signal clutter and interference—and commercialism.

Sarnoff attended the conference representing the radio combine, and on commercialism he and Hoover marched pari passu. In the meeting's main address, Hoover confronted commercialism in caustic terms: "If a speech by the President is to be used as the meat in a sandwich of two patent medicine advertisements, there will be no radio left." It was inconceivable, he continued, "that we should allow so great a possibility for service, for news, for entertainment, for education . . . to be drowned in advertising chatter." To Sarnoff fell the job, which he relished, of drafting a resolution, which the conference endorsed, that direct advertising "be absolutely prohibited."

Yet the conference was no more successful in aborting AT&T's toll service than in eliminating signal conflicts. The local broadcasters present seemed more fearful of being blotted out by the superpower stations of the radio combine than they were of a toll service. The fact was that many local stations were desperately searching for some form of financial support. As Sarnoff had predicted, the novelty of simply listening to an airborne signal was wearing off, and the vast unseen audiences were making their displeasure known through letters, telegrams, and telephone calls. From the wealthy to the impoverished, from the educated to the illiterate, Americans were demanding better radio programs and more of them; and that meant paying for talent, because the novelty of appearing before a microphone to get free publicity was also wearing off.

Gifford's representatives continued to insist they were opposed to "direct advertising," drawing a subtle semantic line between it and toll messages of "public interest." At the same time, they were preparing to project their toll service into America's hinterlands by utilizing a network already in place, one that they owned. The telephone cables that carried the human voice from city to city were just as capable of carrying radio signals. So AT&T hit upon the idea of utilizing them to carry WEAF's programs to other large city independent stations—provided, of course, that they would carry the toll messages as well. By 1923, a plan had been developed for the first regional network utilizing telephone long lines, and phone emissaries were dispatched to selected cities, where the transmitter had been built by AT&T, with contracts of affiliation in which the toll principle of fixed-time charges for fixed periods was embedded. Within a year, twelve stations had joined their program fortunes to flagship station WEAF. The first network extended from Boston, Providence, and Buffalo in the northeast to Washington, D.C., in the south, and it penetrated the heartland through Philadelphia, Pittsburgh, Cincinnati, and Detroit, with the farthest western outpost at Davenport, Iowa. Each of the stations was capable not only of receiving remote programs but of originating for the network as well through the availability of local telephone pick-up lines. This suggested the prospect of remote live broadcasts of sporting events, political conventions, and symphony concerts for audiences in the millions. A national contour for radio was becoming discernible. President Coolidge was among the first to utilize the toll network facilities, thus providing the meat for the commercial sandwich that Hoover had feared, for a 1924 speech heard by an estimated audience of 10 million.

The phone company's sudden challenge to broadcast leadership finally stirred the radio combine to action. Sarnoff suspected that a copy of his letter to Rice had been purloined by the phone people and had inspired their wire network, although he could never prove it. Regardless, he now proposed to counter it with a superpower network of nine stations, three each to be owned by GE, Westinghouse, and RCA, and the idea was accepted in principle. The stations, according to his plan, would be "located at suitable points in the country and interconnected by radio itself," so that all units would send out the same program simultaneously. To Sarnoff, radio relay signals seemed a quick and effective antidote to the spread of wire and tolls, and he hastened to Washington where he sought, with febrile intensity, to persuade the government to grant necessary licenses. Time, he knew, was his enemy.

Hoover was well disposed toward Sarnoff, appreciative of his support in the anticommercial struggle. He quickly agreed to issue an experimental license for a 50,000-watt transmitter, more powerful than any on the air, which Sarnoff proposed to construct in New Jersey. But when word of the grant appeared in the press, a firestorm of opposition developed. Local stations claimed they would be smothered by its more powerful signals. His reputation as radio's policeman stirred protests from other set manufacturers, whose reaction was that anything strengthening the radio combine was harmful. Hoover told Sarnoff ruefully that everyone with any relationship to radio except himself seemed to oppose the license grant.

As an interim measure, since it was obvious a protracted effort would be required to obtain all the licenses, Sarnoff decided to copy the phone company's tactics and initiate a rival RCA network, linking up its stations by telephone lines which would be leased from AT&T. Westinghouse station WJZ had been fused into the broadcast operations of RCA at Aeolian Hall, thus providing a flagship for the new network, which would initially be joined with RCA's Washington outlet and the Westinghouse and GE stations in Chicago and Schenectady. And it would be a public service network, its costs underwritten by the radio group until a pattern of public or industry support had crystallized.

But when he approached the phone company, his stance that of a normal commercial customer, Sarnoff was informed that AT&T would not lease its telephone circuits to RCA for broadcast transmissions. The fissure was widening, and Sarnoff was certain responsibility rested with Gifford. The reason given was that RCA and its electrical overseers were violating the original cross-licensing agreement, which confined them to the receiving end of the business. "Transmission by wire is ours. Stay out of it" was the message Sarnoff remembered receiving, and it angered his superiors as well as him. At a hurriedly called boardroom meeting, battle lines against the wire goliath were drawn. Sarnoff was authorized to seek an alternate means of linkage of the radio group stations, and his engineers suggested renting Western Union and Postal Telegraph lines, which he promptly did. Preliminary tests conducted between New York and Schenectady confirmed the technical feasibility of moving radio signals over telegraph lines. So a second, rather minuscule, network was born, reaching to Washington, Boston, Chicago, Pittsburgh, and Schenectady, and in time for a crucial competitive test with the larger toll group in the coverage of the forthcoming Coolidge-Davis presidential election of 1924.

To Sarnoff's chagrin, the telegraph lines failed him. In extended coverage such as the presidential campaign, the signal transmissions weakened as time elapsed, their quality degrading into virtual incomprehensibility. He recognized the clear superiority of the telephone lines, as the election coverage demonstrated, and he brooded over how to force access to them from the company he now regarded as his principal enemy.

Thus far not a line about the rupture between the erstwhile partners had appeared in the nation's press. While Sarnoff had spoken out forcefully in support of noncommercial broadcasting, he had not singled out AT&T, or Gifford, for personal criticism. Nor had the phone company breached its traditional wall of silence concerning internecine disputes. The press was, at the time, remarkably benign and pliable in its coverage of business affairs. While it reported fully on public monopoly concerns about radio and congressional attacks on the radio and telephone combines, little effort was made to probe beneath surface controversies. The corporate press release, rather than the investigative reporter, seemed to provide most of the information for business magazine and news stories. The only partisan bite was injected in editorials and editorial page cartoons, which often reflected the parochial interest of the publisher. Had the subsurface radio conflict occurred in a later generation, it likely would have been exposed quickly on front pages and then been ventilated on a running basis throughout the four years to resolution. While lacking the venery of the Teapot Dome scandal of the time, with its attempted theft of the government's oil reserves, the battle for control of radio also featured men and companies of great public stature, and the prize being sought was as precious as the oil reserves, for it too involved one of the nation's crucial resources, its airwaves.

The success of AT&T's toll network was being paralleled by its technical advances in the design of home receivers. In 1924, Gifford received a report from his legal staff that the Bell Laboratories had succeeded in designing a home radio set free of any RCA patent encumbrance. In its annual report to management, the engineering department in the same year said, "The types of receiving sets which have been designed cover the whole field efficiently and we are in a position to meet any commercial demand." So AT&T now possessed the weapons to attack RCA in the area from which it derived more than 90 percent of its revenues, a total of nearly $51 million in 1924. And the phone company had seized on a clause in the cross-licensing agreement to give legitimacy to the production of its first sets, a clause permitting it to manufacture receiving apparatus when "part of or for direct use in connection with the transmitting apparatus made by it." The exception had been intended to allow the Bell System to operate a two-way radio network as part of its internal communications system.

The first indication that Gifford had more than internal uses in mind came with the dispatch of a newly manufactured AT&T cabinet-style radio to the White House. Apart from the superb quality of its superheterodyne reception, it was a handsome piece of furniture and the president known as

Silent Cal was vocal in his praise to White House staff members and Bell's Washington representatives. Within days, word reached New York of the gift, and alarms sounded through RCA headquarters. To Sarnoff, it was conclusive proof of Gifford's duplicity, and he urgently memoed Harbord that this invasion of "our exclusive field" placed the entire industry in peril of a telephone takeover. The soldierly RCA president, whose love of battle had never waned, in turn urged Young via memo to mount a no-quarter attack. Otherwise, a Carthaginian settlement was in prospect, because they'll "probably put us out of business."

It was at this point, in Sarnoff's remembrance, that the dispute took an unsavory turn. He became outspoken to associates in the industry, including some lower-level Bell executives of his acquaintance, about Gifford's perfidy in twisting the clause in the cross-licensing agreement into an entering wedge for the home market. Word undoubtedly reached the AT&T leader of Sarnoff's remarks, and he reputedly responded (according to comments later reaching Sarnoff secondhand) that the real roadblock to a settlement of the dispute was the abrasive "Jewish" general manager of RCA. To Sarnoff, this explained Gifford's attitude toward him from the beginning. He was anti-Semitic. Then, as if validating that assumption, Sarnoff said that Gifford arranged a private meeting with Young at which he suggested that the climate for negotiating a resolution of the differences between the former partners was being poisoned by Sarnoff. If he were removed, the AT&T leader told Young, a more tranquil negotiating environment would ensue.

When Young later told him about the meeting and Gifford's request, Sarnoff responded that the reason was because he was Jewish and Gifford was an anti-Semite. The telephone company, he asserted, was known for its hostility toward Jews, and Gifford was one of those responsible for its exclusionary policy. Sarnoff said he offered to step aside in the controversy, but Young said he would not hear of it, any more than he would consider dismissing him. By that time the relationship between the two men had become almost Damon-and-Pythian. While Young respected Harbord and worked well with him, it was on his young general manager that he felt the future of RCA rested, and in the aftermath of the Gifford meeting he gave Sarnoff that assurance.

In retelling the story, which he did occasionally in later years to members of his family and RCA associates, Sarnoff contended that Gifford's effort to oust him was neither surprising nor dismaying. He possessed complete confidence in the strength of his ties to both Young and Harbord, and he felt that if anyone could block AT&T's radio incursion it was he. Beyond that, if Gifford were successful in taking over the industry, he wouldn't wait to be fired. He'd quit. RCA would regress into a minor international wireless company, and he wasn't interested in a career in that type of business. He felt the wave of the future was in electronics for the home, and he intended to ride it. He remembered himself, rather than being depressed, as being exhilarated by the prospect of a decisive battle. He was David challenging Goliath, with the battleground narrowing down to either the courts or arbitration because there seemed no other means of resolution.

The original cross-licensing agreement contained a provision for arbitration of disputed interpretations of functions. If arbitration was invoked by mutual agreement, it was to be binding upon each party "as finally and conclusively as an adjudication of a court." Further, each party "agrees that it . . . will not take any proceeding to modify it or set it aside." In addition to its finality, arbitration possessed the virtue of privacy, with no public laundering of the struggle, and it was to this forum that Sarnoff now proposed to Young and Harbord that the dispute be taken. If AT&T rejected it, then he suggested going to court and seeking an injunction against the phone company's entry into the home set market. Then the battle would blaze in the headlines, and Ma Bell's drive for radio control would be exposed.

Sarnoff felt it was an all-or-nothing situation. For hours, with RCA lawyers, he had pored over the fine print of the complex cross-licensing agreement, and he had become persuaded that RCA's chances of being upheld by an impartial arbiter were excellent. Besides, if they did nothing, AT&T would overwhelm them in the home receiver market, so what was the choice? Sarnoff was arguing for a bet-the-company gamble, the first of several in his career, and the RCA board agreed. It empowered Young to inform Gifford that unless the dispute was arbitrated, RCA would have no alternative but to seek injunctive relief in the courts.

Unknown to the radio group, Gifford had also been considering the arbitration route. While the dispute had been kept secret, the fact of AT&T's ambitious foray into broadcasting and the growing success of its toll network were well known. In Washington and the press, a chorus of criticism was swelling. Editorialists concluded that Hoover had AT&T in mind when he issued a statement that "it would be most unfortunate for the people of this country to whom broadcasting has become an important incident of life if its control should come into the hands of any single corporation . . ." Even within the Bell System's officer ranks, and particularly among wire executives, concern was being expressed that a groundswell of hostile public opinion over its radio incursion might jeopardize the phone monopoly on which the company's existence depended. Undoubtedly, Gifford had good reason to fear the seismic-shock effect of a courtroom battle.

Telephone and radio historians dispute whether the initiative for arbitration came from AT&T or the radio group. In either event, by early 1924 an agreement to arbitrate was reached between Gifford and Young, and a Boston lawyer experienced in such proceedings, Roland W. Boyden, was selected as referee. Hearings were to be rotated between the Manhattan offices of the various law firms involved, and under iron security arrangements. Every participant and attendee was carefully screened. Even within the contending companies, only a handful of executives were aware of what was transpiring. At stake was the future of the nation's fastest growing industry, probably the most significant arbitration proceeding in American history, and it was shrouded in conditions of wartime secrecy.

The phlegmatic and professorial Boyden was not inclined to haste, and months elapsed as he heard executive and technical witnesses, listened to the protracted arguments of counsel, and studied the mounds of documents placed in evidence. In the latter stage of the proceedings, Boyden's wife died and hearings were postponed for several weeks. It was late 1924 before the referee's draft decision was submitted to the contending groups for their comments before final issuance.

On almost every issue in contention, Boyden found for the radio group and against the phone company. It was a victory of such sweeping dimension that even the optimistic Sarnoff was stunned. Boyden ruled that the manufacture and sale of the receiving sets was the province of the radio combine, and AT&T was the transgressor. Beyond that, since AT&T had withdrawn from ownership in RCA, it had no further rights to use of radio group patents in broadcast transmissions. And RCA, if it wished, had the right to collect tolls for broadcasting. To Young, returning from Europe by ship and acquainted with the findings by an elated wireless message from Harbord, the victory was almost too complete. By nature, he was a reflective, pipe-puffing conciliator, and he immediately sensed that some form of overture must be made to a foe who could only be irate and disbelieving.

After both sides had submitted comments, a pro forma exercise that did not influence Boyden's judgment, the referee issued his binding ruling, identical with the draft except for minor word changes. But before Young could practice his conciliation, the phone company struck back. Despite its commitment to the finality of arbitration, Gifford engaged one of the nation's eminent lawyers for an advisory opinion on the legality of the Boyden ruling. He was John W. Davis, unsuccessful Democratic presidential candidate in 1924, a former solicitor general of the United States and a principal drafter of the Clayton Antitrust Act. And Davis's advisory memorandum, which AT&T forwarded to Young, proved as much a bombshell as the Boyden decision.

In essence, Davis held that the cross-licensing agreements of 1920 and 1921, which were the basis for the Boyden arbitration, were themselves illegal. They constituted a conspiracy in restraint of trade and thus violated the antitrust statutes. If the Bell System were to abide by the arbitrator's ruling, it would, in effect, be abetting a conspiracy. In Davis's judgment, the patent plinth that Young and Sarnoff had so carefully constructed, with the government's encouragement, could not stand the test of judicial scrutiny. Implicit was the threat that if RCA challenged AT&T in the courts, the result might be its own dismemberment.

Sarnoff viewed the advisory memorandum as a meretricious legal maneuver, instigated by Gifford to avoid the drastic consequences of arbitration. Yet he also recognized the peril to RCA if the Davis memorandum found its way into the hands of the press or an unfriendly congressman. Despite his aversion to Gifford, he concurred with Young's view that a renewed effort at conciliation be attempted. He had heard rumors of the strong currents within the phone company for abandonment of radio, and he surmised the Boyden decision must have strengthened them. Perhaps there was some basis for compromise. After nights spent noodling on a legal pad in his office, Sarnoff completed an internal memorandum that suggested a new approach and that was submitted to his superiors on February 5, 1925. Its key proposal was contained in one sentence: "Put all stations of all parties [the radio group and the phone company] into a broadcasting company which can be made self-supporting and probably revenue producing, the telephone company to furnish wires as needed." The toll network would be united with the stations of the radio group to form the genesis of a national chain. The connecting lines would be leased on an annual basis from the phone company, thus providing it with a significant new source of income that would grow as the network grew.

Sarnoff's memorandum signaled the abandonment of his long battle against commercialism. The words "revenue producing" could mean only advertising, whether under the guise of toll messages or direct. But he did not yield on the question of control of the proposed new company. That had to be within RCA's orbit. On all points Young and Harbord endorsed his recommendations, and Gifford was soon approached with the unified company idea as the basis for further secret negotiations.

Nineteen twenty-five was an important transition year for the Bell System. Gifford succeeded the retiring Thayer, and he wanted to resolve the nagging radio problem before it became a stain on his presidency. Was the radio candle really worth the wire cake? He knew that his senior executives had been badly shaken by the arbitration decision. Like them, he did not enjoy seeing at his breakfast table editorial cartoons of a gluttonous Ma Bell feasting on its telephone monopoly. Perhaps the time for a softer stance on radio had arrived, and Gifford agreed to secret negotiations centered on the unified company idea. He selected Edgar Bloom, head of his Western Electric subsidiary, as his negotiator.

For RCA, Young chose the man Gifford had wanted fired. Perhaps it was impolitic, but Young could be steely on matters of justice. Sarnoff was the father of the idea to be negotiated out, he was the most knowledgeable on all aspects of radio, and he possessed the youthful stamina—he was then thirty-four—to weather marathon negotiating sessions. So in the late summer of 1925 Bloom and Sarnoff came together with no one else present. They alternated offices for their meetings, which often extended far into the night. They were compatible personally, and the lack of tension perhaps sped their progress. Sarnoff later professed amazement at how swiftly key points were disposed of. "It was like a dam breaking," he recalled. "All the logjams were suddenly washing away."

Within weeks, the two negotiators hammered out an agreement that would shape the future of American radio. In a sense it was an abdication as much as an agreement, for it signaled the phone company's withdrawal from radio. AT&T would sell its flagship station, WEAF, to the radio group for $1 million ($200,000 for physical facilities and $800,000 for goodwill). Through the new broadcasting company it would form, RCA would take over the existing toll network and would lease interconnecting telephone lines under a ten-year contract that guaranteed AT&T $1 million annually. As a face-saving gesture, the radio group granted the phone company the right to manufacture its own radio receivers, but there were verbal assurances that it would never be exercised, and it never was. Except for the leasing of telephone lines to radio broadcasters, who would soon become its largest single customer group, the phone company's chapter in radio history had concluded.

How conclusive the Bloom-Sarnoff negotiations were in stimulating AT&T's dramatic change of course has been a subject of dispute between broadcast and phone historians. Some contend that the two negotiators were simply crossing *t*'s and dotting *i*'s and that the phone decision to withdraw preceded the negotiations. But Sarnoff never accepted that view. Before the substantive points were addressed, he said, long discussions ensued on the outlook for radio if both parties continued in it. Sarnoff assured Bloom that a court battle of great ferocity would erupt, that RCA and the electrical companies would seek to mobilize all the forces opposed to a dual communications monopoly—in the Congress, the executive branch, the press, and the radio industry—and that AT&T would find itself in a harsher environment than it had ever encountered. And perhaps RCA might even consider entering the telephone market, backed by the resources of the electrical companies, if it were squeezed out of radio. To his associates years later, Sarnoff insisted that he was able to persuade Bloom, and through him the telephone management, that even if AT&T succeeded in radio, the destructive impact on its telephone business would be too great to accept.

The Sarnoff-Bloom accord was ratified by the RCA Board of Directors at its first monthly meeting in 1926. It also authorized the creation of a new broadcasting subsidiary that would be owned 50 percent by RCA, 30 percent by GE, and 20 percent by Westinghouse. To Sarnoff the percentage apportionment, which he had recommended, was significant because it told the industry that the lead role in network broadcasting would be played by RCA. The name selected for the subsidiary enterprise was the National Broadcasting Company. The general manager's suggestion of Public Service Broadcasting Company had evanesced along with his noncommercial dreams.

Several months were required to refine the language of the peace treaty. In its final form, the contract contained twelve codicils that embraced all conceivable aspects of future relationships between the two parties in radio. The recently formed Broadcasting Company of America, in which AT&T had grouped its toll network and station interests, was dissolved, with its facilities and personnel transferred to NBC. A service contract for use of the interconnecting telephone links was included. On July 22, 1926, the agreement was signed, and for the radio group the signature was Sarnoff's. This was Young and Harbord's way of saluting his pivotal role.

Only then did the story of the historic transfer of broadcast responsibility begin to emerge, but the reasons were carefully adumbrated. On July 22, the *New York Times* carried a two-column story at the top of page one announcing that AT&T "will quit the broadcasting field," and the reasons were those contained in a phone press release that was more obfuscatory than enlightening. AT&T had always sought, the release explained, to improve the quality of its service by examining new means of electrical communications and this led to its experiments in broadcasting as a commercial enterprise. Public reaction to its "high class" programs had been carefully analyzed. "The further the experiment was carried," the statement continued, "the more evident it became that while the technical principle was similar to that of a telephone system, the objective of a broadcasting system was quite different from that of a telephone system. Consequently it has seemed to us after several years of experimentation that the broadcasting station that we built up might be more suitably operated by other interests. If WEAF has helped to point the way to that future it has served a useful purpose. In the hands of the Radio Corporation of America with a concurrent experience in radio broadcasting the future of the station WEAF should be assured."

The seven-paragraph story made no reference to any conflicts or disagreements, nor did it touch on the transference of network control. To the reader, it must have seemed a rather routine AT&T withdrawal from radio through the mechanism of a single station sale. In a sense, what was omitted was more significant than what wasn't. RCA was absorbing a toll network that in 1925 collected revenues of $750,000 and made a profit of $150,000, and that would soon become a marketing force of unprecedented power. And by committing to the relay of radio signals over telephone wires, it was abandoning, in the face of overwhelming opposition from local broadcasters, its concept of a superpower station network. Yet RCA was as pleased as the phone company at the low-key press coverage of the pact. It offered no comment, "all the officials who could be reached being in total ignorance of the transaction," according to the *Times*. Young and Harbord were out of town and Sarnoff was incommunicado. They had decided that any verbal poultices they attempted to apply to Ma Bell's wounds would seem saline in content.

For the architect of the agreement, it was the greatest victory of his brief career. Yet Sarnoff's euphoria was tempered by the realization that he had lost the battle for a tithe-supported public services network. In 1925, a committee of the radio group had been created, with Sarnoff a member, to examine alternative ways of creating a financial base for radio, and it concluded that only advertising support was feasible. He did not demur. Toll messages had spread too far, too quickly. Independent stations were embracing the toll concept, and efforts by various public organizations to obtain remedial legislation languished in the Congress. Even Hoover, only three years after proclaiming advertising on the airwaves "unthinkable," made no further public protest, absorbed as he was in his impending run for the presidency. After the peace treaty, the word "toll" was quickly and quietly interred, but the commercial underpinnings of broadcasting were firming, and Sarnoff philosophically accepted advertising as a fact of life. Thirty years later, he did not delete from his authorized biography a description of his early opposition as "soft headed," which was undoubtedly the most critical phrase applied to him in the adulatory volume.

On September 9, 1926, the National Broadcasting Company was incorporated under the laws of Delaware. Full-page advertisements signed by Young and Harbord appeared in metropolitan newspapers to herald its arrival, and they were couched in the loftiest of inspirational terms. NBC would provide "the best program [*sic*] available for broadcasting in the United States." Any use of radio, the ad said, that "causes the public to feel that the quality of the programs is not the highest, that the use of radio is not the broadest and best use in the public interest, that it is used for political advantage or selfish power, will be detrimental to the public interest in radio, and therefore to the Radio Corporation of America." Then, to lay to rest any further talk about monopoly: "The Radio Corporation of America is not in any sense seeking a monopoly of the air. That would be a liability rather than an asset . . . If others will engage in this business, the Radio Corporation will welcome their action, whether it be cooperative or competitive." There was also reassurance for set competitors: "If other radio manufacturing companies . . . wish to use the facilities of the National Broadcasting Company for the purpose of making known to the public their receiving sets, they may do so on the same terms as accorded to other clients." That was as close as the ad came to conceding the commercial structure.

There were 5 million radio sets in American homes when NBC was formed, and RCA decided to reach out to them through a bifurcated network arrangement, since it now owned two stations in New York. WEAF would become the flagship of the Red network, linking up with stations that mostly had been affiliated with the telephone toll group. WJZ would be the center-piece of a Blue network formed around the stations owned by GE, Westing-house, and RCA. The names derived from the color of grease pencils used by engineers in mapping out the line routes for station interconnections. Soon the Red and Blue nomenclature would be as familiar to Americans as radio itself, even though it still had twenty-one million homes to reach.

Sarnoff toyed with the idea of asking Young to let him serve as chairman of NBC, in addition to his RCA responsibilities. After all, it was his concep-tualization and his negotiating skills that had made it possible, and he knew the position would attract enormous public visibility. But he soon discerned that Young had other ideas and he did not pursue the thought. His time would come. In 1966, his official biography would say that Sarnoff was NBC's chairman of the board "in the initial years," but that was a misstate-ment. Young had decided to couple his own growing public stature to the new venture. Since late 1922 he had been chairman of GE as well as RCA and now he would oversee the emergence of the network. He had already decided to create an advisory council of eminent Americans to serve as a form of corporate conscience for NBC, and thus ensure that the public interest was safeguarded, and he felt his chances of attracting the best people would improve is he were personally involved. So he would become chairman of the NBC Advisory Council. Perhaps this was the reason, or perhaps it was the glamour attached to the new venture, but Young was able to assemble a galaxy of eminent Americans that any president of the United States would have coveted as a cabinet. Among the council's first members were Charles Evans Hughes, former Republican presidential candidate, former secretary of state, later chief justice of the United States; Elihu Root, former secretary of state; Dwight Morrow, distinguished banker and diplomat; John W. Davis, the former presidential nominee whose legal misgivings over RCA's foun-dation did not deter him; and William Green, president of the American Federation of Labor.

For president of NBC, the man who would be its operational chief, Young decided to go outside radio. Although there were experienced station executives available, like Charles Popenoe, general manager of WEAF, the chairman wanted someone schooled in dealing with the nuances of public opinion. As Young later explained in a *Saturday Evening Post* interview of June 14, 1930, "It occurred to me that the problem [facing NBC] would be largely one of external relations—dealing with mass psychology." What was the public's appetite in the way of radio programs, and how could shifts in that appetite be discerned and quickly responded to? At the time there were no Nielsen or Trendex rating services to provide audience measurements. So the man Young turned to was one he personally knew, whose job had been molding, and reacting to, public perceptions of the electrical industry.

He was Merlin H. Aylesworth, managing director of the National Electric Light Association and former chairman of the Colorado Public Utilities Commission. Aylesworth had built his reputation as a remorseless foe of public power, which he equated with socialism, and he knew nothing of radio, not even owning a set. Nevertheless, he proved an effective choice for the $50,000-per-year network presidency, for he was witty, urbane, and articulate, and he was adept at enveloping the mission of NBC in phrases of grandeur—"The enormous power concentrated in the hands of a few men controlling a vast network of radio stations" constituted a "sacred public trust."

On November 15, 1926, the Red and the Blue networks were launched simultaneously with a four-hour broadcast that was surrounded by all the klieg-lit panoply of a Hollywood premiere. While crowds swirled outside New York's Waldorf Astoria Hotel, the nation's power elite, in formal dress, gathered in the Grand Ballroom. Leaders of finance and industry, publishers and editors, congressmen and diplomats mingled with stars of the entertainment world. Twenty-five stations, extending as far west as Kansas City, were joined to the Waldorf, the largest network yet formed, and Aylesworth, who suavely greeted the guests, forecast for the program an audience of 12 million Americans, who would be entertained with a potpourri of culture, humor, and popular music. In the ballroom, Walter Damrosch conducted the one-hundred piece New York Symphony and the Metropolitan Opera star, Tito Ruffo, sang several arias. The dance bands of Ben Bernie and Vincent Lopez were among several picked up from remote locations. From Independence, Kansas, Will Rogers did his famous impersonation of President Coolidge's flat twang, and from her Chicago hotel apartment soprano Mary Garden chimed in with "Annie Laurie." The renowned vaudeville comedy team of Weber and Fields made its radio debut before the Waldorf microphones. Members of the press who were present lavished superlatives on the program, which extended beyond midnight. For the first time, many Americans were able to read about a program they had already heard. The Washington *Post* summed it up: "Radio . . . has put aside its swaddling clothes and has become a potential giant." The cost of the program, including telephone line charges, ballroom rental, and entertainment of guests, was estimated in the press at $50,000. Aylesworth insisted it was far less, but it would have been far more had the talent been paid. For the privilege of participating in this dawn of a new epoch, as it was widely described, the stars and musicians had contributed their services. But they were among the last to do so. The payment of talent, soon to be enormous sums, would accompany the rise of networking.

Among those in the grand ballroom were the immigrants from Russia and France, driven there by limousine, David in a new tuxedo, Lizette elegantly coiffed and in a floor-length gown by a Fifth Avenue couturier. They were not only rubbing elbows with America's elite, they were joining the fraternity. His salary was now $60,000, fortified by an expense account so elastic he was able to joke to a friend, "I may not be a millionaire yet, but I'm beginning to live like one." The struggle and the concentration of his early years were finally being rewarded. While his biographer would later describe Sarnoff as the putative hero of the Waldorf gathering, that was unlikely because his central role in NBC's creation was known to only a few in the room and had not yet been recognized in the press. And he was not an officer of the new network, nor even a member of its board of directors, which consisted of senior executives of GE, Westinghouse, and RCA, with Young and Harbord representing the latter.

Nevertheless, 1926 was in many ways an annus mirabilis. He had bested Gifford and the goliath. More than ever, he was convinced that he, an immigrant Jew, could surmount any opposition, no matter how powerful. The network that he conceptualized four years earlier was now in being, under the hegemony of RCA. Its broadcast signals were already sweeping across the plains of Kansas and were projected, within two years, to reach the western littoral, unifying America with wireless sound. His plan for an independent, all-inclusive RCA was nearer fruition, for the essential underpinning of network broadcasting had been achieved.

5 / *Independence Achieved*

The trajectory of Sarnoff's career in the twenties was not unlike a trendline charting the performance of the American economy, which soared and awed the nation. The superficialities of the Jazz Age could not obscure real economic growth of unprecedented proportions. In eight inflation-free years ending in 1929, the national income increased from $59 billion to $87 billion annually. Over 34 percent of the world's production of manufactured goods came from the United States in '29, compared with Soviet Russia's 10 percent and Japan's 4 percent. In his final State of the Union message on December 4, 1928, the businessman's president, Calvin Coolidge, observed that no Congress had ever convened under more pleasing circumstances. "The great wealth created by our enterprise and industry, and saved by our economy, has the widest distribution among our own people, and has gone out in a steady stream to serve the charity and the business of the world. The requirements of existence have passed beyond the standards of necessity into the region of luxury." Few questioned the durability of the growth. Even historians of the era viewed the economy's performance as a watershed development of civilization, moving the nation, in Charles Beard's *The Rise of American Civilization,* "from one technological triumph to another, overcoming the exhaustion of crude natural resources and energies, effecting an ever widening distribution of the blessings of civilization—health, security, material goods, knowledge, leisure and aesthetic appreciation."

Demand for consumer goods fueled the boom, with the principal thrust derived from mass production in two industries, automotive and electric. By 1929 one of every five Americans owned a car, and five-sixths of the world's automotive production was in the United States. The web of dirt and macadamized roads that accommodated the vehicular outpouring gave the nation a new cultural and commercial cohesiveness. Far from a mere trickle-down agent of wealth distribution, the automobile initiated a massive spread of affluence through the middle and lower classes, with the average worker's wages increasing by more than 40 percent, an affluence reaching even the immigrant groups of the Sarnoff generation, loosening their Old World ties and hastening their assimilation into an indigenous culture being created by radio and motion pictures. The car gave America in this Arcadian era a measure of upward mobility that no race or culture had ever experienced.

Henry Ford's Model T and home electrical appliances, particularly the radio, became the symbols of the vast social transmutation. From the introductory year of 1920, when sales totaled $10 million, radio expenditures had mounted to more than $400 million annually by the decade's end. Originally the plaything of wireless buffs, then in ornate cabinetry the status symbol of the rich, radio was becoming a household utility, as essential as the telephone or the refrigerator. Home receivers, which retailed from $25 to $500, were being manufactured at the rate of seventy-five thousand monthly. No product, not even the automobile, had achieved such sales velocity so quickly. The output of other electrical appliances—power tools, lamps, toasters, and refrigerators—which tripled in the same period, passing the $2 billion level in annual sales, seemed measured by contrast.

The ultimate certification of radio's growing impact came on America's bourses, where low margin requirements and easily accessible credit had induced a mania of speculative fever. As the boom crested in '29, one of every four American families was playing the market on one or more of twenty-nine different stock exchanges. More than bootlegging or Florida real estate, trading floors strewn with ticker tape became the focus of dreams of instant wealth. And no one stock came to synthesize the national yearning more than that of the recently formed Radio Corporation of America. The automobile may have provided the essential underpinning of the boom years, but RCA—or simply Radio as it was known in the jargon of Wall Street— became the lightning rod of the speculator because it brought to the marketplace the glamour of new technology. An investment of $10,000 in 1921 in profitable, dividend-paying General Motors was worth $400,000 eight years later; a similar par value investment in RCA in 1924, when its shares were first traded on the New York Stock Exchange, would have returned at the crest of the '29 market more than $1 million, eight years before the first dividend would be paid on its common stock. In '28 alone, Radio vaulted from 80 to 420, and its stock was soon after split five for one.

In the gambling argot of the era, it was a blue chip, the bluest of the blues, a combination of IBM and Silicon Valley a half century later. Many of its eighty-five thousand shareholders were young and newly affluent. Like having a Stutz Bearcat, ownership of a block of Radio was de rigueur for the "in" generation. If anyone could be said to symbolize this new class, it was the novelist F. Scott Fitzgerald. From the proceeds of his best-selling *This Side of Paradise* and *The Great Gatsby,* Fitzgerald invested in RCA, soon quadrupling his resources and permitting the chartered yachts, the European villas, and the lavish dusk-to-dawn parties that made him and his wife, Zelda, the epitomization of the Jazz Age.

Most of RCA's stock as it gyrated upward continued to be held by the electrical companies, and, at a time when stock options were yet to be an executive-suite perquisite, management did not reap rewards commensurate with the speculator. The modest RCA holdings of Owen Young and Sarnoff were initially acquired through their own purchases. However, as Radio's star ascended in Wall Street, both men were placed on elite lists by J. P. Morgan & Company and other brokerage firms, lists that consisted of individuals eminent in finance, business, industry, politics, and public affairs. When a public offering of a new stock was imminent, they were given the opportunity to purchase a block at offering value, confident that the soaring market would soon enhance its worth. And they were in illustrious company on these "preferred" lists, coupled to ex-President Coolidge, General John J. Pershing, Bernard M. Baruch, and Walter Gifford of AT&T. Market manipulation through the operation of stock pools was then accepted practice, and Sarnoff in particular counted it part of his rising good fortune to be accorded such opportunities. On one public offering, which occurred while Sarnoff was in Europe, his wife, Lizette, was included for ten thousand shares, which, when sold later, returned a profit of $58,000.

However, in personal financial matters unlike in business and technology, Sarnoff was not inclined to gamble. Poverty had attended him too long to risk its return. His modest stock portfolio included shares of the electrical companies and other issues considered nonspeculative. He made frequent trips to Wall Street in connection with RCA financings or his own transactions, and his circle of acquaintances in the upper reaches of finance widened. Through Young, he met Morgan and his senior partner, Thomas Lamont. But the most important contact he made in Wall Street, because it ripened into a lifetime friendship, was with Bernard Baruch. A generation older than Sarnoff, Baruch shared his Jewish immigrant ancestry, and he had risen rapidly on the national scene as a pince-nez wizard of finance. His service on the War Production Board under Woodrow Wilson had made him a familiar headline figure, and afterward he carefully cultivated the dual image of adviser to presidents and park-bench philosopher to the press on national issues. The two men became firm friends and Baruch, who had amassed a sizable personal fortune in the market, became for a brief period Sarnoff's personal financial adviser. He also broadened Sarnoff's national and international exposure through introductions to such intimates as Franklin D. Roosevelt and Winston Churchill. Another Baruch crony, the flamboyant Herbert Bayard Swope, editor of Joseph Pulitzer's influential New York *World,* also became a close Sarnoff friend and later his public relations adviser at RCA. As a seeker of power, Sarnoff respected it in others, and his expanding list of friendships with men of power in finance, politics, and publishing provided certification to himself of his own growing eminence.

More than personal gain, the real significance of the upward thrust of RCA common, in Sarnoff's view, was the leverage it provided for growth into new areas. He had observed how skillfully Young had traded RCA stock for patent rights in the original cross-licensing agreements, with not a dollar expended by the corporate treasury. Now he began to consider how the same technique could be employed in the acquisition of a manufacturing facility, which was the next target in his corporate independence drive. As early as 1922, he had foreseen the possibility of a marriage between the radio and phonograph industries. The manufacturing lines for both instruments were similar, as was their purpose in the home—to entertain. On his instructions, RCA engineers had created a prototype home instrument incorporating both a record player and a radio. Sarnoff had invited executives of the largest American phonograph concern, the Victor Talking Machine Company of Camden, New Jersey, to his New York apartment for a demonstration. While they had professed interest in the merged machine, they had refused a joint venture, fearing the radio, newer and more popular, might eclipse the phonograph, which was already suffering competitively. So Sarnoff had turned to the second largest recording company, Brunswick, and negotiated a $1.5-million contract for RCA radios to be placed in Brunswick phonograph cabinets. Introduced in 1924, the combined radio–record player had won quick public acceptance, and a year later the Victor Company had bowed to competitive pressure by signing with Sarnoff for a joint instrument to be marketed through its phonograph retail stores. The trademark it bore—the little terrier Nipper listening to His Master's Voice emerging from a gramophone—was to become the most famous in business annals.

With the stock market continuing its seemingly endless ascent in early '28, Sarnoff proposed to Young and Harbord the acquisition of Nipper's master. In the sprawling Victor Company facilities at Camden, he visualized the concentration of all radio manufacturing for the electrical companies, under the control of RCA. The same lines producing radio-phonographs could easily absorb production of Radiolas from GE and Westinghouse. The time was ripe, Sarnoff argued, to wipe out the competitive disadvantage of divided manufacturing responsibilities by buying the Victor Company on the open market, using the gilt-edged securities of soaring RCA as the inducement to the public to sell. Two years earlier, the founder of the Victor Company, Eldridge Johnson, had disposed of his controlling interest for $27 million to a banking consortium which, in turn, had sold Victor to the public through a stock offering that netted $53 million. Through payment of a substantial premium in RCA common and preferred, Sarnoff was confident sufficient shares could be recaptured for control. He described his plan to the RCA Board of Directors and bluntly assured its electrical company members that unless they gave their approval they would soon have a wasting asset on their hands. Without the greater efficiency of a unified production facility, Sarnoff insisted, RCA could not indefinitely withstand the competition of independent manufacturers. As its share of the market eroded, its blue chip image would crumble, leading to a collapse of its inflated price-earnings ratio and causing enormous paper losses to the electric companies and their shareholders. His scenario was apparently compelling, if not alarming, for the board created a high-level committee to examine his proposed Victor acquisition on a priority basis.

More than ever, Sarnoff felt he was dealing from a position of strength. His success in negotiating the telephone pact had prompted Young to propose his election to the RCA board in 1927. Now he could personally prod the board along the path he intended to follow and he could gauge more precisely the depth and intensity of his opposition, which he knew would emerge sooner or later. Sarnoff was also being credited within the radio combine for his conceptualization of network broadcasting. A year after its founding, NBC was finding it difficult not to exceed its original goal, which was simply to promote the sale of radio sets. A long line of advertisers was clamoring for air time to sell their products and for mass-appeal programs through which to exploit them. Profits for NBC suddenly loomed not only as a probability, but as an inevitability. Far beyond his public service intentions, Sarnoff had dreamed up what would become one of the greatest profit-making machines in economic history.

In the summer of 1928, General Harbord requested a two-month leave of absence from RCA, without pay, to campaign for his friend Herbert Hoover, the Republican nominee in the forthcoming presidential election. Young promptly granted it and designated Sarnoff as acting president, thus hardening the seal of succession. And soon after Harbord's return, Young gave Sarnoff the title of executive vice-president and increased his salary to $80,000 annually. Then thirty-seven, only twenty-eight years removed from the Uzlian ghetto, Sarnoff was making more money than the president of the United States and as much as baseball's Sultan of Swat, Babe Ruth. In 1986 dollar values, his salary was approaching the million level. He was nearing the top of the industrial rung.

While the committee of the radio group evaluated his Victor proposal, Sarnoff looked for additional areas to exploit. In his developing credo for expansion, he made the confident assumption that any ancillary services growing out of radio should fall within the province of RCA. Thus, when a system of sound coupled to film emerged from GE's research laboratories, Sarnoff persuaded Young that it belonged in his marketing domain, since it involved the use of radio amplifiers, vacuum tubes, and loudspeakers. Unfortunately, the new system, which would be named Photophone, had been caught up in the cumbersome committee approval cycle of the radio combine. Before Sarnoff could shake it loose, a rival system of motion picture sound, engineered by AT&T's Western Electric and known as Vitaphone, was offered to Hollywood. In 1926, Warner Brothers employed it for the first time with a feature picture, *The Jazz Singer,* starring Al Jolson, and the impact was seismic. The public flocked to theaters, fascinated by the novelty of sound synchronized with motion. A $100,000 film returned several million dollars in profits and Hollywood was thrown into turmoil. The major studios raced to sign up for the Bell sound system, sensing the end of the silent era. By the time RCA was ready to challenge, 90 percent of the industry, including the five major studios, had contractually committed to the Bell system.

So Sarnoff found himself again facing his powerful telephone rival, with the only option available being to seek out remaining niches in the market. His search for an alliance with independent producers led to Boston, where a friend, Louis Kirstein, introduced him to a rising young Irish-American financier, Joseph P. Kennedy, who controlled a struggling film production unit named Film Box Office (FBO). In addition, Kennedy held a substantial interest in a vaudeville circuit known as Keith-Albee-Orpheum, which owned two hundred theaters dispersed nationally. The synergism between his interests and RCA's sound system quickly became apparent to both men. And as Sarnoff and Kennedy explored merger possibilities through numerous meetings and telephone conversations, they also discovered a personal synergism at work—perhaps because of common antecedents. Kennedy was the son of Irish immigrants, and he was fighting his way out of Boston's Irish ghetto at approximately the same time Sarnoff was hawking his penny tabloids on Manhattan's Lower East Side. Both men prided themselves on being self-made and both yearned for establishment acceptance. Where Sarnoff lusted only for power, Kennedy lusted for power and money. Their friendship would ripen through years of collaboration on various RCA-related ventures, and David and Lizette would occasionally visit Kennedy and his wife, Rose, at the family compound in Palm Beach, Florida. Only in 1960, more than thirty years from their first meeting, did the relationship terminate with bitter finality. Sarnoff worked for the election of Richard Nixon as president against Kennedy's son, John Fitzgerald, and the father was unforgiving.

Kennedy imparted to Sarnoff a philosophy of living that he never forgot. More important than the substance of the individual, according to Kennedy's doctrine, was the appearance he projected. It was the perception that counted, the image that the public held. In terms of Sarnoff's career, this suggested that if the public accepted him as the hero of the *Titanic* disaster, as the infallible prophet of the technological future, as the founder of RCA, then history would be frozen in that heroic configuration. Long before the words "image making" had entered the business lexicon, Sarnoff had learned their meaning, and their importance, from his Boston friend.

In October 1928, Kennedy came by train to New York to complete a deal for which Sarnoff had already won agreement in principle from RCA's board. They met in the Oyster Bar in Grand Central Station and out of their supper together a new Hollywood force emerged. The radio group would invest $400,000 in FBO to stimulate its production of feature films. In return, Kennedy would induce a merger of FBO with Keith-Albee-Orpheum, whose vaudeville theaters would be converted to motion picture outlets equipped with RCA sound. For good measure, Kennedy agreed to throw in another small film producer, Pathé Pictures, in which he also had substantial holdings. The merged entity would be known as Radio-Keith-Orpheum (RKO) motion pictures. In exchange for Photophone sound equipment, RCA received a stock interest in RKO which would ultimately total 25 percent of the shares outstanding and Sarnoff would become its chairman of the board, in addition to his RCA responsibilities. To Kennedy went a fee of $150,000 for arranging the merger plus substantial holdings in RKO stock, which he would later sell at the market's peak for a profit approaching $20 million.

So Sarnoff had his entering wedge in motion pictures and he exploited it boldly. With an experienced Hollywood producer as president, RKO soon became profitable. Its first stars were Constance Bennett and Ann Harding, but its greatest box office coup came through the pairing of two young dancers whose balletlike grace captured moviegoing America. Fred Astaire and Ginger Rogers made ten musical features for RKO which set box office records and brought the new studio to parity with the five older majors.

In addition, Sarnoff widened the market for RCA Photophone by assuming the uncharacteristic posture of an antimonopolist. When the competitive Vitaphone sound system sought to perpetuate its sound monopoly with the five majors, he threatened court action to break up this "unlawful concentration." The exclusive clause soon disappeared from motion picture sound contracts and the market ultimately would be divided approximately evenly between the two major systems.

From music boxes to a radio network to motion pictures, the relentless RCA general manager was spreading his entertainment empire. Next, he turned to the automobile, the symbol of America's prosperity, to link it to radio. In 1922, in one of his early internal memos, he had forecast radio usage on all moving vehicles—airplanes, trains, ships, and cars. Portability, he wrote, was one of radio's inherent qualities and it must be exploited as technology permitted.

By 1929, General Motors had perfected a technique for implanting radio receivers in the dashboards of its new models, and Sarnoff saw an opening for another joint venture. His record of success was by then so unblemished that he was given a virtual free hand to negotiate with the automaker. The deal that was put together in Detroit and New York called for formation of a new company owned 51 percent by GM and 49 percent by RCA, with a capitalization of $10 million provided equally by the two partners. The manufacturing of radios not only for cars but for the home market would be done by GM at its Dayton, Ohio, plant, under patent license from RCA, and with the sets to be distributed through car dealers. Apart from being an expensive new extra to be offered with its latest cars, radio appealed to the auto giant because of its cyclical sales characteristics. Cars sold mainly in the spring and summer, radio in the fall and winter; thus, GM dealers would have year-round product. To Sarnoff, the appeal, apart from a steady stream of licensing income, was the prestige to be gained by coupling RCA with GM. It appealed to his oligarchical sense: one giant of industry and one future giant uniting in a joint venture that glorified the efficiency of bigness. And it added another title to his swelling portfolio as he became a director of the General Motors Radio Corporation.

The radio group committee studying the proposed Victor merger agreed in early '29 with the wisdom of the acquisition and the unification of radio manufacturing facilities. Like the stock market, Sarnoff seemed unstoppable. Only board ratification and the signing of contracts stood between him and the major achievement of his unification campaign. However, before it could be consummated, Sarnoff was deflected for nearly five months on an international mission that exposed him for the first time to the rarefied atmosphere of diplomacy and statecraft and, again, it was because of his mentor Young's respect for his negotiating skills.

America's unprecedented prosperity had not reached to Germany. A decade after the armistice, Germany's experiment in democracy was foundering. Saddled with a crushing impost of war reparations, the Weimar Republic was caught in an inflationary spiral that threatened its survival, under attack from the left by the Soviet-supported German Communist Party, and from the right by the emerging Fascist party of Adolf Hitler. A series of frantic warnings had gone to the Allied governments that a collapse of the republic was imminent unless its debt payments were eased. In the final days of his administration, President Coolidge had reluctantly agreed to send an American mission to Paris to examine the reparations problem with representatives of England, France, Italy, Belgium, and Germany, and his choice to head the mission was Owen Young. The farm boy from Van Hornesville, New York, had become one of America's best-known businessmen, challenged in public esteem perhaps only by Henry Ford. In addition to his chairmanship of GE and RCA, he had won wide renown for mediation of complex industry-labor disputes. Young was the first businessman to be anointed in the press with the title of industrial statesman. Also, he was a Democrat, which gave a bipartisan cast to the American mission, whose other senior members included Republican banker J. P. Morgan; his senior partner, Thomas Lamont; and an eminent Boston lawyer, Thomas W. Perkins. Each of the mission members was permitted a chief assistant and Young's choice was Sarnoff.

In this exalted company, equipped with his homburg and cane, the young RCA executive set sail on the *Aquitania* in February 1929. Reluctantly, he and Lizette had concluded that she must remain behind to care for their three sons, Robert, Edward, and the youngest, Tom, who had been born only two years earlier. So he was by himself in his own first-class cabin, supping nightly at the captain's table with princes of finance and industry.

It was twenty-nine years since his first Atlantic crossing in steerage and he relished the contrast. At the French port of Cherbourg, a tender with French protocol officers greeted the ship, swept the Americans through customs and onto a private railroad car which bore them to Paris, where they were ensconced in luxury quarters at the Ritz Hotel.

Headquarters for the negotiations, which were expected to conclude within a few weeks, were at the newly completed Hotel George V, and it was here that the first plenary session of delegates convened. It quickly became apparent to Young that the differences were more intractable than he had feared. The European Allies were unforgiving in their demands, and Germany was insistent that it could no longer afford the reparations level agreed upon in the Versailles Treaty. While America was not a creditor nation of Germany, having forgone indemnities in the peace treaty, her stake nonetheless was great because the Allies linked their ability to pay war debts to the United States to their continued collection of German reparations.

Protracted negotiating sessions, many through the night, seemed only to harden the division between Sir Josiah Stamp of the Bank of England, Emile Moreau of the Bank of France, and Germany's principal negotiator, Dr. Hjalmar Schacht. A leading German newspaper, *Deutsche Allgemeine Zeitung*, commented glumly that the prospects of a settlement diminished the nearer the conference got to "the crucial problem of how much Germany can honestly promise to pay." Threats of a walkout by the various delegations were commonplace, and only Young's stubborn insistence that a solution could be found, plus the fear of world disfavor toward any nation that disrupted the conference, kept the talks going as weeks and then months elapsed. To maintain the appearance of progress, Young divided the delegations into subcommittees to examine pieces of the problem, hoping that ancillary agreements might frame a better negotiating climate.

Initially, Sarnoff's role was that of a self-professed bellhop. The chief assistants waited outside the George V conference room during negotiating sessions and were called in whenever needed to develop additional information or provide figures. Thus they jokingly called themselves the Bellhops Club, and two of them, Sarnoff and Ferdinand Eberstadt, later a leading New York investment banker and lifelong Sarnoff intimate, became the principal channel for information to the American delegation. As he had in the radio-telephone negotiations, Sarnoff displayed an ability to strip away tangential matters and bring issues into clearer focus, and he soon found himself more inside the conference room than out.

Finally wearying of fruitless committee meetings and plenary sessions, Young decided to try personal diplomacy. He began a series of private meetings with the various delegation heads, with only Sarnoff accompanying him. Together they went to England for a weekend with Sir Josiah Stamp and followed that with a series of private dinner meetings with Schacht at Parisian restaurants he enjoyed. Curiously, a strong personal rapport began to develop between Sarnoff, the Russian Jewish immigrant, and Schacht, the sophisticated German financial expert, who would a decade later collaborate with Hitler in financing his vast military buildup and would wind up a defendant in the Nuremberg war crimes trials.

Schacht's university doctorate had been taken in the Hebrew language, which he spoke fluently and which Sarnoff still understood somewhat haltingly from his early rabbinical studies. The German delegate began inviting Sarnoff alone to dinner and Young encouraged him to accept. In a small private dining room at Schacht's favorite West Bank restaurant, they held leisurely discussions that ranged from German opera composers to the Hebrew prophets to the precise reparations figure Schacht felt Germany could tolerate. Thirty-eight years later, on the last European trip of his life, Sarnoff would return to the restaurant and persuade the maître d' to search out a musty guest book for 1929. To Lizette and an accompanying couple he would proudly display the faded signatures, adjoining one another, of Hjalmar Schacht and David Sarnoff.

Slowly, perhaps under the weight of personal weariness, or perhaps because of increasing world demand for a settlement, the rival delegations began to nudge toward a compromise on a lessened level of reparations, supported by the creation of a Bank for International Settlements, which America would help to underwrite. After four and one-half months, the dam again seemed ready to break—as it had in the radio-telephone negotiations— and Sarnoff again found himself in the pivotal negotiating role because of the relationship he had cultivated with Schacht. In a 1982 biography of Young by his daughter and son-in-law, Josephine and Everett Case, it was acknowledged that "yeoman efforts" by Sarnoff "finally got Schacht off his high horse." In Sarnoff's later recollection, his crucial meeting with the German occurred in late May 1929, at Schacht's suite in the Royal Monceau Hotel. The young American came equipped with a compromise reparations figure to which the Allies had finally secretly agreed, and with a key proviso added—that German payments be hinged to the performance of the German economy at certain minimal levels. This was the escape hatch, according to Sarnoff, that he had devised and that Young had sold to the Allied delegations. To his joy, it also made the agreement palatable to Schacht. Again, the logjams began to clear away in areas of lesser disputation. A series of collateral agreements led to announcement on June 4 of the main agreement in a final plenary session at which Young presided.

The world's press hailed consummation of "the Young Plan." The great American conciliator of industrial disputes had tested his negotiating skills in the international arena with spectacular results, devising a formula that was confidently expected to heal the last wounds of World War I. From recently inaugurated President Hoover came a wireless message of congratulations to the mission chairman for "this most important step toward the restoration of international confidence and national stability." Democracy itself, it appeared, had been saved in Germany. New York's Mayor Jimmy Walker proposed honoring Young with a ticker-tape parade up Broadway, but the self-effacing industrialist declined because he was racing back to his son's wedding. The American press began speculating on Young as a possible Democratic presidential rival of Hoover in 1932. From Adolph Ochs, publisher of the *New York Times,* Young received a wireless message that he had established himself "as the wisest and greatest peacemaker of your time," and predicted that "you will be in the White House if not in four years in eight years."

Little press attention focused on Young's chief assistant. After all, it was the Young Plan, not the Sarnoff Plan, that monopolized the headlines and editorial cartoons. Within the American delegation, however, there was abundant acknowledgment of Sarnoff's vital role. J. P. Morgan, his yacht standing by to whisk him off to Scotland for grouse shooting, presented Sarnoff with a prized meerschaum pipe as a gesture of gratitude. Thomas Lamont's papers, opened at the Harvard Business School in 1981, contained a copy of a wireless message sent to Lizette Sarnoff by Lamont which said: "I want to send you sincerest congratulations on David's work. You must know that for weeks past we relied upon him in extraordinary measure and his work was wonderfully effective." Young wirelessed Lizette that "David did the job of his life." A year later, in a *Saturday Evening Post* interview, Young, always generous in apportioning credit to his protégé, would describe him as "our principal point of contact with Dr. Schacht [who] had confidence in Sarnoff and believed in him." Summing up in the same article, Young said "there came a time when only one man could save the situation, and that arose toward the end with Sarnoff and the German delegation."

But that was in retrospect. At the time, despite the accolades of his colleagues, the world knew nothing of his Bunyanesque role. When Sarnoff returned on the *Aquitania,* gone nearly five months, a joyful Lizette and his family greeted him. But no brass bands played, there were no welcoming home speeches, no flashbulbs popped. For the second time within three years, first in the radio-telephone negotiations, he had been the key figure in accords of historical significance, only to find his achievements penumbrated. Determination welled up in him as he rode back to his apartment that never again would he be a supporting player as the dramas of his life unfolded. He would be center stage, with the spotlight locked on him. His life would be cast in the heroic mold in which he saw it, from struggling immigrant to dominating industrialist, a starring role from start to finish.

Back at RCA, Sarnoff quickly found himself center stage in an internal power struggle. When he departed for Europe, he had believed that all aspects of the merger of the Victor Company with RCA were in place. The plan, which he had left with Harbord and which had been endorsed by a review committee of the electrical companies, called for consolidation of all radio manufacturing facilities of the combine in the Victor plants at Camden under RCA suzerainty. But now to his consternation, he found that a key element of the plan had been altered during his absence and that Harbord had gone along with it. While the radio facilities would be unified in a separate company, control would be vested in the electrical companies, with RCA participating simply as a minority stockholder and still confined to its sales agent role. Rather sheepishly, Harbord said he had signed the revised agreement at the urging of RCA's legal counsel, Cravath, Swaine, and Moore, which happened to represent Westinghouse as well. To the irate Sarnoff, this was a flagrant conflict of interest; the lawyers, he decided, had simply duped the elderly Harbord, who had not been involved at all in the Victor negotiations until Sarnoff departed. Sarnoff quickly concluded that the issue was fundamental, not subject to negotiations like a reparations pact. He demanded that the RCA board reopen the agreement, suggesting to Young that its GE and Westinghouse members, Gerard Swope and Andrew Robertson, had taken advantage of their combined absences to shift control away from RCA. To Sarnoff, it was an attempt to maintain the status quo, which he would not tolerate. Either restore the agreement or he would resign.

Again he was on the shores of a personal Rubicon, again his future in the hands of one man—and again Young did not disappoint him. The chairman, cast in his familiar role as arbiter, called a special meeting of the RCA board to permit Sarnoff to present his case, which he did with compelling logic. Committee control had not worked in radio manufacturing. Why would it, under the Victor merger, with a broader range of manufactured products? The possibilities of effective integration were infinitely less under multiple management than with a single guiding source. If Sarnoff's contention was correct, if the continued separation of marketing and engineering and manufacturing was a formula for competitive failure, the penalty in the long run would be borne by the electrical companies and their shareholders, for they were RCA's principal owners. In his presentation Sarnoff was given free rein by Young, with no holds barred. No minutes were kept of the interplay, but in Sarnoff's memory the boardroom echoed after his presentation with spirited and at times caustic exchanges. At one point he threatened to walk out of the room and let the industry and public know why. Perhaps, he suggested, others in the worlds of business and electronic technology would place a higher premium on his services than did the electrical companies. Swope and Robertson did not yield easily. They distrusted the belligerent acquisitiveness of their younger associate, and they apparently sensed that if Sarnoff won the integrated control he sought it would be only a further stage in the loosening of RCA's moorings, and in the creation of a potentially powerful independent enterprise that might one day scourge them competitively. Harbord, of course, swung to Sarnoff's side, bluntly admitting he had misunderstood the implications of the document he signed on advice of counsel. So it was with Young, the senior and most respected board member, the founder and early shaper of RCA, that the decision rested.

Sarnoff said later he did not fear the outcome, for he had other career options in mind if the verdict went against him. In Paris, as the reparations talks neared an end, Morgan and Lamont had approached him on the possibility of becoming a J. P. Morgan partner, with the prospect of enhancing his income by infinitudes. A summer earlier, in '28, he and Lizette had vacationed in Italy with the Marconis, cruising the Adriatic Sea aboard the inventor's famous yacht, the *Elettra*. On numerous nights, while their wives played cards in the cabin, the two men had sat on the bridge, observing the stars and discussing new developments in the electronic art. As always in Marconi's presence, Sarnoff's enthusiasm for technology was rekindled. They discussed becoming a team, creating joint international enterprises in new technology, with substantial Wall Street funds perhaps available because of the inventor's fame and Sarnoff's growing managerial renown. While the talks were more reverie than a plan of action, Sarnoff had not entirely dismissed them. He was confident Young would support him in whatever new venture he might undertake. The chairman's admiration for his younger colleague seemed boundless. Frequently, in speeches or press interviews, he would refer to Sarnoff's career as "the most amazing romance in business history."

When Young's verdict came, it was unequivocally for Victor's integration under RCA. Sarnoff got precisely what he wanted. Was it because of a sense of gratitude for his reparations services? Was it because Young feared an internal schism that might emerge publicly and damage the reputation of all his companies? Or did he sense the inevitability of RCA's independence, propelled there by his implacably determined protégé? Even Sarnoff was never certain, for Young never told him, but ratification of the chairman's decision by the board swiftly followed. Even the Westinghouse members were not prepared to challenge the most eminent figure in their industry. The contract signed when Young and Sarnoff were abroad was scrapped, along with the company, Audio Visual Appliance, set up by the electrical companies in their absence. The RCA Victor Company was incorporated in 1929 in Delaware, its stock owned 50 percent by RCA, 30 percent GE, and 20 percent Westinghouse, and its chairman of the board David Sarnoff. The acquisition of the old Victor Talking Company through a public stock exchange for RCA preferred and common was swiftly accomplished and the production of phonographs, records, and combination radio-phonographs started phasing into radio production at Camden. The little terrier Nipper had a new master, and he was a man with a mission. In the words of a *Fortune* magazine article, Sarnoff had "got what he wanted."

Apart from its internal struggles, RCA was prospering, with the radio tail wagging the international wireless dog. In the decade since its founding in 1919, revenue had increased from $2 million annually to $182 million, with more than 90 percent coming from sales of radio devices and licensing income. Despite its occasionally laggard market share in radio sets, RCA's profit increased in '29 to $15.9 million because the public continued buying sets in record numbers. The number of employees had increased from five hundred to twenty-two thousand worldwide, and total assets to $189 million. Even the National Broadcasting Company, now linked coast-to-coast, could scarcely help returning a profit of $3 million from vaulting advertising sales.

It all seemed almost too good to be true, this seemingly unstoppable upward march of the company and the economy. And it was soon shown to be, beginning in the fall of the last great boom year, 1929. On October 30, the show business weekly, *Variety,* headlined: WALL STREET LAYS AN EGG. The orgy of margin trading came to an abrupt halt. The cycle of economic growth had peaked in June, but the impact of a precipitous downturn did not work its way through the market until autumn.

Heavy selling began on October 21, when the ticker tape for the first time could not keep up with orders. As buy orders simply evaporated, panic selling set in. Speculators who failed to respond to margin calls found themselves wiped out, their homes, businesses, and savings gone. No fall of this magnitude had ever occurred before. It became a financial Armageddon. Eleven Wall Street figures of varying prominence committed suicide within a period of days. Crowds began congregating daily outside the New York Stock Exchange, morbidly curious witness to the collapse of great fortunes just as the knitting housewives of Paris more than a century before had observed the arrival of tumbrils in the Place de la Concorde to feed the guillotine of revolutionary justice.

On Black Tuesday, October 29, the wipeout of stock values extended beyond speculative issues to the bellwethers of industry, and the downward toboggan would continue, except for short aberrational upturns, for three years. No longer a gauge of industrial values, the market became a breakaway engine of disaster, pulling the economy along with it. Superbly managed General Motors saw its stock fall from 73 to 8, United States Steel from 262 to 22. Even RCA, the Radio of the twenties, precocious child of the Jazz Age, collapsed from a post-split high of 110 to less than 20, changing dreams to alcoholic traumas for Scott and Zelda—and perhaps many other of its "in" shareholders.

But Sarnoff was not among them. During his youth, his mother, Leah, in cataloging to ghetto neighbors the virtues of her various children, would describe David as the "lucky" one. She was prophetic, for in June 1929 he sold his modest portfolio of stocks, every share he owned. His decision, he later confessed, was purely visceral. Neither Baruch nor any other Wall

Street friend had advised him to sell. Perhaps there was a wariness born of his impoverished childhood; more likely, the fact was that amassing great personal wealth had never motivated him. His daring, his greed, came in the drive for power and fame. Unlike his mentor Young, who had played the margin game and emerged from the crash deep in personal debt, Sarnoff managed on the basis of his comfortable stock profits and his enlarged salary to move during the depression's trough years to a larger apartment on the Upper East Side with an adjoining annex for his sons and their nurse.

His luck also held at RCA. The shock of personal disaster contributed to Young's decision to lighten his executive load by relinquishing the chairmanship of RCA and becoming chairman of its executive committee. He picked Harbord to become chairman, and his choice for president was Sarnoff. On January 3, 1930, the RCA board, without a dissenting vote, confirmed the thirty-nine-year-old immigrant as RCA's third president. Even Swope and Robertson, his foes in the unification battle, capitulated to Young's insistence by seconding Sarnoff's nomination. Less than thirty years from his arrival in America, eleven years since his start with RCA, he was now RCA's unchallenged leader, with an elderly and pliable chairman to do his bidding, and with opposition to his unification policies collapsed.

Sarnoff accepted his new eminence modestly. When a *New York Times* reporter interviewed him for a three-column story on his life, he advised him: "Forget the sob stuff . . . the Alger stories are out of date." His interest, he told the reporter, lay not in the past, but in the future. Now he had the visibility to be the prophetic voice of American communications, and he would play that role without surcease for the remainder of his life. He, who could not speak a word of English at age nine, "is probably doing more than any man who ever lived to make English the language of the world," the *Times* said in admiring allusion to his leadership of radio and international communications. Later, when he had consolidated his position of industry leadership, when he was its elder statesman, Sarnoff would concentrate on the romanticization of his early years; then, he would want it told as he saw it, "for my grandchildren." For now he was content with the *Times* description of him: "He sits behind a glass-topped desk in one of the world's tallest skyscrapers as head of a gigantic organization whose worldwide influence is a byword on two continents. Between the boy and the executive lies a quarter of a century filled with years of struggle in the face of great odds, of obstacles surmounted, of enormous energy, tremendous perseverance and hardships endured before the heights of success were scaled."

In Sarnoff's view, the scaling had only begun. His first goal as president was for RCA to acquire all the stock of NBC and RCA Victor, and once again he seized on the mechanism of a stock transfer to accomplish it. Within two months of his election, he had presented the electrical companies with a plan that would close the unification circle, and this time, to his surprise, he encountered no resistance. Perhaps his owners were weary of fighting him. Or perhaps they felt, with the depression deepening and with radio sales starting to slacken, that RCA might become more millstone than asset. GE and Westinghouse agreed to sell their 30 percent and 20 percent interests in NBC and Victor; a loan of $32 million in connection with the Victor purchase was forgiven; all patent licensing income from radio apparatus, previously split 60–40 between RCA and its parents, went to RCA, and the radio research and engineering facilities of the electrical companies were transferred intact. The book value of the assets transferred amounted to $53 million. In exchange, the owners received 6,580,375 shares of the recently split RCA common, which dropped to a new low of 11.5 as the deal was consummated.

The new president had no qualms about the amount of stock he had surrendered. While the electrical companies increased their ownership share, now they would no longer be interfering partners with committee oversight. And RCA had shouldered no new financial burdens, since no dividends were being paid on its common. Without spending a cent of RCA money, he had pulled together the largest electronics enterprise in the nation by arranging what radio historian Gleason Archer would later describe as one of the largest asset transfers in industrial annals. RCA's assets surpassed $200 million, and Sarnoff was sure the depression would be short-lived, as most others in America had been. He believed President Hoover's assurance that prosperity was "just around the corner." The fact that RCA's profits in the first year of his presidency dropped from $16 million to $5.5 million, a reflection of softening consumer sales, did not unduly disturb him. When the upturn came, the efficiencies of his streamlined new organization would promote vastly greater profits, and he would prevail on his electrical overseers, through Young—as he always had—to permit a buy back of the RCA stock, thus finally severing the electrical umbilical.

What Sarnoff, like so many of his business peers, failed to perceive was the cataclysmic depth and duration of the downturn. Bank failures began to spread, credit to business dried up, consumer spending collapsed. As factory after factory shut down, unemployment soared from 3 percent in 1929 to more than 28 percent three years later. Prices fell through the floor. In Los Angeles, two quarts of milk were scaled down to five cents in a price war between competing dairies. With home mortgages foreclosed, "Hoovertowns," shanties built of cardboard and wooden slats, were thrown up by the homeless in municipal parks and unoccupied public lands, apples were sold on street corners for pennies by the skilled and unskilled alike, and "Mister, Can You Spare a Dime" became the haunting theme ballad of a nation in distress.

A new cynicism started to pervade America, and much of it began to focus on business. The index of industrial production dropped from 114 in

'29 to 54 in '33, manufacture of durable goods declined by 77 percent, and business construction fell from $8.7 billion to $1.4 billion. The mightiest industrial engine in human history was stalled and soon editorialists and historians began questioning whether the prosperity of the twenties was built on a meretricious base. Business had been sanctified through Coolidge's laissez-faire policies, and now both he and they were being reappraised. "His frugality sanctified an age of waste . . . his taciturnity an age of ballyhoo," was the caustic later judgment of liberal historian Arthur Schlesinger, Jr.

In the Department of Justice, after the benign antitrust neglect of the Coolidge years, pressures were building from Congress and elsewhere to punish business transgressions—and RCA became the flash point that ignited them. As the declining radio set market eroded profits, threatening insolvency to scores of manufacturers, the payment of patent licensing fees became the most chafing symbol of unfair business practices. At hearings before the Interstate Commerce Committee of the Senate in 1930, the president of Grigsby-Grunow, maker of the popular Majestic set, testified he had paid RCA over $5 million in royalties but did not know what he was paying for, other than immunity from legal action, since his RCA license did not divulge what patents were covered. "The radio combine had so terrorized the industry, and the dealers and the jobbers everywhere," B. J. Grigsby testified, "that they were afraid to handle what they called 'un-licensed' sets. Our bankers said they would not finance us unless we took out a license. They said they would not finance a patent fight against such a monopoly . . . The merits of the patents had nothing to do with it."

On the evening of May 30, 1930, Sarnoff was guest of honor at a stag dinner to celebrate his election to RCA's presidency. As he entered the Fifth Avenue apartment foyer of his host, Frank Altschul, wealthy head of the investment banking firm of Lazard Frères, a figure accosted him out of the shadows. Twenty-four years earlier, he had used the same technique, as a Marconi office boy, to meet the great inventor, and the memory flashed through Sarnoff's mind. But this was no well-wisher, not even a job supplicant. This was a United States marshal, and his outstretched hand bore a formal complaint from the Department of Justice, charging that the patent pool on which RCA was founded and the subsequent cross-licensing agreements were in violation of the antitrust laws, an illegal restraint of trade. All the original signatories were listed as defendants—GE, Westinghouse, AT&T, RCA—plus the GM Radio Corporation.

Quickly scanning the summons, Sarnoff pocketed it and went through the evening's festivities without mentioning it. Afterward, he asked a few RCA executives who were present to join him at the office, and together, until dawn broke, they analyzed the devastating implications of the summons. Now the battle was not for freedom, it was for survival. If the government's legal thrust succeeded, the pool would be dissolved, the licensing agreements abrogated, the manufacturing and engineering units dispersed, and RCA would thus be dismembered. What would be left? A small international wireless business that could be run by technicians and clerks. Even NBC might be eviscerated, for a conviction on monopoly charges, under the recently enacted Federal Radio Act, would mean forfeiture of the operating licenses of the powerful clear-channel stations owned by the radio group.

Publicly, the response of the radio group the following day was calm. Bearing Young's name, the release recited the history of RCA's origination at the government's instigation and concluded by welcoming "this test of the validity of its organization . . . in every step of which the government has been advised." Privately, a sense of outrage swept through the organization that a business-oriented Republican administration would thus betray them. Among many of the senior executives, including Young and Sarnoff, President Hoover was considered a personal friend, but inexplicably he had not moved to intervene when his attorney general, William Mitchell, and the head of the antitrust division, Judge Warren Olney, announced the action, producing headlines across the nation. Later they would learn that Hoover had actually encouraged his top legal experts in their interpretation of the antitrust statutes. Already under siege for his depression policies, he was not prepared to risk a further political explosion. So the battle lines were drawn, with perhaps the most imposing phalanx of legal talent ever marshaled—John W. Davis, Charles Neaves, Thurlow Gordon, Paul Cravath, ex-Senator George Wharton Pepper—leading the defense; in Young's phrase, "a multitude of lawyers."

Months would elapse in file searches, deposition taking, interrogatories, and legal conferences before the government's suit could be brought to trial. Meanwhile, at Sarnoff's insistence, the transfer of engineering and manufacturing facilities to RCA, which had just begun, continued to completion. To do otherwise, he argued, would be to concede the validity of the government's case. On September 19, the converted Victor plant was splashily dedicated, with Sarnoff proclaiming Camden the new radio capital of the world. But despite the brave front, RCA's troubles worsened. As legal bills mounted, radio sales continued to fall. In 1931, total company profit would be less than a million dollars, and in the subsequent two years losses would be experienced, the first in RCA's history.

As he passed his fortieth birthday in 1931, RCA's president found himself in a drama being played on many stages. He became the contact with the antitrust department on behalf of all the defendants; he coordinated legal defenses between the radio and telephone interests, and between GE, Westinghouse, and RCA. Often he would have lengthy and introspective review meetings with Young, who sought to stand above the fray, although he was its central figure. But even Young was not immune from the ire of the liberal press. "If anyone can find in the history of Standard Oil or steel more ruthless examples of corporate buccaneering than attended the rise of the Radio Corporation under Mr. Young's enlightened guidance, I should like to hear of them," wrote Paul Y. Anderson in the *Nation*. In one sense Young was the symbol of radio monopoly, but he was also considered the nation's preeminent industrial statesman, a potential rival of Franklin D. Roosevelt for the Democratic nomination in 1932. The paradox of his position was furthered by efforts of the Hoover administration to enlist Young's services as leader of a business coalition formed to recommend anti-depression measures. Caught in these political and professional crosscurrents, Young relied increasingly on Sarnoff to achieve a solution of the seemingly intractable antitrust challenge.

Attorney General Mitchell described the case as perhaps the most complex in antitrust annals. No other company in history had been given a patent monopoly by the government at its birth, and then had the government turn on its own creation. The issues were unprecedented, and as Sarnoff wended through the legal labyrinth he became persuaded that a fresh approach would be required to resolve them. The questions that kept coming back to him: Were the interests of RCA and its owners really the same? What if RCA supported the government's demand for a breakup of the combine? Could this be the route to the independence he had always cherished? Could the electrical companies be persuaded to abandon their ownership on terms sufficiently favorable to permit RCA's survival alone? The more Sarnoff asked the questions, the more he became convinced that a breakup, sanctioned by a consent decree, was the only solution—and the real job was to persuade not the government, but the electrical companies. AT&T had already reached a settlement by agreeing to cancel its cross-licensing agreement, and had long since sold its stock interest in RCA. Only one man could persuade the electrical companies, and that was RCA's creator, Young.

So Sarnoff began a campaign, subtle at times, persistent at others, to persuade Young and the other owners of the dire consequences of protracted litigation with the government. In its weakened financial condition, he argued, with its tubes and sets a glut on the market and with RKO forced into receivership by a box-office collapse, RCA could not afford it. If the company were found guilty of monopoly, the group's radio stations, still profitable, would be forfeit, and the electrical companies would be hit with multiple lawsuits from disgruntled shareholders and competitors fighting over the remains of the RCA carcass. Better, he argued, to make a magnanimous settlement, free up the patent pool to all comers, and give RCA sufficient resources to stand alone, at least temporarily. In endless meetings Sarnoff pressed the case for independence. Mostly, the meetings were chaired by a weary Young, burdened by political pressures from every quarter to make the presidential run, deeply in debt, and troubled by his wife's serious heart ailment. One of the participants, Walter C. Evans, of Westinghouse, later wrote: "I distinctly recall Mr. Young slouched down in an arm chair in the RCA board room with the appearance of being more than half asleep. When the controversy reached a complete impasse, his eyes would open only a slight amount and he would suggest the compromise which solved the question."

Over a period of months, Sarnoff hammered out a series of basic principles in which Young, who had taken himself out of the presidential race, and his associates concurred. The pivotal one was that RCA "must remain an effective unit in the radio and associated fields." To ensure it, GE and Westinghouse would agree not to compete with RCA in radio for two and a half years. After that they would license RCA patents like other competitors. They would meet the government's unyielding demand for total separation by distributing their RCA stock on an equitable basis to their own shareholders, and would never attempt to influence the voting of it. They would all resign from the RCA Board of Directors.

Thus were the terms of divorcement reached in the autumn of 1932, prodded by the setting of November 15 as the date for the government's trial to open. Marathon negotiating sessions, weekends, night long, completed the housekeeping details, with Sarnoff pleading RCA's current impoverishment and Young not unsympathetic. Half of RCA's $18-million debt outstanding to its parents was canceled, the other half to be met by the issuance of debentures and the transfer of RCA's new headquarters building at Lexington Avenue and 51st Street to GE. The valuation placed on it was a generous $5 million and it would become GE's own headquarters. On November 11, three days after Roosevelt had swept to a landslide victory, the plan was delivered by Sarnoff to the Justice Department, which had been kept apprised of the negotiations, occasionally injecting its own suggestions but clearly sympathetic toward Sarnoff's thrust for independence. The trial date was postponed a week. Minor modifications were requested by the Justice Department, quickly agreed to, and on November 21 a consent decree was signed and the trial canceled.

In much of the press, the Congress, and the radio industry, the decree was jubilantly hailed as a landmark government victory against monopoly, even though it came too late to help the Hoover administration. Parallels were drawn with the packers' decree of 1920 and the dissolution of Standard Oil in 1911. The Sherman Act and the principle of free competition had been vindicated. The stock market responded with a heavy sell-off of RCA shares, shareholders apparently reasoning that no longer would RCA have the resources of the electrical companies to sustain it. Now, it would be on its own, and at the lowest point yet of the depression. While the patent pool was intact, it had been opened to all and stripped of its more coercive features, and the favored status of the cross-licensing partners eliminated.

In Sarnoff's mind, the negatives paled in comparison with the central fact of independence. He was as jubilant over the decree as the most extreme of his enemies, and even boastfully so. "They [the government] handed me a lemon, and I made lemonade of it," he told associates. Radio historian Erik Barnouw later agreed: "Miraculously, RCA emerged as a strong and self-sufficient entity. No longer owned by others, it had its own destiny in hand. It owned two networks, broadcasting stations, manufacturing facilities, international and ship-to-shore communications facilities. It controlled a majority of clear channel stations."

Among the main actors in the drama, Young was the most ambivalent about the outcome. Only the weight of his immense prestige had tipped the scales in Sarnoff's favor. Now he was faced with an agonizing choice: either GE or RCA, but not both. The more daring challenge would be to stay with RCA, his creation, and steer it through the economic shoals to safe harbor. He could recapture the chairmanship from Harbord, who had been more the onlooker than a participant in the legal battle, relying on Sarnoff as his strong right hand. The pressures on him to do so became intense. He had been negotiating with the Rockefeller interests a new headquarters lease for RCA and NBC in the vast mid-Manhattan office complex they were constructing, to be known as Radio City. Winthrop Aldrich, a Rockefeller in-law, told Young bluntly they preferred dealing with him rather than RCA's abrasive president. Sarnoff's old nemesis, Walter Gifford of AT&T, which provided NBC's interconnecting lines, insisted that Young was the only one he would talk to at RCA. And NBC's president, Deac Aylesworth, who would have to report to Sarnoff, informed Young, as the chairman later recounted, that "if I got out he got out too . . . he did not have to stay as Sarnoff's man and he would be damned if he would."

The more prudent course would be to continue his overseership of GE, which was the nation's leading electrical power company, more than triple the size of RCA and sure to weather the depression, barring total economic collapse. Young's personal situation weighed heavily in his evaluation. His stock market forays had left him more than $3 million in debt, and it was collateralized by virtually everything he owned, including his cherished collection of rare books. His devoted wife, Jo, was a semi-invalid and he wanted time to be with her. Under terms of the consent decree, he had five months from its date to resign from the RCA board, or sever with GE. Sadly he chose the former. The personal considerations were paramount. On May 4, 1933, Young resigned as a director of the company he had created.

Clearly, this was the outcome Sarnoff desired. Despite his reverence for Young, he considered himself the architect of RCA's independence. At age forty-one, portly, aggressively self-assured, a tycoon in manner and dress, Sarnoff felt the time for sharing control of RCA had passed. For nearly two years, he had devoted virtually every waking minute to the government case, eschewing social engagements, sometimes canceling vacations, and virtually abandoning his home life. At times he felt, guiltily, almost a stranger to his three sons in their formative years. But the patient Lizette never complained at the dual parental role forced on her. She was a poem of a woman, as important in her way to his struggle as Young had been.

In his public attitude to Young, Sarnoff was still the loyal disciple. At his urging, the RCA board petitioned the Justice Department of the new Democratic administration for a waiver that would permit Young to continue as an RCA director for two and one-half additional years. When it was unceremoniously denied, Sarnoff drafted an eloquent board resolution of tribute to the company's founder. Young's brief response of thanks, "misty eyed," went not to board chairman Harbord but to "Dear David," the president who would guide RCA's destinies, almost single-handedly, for the next three decades.

6 / The Television Era Begins

As Sarnoff achieved paramountcy of an independent RCA in 1933, poverty of pandemic proportions deepened in America. Thomas Wolfe, chronicler of the nation's despair, wrote of masses of derelicts, part of the 28 percent of the populace without any income, clustered in Manhattan's public lavatories seeking shelter and warmth, an "abyss of human wretchedness and misery," only blocks removed from skyscrapered pinnacles of affluence and power, "the giant hackles of Manhattan shining coldly in the cruel brightness of the winter night."

Into one of those pinnacles, the newly completed sixty-five-story centerpiece of Rockefeller Center, between 49th and 50th streets and Fifth and Sixth avenues, Sarnoff moved RCA's headquarters in June 1933. Despite Winthrop Aldrich's profession of disdain for him, the Rockefellers welcomed their new tenant with open arms, even to substantial last-minute concessions on the terms of its lease. Without RCA and its now wholly owned broadcast subsidiary, NBC, the concept of a Radio City, which had already caught the public fancy, would be meaningless. On the fifty-third floor of the newly christened RCA building, Sarnoff ensconced himself in a large white-oak paneled corner office, richly carpeted, which commanded a sweeping view of the Hudson River and the Palisades of New Jersey to the north and northwest, and the sprawling clutter of Long Island to the east. Only to the south, to the lower Manhattan of his ghetto youth, was the view blocked by his private barbershop, lavatory, and dressing room. This would be his command post, the nerve center of an electronics empire that would grow to 130,000 employees, for the remainder of his life.

At the time of his move, Sarnoff was forty-two, still younger than most of his business associates and peers but no longer the youthful protégé soliciting the support of older men. While he maintained a cordial relationship with Owen Young, the day-to-day intimacy soon disappeared. There were occasional exchanges of congratulatory notes over a speech or a positive earnings report and less frequently a lunch or dinner given over mainly to reminiscences. The blunt fact was that Sarnoff no longer felt that he needed Young, and he reasoned that the appearance of a continuing intimate association might suggest to some that the elder man was still influencing policy at RCA.

But to the other father figure of his past, Marconi, Sarnoff still maintained ties of unwavering affection. When the inventor asked him for help in 1934, in drafting a new employment contract, Sarnoff went to London to oversee in person the negotiations with British Cables and Wireless, Ltd., which was the successor company to British Marconi. At the time Marconi was a member of the Italian Grand Council of Fascism under the leadership of Benito Mussolini. He was a national hero in Italy, a senator and a marchese, and it became a matter of state concern that he be properly treated by the British firm. To Sarnoff, of course, it was a matter of personal loyalty, and he succeeded in obtaining for Marconi a renewal contract as scientific adviser on terms that the inventor considered highly favorable.

Later, reporting to the RCA board on his negotiating efforts, Sarnoff said that "it is interesting to mention the personal affection which Mussolini holds for Marconi as evidenced by the fact that Mussolini sent his personal counsel with Marconi to London in order to help the inventor with his problem. Marconi introduced me to Mussolini's counsel, who was naturally in favor of the suggestions I made."

Sarnoff was spared, by Marconi's death on July 19, 1937, the hard choice he would have had to make between his personal ties to the inventor and Marconi's allegiance to the Fascist cause, since Mussolini, of course, later joined Hitler in warring on America. When Sarnoff received the news of the inventor's death at age sixty-three, he ordered a special commemorative program on the NBC radio network, on which he personally appeared and said: "The world has lost a great man. Science has lost a great genius. I have lost a great friend."

Even though his greatest struggles—and triumphs—lay ahead, Sarnoff considered his early forties his prime years. "Your status in life is pretty much set by the time you're forty," he later told a young associate. "Sure, great things can happen after that, but by that time you've either made it or you haven't." Indisputably, he had—president of RCA weeks before his fortieth birthday, chief executive two years later, with all the autonomy a pliant board and chairman could bestow upon the leader of a publicly held company. If assuredness that bordered on cockiness began overtaking his demeanor, it could perhaps be attributed to the swiftness of his rise. He could measure it in terms of those he had vaulted past, like Edward Nally, his early boss at the Marconi Company, now his respectful board associate. He could measure it by the camaraderie of those he held in awe as a youth. He could measure it by the almost adulatory outpourings at anniversary banquets given him by his associates, beginning with the conclusion of his twenty-fifth year in communications and continuing each five years thereafter. Yet his appetite for praise was never sated, either verbally or in print. This was the assurance he appeared to need of the reality of his transformation from immigrant to industrial nonpareil. One of his closest friends, David E. Lilienthal, an RCA consultant and once head of the Atomic Energy Commission, said Sarnoff "doted on publicity as much as anyone I have ever known."

Despite the opulence of his new environment, Sarnoff found himself beset by problems that threatened the durability of his freshly sovereign enterprise. A sudden collapse of the radio set market in 1932 had forced him to lay off hundreds of production line workers in Camden, only two years after he had christened it radio capital of the world. He slashed executive salaries ruthlessly, including his own—from $80,000 to $50,000 annually. Even the movie industry, supposedly depression-proof because it peddled escapism, could not surmount the scarcity of spending money. Double features were offered for admission prices as low as a nickel. RKO's early burst of prosperity soon evanesced, and Sarnoff's requests to the banks failed to elicit sufficient funds to keep the new company out of receivership. RCA had to come up with $3 million for a final payment on RKO debentures, bringing the company's total investment to more than $16 million. Ultimately, as movies restored their box office appeal, RKO would regain its fiscal stability and RCA would recoup most of its investment through sale of the debentures. At the time, however, it represented one more drain on a burdened treasury. Even the company's international wireless business, which had shown steady growth since RCA's founding in 1919, dropped precipitately as the nation's foreign trade declined to the lowest level in nearly three decades. The depression had become worldwide, and even RCA's technical skills provided no immunity.

With the forced resignation of its ten GE and Westinghouse representatives, the RCA Board of Directors dropped to eleven members, including insiders Harbord, Sarnoff, and Nally. Sarnoff was in no haste to build it up again. First he wanted to solidify personal relationships with those outsiders who remained, a cross section of business, cultural, and technical leaders with no financial ties to GE or Westinghouse. Their loyalty not only to RCA, but to him personally, became an early tenet of his management creed; indeed, he often said he felt he was nourishing himself through the care and feeding of his directors. Similarly, he kept his corporate staff small, with only seven officers listed in the 1932 annual report, perhaps the smallest headquarters cadre of any major corporation. Manton Davis, general attorney; Otto Schairer, head of the patent department; George De Sousa, treasurer, who had hired Sarnoff as an office boy twenty-six years earlier; and Lewis MacConnach, secretary, were career employees and known throughout the company as Sarnoff men. The later charge that RCA suffered from one-man governance—a charge that Sarnoff never sought seriously to rebut—perhaps had its genesis in the fact that he controlled the decision-making process initially through this small, tight-knit headquarters group of loyalists who evinced no desire to challenge his authority. It was a management as far removed from the layered committee structure of the electrical companies as he could make it.

A less self-confident man than Sarnoff might have been sobered by the initial results of his independent stewardship. In 1932, RCA suffered its first loss—$1,133,585.65—since its formation in 1919; a year later the loss had been pared to $582,093.55, but radio sales had declined by 34 percent, and the cash surplus accumulated in the boom years was being siphoned off. Yet, curiously, Sarnoff always contended that those trough years were among the most exhilarating of his career. Above all, he relished his new freedom of action. The challenge of steering through the economic shoals invigorated him. "There can be only one captain on the bridge," he would tell friends, employing a metaphor of the sea because it contrasted in his mind with his first voyage in steerage, "and I happen to be that fellow for this ship at this time." One of his early associates, Meade Brunet, who later headed RCA's international division, could remember the contrast between Sarnoff's supremely confident attitude and the subdued demeanor of those around him. "He never doubted that we'd make it, and he had no patience with those who did," Brunet recalled. "Even when he was wrong, he was the most assured man I've ever known."

Despite his reduced salary, Sarnoff's personal life prospered. It was one of the depression's ironies, as James Thurber pointed out in the *New Yorker* magazine in 1932, that those who had an income or possessed money got far more from it. Taxis in a smaller fleet became cleaner and their drivers politer; transatlantic liners slashed prices by a third, and improved their service and cuisine; the best hotels, like the Ritz and Pierre in Manhattan, dropped their room rates to $6 nightly, yet were seldom crowded; department stores slashed retail prices by more than half, and bargain basement sales became a way of life. Fads continued to flourish. Ely Culbertson's bridge books sold up to 400,000 copies annually. Stripteasers made up to $500 weekly, with their performances often sold out. For those who could still make money, Thurber wrote, the depression offered the best of times—and Sarnoff was among that cosseted group. He educated his sons at private schools, beginning with Columbia Grammar in New York City and progressing to Phillips Academy in Andover. Later his progeny would attend Harvard, Stanford, and Brown universities, fulfilling the father's vow that there would be no more grade-school dropouts in the Sarnoff family.

His still large income and his corporate stature offered entrée into higher social echelons than the Uzlian Sarnoffs had ever dreamed of. In this area, he was guided to a degree by Lizette, who was developing a matronly panache of her own. As her children left the nest, she became increasingly involved in outside interests. She took bridge lessons with ladies from the oldest New York families, she became an accomplished amateur sculptress and an indefatigable fund raiser for the New York Infirmary and later the Einstein

Medical College. As a sideline, she developed a repertoire of earthy jokes, replete with sexy punch lines, that were the delight of her growing body of friends. Occasionally they discomfited her husband because they seemed incompatible with the accepted demeanor of the wife of a corporate leader, but this didn't cow her. She matched his cigars with cigarettes, chain-smoked in a tapered holder, that ultimately rasped her vocal cords, giving her French-accented words a husky and throaty quality that seemed to impart intimacy in personal conversation.

Lizette possessed a personal warmth that tended in social gatherings to counter the more formal, sometimes even foreboding, mien of her husband. With his RCA associates and their wives, she developed easy and informal relationships. Those who were exposed to her often came to adore her for her humor, her ability to put them at ease, and her great sense of loyalty to those she felt had served her husband well. In Paris once, she accompanied the wife of one of his aides to the Flea Market. When the wife expressed a desire to purchase a pair of silver peacocks, Lizette said, "Let me handle it." In her native French, she haggled for five minutes over price, finally beating it down to what she and her companion considered an acceptable level. Later, the awed wife told her husband, "Lizette fought for me like a fishwife. She wasn't going to let them gyp me out of a single franc."

Had Sarnoff sought social stature comparable to his professional position he probably could have achieved it, with the aid of his formidable consort. For Lizette was not only a handsome woman, addicted to the latest in fashions, her carefully coiffed brown hair fashionably streaked in gray, but she possessed great personal aplomb. Not even the most glittering White House gatherings, of which she attended many with her husband, could ruffle her poise. She relished the spotlight. "I'm a ham at heart," she once confided to a friend. But her husband, to whom she was slavishly devoted, was never really comfortable in a society milieu. "I have never tried to be socially successful," he told an interviewer in the latter years of his career. "I find teas and parties a bloody bore. I have fun listening and talking to intelligent people at small gatherings, but these public parties I find unbearable."

Occasionally, however, society columns in the New York press would report David and Lizette on passenger lists for Caribbean cruises, in the company of Vanderbilts and Goulds. Lizette would sometimes venture forth alone on Atlantic crossings for reunions with members of her family who remained in Paris. On one such occasion, she was interviewed by shipboard reporters seeking information about her increasingly famous husband, and she responded in French that he was, she hoped, paying attention to business.

As 1933 ended, the business of RCA was improving and its deficit narrowing, although the economy continued to languish despite the flood of pump-priming legislation that Congress had passed at Roosevelt's behest. Unlike many manufacturers who had inhaled their profits from radio set sales in great gulps during the boom years but then shifted to white goods in a misguided search for more stable and depression-proof products, Sarnoff kept RCA toeing the radio line. He was confident that once the initial numbing effects of the crash had worn off, sales would pick up and profit margins would be restored. His perception proved correct, and to a greater degree than even he surmised. Unlike movies, the theater, and vaudeville, radio provided at no cost the diversion and escapism that the public so desperately sought. It also provided a reassuring lifeline to the real world through the fireside chats President Roosevelt had begun to broadcast. RCA field salesmen began relaying back to Rockefeller Center their conversations with social workers who reported that impoverished families would meet rent payments by sacrificing their refrigerator, bathtub, and telephone, even their bedding, before their radio. Sales were also stimulated by RCA's introduction of a new line of portable receivers, retailing for as little as $20, which unshackled radio from the family living room. Away from parental oversight, amorous young couples could now listen on the beach and under the stars to the crooning of Rudy Vallee and a youthful Bing Crosby. Industries seeking desperately to reach what remained of the buying public turned to broadcasting to carry their product messages, and NBC's profits moved steadily upward in contradistinction to economic trend lines.

By 1934 Sarnoff had returned RCA to profitability. On gross sales of $79 million, net earnings were $4,249,263.67. Dividend arrears on class A preferred stock were paid up, the company had no bank indebtedness, and its treasury possessed a comfortable surplus of $13.5 million. Few American enterprises in that fifth depression year possessed a more sturdy balance sheet. It was a pendulum swing of dramatic proportions, and it was caused primarily by the resurgence of radio sales and the growth of NBC.

By then, however, Sarnoff's thoughts were turning to a new technology that would virtually supplant radio, would transform societal living patterns as much as or more than the printing press and the automobile, and would provide the RCA leader with the greatest challenges of his business career. It was the wireless communication of moving pictures, known as television.

To many Americans of the post–World War II generation, television seemed to spring forth Minerva-like, a product of the same inventive genius that had created radar and guided missiles and nuclear explosives. In reality, its scientific pedigree reached back a century. Long before Marconi's landmark discovery of wireless communications, researchers in universities of Russia and Europe were theorizing how to transmit visual information by electrical impulses over wires. In the United States, Alexander Graham Bell's demonstration of voice communications by wire in 1876, following upon Samuel F. B. Morse's invention of wired telegraphy, led to widespread speculation in technical journals on the possible progression of distance communications from code to voice to visual information. Bell himself prepared technical designs for a system of transmitting moving pictures over telephone wires, although it never proved economically feasible during his lifetime. In 1884, a twenty-four-year-old German inventor named Paul Nipkow developed and received a German patent on a mechanical spinning disc concept of picture transmission. Perforated with thousands of tiny holes, the Nipkow disc, when rotated in front of a focused image, permitted tiny light and dark bits to filter through, each of which was converted into an electrical impulse by a photoelectric cell. At a nearby receiver, linked by wire, a comparable disc rotated in precise synchronization with the transmitting disc and reconverted the electrical pulses of light and dark into the same focused image on a viewing screen. This was the first primitive concept of picture transmission, but the real impetus to television's development came through Marconi's invention at the nineteenth century's end, which liberated communications from wires and encouraged scientists from many nations to begin testing visual transmissions in the less confined airwaves.

Soon after World War I, demonstrations of picture transmission by wireless, all embodying the Nipkow concept, were conducted in France, Germany, and England. By 1923, a British pioneer, John Logie Baird, had developed a cumbersome disc transmitter, and two years later he launched a series of test transmissions to receivers placed in London department stores, drawing throngs of the curious to witness flickering images of people and objects in the first public television demonstration. In the United States experiments were also under way with the mechanical disc, with AT&T and GE among the leaders. In his Schenectady laboratories, Ernst Alexanderson, the inventor whose alternator gave birth to RCA, attracted wide press attention when he sought to duplicate his earlier success with a refined version of the Nipkow transmitter. By the middle twenties the word "television" was an accepted addition to the scientific lexicon. But long before that, as early as 1907 in fact, *Scientific American* magazine had employed the word to explain the conversion of light waves into electrical waves and then their reconversion in a coherent pattern at a receiver. In 1910, the Kansas City *Star*, reporting on primitive French TV experiments, confidently assured its readers that television was "on the way."

In his office boy years at Marconi, when he browsed in the technical literature at the inventor's Front Street library, Sarnoff had become aware of the theory of television. In scientific publications and in translated accounts from German newspapers, he had absorbed Nipkow's concepts. He discussed the approach and its potential realization with RCA and GE engineers, including Alexanderson. By 1923 he was persuaded that television would be the "ultimate and greatest step in mass communications," and he had so informed the RCA board in another of those prophetic memoranda that were becoming his trademark. "I believe that television, which is the technical name for seeing instead of hearing by radio, will come to pass in due course," he wrote. "The problem is technically similar to that of radiotelephony though of more complicated nature—but within the range of technical achievement. Therefore it may be that every broadcast receiver for home use in the future will also be equipped with a television adjunct by which the instrument will make it possible to see as well as hear what is going on in the broadcast station."

Sarnoff's first television memo, unlike his radio music box proposal, was more informational than a call for action. By his own estimate, a workable commercial system was at least a decade away, and even that proved overly optimistic by more than a decade. It was his way of telling the board that he, the new general manager, was tracking television, and that there was more substance to the emerging technology than the fantasy of Buck Rogersish newspaper cartoons might imply, or the lurid science fiction of Hugo Gernsback's *Modern Electronics,* which was enthralling youthful Americans of technical bent. At the time, Sarnoff was too absorbed in policing the patent pool and fighting free of electrical company committees to be more than a passive bystander at television's emergence in America.

The first public demonstration of working apparatus invented by an American occurred in 1925. Charles Francis Jenkins, a squat, baggy-eyed tinkerer out of Dayton, Ohio, who apprenticed as a movie engineer, stole a march on the scientists of the great corporate laboratories by transmitting a film of a Dutch windmill in motion from Anacostia, Virginia, to Washington, D.C., a distance of about five miles. His system embraced Nipkow's mechanical concept, but in place of spinning discs Jenkins employed prismatic rings that rotated horizontally and vertically, scanning the film across a photoelectric cell. The result was a rather blurred silhouette reproduced on a 6-by-8-inch screen. It was picture postcard television, as primitive as the first movie flickers, but to Jenkins, the quintessential little man of invention, a throwback to the attic inventor of radio's formative years, it was the beginning of a new era which would link the nation with "radio vision," as he first called it. Representatives of the press and high government officials, including Secretary of the Navy Curtis D. Wilbur, witnessed the demonstration in Jenkins' Connecticut Avenue laboratory in Washington, and the *New York Times* was sufficiently impressed to accord it several paragraphs on page one.

Nevertheless, there was no great outpouring of interest from a public still in thrall to radio. The technique was simply too crude in comparison to the large-screen clarity of movie theaters. It required the promotional resources of a large corporation wedded to an improved system of transmission to begin attracting the public's interest. With considerable fanfare in 1926, GE took the wrappings off Alexanderson's system, a form of projection television featuring a large mirror drum and a two-foot scanning disc. The receiver screen was lit by a neon glow lamp which imparted a pinkish tinge.

A year later an AT&T research team headed by Dr. Herbert Ives transmitted pictures over wire lines between Washington and Whippany, New Jersey. The screen was only 2 by 2½ inches in size, intended, according to AT&T, to be a visual adjunct to the telephone. But the clarity of the picture was sufficient to set off excited tremors in the press. From Washington, Commerce Secretary Hoover spoke to an AT&T vice-president in New Jersey, and his features were easily discernible. An AT&T engineer, Edward Nelson, did a Negro dialect monologue in blackface. MORE THAN 200 MILES OF SPACE ANNIHILATED proclaimed a front-page headline in the *Times,* with subheads LIKE A PHOTO COME TO LIFE and TELEVISION TRIUMPHS. Sarnoff was no less euphoric over one of the GE demonstrations he witnessed in Schenectady. "An epoch-making event," he told the press, comparable in importance to Marconi's first wireless transmission on his Italian farm.

Now the public began to stir. Letters to manufacturers and newspapers asked when a regular service would begin and how receiving sets could be obtained. The first to respond was Jenkins. From the Federal Radio Commission, Jenkins obtained an experimental license to begin regular telecasts over Washington station W3XK. He transmitted via shortwaves an hourly diet of film shorts and half-tone stills, some of which were received with fair legibility as far away as Alabama. Wall Street was impressed. Perhaps a new RCA was in the making. Speculative fever was then at its peak, fueled by a society imbued with the concept of instant riches. Anything that related to new technology was fondled. Almost overnight, investment bankers underwrote for $10 million the Jenkins Television Corporation, with a capitalization of one million shares. The scion of a distinguished family of merchant princes and bankers, Anthony J. Drexel Biddle, Jr., lent his gilded name to the new corporation as chairman. In a manufacturing plant in Jersey City, Jenkins' mechanical disc receivers were assembled for sale through radio retail outlets, priced from $85 to $135. They were a luxury item for the upper classes, comparable to $500 or $1,000 sets at today's dollar value. For the less affluent, Jenkins offered do-it-yourself receiver kits for $47.50, complete with magnifying lens for viewing a picture that in its smallest dimension was 1½ inches square. Although precise figures were never revealed, the press estimated that several thousand Jenkins Universal Television Receivers were purchased in the first year. The *Times* reported that radio retailers were expecting to reap a rich harvest from "the seeds of television." A minor television boom was under way in 1928, and its father was not the dominating leader of RCA, but the snub-nosed, rumpled, and unquenchably enthusiastic Jenkins.

He constructed a $65,000 studio at 655 Fifth Avenue in Manhattan, and began televising monologues by actors and actresses, including Ethel Barrymore, Lionel Atwood, and Gertrude Lawrence. Estimates of the viewing audience ranged up to 100,000. But because his license was experimental, not commercial, Jenkins could not solicit advertising. His revenue depended on the sale of receivers, and that in turn depended on his ability to program adequately.

Jenkins' relentless television push stimulated others to obtain experimental licenses. GE began a limited telecasting schedule in Schenectady, mainly to technical employees whose homes were equipped with test receivers built by Alexanderson. Most of the TV licenses were obtained by radio station owners, nervously uncertain what television's effect would be on their profitable audio service. On the West Coast, the Don Lee radio station group started telecasting feature films. In the midwest, the Chicago Federation of Labor launched the first experimental service, sensing its propaganda value for the labor movement. By the end of 1928, the Federal Radio Commission had granted twenty-eight experimental licenses. Abroad, the British Broadcasting Corporation had launched a regular schedule of telecasts in the London area, and French and German services were gestating. In many respects, the pattern for a repeat of radio's explosive eruption seemed to be forming.

Yet it failed to materialize because two developments conspired against it. First was the onset of the depression, which closed off the money sluices of Wall Street to uncertain technical experiments. Second was the growing conviction of various industry leaders, Sarnoff foremost among them, that the mechanical concept on which television had been built was the wrong technological approach. A half century of intense experimentation and field testing had failed to conquer such inherently limiting factors as the small size of the screen, which could be enlarged only by a proportionate increase in the size of the spinning disc, thus rendering the receiver too large for comfortable accommodation in the home. Similarly, to refine picture transmission, ever bulkier transmitter equipment was required, thus constraining the mobility of telecasts. Despite occasional good picture quality under carefully controlled conditions, the clarity of reception was difficult to sustain over extended periods, and there were frequent mechanical breakdowns. In Sarnoff's judgment, slowly arrived at after a decade of observation, it represented a marriage of the horse and buggy with electronic technology, and it wasn't working, and wouldn't.

In 1929, when Sarnoff was forcing the unification of the radio group's manufacturing and research facilities under RCA, he was visited in his New York office by a young Westinghouse scientist named Vladimir T. Zworykin, who had been doing television research on his own initiative and who shrewdly gauged that RCA's general manager, whose reputation for venturesome outreach in new areas of technology was spreading, represented a possible corporate patron. The same age as Sarnoff, Zworykin was also a Russian émigré. His ship-owning family came from Muram in the eastern central region and was as affluent as the Sarnoffs from the southern steppes were poor. As an engineering student at the University of St. Petersburg, Zworykin had become the protégé of Professor Boris Rosing, a pioneer in the theory of electrical scanning. In 1907, Rosing had applied for a patent on his concept of an "electric eye," which employed a cathode ray tube whose fluorescent screen could be excited by a bombardment of electrons, thus producing a crude television image without a mechanical scanner. When Zworykin came to the United States in 1919, fleeing the Russian Revolution, which swallowed up Rosing, he determined to advance his teacher's early work by developing a completely electronic television system in which all mechanical devices were eliminated. By 1923, working at Westinghouse, he had cleared the first hurdle, inventing a cathode ray scanning tube, known as the iconoscope, that gave the television camera an electronic eye. As a pickup tube, the iconoscope promised a quantum leap over mechanical scanning apparatus in clarity, light contrast, and mobility, but his first demonstration to Westinghouse executives proved disappointing. The camera apparatus was primitive, the picture occasionally unstable, and Zworykin's superiors, dedicated refrigerator merchants, refused to commit the substantial development funds they judged would be needed.

When Zworykin faced Sarnoff across the desk for the first time, he had gone through several discouraging years attempting to interest others in his all-electronic concept. In a burst of frustration, he had left Westinghouse to work for a small midwestern electronics firm but, finding no encouragement there, had returned to the big electrical company, where word filtered into his engineering laboratory of Sarnoff's drive for research unity. So he had short-circuited organizational lines, and in his heavily Russian-accented English he outlined to an intent Sarnoff his concept of an electronic camera eye that would replace the spinning disc. He conceded the primitive nature of his laboratory apparatus and the need for extensive developmental work. When Sarnoff asked the cost, Zworykin estimated $100,000 to achieve a workable video system. This proved to be one of the classic cost underestimates of technological history—by about $50 million—but Sarnoff did not quibble with it then or later. He was caught up by the intensity of the slight, sandy-haired inventor whose blue eyes sparkled behind thick-lensed glasses. For more than an hour, the two Russian émigrés pursued a question and answer dialogue, the enthusiasm of both steadily heightening. Again, Sarnoff had discovered someone on his wavelength and, without bothering to check with his superiors, he pledged to underwrite an expanded research effort by Zworykin at the funding level he requested. Within a year, with the unification of radio group research effected under RCA control, Sarnoff made good on his pledge. Zworykin moved to the RCA research center at Camden and, with a staff of four engineering assistants, began in earnest the pursuit of an alternative to the mechanical disc.

The Sarnoff-Zworykin encounter proved to be one of the most decisive in industrial annals. It brought together television's leading inventor and the executive who would guide its development. Their spirit of kinship, perhaps forged out of a Russian cradle, would endure for Sarnoff's life, and would lead to a fundamental alteration in the direction of technology and its management. A year earlier Sarnoff had hinted at the magnitude of this change when he told a Harvard Business School audience that a new breed of manager, skilled in the understanding of technology and capable of interpreting its future directions, would be required to maintain America's industrial supremacy. Now, for the first time, he would have a chance to prove that thesis. In radio, he had been the surrogate of others, negotiating patent licenses, policing the industry, warring against the telephone company, but often subordinate to policy interests that conflicted with his own ambitions. The convergence of Zworykin's inventions with the emancipation of RCA gave him the opportunity to create, nurture, and shape a new body of technology, beginning at its infancy. It involved a unique concept of management, with the supreme executive authority of the corporation linked, without intermediaries, to fundamental research. For Sarnoff, it meant a form of shuttle management, from the empyrean tower of Rockefeller Center to Zworykin's small, cluttered Camden laboratory, and he made the trip often to observe, inquire, and exhort. In New York, he was an immaculately garbed corporate paladin; in Camden, he went to shirt sleeves in the bright lights and intense heat of the television labs, sweating, cigar or pipe clenched within his jaws. "It was a question of confidence," he would later say. "The technical people had to know management was behind them, and I was management. I let them know I believed in them more than they believed in themselves." Thus was born the Sarnoff concept of hands-on management of technology. When he had talked to the Harvard students about a new breed of manager, he had meant, of course, himself.

Soon after RCA's independence, with the depression at its nadir, Sarnoff had seen enough of Zworykin's progress to arrive at perhaps the most significant decision in television's history. He decided to jettison the accumulated technical knowledge of a half century, cut loose from the spinning disc that underpinned TV's first boomlet, and lead the industry in the development of a new, all-electronic approach in which transient pictures would be transmitted and received without mechanical moving parts. To emphasize that the bridges were burned behind him, he made a dramatic announcement to RCA shareholders that he was committing $1 million to intensified research in electronic TV. Zworykin's engineering staff was sextupled, provided with an enlarged testing laboratory, and Zworykin was given the title of director of electronics research.

In a sense, the depression was Sarnoff's ally. Sales of Jenkins TV receivers dried up by 1932, and the Wall Street bankers who had embraced his initial overtures now were coldly unresponsive. Without advertising revenue for his experimental telecasts, Jenkins lacked sufficient funds to maintain a continuing schedule of entertainment programs of the type the public was demanding. Letters from set owners pleaded for more lavish theatrical productions and sporting events, which Jenkins was incapable of mounting. In 1932, the blue-blooded chairman, Biddle, had abdicated, and shareholders of the Jenkins Television Company were informed by President Leslie S. Gordon that "commercial development of television has been slower and more costly than originally contemplated." He requested permission to sell the company's assets to De Forest Radio, another small and struggling enterprise that had been created by the pioneer inventor of the Audion tube and that a year later would itself plunge into receivership. Telecasts from Jenkins' Washington station ceased and his New York studios were abandoned. In the hostile economic environment of the thirties, the Jenkinses and De Forests were swallowed up, along with tens of thousands of other small businesses. Taps were sounding over the era of the individual inventor, and Jenkins was its television paradigm. Within two years of his company's collapse, the little man from Akron who had fathered the first video boom in America died penniless and, according to associates, brokenhearted at the collapse of his enterprise.

For a quittance of $500,000 Sarnoff acquired the assets of the defunct venture. These included several De Forest patents that he felt would strengthen RCA's coverage, plus engineering personnel experienced in TV circuitry who were added to Zworykin's growing staff. He also acquired broadcast studio and manufacturing equipment that he felt could be integrated into the different type of system he was planning. Although he knew Jenkins only casually, Sarnoff had always insisted to associates that the inventor's enterprise was too fragile financially and too fenced in by technical limitations to succeed. By now he knew that vast sums would be required to develop a successful electronic system, and that only corporations with renewable technical resources and managements not intimidated by the vagaries of the economy could succeed. Already he was joking with friends that Zworykin was not only a great inventor, he was "the greatest salesman in history. He put a price tag of $100,000 on television, and I bought it."

By 1932 RCA engineers were field-testing the iconoscope pickup tube linked to a transmitter installed on the roof of a Camden plant. Still pictures were broadcast via ultrahigh frequency over a few miles' distance to a prototype set equipped with another Zworykin invention, a cathode ray receiving tube which replaced the rotating disc and was known as the kinescope. The pictures received were blurry and unstable, but their pedigree was purely electronic, no longer a mechanical hybrid, and Sarnoff judged them of adequate quality to begin serious field tests. An RCA transmitting antenna was implanted at the top of New York City's highest skyscraper, the Empire State Building, and several receivers were scattered about the metropolitan area in the homes of RCA technical personnel. A small television studio, equipped with an iconoscope camera, was constructed at NBC. Still pictures of Felix the Cat, a familiar cartoon character, and of various pretty girls were the broadcast staples. Five separate generations of tests were conducted through the middle thirties, each registering advances in picture clarity, fidelity, and range of reception, which soon extended consistently to fifty miles.

Sarnoff orchestrated the advance. "Finally, I had the authority to move television at my own pace. No executive layers above, no electric committees to question expenditures," he later recalled. He carefully drew the small RCA board into the drama of technological gestation, reporting monthly on progress, taking the board on guided tours of the Camden facility, the Empire State transmitter, and the broadcast studio. Costs had mounted beyond $5 million, but the board continued sanctioning his every request for additional funding, gambling on his belief in long-term rewards. Still, he was cautious publicly in forecasting the ultimate commercialization of electronic television. It wasn't "just around the corner" he told RCA shareholders at the 1935 annual meeting, and when several complained about the unrequited costs, he told them bluntly that without courage, initiative, and sacrifice "a new art cannot be created or a new industry born." Yet there was no serious shareholder unrest because robust profits from radio were more than off-setting the developmental costs of a new service that would ultimately eclipse it. By 1937 the company began paying dividends—twenty cents per share—for the first time on its common stock.

Napoleon, it has been said, could look upon a wildly disordered battlefield and envisage a coherence that would redound to his advantage. Viewing the disarray of television following the collapse of the mechanical forces led by Jenkins, Sarnoff sensed a similar opportunity to rally a new industry under his banner. It would not be enough just to have the best TV camera or the best home receiver. The leader must lead in all areas of the new art—in the construction of transmitters and mobile equipment, in componentry and equipment servicing, in studio construction and networking, in the creation of the entertainment and informational programs that would course through the apparatus of transmission and reception. It was a total system approach to a new industry—"the whole ball of wax," Sarnoff called it—and at the time it was unique on the industrial landscape. The leader would be the pioneer, his compass charting the industry's course, a lodestar to which others of lesser magnitude, the followers, would be drawn. The followers would seek competitive niches in one or more aspects of the system, but only one would be involved in them all, and that would be RCA, led by its own Napoleon.

From this concept, Sarnoff moved on to an even more dynamic gestalt for the management of technology, which he began articulating during the mid-thirties in speeches and at stockholder meetings. *Fortune* magazine would later call it his "missionary approach to the science of electronics." RCA would muster all its research resources behind the electron, the building block of wireless intelligence transmission, one of the tiniest particles of matter in the universe, and would go wherever technological breakthroughs dictated. Thus the company's future would be charted by what Sarnoff described as "supplantive" competition in electronics. Just as wireless had supplanted the cable, just as the radio had supplanted the phonograph, now television would supplant radio. More than manufacturing or marketing or finance, research would become the sine qua non of his new corporate structure—in his oft repeated phrase, "the lifeblood of RCA." And always "cooking in the oven" of research would be the embryonic beginnings of new core technologies that would ultimately supplant those in the marketplace. Within this broad parameter, Sarnoff would guide RCA throughout his career, filtering his management concept like a sacred rubric down through every managerial level to the production line, providing the company with a unity of purpose and congruence of motivation that for many years made the sum of RCA seem greater than its parts.

By 1936 the pieces of the television system were beginning to fit together. RCA engineers had constructed a series of relay stations for transmitting TV signals in the very high frequency band between the Empire State tower and the Camden laboratories. Two-way transmissions soon followed between New York and Philadelphia, and the validity of networking was established. Picture quality continued to improve: "more distinct pictures, lines across the pictures disappear, great detail is visible, so that a sports event, even a baseball or football game, might be televised," the *New York Times* reported of a demonstration of RCA receivers with screens measuring 5½ by 7½ inches, and with the picture projected onto a mirror on the inside of the cabinet's lid. As a safety precaution, a sheet of shatterproof glass separated the viewer from the screen and imparted a green tint to the television image.

By 1937 the first mobile RCA television van appeared on the streets of New York, containing two cameras and a relay transmitter and permitting remote pickups. In July, NBC announced plans to begin experimental telecasts from Madison Square Garden of prizefights and other indoor sporting events. Public demonstrations were staged in semidarkened auditoriums, featuring monologues by the comedian Ed Wynn, the actor Henry Hull in vignettes from *Tobacco Road,* and songs by the popular radio chanteuse Hildegarde. At the most important demonstrations, Sarnoff himself would preside, opening the program with a recitation of television's development and with RCA, of course, in the starring role. Then a soaring extrapolation of the future: "To people in their homes, a complete means of instantaneous participation in the sights and sounds of the entire outer world." Then a prescient summation: To the American people television might soon become "their principal source of entertainment, education, and news."

In part in response to Sarnoff's initiative, in part because of the stirrings of their own scientists, other companies and other countries were discarding their mechanical apparatus and pursuing the electronic route. The leading independent radio manufacturers, Philco and Zenith, were joined by Dumont in the development of receiver circuitry; GE became active in transmitter technology; and AT&T developed a coaxial cable for TV signal transmission. At a cost of nearly $600,000, the phone company installed an experimental cable between New York and Philadelphia and successfully transmitted high-definition television pictures. Whether by RCA's wireless relay stations or AT&T's cable, the new science was assured of a network capability comparable to that of radio. In England, the BBC announced that it was abandoning its mechanical apparatus in favor of the newer technology, under patent license from RCA.

Sarnoff's policy toward his competitors in television was far more liberal than in radio. The terms of the consent decree of '32 ensured that. The patented inventions of Zworykin and his associates would be licensed to the industry—at a fee, of course. On July 7, 1936, RCA's licensees, meaning virtually the entire industry, were invited to a progress demonstration at which Sarnoff presided. There was room for all in this new industry of unfathomable potential, he proclaimed; television was too great in its promise for all mankind to be the exclusive preserve of any one company, and RCA was prepared to share the fruits of its pioneering with all others, including foreign licensees. Among the first of these was Telefunken of Germany, providing the emergent Nazi government with an early TV capability, although Hitler never exploited it, probably because of his absorption in preparation for war.

After Sarnoff's remarks, the industry leaders witnessed a test telecast featuring Bonwit Teller models parading before the camera. Three different sets of design specifications for experimental receivers were unveiled. The atmosphere seemed one of cooperation and harmony, as though Sarnoff were assuring his competitors that the lacerating wars of early radio would not be repeated. Even at that early stage, he was convinced RCA's patents blanketed the television art, and that it needed no inventions of others to proceed into commercial production.

Sarnoff was nearly proved correct, but the work of one inventor belied him, piercing the RCA patent phalanx with discoveries that could not be ignored. Philo T. Farnsworth was a Mormon farm boy, born in Utah and reared in Idaho. In high school he had taken rudimentary courses in electricity and was fascinated by them. He enrolled in Brigham Young University in Provo, Utah, majoring in mathematics and electronics engineering. But the death of his father, like that of Sarnoff's father a generation earlier, forced him to leave school to support his family. In 1926, he opened a radio service shop in Salt Lake City, where he began tinkering with the development of an electronic pickup tube for a television camera. His concept was similar to Zworykin's, centering on picture transmission without a mechanical scanner, but the linear technique he developed was radically different. Where Zworykin's design focused electrons into a beam, Farnsworth conceived of dissecting the electronic image into picture elements, and then transmitting them through a small aperture in an electrical shutter. By 1927, two years before the first Sarnoff-Zworykin meeting, the slender, intense twenty-one-year-old inventor had applied for a patent on his pickup tube, which he called an image dissector. Cylindrical in shape and operating without a beam, the Farnsworth tube represented a fundamentally different approach to electronic image scanning.

Like Zworykin, Farnsworth was an engineering genius who also possessed an aptitude for selling himself and his inventive ideas. First, he attracted developmental backing from Utah friends, then from the Crocker Bank in San Francisco as word of his invention began to infiltrate the radio trade press. By 1929, when Zworykin was first approaching Sarnoff, Farnsworth had already spent $60,000 on the image dissector and it had become apparent to him and his backers that substantially greater sums would be required to achieve commercial readiness. So he turned to the Philco Corporation, which had become RCA's principal manufacturing rival in radio, and Philco established a research laboratory for him at Chestnut Hill, near Philadelphia, in exchange for a license to manufacture sets of Farnsworth design. But after two years and an expenditure of $250,000, the alliance was terminated. Philco's interest was more parochial than Farnsworth's; it wanted a marketable set, and as soon as possible, but he sought a broad range of patents that would embrace all aspects of the new art. Like Sarnoff, Farnsworth was a broad-gauge dreamer, and it was therefore perhaps inevitable that their aspirations would collide.

In 1932, with Sarnoff mustering RCA's resources behind Zworykin's iconoscope, Farnsworth sought to halt the industry giant by filing a patent interference action against Zworykin, claiming priority in the concept of scanning an electronic image. When he was upheld by a patent examiner, RCA appealed the verdict to the Patent Office's appellate division. But, again, in 1936, the Utah youth's claim of prior disclosure was upheld, and the RCA television drive appeared in jeopardy. An appeal of the decision in the civil courts might require years, seriously delaying commercial introduction. Yet RCA apparently could not deliver a marketable product based purely on Zworykin's developments without infringing on Farnsworth's patents. Trapped in this dilemma, Sarnoff sought to purchase Farnsworth's patents outright, but the young inventor would not sell. He would license his patents to RCA, just as RCA licensed to others; on that basis alone would he share the fruits of his inventive genius with the company that had been founded on a patent monopoly. Never before had RCA licensed patents instead of purchasing them, but Sarnoff reluctantly concluded that he had no choice. He directed RCA's legal staff to prepare a cross-licensing agreement with Farnsworth, and, according to legend, the RCA legal official who signed it had tears in his eyes.

By wedding the best features of the image dissector and the iconoscope, a television transmitting system evolved that Sarnoff judged to be of commercial quality. He had been forced to accept a patent partnership with Farnsworth, but strangely he appeared to bear no malice toward the younger man, as he did toward so many others in the industry who had sought to challenge him. Perhaps it was because of their similar underprivileged beginnings, the shared sense of a youthful struggle against great odds. Years later, in testimony at a United States Senate committee hearing on television industry practices, Sarnoff recognized Farnsworth's contributions: "It is only fair that I should mention this—an American inventor who I think has contributed, outside RCA itself, more to television than anybody else in the United States, and that is Mr. Farnsworth, of the Farnsworth television system." Unlike the other little man of television, Charles Jenkins, who failed because of a flawed technology, Farnsworth succeeded in creating a profitable enterprise, the Farnsworth Television and Radio Corporation, which, backed by the banking firm of Kuhn, Loeb and Company, began operations in Fort Wayne, Indiana, and produced a modestly successful line of radios, phonographs and, later, television receivers under the Capehart label. Farnsworth served as its vice-president and director of research. He was not a driving, dominating executive in the Sarnoff mold, but he succeeded in creating an enduring niche for himself as the co-inventor, with Zworykin, of the television system that the nation would ultimately embrace.

With his patent problem in the process of resolution and with the technological progression of electronic TV moving ahead, Sarnoff began focusing his attention on the political questions involved in securing authorization for RCA's system. As interest in television mounted, Congress had responded by passing the Communications Act of 1934, which created the Federal Communications Commission to supplant the Federal Radio Commission that had been established in 1927 to allocate broadcast frequencies among stations and adjudicate technical disputes within the industry. The FCC, whose seven members were nominated by the president on a bipartisan basis and confirmed by the Senate, was given a broader mandate. It would oversee all present and future broadcast communications services, and would regulate the rates charged for commercial messages by cable, wireless, and long-distance telephone. However, the relationship that the Communications Act codified between the government and broadcasters held to the pattern that emerged in radio. Station owners would be licensed for fixed periods by the FCC, and charged with operating in "the public interest, convenience or necessity." Theoretically, license renewal every three years would hinge on adequate fulfillment of that mandate. The legislation affirmed that the air-waves belonged to the people, the broadcasters were trustees of a national asset, not its owners, and their failure to perform in the public interest could lead to license revocation and forced sale of their assets. Yet, ambivalently, the commission was denied control of program content, which would remain, as it had in radio, with the broadcasters. In effect, Congress mandated a competitive and "free" system of broadcasting. The decision on what the American people saw and heard over their airwaves was thus the responsibility of private corporations whose success hinged on profits—profits that the marketplace had already determined would come from the advertising dollars of other private corporations. It was a unique American formula, attuned to the national devotion to private enterprise. Virtually all other broadcasting systems around the world came to be government owned or controlled, with authority over program content as well as technological standards. The dichotomy inherent in the American system—the FCC was a guardian but not a policeman of the airwaves—quickly generated disagreement over the proper relationship between regulator and regulated, and it was most dramatically manifest in television's emergence.

Within the industry itself, efforts to reach technical agreement along the lines proposed by Sarnoff had quickly withered. At Philco and Zenith in particular, the suspicion was deep rooted that RCA would attempt to dominate television as it had early radio, and that the new FCC would become Sarnoff's consort. Beyond that, they saw no reason to rush television's commercial introduction since the rebound in radio sales had restored their profit margins. Why, they asked, jeopardize a flourishing business for which the public appetite was still unappeased by forcing the introduction of an untested new service? Sarnoff saw this as a delaying tactic, and by 1937, when the FCC agreed to address the questions of technical standards and channel allocations for a video service, he had emerged as the foremost proponent of quick introduction.

Assuredly, he was the most visible and articulate leader of the new technology. The title "televisionary" had already been bestowed upon him by the trade press, admiringly by his supporters, sardonically by his foes. Television had, without question, become an obsession to him. It represented the consummation of his long odyssey in search of respect, acceptance, and fame, within a chrysalis of power. Since the industry had rebuffed his co-operative overtures, he was now ready, even eager, to battle for his system. He was buoyed by the support of the RCA Board of Directors, which raised his salary to $100,000, making him one of the higher paid American industrialists. As the battle flared, he purchased a six-story, thirty-room town house in Manhattan's east seventies, complete with servants' rooms, private elevator, and a solarium. Both his professional and personal quarters were now truly baronial, and almost as important to him as the substance of power were these externals that embellished and certified it. This was also reflected in personal idiosyncrasies that began surfacing and that were judged by some to reflect a swelling ego. For example, at his frequent public speeches, he began designating an underling to accompany him. The primary responsibility of this functionary was to carry a black loose-leaf notebook containing his prepared remarks in bold-face, capital-size type, which permitted Sarnoff to speak without employing reading glasses. Only after the head table had been seated would the book bearer approach the podium and rather ceremoniously present his offering to Sarnoff. To a young RCA executive witnessing the ritual for the first time, it seemed not unlike a page bearing a royal proclamation to his monarch, with the court in attendance. After the speech, again almost ritualistically, a text would be forwarded to RCA's Washington office for insertion in the *Congressional Record* by a friendly legislator. Press releases digesting the speech flowed into city rooms and wire services, so that the saga of Sarnoff would continue fresh in the minds of his contemporaries— and of history.

Sarnoff's desire for personal service also became more acute. He stopped carrying cash, and aides who accompanied him were expected to pick up whatever tabs he incurred—to be reimbursed later, of course, by expense account. One of his senior associates, Meade Brunet, once accompanied him to an industry meeting in Chicago where they shared a hotel suite. At checkout time, according to Brunet, his boss ordered him to carry his luggage. "I'll call a bellhop," Brunet responded rather grimly, facing up to Sarnoff's surprised glare. "If you'd let him, he could walk all over you," Brunet later recalled.

The television systems disagreement that the FCC was required to adjudicate centered on the question of transmission and reception standards. The technology demanded a precise synchronization between the density of scanning lines and the number of picture frames transmitted between the broadcast station and the receiver in the home. An inflexible lock-and-key relationship thus existed between the two principal components of the system. It was therefore incumbent on the FCC and the industry to agree upon a single set of standards. Otherwise, the public would find itself in the untenable position of being asked to purchase sets that could receive pictures only from the channels with which they were technically aligned. The system RCA's engineers had developed called for transmission of 30 frames and 441 scanning lines per second, and these were the standards to which Sarnoff, of course, attached his battle flag. But others in the industry who had been experimenting with standards came up with different solutions. The Dumont Company, headed by the veteran electronics engineer Allen B. Dumont, who had been an associate of Lee De Forest in early radio, proposed a 15-frame and 625-line system. Philco urged 24 frames and 605 lines. Others, like Zenith and CBS, saw the standards conflict as proof that television's commercial introduction was premature, the result sure to be an unsettling of a thriving radio business.

Nowhere were the lines of conflict more sharply drawn than between RCA and Philco. From its early years as a manufacturer and distributor of storage batteries, Philco had successfully converted to the production of radios featuring ornate cabinets crafted by leading furniture designers. Their novelty won quick public acceptance, and by 1933 Philco was outselling RCA in radio sets. Now it appeared determined to repeat the pattern in television. Under President Lawrence E. Gubb, a bitter personal rival of Sarnoff, Philco created its own video research staff after terminating Farnsworth, with primary concentration on the production of home receivers. By 1936 it was demonstrating to the press in Philadelphia, its headquarters city, a home receiver featuring a 9-by-8-inch mirror screen, based in large measure, it claimed, on its own patents. Within the industry, and particularly RCA, it was viewed as a desperate stop-Sarnoff effort, which reached a titillating climax when Philco filed suit in New York Supreme Court accusing RCA of unfair trade practices. The complaint contended that RCA had procured company-confidential information from certain Philco female employees by plying them with "intoxicating liquors at hotels, restaurants and nightclubs." Further, it alleged that RCA's agents had sought to involve the girls in "compromising situations," and did, in fact, "induce, incite and bribe said employees." RCA responded that the charges were sheer fabrication. To Sarnoff they offered further proof of his dictum that competition brought out the best in products but the worst in men. The Philco suit, which ultimately was dropped, also reinforced his determination to get approved standards before the industry battle became a tabloid sensation.

In 1936, largely at Sarnoff's instigation, and with the tacit approval of the FCC, the Radio Manufacturers Association created an engineering committee to seek a technical consensus of the industry on standards. Over a year later, the RMA committee reported to the FCC that it had reached an agreement—and its recommended standards were closely attuned to those advocated by RCA and Farnsworth. But it quickly proved a fragile concord. Before the FCC could act, Philco disowned the agreement by claiming the committee was stacked with RCA supporters and others who feared the patent licensing power of the industry giant. Later Zenith and CBS, which was making rapid competitive strides against NBC in network radio and which had created its own research facilities for television, joined in a warning threnody of the disasters facing radio if the FCC acted hastily.

With its hopes for an industry consensus thus thwarted, the FCC backed away from the final step of adopting commercial standards, which would have permitted broadcasters to sell television time as they did radio. The commission simply urged further field-testing along the standards path recommended by the RMA engineering committee.

Rather than encouraging renewed technical efforts, the FCC's decision stimulated a further drumroll of intra-industry attacks by propagandists of both sides. Philco reiterated its charge that Sarnoff was attempting to force the government and the industry to freeze on his standards prematurely. Zenith's McDonald launched a trade advertising campaign warning that television was "premature both for economic and technical reasons." A trade cartoon, inspired, Sarnoff believed, by Zenith, showed him as a giant "televisionary" ape, trampling on the prostrate corpus of the radio industry.

And Sarnoff responded in kind. To him, the conflict had become Manichaean, no longer susceptible to compromise. Freed of the restraints of electrical company ownership, secure in his stewardship of RCA, he poured invective on the McDonalds, Gubbs, and Dumonts, indeed all those in the industry who opposed him. They were "parasites," seeking to fatten themselves on radio to the detriment of a newer service that could reinforce America's technological leadership in the world. It was always thus with the pioneer who led the way and took the risks, he averred publicly and privately. Not until the rewards were in sight would the "scavengers" crawl on the television bandwagon and join the feast. There was deeply felt anger in Sarnoff's words. In his youth he had possessed a quick, flaring temper, nurtured perhaps by the manifest injustices of ghetto life, but he had schooled himself to contain it except in the confines of family and among subordinates, recognizing the impediment it might become to his progress. But no longer. He had cast off the shackles of poverty and servility, and the verbal thunderbolts he unleashed were probably a form of therapy, although he would have scorned the word. To his associates, he seemed to relish the clash of wills. His longtime engineering chief, Charles Jolliffe, remembered him as "never more alive" than in the angry give-and-take of television's emergence.

To those who accused him of haste, Sarnoff responded that he had counseled caution on the commercial introduction of television for over a decade. Even though RCA had spent more than $20 million on television research, more than the rest of the industry combined, and had amassed more basic patents, he had insisted that field tests must establish the basic validity of the system. But now he felt that had been accomplished and he was goaded into action by the FCC's failure to accept the RMA's recommendations. He had decided to go it alone. "Television in the home is now technically feasible," he told the RMA annual meeting in October 20, 1938. "The problems confronting this difficult and complicated art can only be solved from operating experience, actually serving the public in their homes." So he would take the decisive next step and launch a regular service. With his typical flare for the dramatic, he informed the RMA the inaugural program would coincide with the opening of the New York World's Fair on April 20, 1939.

Sarnoff was taking a risk of make-or-break proportions. Sans FCC adoption of commercial standards, operating only with the experimental authority of a test license, which did not permit the sale of commercial time, he was gambling that public enthusiasm would stampede the industry and the commission behind the RCA system. He had studied the massive impact of Alexander Graham Bell's telephonic demonstration at the opening of the Philadelphia Exposition in 1876 and he was counting on igniting a similar brushfire of popular interest. Besides, he calculated that the risks of further delay were unacceptable. Philco and Dumont were pushing the development of rival broadcast standards that if introduced publicly would hopelessly muddle the conflict and confuse the set buyer. So RCA sets began rolling off the production line at Camden and NBC's enlarged television studio at Rockefeller Center was readied to begin a daily schedule of telecasts. Philco and Zenith continued to charge that Sarnoff was attempting to "stampede" the industry, but the FCC remained indecisive, neither condoning nor condemning Sarnoff's plan.

When the World's Fair opened on a lambent spring day in Flushing Meadows, Long Island, Sarnoff was there to share the spotlight with President Franklin D. Roosevelt and Mayor Fiorello La Guardia of New York City. A single mobile NBC camera unit, connected by coaxial cable to a transmitting van, was placed fifty feet from the speakers' platform. It showed the Fair's symbols, the Trylon and Perisphere, in the background; it swept across the Court of Peace, panned the gathering throng, captured the arrival of the president's motorcade and his remarks dedicating the Fair as a beacon of progress and hope in a world soon to be savaged by global conflict. The camera captured its first close-up when the photogenic La Guardia strode up and ogled it, face to face.

But neither the president nor the mayor could upstage the immigrant from Uzlian who had debarked in New York, only a few miles distant, thirty-nine years earlier. This was his day. All the rhetorical skills he had mastered in his adopted tongue came into play as he proclaimed the launching of "a new industry, based on imagination, on scientific research and accomplishment. Now we add radio sight to sound. It is with a feeling of humbleness that I come to the moment of announcing the birth in this country of a new art so important in its implications that it is bound to affect all society. It is an art which shines like a torch of hope in a troubled world. It is a creative force which we must learn to utilize for the benefit of all mankind."

As the portly RCA leader uttered his deeply resonated phrases only a few feet removed from the camera, perhaps two thousand people watched on television. From one to two hundred sets were in metropolitan area homes. Several hundred others watched on monitor screens at RCA's Manhattan headquarters, and additional hundreds at the RCA television exhibit building inside the Fair grounds. But the press carried his remarks nationwide. The New York *Herald Tribune*'s special Fair edition gave him pictorial and text attention nearly comparable to the president's—the same *Herald Tribune* that would collapse three decades later from television's competition for advertising dollars. The initial program lasted three and a half hours, featuring mainly speeches by politicians and Fair officials, and was followed by a regular series of NBC telecasts from the Fair on weekday afternoons and from the Radio City studio on Wednesday, Friday, and Sunday evenings. Finally, it appeared, television was no longer just around the corner. It had turned it.

The initial NBC schedule varied from eight to twelve hours weekly, blending dramas and variety shows with sports and feature films and round-table discussions. From a live baseball telecast of the New York Giants and Brooklyn Dodgers at Ebbets Field and from boxing at Madison Square Garden the schedule ranged to a nighttime dramatization of *Treasure Island* and a seventy-minute feature film, *Young and Beautiful*. Sets priced from $395 to $675 were on the market, and Sarnoff received some industry support when GE and the smaller Andrea Corporation offered sets with 6-by-8-inch viewing screens that were aligned to the NBC broadcasting standards. Set owners were urged to mail letters and postcards expressing their program preferences, and these informal polls soon established sports events as the commanding audience favorite. To meet that demand, RCA embarked on a crash program to turn out additional mobile transmitter units. Studio facilities for other major markets, such as Washington, Philadelphia, and Chicago, were being readied, and the telephone company geared up to link them through coaxial cables. All the pieces appeared to be falling in place for a nationwide sweep of high-definition, all-electronic television, based on the Zworykin and Farnsworth inventions plus the patents accrued by RCA over a decade. A stunning industrial coup by one man and one company was shaping up.

Yet, perplexingly to him, the brushfire Sarnoff had envisaged did not ignite—and certainly not on his timetable. Sarnoff had projected set sales of from twenty to forty thousand units in the metropolitan area in the year following product introduction, and this was more a visceral guess based on early radio sales than a careful market analysis. But three months after the Fair inaugural, only eight hundred sets had been sold and five thousand were stacked in dealer and distributor warehouses. An intensive newspaper advertising campaign by department stores, such as Gimbel and Wanamaker, produced only a meager response, and the frustrated Sarnoff arbitrarily slashed the price of RCA sets by a third. The other set manufacturers followed, but again response was tepid. By early 1940, it was apparent that Sarnoff had miscalculated the impact of his promotional blitz. The public was holding back because it was confused. The efforts of Zenith, Philco, and others had succeeded in sowing doubts about the wisdom of buying expensive sets that might become obsolete if the FCC adopted different standards for a commercial service, outmoding those under which NBC was operating experimentally. "Jumping the gun" was an often heard refrain. The premature launch was "Sarnoff's folly" in the words of *Radio Daily*. His personal drive for glory, his opponents charged, was tearing the industry apart. Two decades later, Sarnoff would tell colleagues this was the most abuse he ever experienced—"I've had plenty of cats and dogs thrown at me, but never like that. Philco and Zenith were more interested in getting me than in creating a television industry."

Under mounting pressure from a confused press and Congress, the FCC resumed standards hearings in April 1940, hoping public concern would stimulate some industry give-and-take. Sarnoff led the RCA contingent to Washington. During hours of testimony, he urged the commission to freeze on the RMA standards. "We can't wait indefinitely," he argued, "to wring out the last technical development." RCA had conclusively demonstrated, he said, that quality picture transmission and reception were at hand, and required only the FCC's blessing to clear the way for a national service in which all telecasts could be received by all makes of sets. But as others testified, the hearings began focusing more on the persona of Sarnoff than on the issue. Dumont reiterated that he had stacked the RMA committee with his puppets. Philco dramatically announced its withdrawal from the RMA, charging it with subservience to Sarnoff and challenging the validity of the technical work done at his research center. Better quality television, with higher definition pictures, would come soon, it implied, if the industry and the commission weren't stampeded by the autocrat of RCA. *Fortune* magazine washed its hands of the battle by describing radio as "a prima donna industry, as full of feuds and temperament as an opera troupe."

With a consensus still unobtainable, the FCC decided on a cautious further step. Its members were more politically than technically oriented and appeared loath to alienate important constituents by acceding to RCA's importunings. The chairman, James Lawrence Fly, an ardent New Dealer, an antimonopolist of deep conviction, seemed more concerned with preventing big company domination of the new art than with which set of standards ultimately prevailed. Rather than confront a Hobson's choice between unyielding factions, Fly's commission suggested a further cycle of experiments leading up to "limited commercial telecasting" by September 1940. But again it failed to freeze standards. It also failed to define what "limited" meant, so Sarnoff elected to apply his own definition. He announced RCA would begin commercial telecasts in September on a regular schedule, and it would offer for sale in the New York metropolitan area twenty-five thousand sets at reduced prices. The plan was set forth in full-page ads in New York dailies. To Sarnoff, the FCC had opened the door a crack, and now he was going to barge through. "Opportunities have to be viewed as though they were a barrel of apples," he later philosophized in justifying his action. "You pick out one you like, rub it briskly, and sink your teeth in it. In other words, you have to pick out the opportunity and make the most of it."

This time the reaction of the FCC was indignant, and Fly, in particular, aligned himself with the anti-Sarnoff forces. Granted an hour of free time on the small, recently formed Mutual radio network, the commission chairman accused RCA and its leader of attempting to gain a television monopoly: big business, meaning RCA, was "bullying the little fellows." On March 22, 1941, the FCC formally suspended the limited commercial authorization, accusing RCA of disregarding the intent of its order, and suggesting darkly "the possibility of one manufacturer gaining an unfair advantage over competitors," which "may cause them to abandon the further research and experimentation which is in the public interest."

Sarnoff professed amazement and consternation with the order, but he complied with it, and the Camden production line shut down. To Fly's accusation of monopoly, he replied that it was a "mildewed red herring." To the commission's call for further experimentation, he insisted that the public interest would be better served by extending television to "as many homes as possible," rather than by technical improvements that "merely add to the size or definition of the picture now enjoyed by the few." To Fly's warning of the "great danger in taking this young stripling [television] and selling him down the river for a few pieces of silver," Sarnoff responded publicly that the chairman was more interested in protecting RCA's competitors than in getting TV off the ground. To associates, he claimed that the Judas allusion was aimed at him as a Jew. He was so incensed that when President Roosevelt, whose relationship with Sarnoff had become close through NBC's inauguration of the fireside chats and its extensive coverage of presidential speeches, made the rather unusual suggestion that he get together with Fly at lunch (to be paid for by FDR) and work out their differences, Sarnoff politely demurred. Fly's solecisms had cut too deeply. "Our dispute is in the head, not the stomach," he told the president.

As the war of words continued, the RCA leader found himself supported by a broadening constituency. The sudden and seemingly arbitrary nature of the FCC's reversal struck many as bureaucratic overkill. Senator Ernest Lundeen of Minnesota, chairman of the committee with oversight responsibility for communications, went on NBC and Mutual to decry the throttling of a new industry "by a government bureau exercising power never granted by Congress." The *New York Times* called the FCC's action "absurd and unsound," and the Philadelphia *Enquirer* lamented the "bureaucratic blackout of television." In *Newsweek,* Professor Raymond Moley, a former New Deal brain truster, wrote of "an alien theory of merchandising," through which the FCC was attempting to protect the consumer "beyond acceptable bounds." A few in the industry, including GE and Farnsworth, expressed support for an early commercial introduction. Reacting to the outcry, the Senate called a committee hearing, chaired by Senator Burton K. Wheeler of Montana, to determine whether the commission had exceeded its authority.

The stars were Fly and Sarnoff in face-to-face confrontation. The FCC chairman held his ground, deploring the "blitzkrieg" tactics of RCA which he said flaunted the intent of the commission's "limited" order and threatened to impede further technical advances. Sarnoff's astute response was to promise the depressed American economy a massive new stimulant—a billion-dollar industry that would create a half million new jobs—if he could get the FCC off his back.

Without choosing sides, the Senate committee returned the dispute to the FCC, with the strong hint that a final resolution be achieved promptly. This was reinforced by popular rumblings of discontent; a mounting volume of letters to radio manufacturers, the press, and the commission had a let's-get-on-with-it theme. Finally, two years after the Fair opening, the brushfire began to ignite, and the heat was sufficient to persuade Zenith and Philco, most obdurate of the holdouts, to join under FCC auspices in an enlarged National Television Standards Committee, a successor to the old RMA standards committee that Sarnoff had inspired. It was to be headed by a respected GE research scientist, Dr. Walter R. G. Baker. The committee was to be purely engineering and free of corporate pressures. The FCC strongly implied that if the committee could achieve consensus, it would accept whatever the decision was. After several months of meetings, the technicians fashioned what industry and government could not—a consensus on a 525-line picture, interlaced, with 30 frames per second. For RCA, this posed little difficulty in readjusting transmitters from 441 lines and in realigning reception standards, free of charge, for the few hundred sets in the public's hands.

The system finally adopted by a relieved FCC came close to RCA's prescription and Sarnoff, who had remained discreetly aloof from the NTSC deliberations, was satisfied with it—so much so, in fact, that he again resorted to full-page ads claiming the NTSC system was in reality the RCA system. An infuriated Philco countered with ads saying the industry was responsible for American television, not RCA. Amidst a welter of claims and counter-claims, an unfettered NBC launched commercial telecasting in the United States on July 1, 1941. The first commercial, over its New York station, WNBT, was a Bulova clock face, with a second hand ticking off a minute. The price was $4. Forty-five years later the price for two thirty-second commercials in the Super Bowl, over the full NBC network, had increased by $1,099,996.

But still Sarnoff was to be denied his total victory. The winds of war, sweeping across the continents of Europe and Asia, were reaching toward America. Roosevelt's promise, in his unprecedented third-term reelection campaign in 1940, not to send America's sons into foreign battle seemed less unequivocal as Hitler's Panzers debouched over Europe and Africa, and Hirohito's armies engulfed Manchuria and threatened all the Far East. The economy was edging toward a war footing and television's emergence suddenly seemed less a pressing national priority. The explosion in set sales that Sarnoff had forecast again did not occur, and this time he made no attempt to force it. "By the summer of '41, I was convinced we could not avoid war," he later recollected, "and I knew RCA would be in the thick of it. Our technology would be indispensable for military communications. It was just too late in the game for television." A primary concern to Sarnoff was the situation facing Europe's Jews. He had been appalled by the menacing anti-Semitism of the Nazis. Reports of the notorious "Kristallnacht" in Berlin, in which Jewish shops, homes, and synagogues had been smashed, looted, and burned, left him with mingled feelings of apprehension and rage. Now he began shuttling to Washington for meetings with the Signal Corps and other branches of the armed services to plan RCA's integration into the defense buildup. The cathode ray tubes designed for television would soon find new application in radar and other electronic measuring and sensing devices for the armed services. At a private White House meeting with Roosevelt in the summer of '41, he assured the president that RCA's global communications network could be swiftly integrated with military channels. As the world's largest producer of electronic tubes, RCA was prepared, he told Roosevelt, to convert its plants, machinery, and manpower overnight to war production. When news of Pearl Harbor reached Sarnoff on Sunday afternoon, December 7, his first response was to fire off a telegram to the commander in chief: "All our facilities are ready and at your instant service. We await your commands."

By April 1942, when commercial production of television equipment was officially banned, only a few thousand sets were in the public's hands and all of RCA's electronic output had already been consigned to the armed services. NBC's commercial television schedule had been canceled, and its cameras and studios became a training center for air raid wardens and civil defense workers. Characteristically, Sarnoff focused all his formidable resources on the challenge immediately ahead. For the past decade it had been television. Now it was war.

7 / *Military Involvement*

In the early morning haze of December 7, 1941, 353 Japanese bombers and fighter planes launched from aircraft carriers swept past the Hawaiian Islands' Diamond Head and struck at the heart of America's Pacific fleet, moored on a somnolent Sunday at the naval base of Pearl Harbor. It was the most devastating surprise attack in the history of warfare. Six of eight battleships were sunk or seriously damaged, all but sixteen American bombers of the Pacific command were destroyed on the ground at Hickam Field, and 2,400 American soliders and sailors were killed, most incarcerated in watery graves beneath Pearl Harbor. Within a matter of minutes, the nation's strike capability in the Far East had been paralyzed. Not only the great battlewagons, but destroyers and other support vessels were reduced to smoking pyres by the bombs and torpedoes of the Empire of the Rising Sun, whose newspapers proclaimed that America had been reduced to a third-rate world power. Nearly half of the entire United States Navy had been knocked out of action.

Word of the sneak attack was borne to mainland America by military communications and commercial cable and wireless companies, including RCA Communications, which was now the name of the international wireless subsidiary. A nation at peace was enjoying a typically placid Sunday afternoon, witnessing or participating in sports events, attending movies, or gathered at the family table on the day of rest. It learned of Pearl Harbor from NBC and the other national radio networks, which interrupted regular programs with bulletins quoting President Roosevelt's brief announcement that the Japanese had attacked Pearl Harbor from the air. Throughout the afternoon and night, millions of Americans remained glued to their radios, absorbing additional information as the magnitude of the disaster unfolded. Their initial reaction was shock, and then anger, and then, in some cases, panic. Would the Japanese bombers attack the West Coast? Would the carrier fleet move beyond prostrate Pearl Harbor and launch an invasion of Los Angeles or San Francisco or San Diego?

Even the armed forces were caught up in the panicky uncertainty. At Camp Callen, a recently constructed army training base on a bluff overlooking the Pacific north of San Diego, crates of newly arrived rifles were broken open and hastily parceled out to draftees, some with less than four weeks' training. The recruits were ordered onto the chilly Pacific beaches, equipped with a few telescopes, and instructed to report any Japanese ships they sighted and repel any attempted invasion. One recruit noticed that the barrel of his rifle was still packed with petrolatum, making it inoperable even if he had known how to fire it. He asked his sergeant what to do. "Use it as a club when the Japs come," was the gruff rejoinder. Parents of students in West Coast universities, such as Stanford, began telephoning their offspring, urging them to return home. Reports of the sighting of aircraft with the red ball of the rising sun on their fuselage were received by newspapers and radio stations. Few Americans slept well on the night of December 7.

The following day, President Roosevelt reported to a joint session of Congress on the "day which will live in infamy" and called for a declaration of war against the Empire of Japan. By unanimous vote of the Senate and with only one dissenting pacifist vote in the House, a Congress that only months earlier had passed a draft act extension by a one-vote margin now plunged the nation into the spreading world conflict. Three days later, Japan's Axis partners, Germany and Italy, declared war on the United States, and Congress responded with a joint resolution accepting the state of war "which has been thrust upon the United States."

As the Japanese failed to appear on the Pacific shores, the initial panic ebbed, and a sense of determination pervaded the nation. Not since the founding days of the republic had Americans drawn so closely together as in the common purpose of avenging Pearl Harbor. The bitter division between isolationists and interventionists evanesced overnight. President Roosevelt's famous promise in the 1940 campaign—that he would "never, never" send American soldiers to fight in foreign wars—was quickly forgotten. The leader of the antiwar forces before Pearl Harbor, Senator Burton K. Wheeler of Montana, summed it up: "The only thing now to do is to lick the hell out of them."

Volunteers swamped recruiting offices of the army and navy. Women rushed to enroll in the Red Cross. Thousands of construction laborers volunteered to go to Pearl Harbor to repair the damage. A War Production Board was established and with astonishing rapidity major American industries, among them RCA, converted to war production. During the ensuing four years of history's greatest conflict, which spread to fifty-six nations, America more than lived up to its boast of being the arsenal of democracy, producing 296,000 aircraft, 71,000 ships, and 86,000 tanks.

Before the Axis forces were finally hammered into unconditional surrender in 1945, more than 15 million Americans had served in the armed forces, 10 million of them in the army alone. And one of them was the portly, graying president of RCA.

Had he chosen, Sarnoff could have avoided active duty in World War II despite his status as a senior officer in the army reserve. At the time of Pearl Harbor, he was fifty years old and the chief executive of one of the nation's most essential industrial concerns. Out of RCA's factories during the four years of conflict would pour more than two thousand types of vacuum tubes needed in military communications. Its scientists would play a key role in the development of radar and electronic navigation systems, known as loran and shoran; electronic gun control systems; an underwater sound detection device, known as sonar; magnetron tubes of immense power; and small personal communications devices, known as walkie-talkies. Its factories would turn out more than 20 million miniaturized tubes. For the navy alone, RCA would create twenty-six different communications systems to link together the far-ranging battle units of its fleet. As the war neared its successful conclusion, Secretary of the Navy James Forrestal would write Sarnoff that "among the companies which gave our fleet the power to attack, yours has been pre-eminent."

But to Sarnoff, it was not enough to be an essential industrialist in wartime. To satisfy his lifelong craving for acceptance as an American, he felt a compelling need to wear the uniform of his adopted land in its time of greatest peril. His view of the war was one-dimensional. Survival of all the values he cherished was at stake, survival of the democratic precepts under which his career had flourished, even the survival of his coreligionists threatened by the incinerators of Nazi Germany. No American was less encumbered by doubts about the rectitude of the Allied cause, and every fiber of his being demanded active involvement.

His awareness of the military, and of the use of force as a decisive factor in human affairs, was deeply rooted. During his childhood, Cossack cavalry would roam from village to village across the vast sweep of the Russian pale, a menacing symbol of the authority of the czars. To the inhabitants of Uzlian, the sound of cavalry hooves was a tocsin of intimidation, intended to provoke the migration of Jews, like the Sarnoff family, out of Russia. On his exodus from his homeland, the youthful David had encountered close up in the city of Minsk the fury of the Cossacks vented against an unarmed civilian mob. But in America, he began to view the military through a different prism. Soon after his arrival in the East Side ghetto, he had walked to upper Broadway and stood on the sidewalk to watch khaki-clad soldiers, veterans of the Philippine campaign, marching to the cadenced music of military bands and the cheers of a flag-waving populace. The jingoist Hearst and Bennett newspapers that he read as a youth trumpeted the dawning age of American imperialism and glorified the military role in it. Territorial expansion, backed by military force, was their editorial credo. Generals, more than philosophers or statesmen, were the heroes of the hour. And Sarnoff absorbed it all with youthful certitude. When he left school after the eighth grade, he was already persuaded that militarism represented patriotism of crystalline purity.

His first endeavor to wear an American uniform had been rebuffed in World War I when the navy turned down his application for a commission, holding that his contract work as Marconi's commercial manager was essential to the war effort. He was twenty-six then, and eager to engage in naval combat as a communications officer with the fleet. He suspected that anti-Semitic bias in the navy's professional officer corps, which he had often heard rumored in the communications industry, was behind the turndown, but it did not dampen his ardor to wear a uniform, even if it had to be when the country was at peace.

The military ranks finally opened to him as a result of Young's decision in 1922 to bring General Harbord to RCA as its president. For two years, as the company's general manager, Sarnoff worked closely with the elderly soldier, schooling him in the communications art, winning his confidence and his friendship. A widely acclaimed hero of World War I, Harbord embodied all those soldierly virtues that Sarnoff had been steeped in as a youth. Harbord exalted patriotism as the noblest of human virtues, a view that his young associate shared. When, in 1923, Sarnoff first confided to Harbord his yearning to serve, the response was instantly favorable. Harbord suggested that he apply for a commission in the army's Signal Corps reserve and offered to use his contacts with senior officers of the War Department, many of whom had served under him in France. Within days, Sarnoff's application for a reserve commission was in the mail, accompanied by a letter of endorsement from Harbord which suggested that it would be in the army's best interest to establish this connection with the fastest-rising young executive in America's communications industry.

On December 11, 1924, a day that ranked in his memory with his later appointment as RCA's president, Sarnoff received official notification that he had been commissioned a lieutenant colonel in the Signal Corps reserve. It was a higher rank than he had expected, and by any yardstick impressive recognition for a thirty-three-year-old without prior military experience. West Point graduates of that peacetime era, like Eisenhower and Patton, devoted thirty years to regular service before winning the silver palm leaves of a lieutenant colonel.

The requirements of reserve service were not taxing, but Sarnoff approached them with all the intensity of his civilian work. Two weeks a year were devoted to active duty at Fort Monmouth, New Jersey, or at Signal Corps headquarters in Washington. Fortunately, it was sedentary duty, involving his indoctrination in the corps's role in the modern army, and he was spared physical training, which he would have detested. In 1926, in the midst of his struggle with the telephone company over radio networking, Sarnoff found time to attend field grade officer courses at the Army War College in Washington. There he rubbed shoulders and became casually acquainted with some of the young officers, like Mark Clark, who would later lead American armies on European and Asiatic battlefields. Often, he would devote weekends to Signal Corps technical seminars. Whenever possible, in New York or Washington, he would attend military banquets in his smartly tailored uniform, the silver palm leaves gleaming on his shoulders.

"No one," General Harbord told RCA associates, "ever wore the uniform more proudly."

A year after Sarnoff became president of RCA in 1930, the Signal Corps rewarded the enthusiasm of its new recruit by promoting him to full colonel in the reserve, and this was the rank he held when America became involved in world conflict a decade later. Promptly, he communicated to the War Department, and to Harbord, his desire for active duty. In the summer of '42, he was called up for two weeks' service as chief of the Signal Corps Advisory Council. Later that year, he put in two additional months in Washington as special assistant to the chief signal officer, concentrating on the elimination of bottlenecks in the shipment of communications equipment to foreign fronts.

Between these stints, which simply stimulated his appetite for a more active role in the conflict, and preferably abroad, Sarnoff presided over the total conversion of RCA to defense production, which in sum exceeded a billion dollars and permitted the company to maintain modest profitability through the war years. He found time to speak occasionally at war bond rallies, once sharing the spotlight with movie stars Betty Grable and Bob Hope. And he also presided at the dedication in 1941 of a project on which he had planned and worked for several years—a new centralized RCA research facility at Princeton, New Jersey, which brought together the company's thirteen hundred scientists and technicians in the nation's largest research center devoted purely to the electron.

The opportunity for greater military involvement suddenly arose in the spring of 1944, when plans were maturing for an Allied invasion of Europe across the English Channel. The War Department had received an urgent request from the supreme commander of the invasion forces, General Dwight D. Eisenhower, for the best communications expert available to assist him in organizing and coordinating the labyrinthine wireless circuits that would be required for both military and press purposes when the assault on Europe was launched. Major General Harry C. Ingles, the army's chief signal officer, who had gotten to know Sarnoff well during his Washington service, recommended the RCA leader, and the War Department concurred.

Without knowing his precise assignment, Sarnoff was ordered to active service for sixty days and instructed to proceed to Europe on the first available military air transport. There was time for only a brief farewell with Harbord and the RCA staff, and for issuing a company order that his senior scientist, Charles Jolliffe, would serve as acting president in his absence. This told the organization that the focus on technology must continue. Lizette, who was also in uniform as a member of the Ladies' Auxiliary of the Red Cross, heading a large volunteer unit at the New York Infirmary, saw him off on his first air passage to the continent he had left on a refugee ship forty-four years earlier. On the wintry day of March 20, 1944, he arrived in bomb-scarred London and was billeted in Claridge's Hotel, then occupied mainly by senior American officers. Early in the morning of his second day there, wearing an Ike jacket and battle khaki, he appeared at Eisenhower's office in SHAEF, accompanied by the chief of staff, General Walter Bedell Smith.

This was Sarnoff's first meeting with Ike, and the beginning of an association that lasted until the latter's death. Although they were roughly of the same age, Sarnoff responded to his commander as he had to Young and Marconi at their initial meetings. Immediately, he later said, he sensed they were "on the same wavelength." The famous Eisenhower smile captivated him. He listened with total absorption while his "Boss," as he would later address him in written correspondence, spelled out the dimensions of Colonel Sarnoff's responsibilities.

His title would be special assistant for communications to the supreme commander, and his first job would be the construction of a broadcasting station powerful enough to reach all the Allied Forces under Ike's command in the European and Mediterranean theaters. It had to be ready by D day, and while Sarnoff was not made privy to that top secret date he was impressed with the brevity of time available. Second, he was to prepare a plan for coordinating all the communications channels between headquarters and the invasion forces. This was to include an allocation of circuits between the print and broadcast media of the Allied nations who would be flashing to the world the story of invasion. While Eisenhower said he wanted no favoritism shown to American reporters, he wanted to be certain they were not scooped by the aggressive British press or the BBC. In the commander's words, this would require of Sarnoff velvet glove and iron fist diplomacy. But he would have the authority of the supreme commander to overcome roadblocks and to requisition the necessary equipment and manpower. As he saluted as the conference ended, Sarnoff was told to report back periodically through Bedell Smith on his progress.

His task was even more challenging than the elated newcomer had hoped for. His position had been specially created, outside the military table of organization. With his link to Ike, his authority could on occasion supersede that of flag rank officers in American and British communications. Further, Sarnoff knew he had the background for the job. Just as he had rationalized the fragmented radio industry in its formative years, now he would rationalize the communications infrastructure for the greatest military adventure in history.

Working out of the British Ministry of Information building in London, Sarnoff plunged into eighteen-hour days. First, he made the rounds of the American and British Signal Corps establishments, becoming acquainted with their senior officers, inspecting their wireless transmission and reception apparatus, and evaluating the qualifications of the operator personnel. With the assistance of Major General F. N. Lanahan, Signal Corps chief for the

American forces, and senior officials of the British Post Office (which controlled wireless communications), he selected a secret site for the powerful clear-channel station Eisenhower wanted, drew up plans for construction, requisitioned the needed transmitter and an experienced staff to operate it. The station was on the air by Ike's deadline, and before the invasion.

Simultaneously, Sarnoff was evaluating the communications apparatus for the invasion, which he said he found fractured beyond belief. The American and British commercial companies, Western Union and Cable and Wireless, Ltd., had their separate plans for handling D day traffic, as did the British and American Signal Corps units, as did the British Broadcasting Company, the three American networks, and the various radiophoto concerns. "Some things had to be undone and changed . . . others had to be created," he wrote his Signal Corps superiors in Washington, to eliminate "this picture of confusion." With the clock moving "uncomfortably close to twelve," he called meetings at the Ministry of Information of all the civilian and military units involved and set forth a plan he had hastily devised for a unified signal center at the MOI headquarters through which all D day traffic would flow. A common photo pool would be headquartered there. Censorship of news dispatches would be concentrated there. His goal was total centralization of all communications, the same concept of centralization he had learned with patents in the radio pool two decades earlier.

Sarnoff also sought a closer meld of military and commercial communications. Only one shortwave circuit existed between London and New York for the American broadcasting networks, and he persuaded the Signal Corps, in Washington, to authorize another London transmitter. Through judicious use of Eisenhower's name, he also persuaded the British Post Office to lease one of its channels to the American networks. Through Sir Edward Wilshaw, chairman of Britain's Cables and Wireless, Ltd., he got approval for two additional transmitters. He estimated the combined civilian-military facilities would be sufficient to handle between 500,000 and 600,000 words daily, and he judged that would be adequate to handle the unprecedented message traffic the invasion would generate. To ensure its orderly allocation, a Traffic Control Committee was established, with Sarnoff as chairman.

A quarter century later, Sarnoff recalled that his most difficult job was a political one. He had envisaged the creation of an Allied Forces Network, in which all broadcast facilities of the American forces, the British, and their military allies would be pooled. But resistance from the BBC threatened his plan. Brendan Bracken, the British Minister of Information, feared a preponderance of the coverage would go to the American forces because of their numerical superiority in the invasion. There was only one higher level of the British government to which to appeal, and at Sarnoff's request Eisenhower arranged a meeting at that level. At 10 Downing Street, he met Winston Churchill for the first time since Bernard Baruch had introduced them at a social gathering in New York years earlier, when Churchill was in political limbo.

As Sarnoff sketched out his program for communications unity, the British prime minister, burdened by a multitude of preinvasion problems, listened patiently and intently. He was already aware of the friction generated by the American's proposal. "He told me that while he personally sympathized with the British position," Sarnoff recalled, "the need for Allied unity in the days ahead was paramount. So he would go along with it. He overrode Bracken."

To ensure that communications moved in tandem with the invasion forces, Sarnoff proposed, and had approved by SHAEF, the creation of a mobile Army Signal Center to move behind the front, available to correspondents and the commanders of battle units, again intermingling commercial and military circuits. To ensure that this complex interplay was properly understood, he conducted briefing sessions for British and American Signal Corps units along the Channel coast and aboard the American battleship *Ancon,* which was equipped with advanced electronic gear and which was scheduled to anchor in mid-Channel, a floating relay point for intelligence from the Continent.

The two months of this scheduled active duty sped by, but Sarnoff had no intention of returning home. Again, he was where he most preferred to be, at the epicenter of history, a player, if not one of the leads, in the theater of great events. On occasion, as his staff car wended through the streets of rubbled London, still not recovered from the massive German aerial assaults of '40 and '41, he caught glimpses of Dickensian neighborhoods that afforded poignant reminders of his own ghetto upbringing. His admiration for the British people, their stoicism in the face of deprivation, their obdurate will to victory, had been enhanced greatly, perhaps in echoing response to his own early struggles.

Despite his modest standing on the pyramid of rank—London in those preinvasion days had more admirals and generals than cabbies—Sarnoff's stature as head of one of the world's great communications companies, including NBC, gave him access to exalted circles enjoyed by few, if any, other colonels. Occasionally, he was one of those privileged to dine with Ike and his senior staff at Claridge's or SHAEF headquarters. Churchill and his wife, Clementine, invited him to lunch at 10 Downing Street, where they discussed the future of television and whether FDR would seek a fourth term in the next election. He met with the opposition Labor leaders, Clement Attlee and Ernest Bevin, and the fiery Welsh leftist Aneurin Bevan; he was the guest of honor at a dinner given by the directors of the *Times* of London; and he was made an honorary member of the British Institute of Radio Engineers at a dinner presided over by Lord Mountbatten, soon to become Viceroy of India.

Ten weeks after his arrival in Europe, the invasion of Hitler's fortress Europe commenced. A day earlier, Sarnoff had been alerted to stand by at his office in the Ministry of Information. The first invasion flash reached the MOI at 7:31 A.M., and a minute later it had circled the globe over the transmitter network he had pieced together. In the first day, 570,000 words were processed through the Signal Center, and the unfolding story of the massive cross-Channel thrust was recounted over the Allied Forces Network with a thoroughness never before attained in military communications. Not until the Viet Nam war, when television came into play, would the world know so much about a military action as it unfolded.

Sarnoff remained at his headquarters most of two days and two nights, snatching moments of sleep on an army cot. By then, he was assured that eyewitness accounts from the front were coming through without serious interruption. He was elated by a message received at SHAEF from the correspondents of the American broadcast networks, including Edward R. Murrow of CBS, expressing gratitude for the cooperation they had received. To Sarnoff personally came a letter from the London Bureau Chief of the Associated Press, Robert Bunelle, saying "hats off" for his job of demolishing red tape. And from his Washington boss, General Ingles, came word that "your estimate of the situation and your performance of a difficult and exacting task has been outstanding."

Three weeks after the invasion commenced, Sarnoff considered requesting permission to return home and revert to inactive status. It had been three months since he left RCA, and he had not since 1930 been removed that long from the guidance of its affairs. But then he received notification, on June 29, that he had been recommended for promotion to brigadier general by General Landham at SHAEF. This would provide the ultimate certification of the value of his military service, and he determined to remain on active duty until it had been finally confirmed through the slow-grinding promotion mills for flag rank officers, at the Pentagon and the White House. The job Eisenhower had given him was essentially accomplished and the war was entering a new phase. Against bitter German opposition, Allied infantry and tanks deepened their penetration of the hedgerows of Normandy. Soon after Ike opened an advance headquarters at Granville in France, Sarnoff joined him there, still a special assistant for communications, in late July 1944. One of his first assignments was to review the communications structure of the Mediterranean theater. He flew to North Africa on a DC-3 military transport plane and offered recommendations for ensuring the cohesion of the Signal Corps units that would participate in the impending American invasion of the Riviera beaches of southern France. From there he flew to Rome, working briefly as a communications adviser for General Mark Clark, whose 5th Army was slogging up the Italian boot against heavy German resistance. He also found time to drive several hours to Marconi's farm for an emotional reunion with the inventor's widow, who had remained in Italy through the war.

Before he left England, Sarnoff had his first exposure to enemy action. He was in London when Hitler unleashed his V-1 guided missiles, and he shared with the civilian population the experience of crouching in a bomb shelter, listening to the eerie wail of the pilotless rockets and the ensuing explosions throughout the battered city. Soon after, during an inspection tour of forward Signal Corps units in Normandy, he was pinned to the ground during a brief firefight between attacking German forces and American infantry. Years later, reviewing the many crises in his career, including his brief exposure to enemy fire, he would insist that "I've never known fear." It was a sense of prudence, he claimed, that motivated him in such instances, prudence to protect himself, whether his life or his career.

At Ike's headquarters in France, Sarnoff's primary responsibility was to plan for the restoration of France's shattered communications as the liberation proceeded. The key was the revival of a direct radio-telegraph link between Paris and New York, which had been severed since the Nazi occupation. By late August, American forces were near the banks of the River Seine, with German forces in Paris in panicky retreat, demolishing as they went. On August 25, word reached Granville that an American division had entered the city, hysterically acclaimed by the Parisian population.

That same day, accompanied by an aide and his driver, Sarnoff set off by jeep for the French capital, two hundred miles distant. Driving as rapidly as possible past truck convoys and tank columns clogging the dusty and pitted roads, the battlefield stench of rotting carcasses of horses, cows, and men assailing his nostrils, Sarnoff reached Paris at midnight on the twenty-fifth. As he would later pridefully recall, he beat General de Gaulle into the City of Light by a day. After a few hours' sleep at a U.S. 4th Division bivouac, he checked in at the newly established American military headquarters and then headed for Boulevard Haussmann and the headquarters of the French Wireless Company and its subsidiary, Radio France.

Sarnoff knew the route by heart. He had spent more time in Paris than any foreign capital . . . the long weeks of reparations negotiations with the Young mission . . . frequent visits with Lizette to the city of her birth . . . negotiating sessions in Paris over wireless circuits and licensing agreements with the government-controlled French Wireless Company and its chief, Emile Girardeau, who had become his personal friend and whom he had entertained at his New York home.

On most of his Parisian trips, Sarnoff had occupied a suite at the Ritz, which he came to consider a home away from home. Then his uniform was the tailored three-piece suit of the business chieftain, with homburg and cane, which, to his pleasure, always impressed Lizette's Parisian cousins. But now, as he burst through the doors of the French Wireless headquarters, he was in battle dress, helmeted, his uniform coated with dust, boots muddied, a stubble of beard, the pistol at his hip readied.

To his astonishment, the headquarters was exactly as he had remembered it on his last prewar visit, and he was overwhelmed by a sense of déjà vu. The French staff was busily working, and rushing to embrace him was his old friend Girardeau, the pioneer of French wireless. Quickly, the volatile Frenchman poured out the story of his Occupation experience. As soon as the Germans arrived, he and his staff had been ordered, under penalty of death, to continue the operation of French Radio under the Nazi military government and Joseph Goebbels' Propaganda Ministry in Berlin. So he had complied, to save not only himself and his staff but their families. But now he was fearful of being branded a collaborator by Resistance fighters of the French underground, with retribution possibly as harsh as the Germans had threatened. He must flee. Would his American friend help?

Throughout his career, Sarnoff had never hesitated to invoke authority when he felt it was needed, and now he invoked it in majestic terms. He was, he assured the frightened Girardeau, the personal representative of the supreme commander, Allied Expeditionary Forces, with full authority to requisition personnel and property. The staff and facilities of French Radio must assist the Allied Forces Network in carrying the message of liberation to their countrymen and throughout Europe. Sarnoff told Girardeau he wanted him and his associates to continue functioning under his direction. He would requisition food for them from military depots and arrange an armed guard of American soldiers to ensure their personal safety. He was enlisting them in the cause of freedom. "Of course, I didn't have any explicit mandate from Ike," Sarnoff later recalled. "But I felt he would have approved. There wasn't any time to weigh the subtleties of collaboration. I needed Girardeau to get my job done, and I trusted him."

A quick examination of the French wireless headquarters assured Sarnoff that nothing had been molested in the Nazi evacuation. Then he asked Girardeau to accompany him to Sainte-Assise, a Parisian suburb where the main overseas transmitting station of Radio France was located. There they found considerable damage had been inflicted by German demolition squads, the 400-foot antenna tower toppled and the 200-kilowatt alternator employed for international traffic smashed. But Sarnoff found the damage could have been worse. In the haste of their departure, the Germans had overlooked many smaller pieces of essential electronic equipment, including a shortwave tube transmitter. Sarnoff instructed the rejuvenated Girardeau to track down all the French radio technicians he could find, lure them with the promise of American food and cigarettes, and start round-the-clock reconstruction. From Signal Corps depots in France, the American colonel secured many of the needed replacement parts, the force of his association with Eisenhower removing obstacles. A French electronics warehouse on the outskirts of

Paris was located, its stocks essentially intact, and truckloads of equipment were rushed to Sainte-Assise.

For two weeks, as most Parisians joyously celebrated the return of de Gaulle and the restoration of the republic, work went forward on a relentless schedule, under Sarnoff's and Girardeau's on-site direction. The antenna tower was restored, the alternator rebuilt. On September 8, radio circuits were reopened between Paris and London and a week later between Paris and New York. France again was linked to the democratic world.

Weeks later, with French radio serving as a relay for messages from SHAEF to Allied forces in Europe and the international circuits functioning efficiently, Sarnoff returned briefly to London, where, on October 12, he was presented his first military decoration, the Army's Legion of Merit. In the usual lush language of such citations, he was hailed for exceptionally meritorious conduct "in the performance of outstanding service" for SHAEF communications and in the restoration of French radio. No lowly foot soldier ever received a medal with greater pride. To Sarnoff, it provided tangible evidence of his Americanism, it further cemented his ties to his country. Soon afterward, back in Paris for his next assignment, which was planning the restoration of German communications services after the armistice, he was honored at a dinner presided over by Girardeau, who had been cleared of collaborationism and restored to his position as head of French Wireless. As the evening's climax, Girardeau announced the French Republic's election of Sarnoff as a Commander of the Legion of Honor—"the thanks of France to the man who took such a part in reestablishing our transatlantic communications."

Despite these coveted emoluments, Sarnoff fretted over lack of news on his brigadier generalcy. And he was becoming increasingly anxious about conditions at RCA. A letter from Lizette informed him that General Harbord had become ill, possibly seriously. He felt his acting president, Jolliffe, lacked the executive skills to preside in a leadership vacuum. Nevertheless, despite the fact his active duty tour had stretched from two to seven months, he accepted membership in the Allied Group Control Council, charged with developing plans for the civilian administration of a Germany nearing prostration under the onslaught of Anglo-American forces from the west and Russian from the east.

As acting chairman of the communications section of the council, Sarnoff worked briefly but intensively with a small staff to develop a blueprint of what he judged would be necessary to restore wireless and wire services and equipment obliterated by Allied bombing. In meticulous detail, he developed a table of organization for the military communications group that would oversee the German civil administration. His plan was accepted by the Group Control Council, and that concluded his final assignment in Europe. He formally applied to SHAEF for permission to return to America and resume, in view of Harbord's illness, his stewardship of RCA, which still had numerous vital defense contracts to complete. Ike's permission was swiftly forthcoming, along with a letter of commendation for Sarnoff's "notable" services to the Allied high command.

On October 28, he arrived in New York, still a colonel, still in uniform. And so was Lizette, in her Red Cross auxiliary uniform, when she emotionally greeted his military transport ship at dockside. Their three sons were all in the service, the two eldest abroad as junior communications officers in the navy and army, so the elder Sarnoffs had an uninterrupted, but brief, reunion at the Manhattan town house. Then he was off to Washington to report to the chief signal officer—after a day spent at 30 Rockefeller Plaza being briefed by Jolliffe and RCA staffers—and to penetrate the mystery of the missing promotion recommendation, which he assumed was circulating somewhere in the bowels of the Pentagon.

Sarnoff's Washington duty stretched out to six weeks, because General Ingles wanted his prize subordinate to make presentations throughout the War Department on the Signal Corps experience in the European theater. Ingles also requested Sarnoff to prepare a comprehensive and confidential written critique for him on the performance of individual unit commanders in the corps. This was time-consuming, and in exchange for Sarnoff's willingness to stay to completion, he was permitted to take occasional days off to oversee RCA affairs in New York and Princeton. In addition, Ingles agreed to track down the promotion recommendation. He soon found it, stuck in the military pipeline somewhere between his office, where it had been endorsed, and that of the Secretary of War. Four months after its initiation in London, it emerged, nudged on by Ingles, from the War Department, and President Roosevelt approved it. On December 7, the third anniversary of Pearl Harbor, the Senate validated Sarnoff's appointment as brigadier general, Army of the United States.

At the end of 1944, three weeks after Ingles had pinned a star on his tunic, Sarnoff reverted to inactive status and resumed full control of RCA. His cumulative active service between '42 and '44 approximated a full year. In peacetime, his sporadic active duty tours, including attendance at the Army War College, consumed another four months. This totaled only a small proportion of a professional career that would extend over sixty-three years, but its impact on him, and the company he led, was vastly disproportionate to the time served.

When Sarnoff reoccupied his fifty-third floor offices at 30 Rockefeller Plaza in January 1945, he was little changed physically, although perhaps a shade grayer. The war had not diminished his girth. He had always prided himself on an erect posture, but now, his associates felt, he was even more ramrod erect. Word quickly seeped through company echelons that he preferred to be addressed by the title of General, and thus he was known for the remainder of his life. In the buttonhole of his suit jacket would appear miniatures of the medals he had won, the Legion of Merit and the Legion of Honor, and others that followed.

Unlike many soldiers who had suffered through the snafus and red tape of the military, Sarnoff emerged from the war with an even greater reverence for the institution and its traditions. The military appealed to his oligarchical sense. He viewed the armed forces as a vast conglomeration of men, weapons, machines, and technology, fused into an effective worldwide striking force by leaders of courage and talent, capable of destroying humanity's predators and reshaping civilization for the better. The military symbolized order, power, daring, and discipline—and these were virtues he revered. It thus followed in his mind that military rank and military decorations were the supreme vouchsafe of patriotism. The higher the rank, the more the decorations, the more one's essential Americanism was validated. Even out of uniform, he felt a continuing sense of kinship to the military establishment. He would, of course, continue to serve it as a reservist, and he would also ensure that the latest advances in electronic technology were adapted to its needs and purpose. This would become a second postwar career to Sarnoff, one to be pursued in tandem with his RCA responsibilities, and in many ways of comparable importance to him.

With the unconditional surrenders of Germany and Japan in 1945, millions of uniformed Americans began returning home, among them numerous generals and admirals who had left America unknown and were now the nation's most visible heroes. Immersed as he was in converting RCA from war to peace production, Sarnoff found time to participate in the round of festivities and the ticker-tape parades in New York and Washington that greeted the conquerors of Hitler and Tojo—the Omar Bradleys and Mark Clarks, the Chester Nimitzes and Bull Halseys. When Eisenhower, the supreme hero, returned months later to become army chief of staff, Sarnoff joined in, whenever he could, the frenzied round of receptions for his revered Boss. Many of the military leaders were now, he felt, his friends, and this became one of the important pluses of his postwar career.

Increasingly, after his return, Sarnoff had reflected with concern on the advanced ages of RCA's senior executives. The ailing Harbord was in his late seventies and unlikely to contribute further. Jolliffe, his wartime surrogate and senior engineering executive, was showing his years, troubled by intestinal cancer that would later require major surgery. Even the board of directors, which had no mandatory retirement age, was beginning to resemble a gerontocracy, Sarnoff felt, the prime exemplar his old Marconi Company associate, Edward Nally, who was nearing eighty-five. Why not, Sarnoff began to ask himself, look for board and executive replacements from those who had managed vast enterprises so successfully for the military? The more he reflected, the more enthused he became.

Acting as his own recruiting agency, Sarnoff began in Washington. First, he persuaded his wartime associate, the chief signal officer, Harry Ingles, to take early retirement and become an RCA director and president of RCA Communications, the global wireless network that had been RCA's first business when it grew out of the Marconi Company in 1919. Next, he asked Navy Secretary James Forrestal to recommend a tough and experienced administrator to oversee the RCA Victor Division in Camden. Thus, from his post as civilian chief of the naval supply organization, Frank Folsom moved to RCA. He, in turn, brought with him to Victor a career naval officer, Vice Admiral Walter E. Buck, the uniformed head of the Supply Corps, and Buck's chief assistant, Vice Admiral Dorsey Foster. Then came, from the Coast Guard, Admiral Thomas Wyncoop to head up RCA's subsidiary RadioMarine, which manufactured wireless equipment for oceangoing vessels. From the Signal Corps came Colonel Thompson Mitchell to backstop Ingles at RCA Communications. Walter Watts, a Signal Corps brigadier general (reserve) became head of the government systems division and later picture tubes and consumer products. Later, the board of directors was replenished with Admiral Buck and Rear Admiral Lewis E. Strauss, who was an early chairman of the Atomic Energy Commission, and by Ike's staff chief, General Walter Bedell Smith, when he returned from Moscow as President Truman's ambassador to Stalin. As a further innovation, Sarnoff induced Captain Mildred McAfee Horton to join the board. She was wartime head of the navy's women's auxiliary corps, known as the WAVES, and she became one of the first female members of a major corporate board.

Sarnoff's recruitment from the armed forces was not unique in postwar America. Many other companies sought to burnish their image through the luster of military stars. General Omar Bradley became chairman of the Bulova Watch Company, and General Douglas MacArthur, after his controversial return from the Far East, chairman of Sperry Rand. But these were essentially public relations choices, as had been Owen Young's selection of a World War I hero, General Harbord, to become president of RCA in 1922, when the company was under heavy attack as a radio monopoly.

What Sarnoff sought in his military selections was substance, not imagery. He felt he could handle the latter. He, after all, was, and would increasingly become, the principal image that RCA reflected to its constituencies. With few exceptions, his choices from the armed services performed key staff and operating functions and remained with the company through to retirement. They were part of the team that ushered in both monochrome and color television during RCA's years of greatest glory.

The impact of the military infusion on RCA's culture is difficult to assess. Probably the addition of many executives with close ties to the Pentagon strengthened its government business, which continued to thrive in the postwar years, when RCA was often listed among the top fifteen defense contractors. Internally, it possibly strengthened discipline, although Sarnoff had always emphasized that. No old boy military network sprang up, creating cleavages with civilian-trained executives. Indeed, a sense of respect for military achievements permeated the organization, beginning at the top. Sarnoff personally felt comfortable in a milieu of shared wartime experience. And it did no damage to his formidable ego to be addressed respectfully as "General" by subordinates whose two or three stars eclipsed his one.

Even with the military galaxy surrounding him, Sarnoff made one further effort to embellish it, and it was an audacious one. And this time, he later admitted, the image of RCA was a major consideration.

In 1947, Eisenhower was in Washington as army chief of staff, apparently determined to return to civilian life but uncertain what to do. He was clearly the most popular man in America, still the premier war hero whose flashing smile and folksy mannerisms made him the envy of every politician. In fact, leaders of both political parties, including President Truman, were urging him to accept their presidential nomination in 1948. But he professed no interest in the presidency and was obviously seeking an escape valve from political pressures through a job somewhere away from Washington.

To Sarnoff, who had maintained contact with his wartime boss through occasional visits in Washington and the exchange of personal notes, the thought suddenly occurred: why not offer Ike the escape valve of RCA? Quickly, he developed a scenario in his mind for an approach to the five-star General of the Armies. He, Sarnoff, would take the title of chairman of the board from Harbord, then near death, and offer the presidency to Ike. He would continue as the chief executive officer, with Eisenhower at his side but unencumbered with administrative responsibilities and free to pursue public service activities. Ike could accompany him to Washington for legislative or regulatory hearings. What a spokesman, Sarnoff thought, the supreme commander would make for television!

Sarnoff had heard that Eisenhower was financially strapped, a supposition confirmed years later by another Ike friend, Bill Paley of CBS. So a handsome salary, far greater than military pay, was in order so that he could maintain a life-style compatible with his international fame. And, of course, all the emoluments of life in the upper corporate strata—year-end bonuses, a chauffeured limousine, unlimited expense account, a large skyscraper office at 30 Rockefeller Plaza, furnished and designed to his own tastes.

In February 1947, Eisenhower came to New York for a reunion dinner with American print and broadcast correspondents who had covered his various battle headquarters. Sarnoff arranged a meeting at Ike's midtown hotel, and he came equipped with a full package proposal in his mind, but nothing on paper. He had confided his plan to no one, fearing a premature leak could squelch it. It was a measure of his extraordinary control over RCA that he did not feel the need to get prior approval of its board before offering the company presidency to an outsider. He simply assumed, and probably correctly, that his board would chorus hosannas if he were able to land the most famous figure, apart from Winston Churchill, in the Western world.

In a lengthy meeting, Sarnoff spelled out the details of his offer, with emphasis on the six-figure salary and on the freedom Ike would have to pursue pro bono publico interests. He could tell that Eisenhower was keenly interested from the frequent questions he interposed. For example, who would report to him? "He was really intrigued, no doubt about it," Sarnoff later recalled. As the meeting ended, Ike said he wanted to go home and think it through in detail and discuss it with his wife, Mamie. He promised to get back to Sarnoff within a few days with a definitive answer.

Ike's reponse came in a latter to Sarnoff in New York dated February 19, and classified personal and confidential. He had considered Sarnoff's suggestion for many hours, he wrote, and had finally come to the conclusion that "I must ask you to drop me from consideration."

"To attempt to put down all my reasons," the letter continued, "would involve a lengthy dissertation on intangibles, but I know that you will have the confidence to believe that these reasons are not wholly selfish ones. They do not involve any other type of personal ambition whatsoever.

"Needless to say, I will always keep entirely confidential and secret the nature of your suggestion, and the fact that you made it will remain with me as one of the most sincere compliments and high honors I have received."

Eisenhower offered to spell out to Sarnoff his reasons for declining in greater detail when they next met personally. This happened several weeks later, according to Sarnoff. "Ike told me that he and Mamie had spent most of one night agonizing over it," he recollected. "They finally concluded life in the corporate world would be a bit too constricting. But it was a near thing. I came within an inch of getting him." Sarnoff surmised, probably correctly, that Ike even then harbored an interest in running for the presidency at some future point, and felt that too prominent identification with big business might undercut the catholicity of his appeal to the electorate.

Later, Eisenhower accepted an offer to become president of Columbia University in New York City. The pay was considerably less than he would have got at RCA, but the position seemed less controversial and Columbia offered something that Sarnoff hadn't—an imposing presidential residence overlooking Manhattan's Morningside Heights that was staffed at university expense. Years later, in June 1966, Sarnoff attended graduation exercises at Columbia to receive an honorary Doctor of Science degree. Afterward, at a reception in the president's mansion, then occupied by Grayson Kirk, his eye swept across the expensive living room, and he muttered to an aide: "This is the place that cost me Ike."

So Sarnoff lost his greatest military prize, but not his ardor for the military.

He continued to attend reserve functions, and to speak out in behalf of military preparedness, warning repeatedly of what he perceived to be the ominous expansionist intensions of Soviet Russia. He became a leader among the cold warriors, a wholehearted subscriber to the later brinkmanship of John Foster Dulles. The choice was between burning to death or freezing, as he saw it, unless America remained strong. A friend of many years described him as almost apoplectic on the subject of his Marxist homeland.

When Eisenhower decided to run on the Republican ticket in 1952, Sarnoff enthusiastically supported him and became his unofficial broadcast strategist, counseling on such matters as the best times for network broadcasts to reach maximum audiences. After Ike had swept to a landslide victory over Adlai Stevenson, he sounded out Sarnoff on the possibility of becoming assistant secretary of defense. But the top defense post had already gone to Charles Wilson, head of General Motors, and Sarnoff politely declined. The subordinate role did not fit his concept of himself as the captain on the bridge, and beyond that the television battle still had to be won, and any other captain on that bridge was unthinkable.

Apart from his active duty and reserve activities, Sarnoff sought throughout his career to conceptualize new uses of the electron for the military. While he had little to do personally with the development of radar, the single most important electronic device to emerge from the war, he became the principal strategist for the conversion of existing apparatus, such as television, into electronic adjuncts of battle. With all the persistence of his radio-music-box youth, he pursued his concepts of electronicized warfare for more than three decades with Signal Corps associates, chiefs of staff, secretaries of defense, and presidents. Often he was rebuffed, but sometimes he succeeded.

A decade before he introduced monochrome television at the 1939 World's Fair, Sarnoff forecast, in a speech at the Army War College in Washington, that a radio-television camera and transmitter installed in a reconnaissance plane might be effective in pinpointing artillery fire by "transmitting a direct image of the enemy's terrain." Several members of the army's general staff were present, and they expressed interest in the idea and encouraged Sarnoff to pursue it. This was all the nudge he needed, and in 1931, just after becoming president of RCA, he started forming a small scientific team to begin laboratory explorations of a variety of possible military television applications. Its key member was the Russian-born Zworykin, Sarnoff's favorite scientist, who agreed to take on the additional responsibility even though then heavily involved in perfecting his image orthicon and iconoscope tubes for commercial television.

By 1935 the Zworykin team had completed design work for the implantation of a miniature vidicon camera in the nose of a flying missile. Characteristically, Sarnoff decided it was too important a development to filter up through military channels. He would present it personally at the highest levels of the nation's military establishment. Accompanied by Zworykin, he met in great secrecy at the War Department in Washington with ranking army and navy officials, Admirals King and Stark, Generals Westover and Tschappat, who was chief of army ordinance. The response to Sarnoff's presentation was positive. Concerned by the expansionist tendencies of Germany and Japan, the military chiefs were receptive to new ideas in weaponry. Out of the meeting came a pledge of technical and financial support for developmental work on the Zworykin design.

By 1937 RCA engineers had completed the prototype of the first television system designed specifically for aircraft use. With borrowed military aircraft, successful field tests were conducted by RCA and NBC engineers of high altitude picture transmission to ground receivers scores of miles away. By 1940 Zworykin's flying bomb design, incorporating radio control and the preliminary design of an aerodynamic carrier, won Washington's authorization to proceed with advanced aeronautic design. In November 1941, under a grant from the National Defense Research Council, three RCA-built TV-guided missiles, the forerunner of the controlled bomb with eyes, were tested successfully at Murac Lake. Sarnoff, who was present, enthusiastically memoed his scientific staff: "The potentialities of television directed weapons seem to be of the greatest importance . . . They [the army and navy] recognize RCA's sponsorship of the project. They consider RCA as the only presently qualified supplier and the only one able to solve the remaining problems. This places a heavy responsibility on us for the furtherance of military efforts which might have an important effect on the course of the war."

By the war's end, RCA had delivered to the armed services 4,400 television cameras and associated transmitting equipment to guide pilotless planes, to direct radio-controlled missiles, including high angle and glide bombs, to enemy targets, to survey enemy terrain, and even to sight guns on naval vessels. In some instances their application in battle was spectacular. In August 1944, a navy-guided missile with an RCA TV camera in its nose was hurled at the lower entrance of Japanese-controlled Rabaul Harbor while its mother ship, a TBF Avenger, circled slowly fifteen miles away. On the TV screen, in the instrument panel, the Avenger pilot guided the missile toward a lighthouse and adjoining radar station. The target disappeared in a flashing explosion, victim of the first sighted bomb.

In the European theater, combat-worn bombers, with RCA cameras in their noses and thousands of tons of explosives aboard, were flown across the English Channel by crews who bailed out. Television took over and the "war wearies" were directed by mother ships into the submarine pens of Helgoland and the rocket-launching sites of Calais. It was on one of these missions, Sarnoff later learned to his sorrow, that the namesake and oldest son of his longtime associate Joseph P. Kennedy was killed when his explosive-laden aircraft blew up prematurely over the Channel.

In the immediate postwar years, as Russia dropped its Iron Curtain around eastern Europe and as the Cold War intensified, Sarnoff volunteered many of his less pressured hours to dreaming up an electronic shield that could be inserted between Russia and America. In a sense, this was his escapism from the day-to-day burdens of running RCA—perhaps like golf and gin rummy to others. Over weekends, he would browse in technical journals, seeking the kernel of an idea that would set him off on new conceptualizations. At lunches or dinners, he enjoyed picking the brains of his top scientists, like Goldsmith and Engstrom, throwing out a grandiose idea and inviting them to shoot it down on technical grounds.

It was out of such interplays, in New York and Princeton, that his concept of an electronic shield emerged in 1948. Several scientists worked with him in reducing the plan to paper, and Sarnoff was so excited by the end product that he applied for, and was granted, a patent in his name. The patent was for an airborne transoceanic radio relay system to be employed in the interception of enemy guided missiles. It proposed a picket line of aircraft spaced about 250 to 300 miles apart, flying serially across ocean spaces that Soviet missiles would cross en route to America. Each aircraft would be a radio relay station, equipped with radar, ultrafax (a high-speed system of facsimile transmission developed by RCA), two-way microwave and broad-band communication circuits, and panoramic receivers to intercept guidance and response signals to and from missiles. The intelligence thus garnered would be relayed to a central control location, permitting swift countermeasures to destroy the missiles far from America's shores.

It was a typically bold Sarnoff conceptualization, offered to the Defense Department with a waiver of patent rights. When a month elapsed without a conclusive response from the armed forces, he wrote directly to President Truman with an outline of his plan and a request for a prompt meeting on what "may constitute one of the greatest aids to our national security in an atomic age." Out of subsequent meetings with Truman (who Sarnoff said expressed "deep interest") and Defense Secretary James Forrestal, agreement was reached to test the system, with the responsibility divided between General F. L. Ankenbrandt of the air force and RCA engineer Loren Jones. It was finally concluded that the proposal, while ingenious, would be prohibitively expensive in sustained implementation. Sarnoff, who accepted the verdict without protest, years later visited the Strategic Air Command headquarters near Omaha, Nebraska, and professed to see elements of his system employed there as part of a continuous air alert. But even if this involved infringement on his patent, which was pure speculation, the possibility pleased him because it suggested a further kinship with the military.

With the cutback in postwar military budgets, TV weaponry seemed fated for the same museum as the B-17 bomber. In a sense, it had been upstaged by radar, which, with greater cost efficiency, could perform functions that television couldn't, gathering intelligence at vaster distances through storms and darkness. But Sarnoff would not permit the idea of battle TV to wither. In 1954, in the midst of TV's commercial explosion, he hatched a far broader concept of military television, focusing his attention this time on applications in ground warfare. He drew on RCA's technical staff for ideas on ways to exploit the shrinkage in weight and size, and the corresponding increase in mobility, of transmitting and receiving equipment in the dawning solid-state age. Armed with a host of potentially new applications of "combat television" as he called it, he persuaded the army that a field test would demonstrate to the American people the army's alert embracement of new technology. His carrot, of course, was live NBC coverage over a full national network. After months of joint RCA-army equipment tests and field manoeuvers, a demonstration was staged at Fort George G. Meade, Maryland, on August 11, 1954.

With Army Chief of Staff General Matthew B. Ridgway and Sarnoff observing together, armored and amphibious units of the 3rd Armored Cavalry Regiment swarmed ashore after a lake crossing to assault a simulated enemy stronghold. Hand-carried vidicon cameras accompanied the first wave—"heralds of a new era in battlefield communications," in Sarnoff's phrase—and flashed back to regimental headquarters a panoramic picture of action on the beachhead. TV-equipped observation planes swept the battle area and beyond, locating the enemy's reserves; tanks equipped with the ubiquitous vidicon observed amphibious thrusts; forward artillery observers pinpointed targets and adjusted fire by TV; prisoners were interrogated, and their captured maps and other documents displayed in front of the camera.

At regimental headquarters, a tent command post behind the battle lines, the regimental commander and his staff observed the flow of action on large screen monitors, punching up pictures that came back via closed-circuit cable and mobile microwave relay stations. In response to the visual intelligence, the commander relayed orders over audio circuits to his battle units at the front, in the air, and on the water.

Covering the action from a remote perimeter were new NBC color cameras which transmitted live pictures over a national hookup in a special nonsponsored hour-long program. To the large gathering of military leaders and electronic executives seated in a circus-size air-conditioned tent erected by RCA, the simulated battle provided a tantalizing glimpse of an ultimate goal. The mobile Signal Corps TV battle equipment was black and white, then the state of the art, but the presence of bulky NBC color cameras portended the future—a combat color system providing the commander with a continuous view of the battle's ebb and flow, permitting him to distinguish between different types of terrain and foliage by color, between natural and camouflaged objects, and between the wide variety of colored markings and signals used by friendly and hostile forces.

It was an expensive demonstration for RCA, with costs exceeding $100,000, but to Sarnoff it provided one of his most rewarding days. In remarks after the demonstration, he said proudly that "today we see concrete evidence that a new era in tactical communications has opened," and General Ridgway offered him warm support: "After its possibilities are thoroughly tested, television ... can take its place beside the atomic cannon, guided missiles and the rocket as part of our modern army." To Sarnoff, Ridgway was generous in his praise: "I doubt that any individual man has contributed more in this vitally important field than you, General Sarnoff, through your vision, your energy, and your persistent patriotism."

The press response disappointed Sarnoff because it did not treat the demonstration as a blockbuster event. Val Adams, a *New York Times* reporter who covered television, suspected it was a publicity ploy and only a half-column back-section news report appeared. In this instance, the *Times* was wrong, for the demonstration proved dramatically that the increasing miniaturization of television gave it a degree of mobility that would change the face of war—although not entirely in the ways that Sarnoff, Ridgway, or any of the scores of officers and electronics executives at Operation Threshold, as the Fort Meade demonstration was labeled, envisaged.

The fact not discussed that day was that the same graphic pictures appearing on the command post monitors—of artillery detonating, close-quarter combat, and all the destructive impact of battle—could be served up in real war not only to the military but to a civilian population a half world away. The war correspondent, as well as the soldier, could play a vital role in "combat television."

A decade later, as America's buildup in Viet Nam accelerated, the mobility of television, with color now included, permitted cameras on helicopter gun ships or with flame-throwing foot patrols. In a sense, television made the nightly network news programs an intelligence center for the public's evaluation of American involvement in Viet Nam. Millions of print words could not rival in impact a same-day TV report of a firefight in Viet Nam, of razed villages, of streams of refugees, of American troops pinned in the cross fire of Viet Cong infiltrators. To a degree that Sarnoff never anticipated, TV became a weapon of antiwar, its impact on the public reaching far beyond the purely military applications he had attempted to refine over three decades.

In his later years, Sarnoff, of course, fully recognized this development, but it did not give him any personal satisfaction. As an unswerving cold warrior, he had fully supported American involvement in Viet Nam. He saw it as part of the essential strategy of worldwide Soviet containment, a strategy to which no think tank expert of the postwar era devoted more time and energy than he. In 1955, he submitted to Eisenhower a lengthy proposal for seizing the propaganda initiative against Russia and her satellites. His "Program for a political offensive against world communism," as it was titled, reiterated his belief that the best way to avoid a "hot" war was to win the "cold" one. The tools he proposed for winning it were electronic, to be made available at cost by American manufacturing concerns, led by RCA. Tiny record players, costing less than $1 to manufacture, would be parachuted in clusters inside Russia along with small vinyl records. The recorded messages in Russian would tell the populace that America was their friend and call upon them to overthrow their Marxist masters. On the up side of the electronic scale, the same message would penetrate the Iron Curtain through powerful radio transmitters which Sarnoff proposed erecting on the borders of West Germany, to be operated by the Central Intelligence Agency.

Eisenhower was sufficiently interested to arrange a Sarnoff meeting with CIA Director Allen Dulles and State Department officials. The idea of parachuted phonographs was dropped as too hazardous, and thus possibly counterproductive; but his concept of penetrating the Iron Curtain with broadcast messages won broad support. Out of it later emerged the Voice of America and Radio Free Europe, to both of which services Sarnoff felt a paternal tie.

Beyond his determination to be the grand strategist, the Von Klausewitz of electronic warfare, Sarnoff acceded to numerous requests through the fifties and sixties to serve on public commissions concerned with military affairs. "I was like the girl who couldn't say no," he confessed. In 1955, at President Eisenhower's urging, he accepted the chairmanship of the National Security Training Commission, which had been created by Congress. The commission's mandate was to revive interest among the nation's young men in service in the military reserves. In the aftermath of a world war and the Korean conflict, patriotic fires were burning low and enlistments in the reserves had fallen off sharply. As commission chairman, it was Sarnoff's responsibility to arrest this trend, and once again he turned to electronic tools to get the job done. With the same intensity that he applied to a crash technical effort, he mustered the broadcasting networks and their stars to sell the concept of a career in the reserves as though it were Pepsodent. Artists of the stature of Bob Hope, Dinah Shore, Perry Como, and Martha Raye offered didactic appeals to America's youth to heed the nation's call. These one-minute "spots" were inserted between advertising messages on approximately six thousand radio and television programs, network and local, during the course of a year. All the air time and the stars' services, at Sarnoff's persuasive urging, were contributed gratis, and a reserve program that was nearly moribund suddenly pulsed with life. Tens of thousands of recruits signed up, and from Sarnoff's administrative budget of $50,000 he returned to the government $12,000, the job accomplished. A quarter century later, when the armed services turned to television to spur recruiting, they purchased time at commercial rates on the networks—at a cost of tens of millions of dollars to taxpayers.

Before his reserve work Sarnoff had, at President Truman's request, chaired a Citizens' Advisory Commission on Manpower Utilization in the Armed Services. Following this, he served on the Rockefeller Committee on Department of Defense Organization and on the New York State Council of Civil Defense. At a critical point in the color television battle in the early fifties, he even acceded to the request of General George C. Marshall that he become national chairman of the Red Cross fund drive, and he crisscrossed the nation between appearances at the FCC and various congressional committees.

Sarnoff's passionate commitment to the military was recognized in countless letters of commendation for his services, and occasionally in something more substantial, such as the Medal of Merit, which President Truman bestowed on him for outstanding contributions to the nation's defense. Even so, he did not feel that the recognition accorded him was commensurate with his, and RCA's, unique history of services. For security reasons, some of them could not be divulged in medal citations, but they were nonetheless known in the highest echelons of the government and were as significant, to his thinking, as the more visible contributions.

Even before Pearl Harbor, Sarnoff had developed close ties with the various intelligence agencies of the government, both military and civil. At the War Department's request, when war threatened in the Far East, he had arranged for copies of messages transmitted to and from Japan by RCA Communications, including diplomatic traffic, to be made available to the military. Months before war broke out, he had inspected RCA's Far Eastern communications centers, including Honolulu, and had submitted a confidential report to President Roosevelt on what he perceived to be the high state of readiness of both military and civil communications units.

In 1947, as the Cold War intensified, a request for similar access to messages sent to and from Russia and eastern Europe was made of RCA (plus the other major carriers, Western Union and ITT) by the National Security Agency and the Federal Bureau of Investigation, then headed by Sarnoff's friend J. Edgar Hoover. This intercept program, under the code name Operation Shamrock, generated a momentum of its own, with intelligence agents copying on a regular basis private messages of interest to them at the Washington and New York offices of RCA Communications, Western Union, and ITT. The degree of Sarnoff's personal involvement was never established, but the fact of his eagerness to employ RCA's resources to thwart the nation's enemies was known throughout the company. Indeed, anything that might serve a patriotic purpose he never questioned. Operation Shamrock was not halted until 1973, two years after his death, when word of the intercept program began to leak into the press, leading to a legislative investigation and public hearings during the Gerald Ford administration. RCA, ITT, and Western Union were harshly upbraided by a House subcommittee headed by Representative Bella Abzug for compromising the privacy of cable and wireless message traffic.

The practice of secret taping of White House conversations made famous in the Nixon Watergate hearings had its genesis in a 1940 gift from Sarnoff to President Roosevelt. It was an experimental recording device, employing a motion picture sound track, developed in the RCA Photophone Laboratories, which worked on sound recording for motion pictures. Its existence was first disclosed in the February 1982 issue of *American Heritage Magazine* in an article by Professor R. J. C. Butaw of the University of Washington, who unearthed several White House sound film recordings while doing research at the FDR Library in Hyde Park, New York.

According to Butaw, the device grew out of Roosevelt's desire to keep track of conversations in the Oval Office to prevent later press misquotations. Word was sent by a White House staff member to Sarnoff in New York of the president's desire, and he promptly had a special film recording machine designed, complete with a new 15½-inch unidirectional RCA microphone small enough to be hidden in FDR's desk lamp. "[Press Secretary] Steve Early was told of this development," Butaw wrote, "and of Sarnoff's desire to present the machine to the President as a gift from RCA . . . an appointment was set up for Sarnoff on June 14, 1940 . . ."

Concealed in the White House basement, the continuous sound machine, minus camera, recorded Roosevelt's meetings for eleven weeks, but then he turned it off. Among the few barely intelligible recorded artifacts still in existence is a Roosevelt discussion with his staff about starting a rumor campaign on the extramarital affair of his Republican rival, Wendell Willkie. Butaw speculates that FDR abandoned the Sarnoff apparatus (which was apparently removed from the White House in the Truman administration) because of dissatisfaction with its quality and fear of political repercussions if it were uncovered.

As the range of his services, overt and covert, broadened, Sarnoff concluded that appropriate recognition should include his promotion to major general in the Signal Corps reserve. He had never been burdened by a sense of false modesty, and he told his military associates within RCA candidly that he would welcome their help in securing a second star. He felt he clearly deserved it. It could be the capstone of his military career, a further tangible certification of the long path he had journeyed out of the Russian pale. There would be nothing subtle or devious about the effort to achieve it, for this would be contrary to his nature. There would be no hints dropped at military social gatherings, no inspired rumors circulated around the Pentagon. He would go right to the top.

Recognizing the importance of seniority in the military, Sarnoff enlisted his highest-ranking board member, General Walter Bedell Smith, four stars, Ike's chief of staff at SHAEF, to initiate the campaign. In 1950, Smith wrote the army's chief of staff, General Joseph "Lightning Joe" Collins, who had been his subordinate in the European theater during World War II, recommending the promotion as appropriate to Sarnoff's selfless service to the military. This was followed by a personal visit to Collins by another board member, General Ingles, two stars, who had taken a fatherly interest in Collins' career during their years of regular duty between wars. Following this personal appeal, Ingles wrote a lengthy letter to Collins enumerating the Sarnoff qualifications for a second star. Initially, the response was encouraging. On June 9, 1950, Collins wrote Ingles (using the salutation "Dear Dad") that "it seems probable that he [the army's chief signal officer] will submit Sarnoff's name to the promotion board." Ingles in turn wrote Sarnoff on June 14, enclosing a copy of the Collins letter, commenting: "Since Collins states there will be one vacancy for a major general in the signal corps allotment, the whole matter looks rather good."

But something happened to alter this optimistic scenario, and Sarnoff was never quite certain what it was. Somewhere in the vast military labyrinth someone was refusing to process the promotion. Why? Had resentment developed within the promotion board at pressure applied from above? Was someone of anti-Semitic bent—an inevitable Sarnoff suspicion whenever he was thwarted—building a case against the second star based on a restrictive interpretation of promotion regulations? As days passed without any word, pro or con, his frustration mounted because time was becoming a factor. Under reserve regulations, his second star would have to be approved by February 28, 1951, his sixtieth birthday, or he would face automatic retirement from the reserve. With the clock winding down to the final days, he persuaded Ingles to make a last-ditch approach.

"I understand," Ingles wrote Collins on February 20, "that General Aiken [then chief signal officer] within the last few days has again submitted a recommendation for his [Sarnoff's] promotion to the grade of Major General in the Signal Corps. If he is not at least nominated for promotion, he will be lost to the Army. His use to the Army in the New York area where he is well known and highly respected is very great. I, personally, can assure you from my own observation among businessmen in New York that it is very much to the advantage of the Army to retain Sarnoff on the active reserve list. I believe that General Marshall, since he knows him well, would concur in this opinion."

But this time, possibly nettled by the pressure, Collins took a different tack in his response to "Dear Dad." His letter to Ingles was dated February 28, Sarnoff's birthday and final day of military reserve service, and said in part: "I would be glad to recommend General Sarnoff's promotion, but by so doing it would violate so many promotion policies we have adopted it would prove very embarrassing. Although he is being transferred to the honorary reserve, this does not mean he cannot be called to active duty when needed in the same manner as regular army retired officers."

So that was that. The Collins rebuff seemed conclusive. But Sarnoff, who had snatched so many victories in life from the brink of defeat, would not accept its finality. At the very core of his character was a compulsive necessity to succeed in all his major undertakings, whether radio networking or television or a second star. He was what he was, and where he was, because he refused to accept the odds, no matter how overwhelmingly against him. The ghetto would have incarcerated him for life if he had accepted, like lesser men, fate's initial ordination. No. Ingles' failure would not deter him. Other avenues would be explored. It never occurred to him that to do so might be brash or impolitic.

Nearly two years elapsed before Sarnoff located another surrogate, out of military channels, for a renewal of the star trek. He was Herbert Bayard Swope, the flamboyant former editor of the New York *World*. Now a well-paid publicist, an intimate of financier Bernard Baruch, Swope numbered RCA among his consultancies. He had many friends in government, and when Sarnoff learned that one of them was Joe Collins, he persuaded Swope to call the army chief of staff, who was soon to retire, and revive the promotion request.

In what terms Swope couched the appeal for the second star is not known, but Collins took more than a month before replying on June 9, 1953.

"Unfortunately, it is simply not in the cards," he wrote to Swope, "much as I would like to be able to do it . . . There is no way we can promote a retired officer except to advance him to the highest grade while on active duty. Since Dave was not a major general on active duty, there is nothing we could do about it . . . my hands are tied."

Beyond the army chief of staff, there was only one recourse—the president as commander in chief. And this time Sarnoff decided to take matters in his own hands, although he had to wait another three years for the moment he deemed propitious. This occurred in 1956, when he reported to Ike personally on the military reserve recruitment program he had headed; after the president expressed gratitude for this service to the nation, Sarnoff told him of his thwarted hope for a second star and mentioned the name of another general, Julius Klein, who, he contended, had been promoted to major general after exceeding the normal retirement age of sixty. Ike promised to look into it, but his response contained in a letter to Sarnoff of May 15, 1956, offered little encouragment.

"Dear Dave. I have a report on your promotion that disappoints me. Evidently, the only legal course available is to accept six months' active duty, then await the decision of a selection board. Obviously for you this would not be a practicable approach.

"You mention Julius Klein. I find that he was promoted in the Illinois National Guard, not in the Federal Reserve, which is quite a different matter."

Despite Ike's discouraging appraisal, Sarnoff weighed seriously the possibility of a return to active duty. He would have to gamble six months of his life, at age sixty-five, and then hope for a favorable promotion recommendation from a board of officers probably unknown to him. Quite possibly, he might be required to serve with a Signal Corps unit abroad, and that would remove him from effective control of RCA at a critical juncture in television's development. Reluctantly he concluded that the price was too great, that the odds, this time, had overwhelmed him.

But Sarnoff did not waste time mourning the failure of a campaign that spanned five years. It was one of his distinctive characteristics that failure did not embitter him. He attributed this to his look-to-the-future philosophy of life—"There's no sense brooding over things you can't change," as he once remarked to a subordinate. In this instance, his ardor for the military remained as keen as ever, and so did his desire to be rewarded for it: if not a second star, then some other form of high level recognition commensurate with the magnitude of his military contributions.

The success of the Fort Meade combat television demonstration in 1954 and the reserve recruitment campaign in 1956 convinced Sarnoff that the Distinguished Service Medal would be an appropriate award. The DSM was the nation's highest military decoration for noncombat service, ranking just below the Congressional Medal of Honor and the Distinguished Service Cross, both of which required conspicuous gallantry under fire. In Sarnoff's mind, the prestige of the DSM equated with a second star. It was normally awarded to senior officers of flag rank at the culmination of their active service careers, and by stretching the prescription only a little, he concluded that he could qualify.

Characteristically, Sarnoff did not assume that the mere mention of his wish to those in authority would permit the DSM to drop like a plum in his lap. It would require careful planning and staff work, followed by a three-pronged approach through military, legislative, and executive channels. First, a five-page, single-spaced dossier of his contributions to the military was prepared, stretching over three decades and scooping up all the minutiae of both active and nonactive service. The original draft was handwritten by Sarnoff himself, carefully polished by his staff, and then transmitted by his RCA generals to the new chief of the Signal Corps, Major General George Bock. Again the reception at that level was all Sarnoff could have wished, with Bock agreeing to initiate a DSM recommendation and monitor it as far as he could through the approval cycle.

Next, an RCA emissary was dispatched to Capitol Hill to enlist the support of Senator Leverett Saltonstall of Massachusetts, an influential senior member of the Armed Services Committee. Saltonstall ducked out of a committee hearing to read the dossier and listen to a relayed request from his friend Sarnoff that he speak to upper-echelon Defense Department personnel. With Back Bay taciturnity, Saltonstall made no commitment, but said he would explore the situation. In Sarnoff's optimistic judgment, that meant he would actively support it. A similar approach was made to James Hagerty, Eisenhower's press secretary, with the scarcely veiled suggestion that a word from the president would sanctify the DSM recommendation. "We'll see what we can do to help the old boy," was Hagerty's rather nonchalant response, but again Sarnoff, by now almost schoolboy eager, construed this as positive. With typical foresight, he began planning ahead on a guest list for the award ceremony.

But again for reasons Sarnoff could only suspect (Pressure? Maybe. Anti-Semitism? Possibly), an alchemic process within the Pentagon bureaucracy transmuted Bock's DSM recommendation into a Decoration for Exceptional Civilian Service. This was the army's highest award for civilian service, and Sarnoff, of course, accepted it with grace and appropriate gratitude at a Pentagon ceremony presided over by Defense Secretary Charles Wilson, with rows of beribboned military leaders as the backdrop. It particularly pleased him that General George C. Marshall, whom he revered, was present for a brief period. But as he departed the Pentagon, medal in hand, he muttered to an aide, "It's not the DSM."

Since army officials had made plain that the Decoration for Exceptional Civilian Service was in lieu of the DSM, and not a stepping-stone to it, Sarnoff, his medal thirst still unslaked, began probing outside the military for further recognition. His next major effort, after a lapse of several years, was directed toward the Medal of Freedom. This was a presidential award established by John F. Kennedy to recognize significant contributions in various areas of national life and carried on in the Lyndon Johnson presidency. Again, there was nothing covert or duplicitous about the campaign, which was directed this time by Sol Polk, a leading Chicago merchant who marketed RCA consumer products and was a longtime Sarnoff admirer. With the encouragement of his candidate, Polk enlisted various congressmen and other government leaders to support his written proposal to the president.

Repeated assurances came from White House staff members to Polk that his candidate was indeed on the list of finalists, and Sarnoff's confidence was buoyed by his close personal relationship with Johnson. They had met in Washington in the early fifties, when Johnson was a rising young Democratic senator from Texas. Over occasional lunches, they had discovered much in common in their backgrounds. Like Sarnoff, LBJ had known extreme poverty in his youth. His father had experienced bankruptcy as a farmer in the infertile Hill Country outside Austin, and he had scratched for his education with menial jobs that paid little better than Sarnoff's newsboy routes. Where Sarnoff had found his escape from the ghetto in the new art of wireless communications, Johnson had found his in the old art of politics, but updated with the enterprising use of radio as his principal tool to reach the electorate across a Texas vastness that rivaled the Russian pale. As his career flourished, Johnson never underestimated the power of the broadcast medium, and those who controlled it. When he became the owner of radio and television stations in Austin, Sarnoff contributed significantly to their success through heavy RCA advertising support and the supply of broadcast station equipment, together with AM-FM receivers, at reduced rates. With Johnson's ascendancy to Senate leadership and later the vice presidency, he commuted between Washington and Texas in a Lockheed Jetstar, which Sarnoff equipped with the most modern RCA radar.

And Johnson was generous in his reciprocity. Major Sarnoff speeches were inserted in the *Congressional Record* with effulgent Johnson introductions. On the frequent occasion of testimonial or anniversary dinners honoring the RCA leader, telegraphed laudations from Johnson became as much a fixture as the menu. "Your work has not only expanded human knowledge," a typical message said at Sarnoff's fiftieth anniversary banquet, on September 30, 1956, "but has contributed to the well-being, the security, and the prosperity of all your fellow Americans."

But again something intervened to thwart Sarnoff. Perhaps it was a question of timing. As protests against America's involvement in the Viet Nam war snowballed in the nation's universities, Johnson found himself under a state of siege. He became, by all accounts, abnormally sensitive to outside pressures of any sort. Perhaps the pressures of the Polk campaign were a sufficient irritant to cross Sarnoff's name off the final list of Medal of Freedom recipients. Or perhaps it was the presence on the White House staff of someone hostile to him. In this instance, Sarnoff suspected Robert E. Kintner, the former president of NBC, who had been discharged for his drinking proclivities. Johnson was a personal friend of Kintner's and, without consulting Sarnoff, had brought him to the White House staff as secretary of the cabinet soon after his departure from NBC in 1966. Had Kintner reciprocated for his discharge by disparaging Sarnoff to the president? Or was it Sarnoff's support of Richard Nixon when he ran against the Kennedy-Johnson ticket in 1960? In the long postmortems that followed the White House announcement of Medal of Freedom winners, Sarnoff and his staff culled all the possible reasons for his omission. Efforts were made through RCA's Washington staff to plumb the mystery of why. But the only answer that came back—that cultural and intellectual contributions to the nation's well-being were the lodestone for selection—never satisfied him. His final judgment was that Johnson was guilty of an egregious slight to an old friend for some unjustified reasons of personal pique. Then he erased it from his mind. There were other medals to be had.

Through the sixties, his last decade of RCA service, much of his time and that of the public relations staff when into pursuit of appropriate awards to further embellish his image. Within the staff, this involved considerable research in the arcane field of decorations and of the qualifications required to win them. Sarnoff personally involved himself, as he did with almost any activity that interested him. For example, at a lunch with his public relations people, he commented that he had read in the *Times* that David Rockefeller had received the annual public service award of the Advertising Council. "Is that something for me?" he asked. "Whom can we explore it with?"

Within the staff, there was a division of opinion over the medal search. Some considered it pure hubris, an almost egomaniacal pursuit and one that was unnecessary in view of Sarnoff's massive and substantive contributions to electronics. Others were more sympathetic, attributing it to the insecurities of his childhood and an overweening desire for acceptance. They viewed it as a search ad hominem for assurance that no one in his adopted land would be unaware of who and what he was—and the "baubles" were his certification.

As most experienced public relations practitioners are aware, a medal campaign by a well-known figure can generate a momentum of its own. The willingness of a recipient to accept an award personally can encourage further awards, and this was certainly true of Sarnoff in his later years. As recognition of his achievements mounted, many awards came to him unsolicited. There were the national commander's award of the American Legion, the gold citizenship medal of the Veterans of Foreign Wars, and the distinguished service citation of the Armed Forces Communications Association. Even the United Nations volunteered its homage with a scroll extolling his contributions to international communications.

All told, more than a hundred awards were showered on the man who had sprung from the ghetto, making him one of the nation's most bemedaled and bescrolled citizens. So there were compensations for the loss of the DSM, the second star, and the Medal of Freedom. Once during a leisurely lunch with an RCA staffer in his executive dining room in 1967, he singled out the award he most cherished. It came on August 31, 1961, when seventeen United States senators gathered at a luncheon in a Senate dining room in Washington to honor his fifty-five years of contributions to military and civil communications. The *New York Times* reported that several senators present said they could not recall when so many senators had come together to honor a private citizen.

Senator George D. Aiken of Vermont, a longtime Sarnoff admirer, presided and presented to Sarnoff a gold-embossed scroll which was signed by the senators present and later by an additional seventeen. The encomiums that flowed like luncheon wine to the immigrant boy who had scaled America's industrial heights bathed him in a warm glow. In a graceful, moving response, he assessed his adopted land's meaning to him and then thanked the senators present "for the friendship you have shown me, for this handsome tribute and this wonderful reception."

While RCA paid for the lunch, helped issue the invitations to it, designed, wrote, and printed the scroll, and later prepared a pictorial brochure of the event which was sent to every United States senator and to the White House, this was not unusual. Corporate underwriting of ceremonial events involving legislators was commonplace in the Washington of that period and RCA's initiative did not detract from the legitimacy and the unique nature of the honor accorded Sarnoff.

A week later, after the last signature had been collected, the scroll was forwarded to Sarnoff's New York office. With an aide, he examined it minutely, each senatorial signature, each word of the testimonial, each sculpted flourish on the scroll. "This beats the DSM," he said.

8 / The Color Television Battle

As speedily as America mobilized in '41 and '42, almost as rapidly did it begin to demobilize following the formal surrender of Japan to General MacArthur aboard the battleship *Missouri* on September 2, 1945. Only 291,000 of the 15,000,000 Americans who served in uniform had lost their lives, a ratio of one to every 450 in the total 1940 population. A generation later, the chances of a civilian's being murdered in urban America were considerably greater. Those who flooded back in late '45 and '46 to an un- scarred homeland were eager to pick up the threads of civilian existence. Many had conserved the tax-free dollars of their service pay, and now they wanted, quickly, to purchase the amenities of peace—automobiles, toasters, radios, refrigerators, apartments, homes. This was also true of the swollen civilian work force of America's mighty industrial arsenal, which had pro- duced $350 billion in war materials between 1939 and 1946. Rosie the riveter itched to spend savings accumulated through long overtime hours on production lines. The war had, in fact, obliterated the last vestiges of the depression, and vast hordes of cash, representing pent-up purchasing power after four years of deprivation, were available to industry as quickly as it could convert to peacetime production.

A young infantry lieutenant colonel from Tucson, Arizona, returned to his home from Germany, much beribboned, in late 1946 and was greeted by the head of the draft board that had enrolled him as a private in the army more than five years earlier. The draft official, Monte Mansfield, happened to be the local Ford dealer, and he was eager to reward one of his most conspicuously successful draftees. "I want to give you the most precious gift I can," he said. "I want to sell you a new Ford." It was indeed a gesture of generous dimensions, for new Fords were just beginning to trickle off the Dearborn production line and hundreds were clamoring for every one avail- able. The young officer was so moved that he presented his benefactor with a cherished war trophy—a gold-plated, swastika-adorned letter opener taken from the captured private train of Reichsmarshal Hermann Göring. Then he paid the full retail price of $1500 for his roadster.

It was in this environment of public yearning for consumer goods of every description that Sarnoff resumed his postwar control of RCA. His war experiences had changed him little physically. His health was excellent. He was a shade grayer, his hairline slightly more receded, with a bald spot emerging at the pate; a second chin was in formation and he was slightly fuller in girth. He also seemed more ramrod erect, more square-shouldered, perhaps because he was now the General and forever more would be. His three sons had returned from the war without injury. Lizette had doffed her Red Cross uniform and was back to sculpting, bridge, and hospital auxiliary work. With the family thus intact, he felt he could face the challenges ahead undistracted.

If anything, his military achievements had burnished his already formidable ego. He boasted to Jolliffe, who had served as acting president during his absence, that while the company's financial performance had been adequate during the war (in 1944, net profit had been $10.2 million on defense-related sales of $326 million), it would pale in comparison to the achievements of the next five years. Immediately after his return, he called together the company's top fifteen executives for a staff meeting in the RCA fifty-third-floor boardroom. Dressed in a new blue suit which Lizette had waiting when he doffed his uniform, Sarnoff seated himself at the head of the table, beneath a portrait of his old mentor, Owen D. Young. With the ailing Harbord at his right, and with Engstrom and Jolliffe among those in attendance, Sarnoff came quickly to the point of the meeting: "Gentlemen, the RCA has one priority: television. Whatever resources are needed will be provided. This time we're going to get the job done. There's a vast market out there, and we're going to capture it before anyone else."

After the false starts of the twenties and thirties, Sarnoff said, all the necessary elements were now in place for swift commercialization. He pointed to wartime advances in electronic circuitry and in the power output and efficiency of vacuum tubes that promised improved picture quality and greater range for television signals. Manufacturing facilities were in place. An electron tube plant, built at Lancaster, Pennsylvania, by RCA with government funds for military production, was available for purchase at the bargain price of $15 million and could quickly be converted to television. In February 1945, anticipating the war's end, the FCC had reconfirmed the prewar NTSC standards which were tailored to RCA's technology. And even some in the industry who had earlier opposed commercial standards, such as Philco and Dumont, were now signaling their readiness to participate in the new era. Television awaited only a leader to launch it, and no one at the meeting doubted who that would be.

As much as Napoleon understood, in Cardinal Newman's phrase, "the grammar of gunpowder," Sarnoff felt he understood the grammar of television. He had thought about it endlessly during the war years. In London, he had discussed its potential impact at long dinners with leaders of the British broadcasting and telecommunications fraternity, with Emile Girardeau in France, with communications chiefs of the various Allied forces, probing for their views of its postwar significance. He had even discussed it briefly with Churchill and Eisenhower and Bedell Smith. "Anytime anybody would listen, I talked television," he recalled. By the conflict's end, he was convinced that television would reshape life in the century's second half to a degree never attained by print or voice communications. Out of his introspections, he had come to view the new medium in almost cosmological terms, as a force of nearly preternatural dimensions, life-transforming in its impact. And increasingly he saw himself as destiny's instrument for bringing it to America and the world. "When I returned, I never doubted what my role and my responsibilities would be," he confided to his old friend Alfred Goldsmith. In discussions with his technical staff at Princeton, he again revived the metaphor of himself as the captain on the bridge, and this time his ship would be not only RCA but the electronics industry, sailing in waters that had first been explored by the discoverers of papyrus and the phonetic alphabet.

In late 1946, before most established industries had completed retooling from war to peace production, the first RCA television sets began rolling off the production line in Camden, equipped with picture and receiving tubes machine-tooled in Lancaster. The 630-TS set, with ten-inch viewing tube, became known as the Model T of television. By year's end, 10,000 had been sold to a reaching public at $385 each. The industry began to join in. A year later, 250,000 sets had been sold, with four-fifths produced by RCA. NBC had resumed commercial telecasts and was adding new studio facilities at Rockefeller Center. Fifteen stations had been built, nearly all utilizing RCA transmitters, and the FCC was processing scores of license applications.

By 1947 it seemed apparent that Sarnoff was right in his assessment of timing and market. He had, of course, paid a heavy price for television, since RCA's investment approached $50 million, which was comparable to more than a half billion in current dollars. But sales were outpacing even his optimistic forecast of a billion-dollar industry by 1955. His formula for industry leadership—the whole ball of wax, as he called it—was proving out. In every area of the new business—transmitters, sets, tubes, components, broadcast facilities, and program generation—RCA was the leading factor. By 1947 NBC had its own stations under construction in Hollywood, Chicago, and Cleveland. Major oil, automotive, and cigarette companies paid NBC $3 million that year in the hope of securing time franchises in the prime evening hours and in order to test commercial techniques for the mass audiences they knew would soon be available. Interest in the Truman-Dewey presidential election, and in the nominating conventions that preceded it, had been heightened by NBC's cameras. The World Series proved a natural for television, and stars of stage, screen, and vaudeville, like Milton Berle, began exposing themselves to the camera's eye.

Four years after commercial introduction, almost half of RCA's gross sales were coming from television. To Sarnoff, whose leadership had already been anointed by the Radio and Television Manufacturers Association with the title of "Father of American Television," the victory seemed more clear-cut and far-reaching than any preceding. The last stragglers, "the parasites" in his favorite phrase, were coming aboard, as he had scornfully predicted they would. Even Zenith capitulated to pressure from its dealers as the five thousand sets per week being produced by RCA were snapped up in their rival's showrooms. As many industry leaders, including Sarnoff, had anticipated, radio was approaching saturation in America, with more than 60 million sets in homes. Sales began declining and price-cutting infested the older service. Even the most astigmatic could see where the profits of the future rested.

Sarnoff was determined that the history of early radio would not be repeated, with RCA losing sales leadership because of the cumbersome committee structure of the electrical combine, which had inhibited his marketing efforts. In 1947, he selected a merchandising specialist, Frank M. Folsom, to head up the RCA television drive. A tough, jowly, blunt-speaking extravert with close-cropped graying hair, Folsom had directed naval procurement in Washington during the war, becoming a close ally of Navy Secretary James Forrestal, who recommended him to Sarnoff. Early in his career, he had served as merchandising manager of Hale Brothers department stores in San Francisco and Portland. From there he had moved to Chicago and become vice-president in charge of merchandising for Montgomery Ward, then under the control of Sewell Avery, who achieved national infamy when President Roosevelt ordered him physically removed from his office by soldiers for resisting wartime controls. In Folsom's judgment, the autocratic Avery, who was reputed to enjoy firing subordinates as a breakfast fillip, was "the meanest son-of-a-bitch who ever lived," and he was not cowed by Sarnoff's reputation for authoritarian management.

The two men hit it off well from the beginning. Folsom was headquartered in Camden at the RCA Victor Division, and when Sarnoff visited him there, Folsom would amuse him with stories of the political infighting in wartime Washington, and with profane descriptions of how Avery terrorized his executive minions at Montgomery Ward. Beyond that, he demonstrated a quick sensitivity to the merchandising potential of television, which endeared him to Sarnoff. His hearty, regular-fellow demeanor also won the friendship of RCA's distributor and dealer organizations, and even some of its competitors, like Zenith's McDonald, whose distrust of Sarnoff was legendary.

In other areas the two complemented one another. Folsom was a leading Catholic layman who soon became a close friend of Francis Cardinal Spellman of New York, a Knight of Malta, and, later, a Vatican representative at atomic energy conferences. As the elderly, ailing Harbord began to withdraw from company affairs, Folsom became recognized as the number two man in the executive hierarchy, even accorded the rare privilege of addressing Sarnoff as Dave instead of General. While Folsom had little interest in, or understanding of, electronic technology, he had an instinctive feel for the selling features of a product. On Saturdays when not playing golf (which his boss considered wasted time), Folsom would browse in dealer storerooms, checking pricing points, studying competitive features, and soliciting the observations of floor salesmen. Because of the complexity of the home receivers (thirty vacuum tubes compared to radio's five), Folsom quickly sensed that service would be the key to enduring sales leadership, just as IBM later demonstrated with computers. In any such high-tech service, equipment breakdowns would be an inevitable part of the growth cycle, and particularly its start-up phase. With Sarnoff's approval, Folsom created a nationwide servicing organization within the RCA Service Company, which ultimately hired and trained two thousand technicians who were on call for repairs in the home of any malfunctioning RCA set. Service contracts were offered with each set, and several home calls per year were commonplace with the early sets. The company was a first in the industry, and it soon gained for RCA a reputation for being concerned with quality in television, a reputation it had lacked in radio.

With the Sarnoff-Folsom team functioning smoothly, and with RCA's omnibus leadership certified by its back-ordered plants, the path of monochrome television appeared detour-free and infinite. The challenge now was tooling up to meet demand—or so Sarnoff thought until a little-noticed development announced seven years earlier, in 1940, mushroomed into prominence, threatening not only the very existence of monochrome television but also his dreams of leadership sui generis of the new industry.

The challenge came from an unlikely source, Bill Paley's Columbia Broadcasting System, which, since its founding in 1927, had emerged through its flair for showmanship and program innovation as a respected, though still junior, rival of NBC. During the years of Sarnoff's intense effort to bring television to market, CBS had dabbled in the new art, creating a small research facility and purchasing from RCA a TV transmitter for experimental telecasts in the New York area. But it was still, in the perspective of the industry, including Sarnoff, a broadcast organization with little technical competence. Consequently, a ripple of surprise greeted CBS's announcement in August 1940 that it had invented a color television system that could be quickly readied for the marketplace, thus making obsolete—it suggested—the need for monochrome television even before it had been commercially sanctioned by the FCC.

To Sarnoff, the suggestion of such a technical leapfrogging, which would make years of black-and-white developmental work obsolete, bordered on the ridiculous. "Horse-and-buggy stuff," he called it. He had no hesitation in communicating that fact to Paley. He had become acquainted with the slender, blond CBS leader, who was ten years his junior, in the late 1920s, and their paths had frequently crossed through broadcaster meetings called to consider common industry problems, such as how to persuade wire services to permit the use of their copy on early radio network news programs. They began lunching together occasionally at each other's corporate dining room. Sarnoff found many qualities in his younger competitor that appealed to him, including their shared Russian-Jewish antecedents. He particularly liked Paley's sense of self-esteem, which rivaled his own, and his willingness to make risky business decisions. Yet their life-styles were far removed. Paley loved the glamour of the New York social scene—a "magical city." After long hours at the office, he would dance and party half the night away. He courted the stars of the entertainment world, and loved to lunch or dine with them. He became part of Long Island's exclusive North Shore social set, an avid and skilled art collector, and he ultimately married Barbara Mortimer, a reigning American beauty and fashion trend setter. Yet Paley was never deflected from his main goal in life, which was to secure network broadcasting leadership.

Privately, Sarnoff admired his younger rival's programming acumen. In the thirties, as CBS was beginning to register important radio gains, he attempted to hire Paley as NBC's head, suggesting he could reap a fortune by selling his controlling block of CBS stock and then becoming the high-salaried head of the senior network, secure with a long-term contract. While flattered, Paley quickly rejected the offer. He had no desire to abandon his position as the unchallenged sachem of an upcoming and profitable broadcasting organization in order to play a subsidiary role in a technological empire. Some of the reasons were hinted at in his memoirs, when Paley described his feelings toward Sarnoff: "We had a long, continuing avuncular relationship down through the years. From the earliest days of radio, when he was the 'grand old man' and I was 'that bright young kid' we were friends, confidants and fierce competitors all at the same time, and we understood each other and our relative positions. I always had the greatest respect and admiration for him. He had a sharp mind and a keen sense of competition. I always thought his strengths lay more in the technical and physical aspects of radio and television while mine lay in understanding talent, programming and what went on the air. I never could learn what made the insides of radio and television work."

It was precisely the latter reason, Paley's lack of technical expertise, that led Sarnoff, in later recollection, to warn him at one of their luncheon meetings that he was getting in over his head with color. "I advised him bluntly to forget it," Sarnoff recalled. Based on RCA's own rudimentary experiments in its laboratories, he insisted that color was years away. This view was also reinforced by other manufacturers' representatives with whom Paley later met.

The fact that Paley did not heed these admonitions was due primarily to a young Hungarian immigrant named Peter C. Goldmark, who had been hired as a research scientist in the CBS Laboratories in 1936. The CBS color system was primarily his invention. He would also invent the long-playing 33 rpm record, which revolutionized the record industry, and a thin-film video recording device which attracted enormous press interest years later but which failed commercially. Beyond his technical skills, the bespectacled and intense Goldmark possessed a genius for public persuasion and press manipulation. And he shared with Sarnoff an almost metaphysical will to fame and public recognition. To a degree that baffled Sarnoff, and in the later stages of the conflict infuriated him, Goldmark managed to persuade many in the government and the press that the CBS system represented the ultimate in color technology. In the RCA leader's often expressed view, Goldmark's skill as a propagandist far eclipsed his qualifications as a scientist.

Sarnoff's reason for attaching little significance to the CBS color announcement was the scientific pedigree of the system. It revived the Jenkins-era spinning disc, the same precept of mechanical transmission that Sarnoff had jettisoned a decade earlier after Zworykin had unveiled his iconoscope. This technical disinterment was so obviously meretricious, Sarnoff reasoned, that it would collapse of its own shortcomings. Thus he did not initially mount a major campaign to halt it, and this proved a serious miscalculation. The commitment of CBS management to Goldmark and his color system approached the fanatical. Many years would elapse—years filled with contentious and often acrimonious conflict between RCA and CBS—before the issue of television's future in color was finally resolved.

Apart from technical merit, or lack of it, Goldmark's color system was based on a concept of ingenious simplicity, which had ancient antecedents. During his school years in Budapest and later at the Physical Institute in Vienna, he had become familiar with Nipkow's mechanical disc concept. Working in his basement laboratory, he put together a television receiver that employed rotating spherical mirrors arranged around the periphery of a small rotating disc. Before emigrating to the United States in 1933, he had received the first television patent issued in Austria. After joining the CBS laboratory staff in 1936, Goldmark had witnessed the motion picture *Gone With the Wind*. It was the first film he had seen in color, and it excited his imagination, particularly the vivid scenes of the burning of Atlanta. How could he transfer the brilliance of those hues to television? Working with a small support staff at the CBS lab, he began experimenting with sets of filters containing the three primary colors—green, red, and blue. He attached them to a motor-driven disc that transmitted the colors sequentially. In reception on the color screen, the persistent vision of the eye mixed them into all the hues of the color spectrum, producing a picture of pleasing clarity.

Goldmark was not the first to experiment with this Waring blender technique of color transmission. John Logie Baird, the monochrome pioneer, had dabbled with it in Britain in the 1920s. In America, the Bell System transmitted crude rotating disc color over telephone lines in 1929. And RCA's scientists, as Sarnoff would later point out repeatedly, had experimented with the technique and even conducted random field-test transmissions of mechanical color in New York in the early thirties.

Yet it was clearly Goldmark who refined the field sequential approach by integrating the disc with modern electronic techniques of transmission and reception. While a technical hybrid, his system worked well with small-screen pictures that could be magnified in an environment of controlled light and movement. In the first demonstrations at his Madison Avenue laboratory in June 1940 for CBS executive vice-president Paul Kesten and a young doctoral graduate of Ohio State University, Frank Stanton, who later became the longtime and highly effective president of CBS, Goldmark won a high level of support. On a three-inch screen viewed through a magnifying glass, a Spanish flamenco dancer dressed in vivid red and white performed "in living color," as Goldmark described it. "It was beautiful," he said. Kesten and Stanton appeared to agree, and they communicated their enthusiasm to Paley. Unlike Sarnoff, the CBS leaders were primarily broadcasters, not technically oriented, and the quality of the picture apparently outweighed any qualms they may have had about technical limitations inherent in the system. CBS still trailed NBC in audience popularity of its radio network shows, and this probably seemed an inspired opportunity to eclipse a dominant rival who was frequently patronizing toward the "second" network. So Goldmark received increased financial backing, expanded engineering support, and the authority to unveil his color system to the industry.

The forum Goldmark chose was the National Television System Committee, which was still struggling, in 1940, to achieve a consensus on monochrome standards. As CBS's representative on the committee, he was aware of the deep division still existing within the industry. Perhaps, Goldmark reasoned, he could render the monochrome dispute moot by providing his colleagues the escape route of color. In August he invited the committee to the CBS Madison Avenue laboratory to view a transmission via coaxial cable of a CBS color broadcast from the Chrysler Building. Colorfully dressed models moved slowly across the small viewing screens, and bouquets of brilliantly hued flowers were shown close up in the small room crowded with industry engineers, including Charles Jolliffe of RCA. "I couldn't have created a greater explosion," Goldmark later claimed, "if I had lit a stick of dynamite." While this was an exaggeration in Jolliffe's view, most of the engineers were favorably impressed by the clarity and definition of the color pictures, and Jolliffe so reported to Sarnoff. Indeed, had the picture been electronically transmitted, it is conceivable that monochrome television might never have emerged as the first nationwide service.

But the use of the rotating disc in CBS's color persuaded most of the industry to continue the search for agreement on electronic monochrome standards, and it was soon thereafter achieved. Only Zenith among the major manufacturers voiced support for CBS color. For the others, too many years of struggle and too many dollars had gone into black and white to see its abandonment at the starting gate. Yet Goldmark refused to heed the industry majority. At his urging, CBS's management decided to seek immediate authorization from the FCC for standards aligned to CBS color.

To Sarnoff, it was still inconceivable that anyone could take the CBS challenge seriously. Addressing one of his regular staff meetings in the RCA boardroom, he said acceptance of CBS color "would set back the cause of our technology by a generation." Then, he added, his tone dark with foreboding: "The RCA will never allow this counterfeit scheme to be foisted on the American people." Silently, his penetrating glance locked with the eyes of each member of his staff, and there was a general nodding of heads. When "true" color came, he continued, it would come within the electronic scanning purview of Zworykin and Farnsworth, and it would be RCA color. Months earlier, in fact, RCA scientists had shown him at Camden a rudimentary laboratory mockup of an electronic color camera without moving parts. The primary colors were transmitted simultaneously, rather than sequentially, in the form of color dots or pulses. Even though the colors were unfaithful, the pictures formless and distorted, Sarnoff decided, against the advice of his scientists, to show their work to the FCC. The demonstration was held in Camden on February 12, 1940, eight months before Goldmark's NTSC unveiling. It was unimpressive, but that did not disturb Sarnoff. "I didn't want to sell the commission on color," he later explained. "I wanted to show that its possibilities were still a long way off. The pictures were terrible, but the principles for electronic transmission were sound. My scientists could make mechanical color as well as anyone. It didn't require any basic discoveries. It was the quick and easy way but it was wrong from the beginning, and I knew it." Even so, his strategy for staking an early RCA color claim later backfired. The primitive nature of the RCA effort became known throughout the industry, and when the rival CBS system emerged months later, the comparison between the two was unfavorable to RCA. Had the FCC been forced to a color choice in 1940, the CBS system would have won, almost by default.

However, the commission was little disposed to face up to color just as the grinding monochrome conflict was being resolved. In 1941, after viewing a Goldmark demonstration, the FCC ruled against commercial broadcasts of CBS color, holding that further field tests were necessary. So the determined Goldmark continued to pursue experimental colorcasts from the Chrysler Building tower transmitter. Even though CBS reported "nothing but enthusiasm" in response to its public demonstrations, the network was unable before Pearl Harbor to rally sufficient public support to persuade the FCC to reconsider. The war, of course, put all commercial television, monochrome or color, on hold.

* * *

In the midst of the ebb and flow of television battle, Sarnoff passed the half-century mark on February 27, 1941. Absorbed as he was in shuttling between his laboratories and executive suite, and in drawing up plans for RCA's participation in the grimmer conflict he saw ahead, Sarnoff paid little heed to the milestone. But later, in a more reflective time, he would describe the fiftieth year as the peak on life's parabola, the year in which the fusion of one's physical and intellectual capabilities permitted one to perform at maximum effectiveness. "By then," he said, "everything should have converged—experience, knowledge, a clear perspective on one's life goals, and sufficient stamina to achieve them. This was certainly true in my case." Then, with a grin, "If I could do it over again on my terms, I'd hold at fifty." To illustrate, he recalled a late afternoon staff meeting he scheduled soon after his fiftieth birthday to resolve a knotty problem concerning television. It proved quite intractable. Darkness fell. When he finally glanced at his watch, it was past midnight, but no one had mentioned it. "I wasn't fatigued," he explained. "Just hungry." The meeting was adjourned, with his younger associates exhausted.

Despite his formidable achievements at mid life, Sarnoff could not be considered a well-rounded man in the Medici sense. While he often promised himself, when the crises abated and his work load lightened, to plunge into literature and philosophy, to assimilate the master works of civilization, he never got around to it. Shakespeare was as remote to him as Babe Ruth's home run production. One of his speech writers, seeking to impart a poetic flair to his rallying of the electronic television forces for battle, drew on a Shakespearean couplet: "Cheerly to sea / The signs of war advance. No King of England / If not King of France." Sarnoff crossed it out of the speech draft, professing not to understand it.

Although not as one-dimensional as Henry Ford, who allegedly never saw a painting he liked, Sarnoff had little interest in, or understanding of, the visual arts. In a general sense, he recognized the depth and complexity of great works of art. But since he could not find the time to plumb those depths, he tended to avoid them. Once, on a rainy afternoon in Paris, when a meeting with French communications officials had been unexpectedly canceled, his wife and an aide suggested a tour of the Louvre. "Why?" he asked. "If you want to take a walk, let's wait 'til the weather clears." And he picked up the phone to call his New York office. Similarly, his threshold of boredom was low when talk veered to modern novels, or fashions, or the latest in parlor games. On one of his Atlantic crossings aboard the *Queen Elizabeth*, he was induced by Lizette to participate in a lotto contest in the main saloon. Within minutes he was softly snoring. Life had always been a serious business. It would not change.

Surely, it was never more serious than in the postwar era when the CBS color threat began to materialize in earnest. In 1946, at a time when Sarnoff and Folsom were tooling up monochrome production at the Camden and Lancaster plants, CBS renewed its color initiative. It requested permission of the FCC to demonstrate what it described as an improved color system, and it added a persuasive postscript to its plea for immediate commercial authorization. Let us take our chance in the marketplace, CBS said; let the people decide which system is superior, our color or NTSC monochrome. This had the ring of traditional free enterprise about it, and for the first time Sarnoff professed concern. To associates, he described CBS as the industry's succubus, seeking to seduce the public with an outmoded technology. But in the press and in government circles, a groundswell of support for the CBS position began to emerge, and Sarnoff realized he could no longer temporize. Through press conferences, speeches, and participation in industry forums, he at last began a public assault on the CBS system, which he contended was flawed by insurmountable technical limitations—small screen size, color fringing and degradation, and lack of capacity for effective mobile coverage. Even though he found himself in the unaccustomed role of appearing to block progress, he insisted that true color—electronic color—was at least five years away, and that its logical precursor was monochrome TV, which the public was already accepting with boundless enthusiasm.

Apart from the CBS technical limitations, Sarnoff maintained the system was fatally flawed for economic reasons. Since the spinning disc transmissions required different broadcast standards from those approved for NTSC monochrome, sets already in American homes would go blank if CBS color were broadcast. Thus the public would be shortchanged the millions of dollars already invested in monochrome sets. In Sarnoff's phrase, which soon became part of the American lexicon, CBS color was "incompatible," meaning that it was incapable of reception on existing sets in either color or monochrome—unless the owner purchased a converter and an adapter to attach to his set. On the other hand, RCA electronic color, when it was ready, would be compatible because its color transmissions would be on the same broadcast standards as those already approved, and could therefore be received in monochrome. Thus the sets already sold would retain their value until that point in the future when color sets were ready as replacements. The virtues of compatibility and the snares of incompatibility became a familiar Sarnoff theme as he sought to educate America on the technical semantics of the unfolding conflict.

CBS recognized its vulnerability on the incompatible aspect of its system. Every monochrome set that rolled off a production line into a home intensified the problem. It therefore became of paramount importance to Paley and Stanton to obtain quick FCC approval of their color so that manufacturers could switch to color production before a growing monochrome population engulfed them. In this race against time, the network's management, urged on by Goldmark and fortified by his assurance that the RCA color system would never achieve technical readiness, demonstrated a willingness to accept a high level of risk. The stakes were that great. Success could move them beyond the role of network broadcasters to television industry leadership, a challenger of RCA in its technical domain. The irrepressible Goldmark had not forgotten that one of his first job applications in America was at the RCA laboratories—and he had been turned down, apparently because there was nothing appropriate to his qualifications available at the time. Now the opportunity beckoned, in Goldmark's words, to cut down to size the "cocky" and "belligerent" Sarnoff.

To build up public support, CBS began running color demonstrations in a fifth-floor suite at 485 Madison Avenue, its New York headquarters. The guests included leading advertisers and their agency heads, plus leaders in business, finance, and government. "I found myself in show business," Goldmark wrote, "giving performances at two o'clock and four o'clock. I must admit I loved it. We handed out questionnaires to collect people's reaction and found nothing but enthusiasm."

With this "strong public mandate," as Goldmark described it, CBS decided in 1946 on another approach to the FCC, which was headed by a new chairman, Charles Denny, a young Harvard-trained lawyer who had risen rapidly through New Deal ranks. To demonstrate color's networking capability, a demonstration was arranged at the Tappan Zee Inn at Nyack, New York, overlooking the Hudson River, a distance of forty miles from the color transmitter at the Chrysler Building. In the show itself, Goldmark employed all his demonstration wiles on the personable Denny.

"I gave the necessary introduction," Goldmark later wrote, "threw the switch, silently prayed a bit in Hungarian, and waited.

"In an instant starlet Patty Painter, our nineteen-year-old heroine from Beckley, West Virginia, filled the tube. Her skin glowed a natural flesh pink, her long auburn-blond hair glistened, and the piquant smile and dancing blue eyes drew appreciative smiles from all of us.

"Denny sat mesmerized. After a few moments he turned to me. 'I wish I could ask her how she feels,' he said with a smile.

"I turned toward him. 'Why don't you?' I said.

"Denny looked surprised. I must admit I had anticipated the possibility of such a request, and I quickly stepped to the phone and called the studio. As Denny watched, an engineer appeared on the screen with a handset and gave it to Patty. He asked her about the lighting.

" 'It's warm but not bad,' she said in a clear and charming voice.

"Denny's face lit up. He said something in reply on how wonderful she looked. The rest of the show went on and was soon over. Everyone looked pleased as they filed out of the suite. I thought we were in."

But they were still not in, and there was consternation at CBS headquarters when the commission held, on January 30, 1947, that its color system still required further field-testing before commercial standards could be adopted. In effect, the commission heeded Sarnoff's plea for additional time to perfect electronic color. The existing monochrome standards were reaffirmed, and sets whose screens would go blank if CBS color were broadcast continued to flood across America.

CBS immediately suspected skulduggery at the FCC. "We felt we had been dealt a foul blow," Goldmark later wrote. "Everybody in the CBS camp noted cynically that six months later Denny accepted a post as vice-president of NBC, which is wholly owned by RCA. . . . A subsequent Congressional investigation of the affair resulted in an amendment to the Communications Act, prohibiting a commissioner from representing a company before the commission for a year after resigning from the FCC."

Goldmark would still not accept defeat. "I couldn't forget color TV," he wrote. "It was a burr in my soul." With Smith, Klein and French laboratories, he arranged a series of medical television demonstrations, culminating in the color televising of an operation at the annual convention of the American Medical Association in December 1949. It drew enormous press attention, including a color spread in *Life* magazine.

Denny's defection to the enemy camp, despite CBS's anger, proved, in one sense, to be of incalculable value to the junior network. As Denny's successor, President Truman appointed Wayne Coy, an executive of the Washington Post Company, which owned broadcast properties affiliated with CBS. As the commission's chairman, Coy began to give Goldmark everything he had hoped for in Denny, and more. From the moment he first witnessed a CBS color demonstration to the commission in Washington, Coy became almost as zealous a supporter of the rotating disc system as the inventor himself. In Goldmark's words, the reaction of the new chairman to the demonstration was "fantastic." Casting aside all semblance of impartiality, the traditional stance of heads of federal regulatory agencies, Coy began lobbying within the commission and among influential legislators for CBS color. One of his first converts was the powerful head of the Senate Commerce Committee, Senator Edwin Johnson of Colorado, who had oversight responsibility for broadcasting. Like the most devoted of acolytes, Coy and Johnson argued the CBS case behind the scenes in Washington, as well as in public forums and regulatory debates.

Caught in this powerful lobbying vise, Sarnoff uneasily sensed that the conflict could turn quickly. He was in daily telephone communications with the chief Washington lobbyist of NBC, Frank Russell. A former newspaperman whose nickname was "Scoop," Russell had for many years tirelessly cultivated Washington's power base with gifts ranging from radios and television sets to weekend vacations. His informational pipelines extended to such powerful senators as Lyndon Johnson and to members of the FCC inner staff. Few lobbyists were more privy to Washington developments, and Sarnoff took seriously Russell's warnings that Coy's spadework on behalf of CBS was beginning to take root. Thus he was little surprised when the FCC voted to hold an immediate demonstration of the rival color systems as a prelude to setting commercial standards. Publicly, Sarnoff welcomed the showdown. Privately, he knew he was faced with a no-win situation. His electronic apparatus was still too primitive to deliver a color picture of comparable quality to CBS's in a demonstration face-off. And the Washington tests in September 1950 proved him correct. The RCA picture was a disaster. "The monkeys were green, the bananas were blue, and everybody had a good laugh," Sarnoff afterward admitted ruefully. Publicly, RCA blamed a faulty coaxial cable link between the transmitter and its demonstration sets. Privately, Sarnoff admitted to being embarrassed and a little annoyed at his scientists, but still undeterred. The headline in *Variety* said it concisely: RCA LAYS COLORED EGG. The press generally reacted favorably to the CBS system and echoed Goldmark's doubts that RCA could ever bring its color to acceptable commercial levels. *Newsweek* magazine, for example, said the RCA color changed shades "like a crazed van Gogh."

Even though the Radio and Television Manufacturers Association warned the FCC to go slow in adopting a technology that might soon be outmoded, the commission majority appeared dazzled by the quality of CBS color and swayed by the partisanship of Chairman Coy. By a 5–3 vote, the FCC approved CBS color in 1951. It became America's only authorized color system, free to begin commercial broadcasting at once, free to compete in the marketplace with a black-and-white service then in its fourth year of explosive growth.

Sarnoff was called at home by Russell with advance word of the FCC decision. He was angered but not surprised. After brooding briefly in his study, he talked with Folsom, Engstrom, Jolliffe, and other senior staff members. The decision was quickly reached to challenge the FCC by every means at RCA's disposal. "No one questioned that we had to hit back," he later recalled. "The only question was how to do it best." As a first step, Sarnoff issued a scathing public statement describing the commission's decision as "scientifically unsound and against the public interest." By that time, eight million black-and-white sets had been sold. Unless the owners paid an additional $50–$100 for a converter and adapter to be attached to the set— "a slave set" Sarnoff called it—CBS colorcasts could not be received. "The hundreds of millions of dollars the present set owners would have to pay to obtain a degraded color picture," he announced, "reduces today's order to an absurdity." He pledged that RCA would not manufacture color sets aligned to the approved CBS standards, nor would it provide converters and adapters for existing monochrome sets. He ordered an intensification of manufacturing and marketing efforts in black and white. "Every set we get out there makes it that much tougher on CBS," he said. At a special meeting of the board of directors, Sarnoff set forth his plan of counterattack. He received the board's endorsement, as he knew he would. In prior actions, the board had approved more than $20 million for color development and field-testing expenditures. It could hardly turn its back on an investment of that magnitude now, any more than Sarnoff could. That would have been tantamount to confessing a massive error in business judgment, perhaps opening the door to shareholder suits charging waste of corporate assets. Beyond his board's support, Sarnoff's position was also strengthened by the announcement of other major manufacturers that they would not build color sets, converters, or adapters for the CBS system. At stake was a flourishing monochrome business which they were terrified of losing. Not even Zenith, despite McDonald's prior support, would make the shift to incompatible color.

Within the company, Sarnoff credited CBS's victory to superior public relations, particularly on the Washington lobbying front, and to the distorted testimony of its technical witnesses. His ire focused primarily on Goldmark, "that scientific charlatan," who had told the FCC that in his professional judgment the RCA system would never emerge from the laboratory. RCA's response would be an all-out military-style counterattack. His eyes flashing with cobalt-blue intensity, Sarnoff assured his associates that "we've lost a battle, not the war."

As a first counterattack step, he mobilized the Princeton laboratories for a crash color development program. Shifts would be increased to sixteen hours daily, continuing through the weekends. No expense would be spared for personnel and equipment, and projects unrelated to color would be temporarily shelved. Bonuses in the thousands of dollars would be paid for significant technological breakthroughs. He was determined to get yellow bananas of perfect fidelity, and not years hence, for now he was battling time as much as CBS. As his proconsul for color, he designated Elmer W. Engstrom, then the corporation's vice-president in charge of research. A devout Christian layman, an admirer of Billy Graham, Engstrom possessed the unruffled type of scientific temperament that effectively interposed between the fiery importunings of his chief and the sensitivities of the research staff. Later, he would describe the crash color program as the most intense, and exhilarating, experience of his career.

To steam up his technical troops, Sarnoff circulated an extract of testimony by Goldmark before the FCC in which he argued against further field tests of the RCA system because "I don't think the field tests will improve the system fundamentally." In the CBS scientist's view, "nothing" could be done to alter that fact. Asked by a commissioner if he advocated that RCA "drop the system now," Goldmark responded: "I certainly do."

To the extract, Sarnoff attached a note that he had personally written: "The above is the most unprofessional and ruthless statement I have ever seen made by anyone publicly about a competitor. I have every confidence that the scientists and engineers of the RCA will answer this baseless charge by the improvements which I have already seen since the first demonstration and which will be made during the coming months."

Then Sarnoff moved on the legal front with a suit filed in U.S. District Court in Chicago to "enjoin, set aside, annul and suspend," the FCC order because it "contravened" the opinions of the industry's most expert technical witnesses and threatened the destruction of a monochrome television industry in which the public had already invested $2 billion.

Next he moved on the propaganda front by hiring the public relations firm of Carl Byoir and Associates, one of America's largest, to alert the nation to the perils of Goldmark and incompatibility. From a relatively simple start, when Ivy Lee persuaded John D. Rockefeller to soften his image by giving away dimes to the public, public relations had just emerged on the national scene in a major way, and Sarnoff was far from alone in enlisting its practitioners. CBS, for example, retained the Earl Newsome firm.

This represented no sudden change of course by Sarnoff, for he had been an early convert to the importance of the art of mass persuasion. Even though he projected himself as the blunt, forthright leader of an industry—the no-nonsense approach—he was among the first to recognize the subtleties involved in the manipulation of public opinion. Years before the color battle, he had hired Edward Bernays, one of the deans of the public relations profession, to spruce up the image of NBC's management. In addition to Byoir, he also retained Herbert Bayard Swope to counsel him on burnishing RCA's image. He also beefed up RCA's internal public relations staff, and he persuaded the Radio and Television Manufacturers Association to raise $1 million for an "educational campaign" for electronic color. (A "slush fund," Stanton called it.) "They [CBS] stole the press. We've got to steal it back," was Sarnoff's charge to his flack brigade.

For several years, the RCA leader had become increasingly disturbed by what he perceived to be a growing bias against RCA and him in the press. In his early career, while he was often berated as a monopolist by competitors, the press had generally fawned upon him. His print profile was that of the scrappy, fearless ghetto graduate who had challenged the goliaths of industry, as in the network struggle, and had emerged victorious. But now color had brought a reversal in roles. RCA and Sarnoff were the goliaths in the eyes of some in the press, seeking to humble a smaller, less richly endowed competitor whose charismatic leaders—the urbane Paley, the statesmanlike Stanton, and the scientific "genius," Goldmark—refused to bow under. Beginning with demonstrations of CBS color in 1946, stories of its superior quality flooded the nation's news columns to a degree that Sarnoff found unbelievable. The press seemed dazzled by it. The *New York Times* considered CBS color images "superior to the technicolor seen in the movies. The hues are softer and more restful . . . A few looks at [CBS] color television and black and white seems drab indeed." The New York *World-Telegram* columnist Harriet Van Horne wrote on February 4, 1946, that the color system developed by the "brilliant young physicist named Dr. Peter Goldmark" was "nothing short of a miracle." The color image was "beautiful beyond description . . . a magic casement, and the vistas it will open should have a profound effect on every phase of the entertainment and advertising business, not to mention the arts, letters and sciences." To the *Wall Street Journal,* CBS "left little doubt that color television has reached the perfection of black and white . . . the color contrasts as good as those of the best moving pictures."

Time magazine provided the ultimate affront. Not only did it rhapsodize over CBS color quality, "as vivid as a van Gogh painting, made black and white television look antiquated," but it bestowed upon Goldmark the laurel wreath of "inventor of color television." Sarnoff read the article just before lunch and he told an associate he had a hard time getting down one of his favorite boiled potatoes. Frankly, he was mystified why he and his public relations people couldn't get across to the press the fatal flaw of incompatibility. Why couldn't reporters grasp the supreme importance of cleansing electronic technology of mechanical impedimenta? Why couldn't they look beyond the picture on the tube? Since, in his mind, his position was unassailable, the only answer must be prejudice in the press against him and his company. That ancient refrain of his childhood began to throb again. Those who opposed him were enemies, and the only valid reason for their enmity had to be his racial antecedents.

A year before the FCC's decision favoring CBS, Sarnoff, perhaps anticipating the need for help in the struggles that lay ahead, had moved Frank Folsom from Camden to New York and made him president of RCA. The way had been cleared by the death of General Harbord in 1947, after which Sarnoff had assumed the title of chairman of the board. Folsom was widely credited with effective stewardship in the monochrome launch, and now he was at Sarnoff's right hand, the junior partner in the color war.

As one of his first steps, the new RCA president summoned the Byoir public relations staff to his fifty-third-floor office, which adjoined the chairman's. He told his secretary, Rita Murray, to hold all calls. For thirty minutes, Folsom briefed the five Byoir men seated in front of his desk on the history and dimensions of the color conflict. It was, he assured them, the most fateful industrial conflict in American history. The future of electronics technology hung in the balance. If the forces of mechanical color triumphed, the march of science would be subverted by the horse and buggy. America's leadership of free world technology would be weakened. Stalin would love it. To one of the impressionable young Byoir staffers, a mental picture formed of dark and deserted scientific laboratories dotting the nation, grass growing in their streets.

Finally, Folsom came to his peroration. The most critical element in the next phase of this epochal struggle would be public relations. The Byoir staffers would be the point men in this assault on the forces of regression, and the battleground would be the nation's press. "You've got to change this bias against RCA and Sarnoff in the press," Folsom said. "CBS has created a lot of sympathy for itself as the underdog, fighting all us big guys in the industry. It's a lot of crap, but so far they've succeeded. They've made Sarnoff out to be powerful and arrogant and a sore loser. They've played up to people in the press who don't like him because he's been successful so much, and he's had to step on some toes to achieve it." Then—and here Folsom paused dramatically—"there are some people who don't seem to like the idea of a Jew having as much power and authority as he has."

Folsom offered nothing specific to back up his charges. He made vague allusions to some *Time* writers and editors giving vent to their latent anti-Semitism by disparaging Sarnoff's color system. The fact that two of the CBS principals in the color war, Paley and Goldmark, were also Jewish drew no mention from Folsom. It became obvious to the Byoir people that the new RCA president was simply parroting the dark, but uncorroborated, suspicions of his boss. Yet they wondered, as they left the meeting, whether RCA's unnamed foes in the press had more sinister intent than the mere endorsement of CBS color.

Unquestionably, racial bias had been a hurtful reality of Sarnoff's life, magnified by his extreme personal sensitivity and his boundless pride. As a schoolboy, he had stalked out of a class when he felt his teacher's depiction of Shylock in *The Merchant of Venice* cast a slur on all Jews. As a rising executive in the radio combine, he had overheard racial epithets whispered at him by jealous junior executives of GE and Westinghouse. The mere fact of his giddying ascent in a Christian-dominated communications technology, the first immigrant Jew to scale its pinnacle, tended to dramatize the difference between him and others in his profession. Executives who deferentially accepted his orders at work spent their evenings and weekends at clubs from which he was barred.

Success did not diminish his suspicions. He was convinced that Zenith's leader, McDonald, was anti-Semitic. When McDonald accused him of employing "Russian tricks" in their television rivalry, Sarnoff insisted that this was simply a code word for "Jewish tricks." When Lester Bernstein, a young *Time* magazine editor, was hired by NBC as a public relations executive, Sarnoff probed him intently about the existence of anti-Semitism among his fellow editors. "I assured him I had never experienced any personally," Bernstein said, "and I didn't believe it existed. He had a hard time accepting that criticism of him in the news columns did not stem from bias, and I'm not sure I changed his mind." In his authorized biography, Sarnoff recalled buying a horse and stabling it in a Central Park riding club so that he could join his then boss, General Harbord, an old cavalry man, in occasional morning rides. When Harbord suggested he would like to sponsor him for membership in the club, Sarnoff responded: "General, my horse can belong to that club, but I can't. It's restricted."

The cumulative effect of these slights, fancied or otherwise, was the conviction, which hardened as the years passed, that all opposition to his goals and aspirations welled from bias. "It's been a fact of my life," he confided to an associate one day at lunch in 1966, when his career neared its end. "It existed when I was a boy. It didn't end with Hitler. It exists today." Only those closest to him could detect that, underlying his dominating, assured presence, a sense of separateness, perhaps insecurity, still lingered. Acceptance in America could not totally obliterate his memories of czarist Russia and the East Side ghetto, and this manifested itself in a number of ways as he aged: through revived studies, seventy years later, of the prophets and the Torah; through intensification of his relationship with his Jewish friends; through his prideful refusal to accept awards at, or speak at, organizations or clubs with exclusionary policies. His concerns, while understandable, were ironic, for to a unique degree the drama and acclaim that surrounded Sarnoff's life stemmed from the stark contrast with his impoverished immigrant origin. While some anti-Semitism did indeed exist in the upper tiers of American industry in his era, as exemplified by Henry Ford and others, there were eminent leaders of American business and finance, like Young and Harbord, Morgan, Lamont and Eberstadt, and two generations of Rockefellers, who formed a cheering section for the young immigrant and were part of his success. Sarnoff recognized this, but the suspicions were woven too deeply into the fabric of his character to be washed away—as Folsom's remarks in the color war illustrated.

On an almost daily basis in 1950, the CBS-RCA conflict escalated in print and over the airwaves. Its weapons were jargon: "horse and buggy" spinning discs and "slave sets" versus the compatible technology of the future; a "mechanical harness" saddled to an electronic art; "degraded" mechanical pictures versus the real-life fidelity of large-screen electronically generated hues. Most manufacturers announced they would continue black-and-white set production and would not produce adapters and converters for CBS color—"Rube Goldberg contraptions," they called them. FCC Chairman Coy and Sarnoff accused each other in print of lying about the commission's willingness to examine further refinements in RCA color.

Dr. Stanton, the flaxen-haired research expert who was by now CBS's president and Paley's right-hand man, went on the CBS radio network on October 15, 1950, to accuse the RTMA manufacturers of "belligerent and misleading" statements. "Some manufacturers have said that the CBS system is degraded, that it is a mechanical system, that its picture size is limited.

These criticisms are not true." Stanton insisted that "present sets can be adapted at reasonable cost; compatibility can be built into all future sets at a lower cost." Then, echoing Goldmark and Coy, he emphasized that the FCC had "concluded that it is improbable that a system can be developed which would be satisfactory in color performance and at the same time be compatible." He pledged that "in less than two months we will be broadcasting twenty hours of color programs each week." A week later, in another sling at the manufacturers, the CBS president said, "We question whether the RTMA really wants compatibility. We suggest that what it really wants is to hold back color, and that it is preserving the issue of compatibility only to achieve that delay."

The net effect of this barrage of technical charges and countercharges was to create a fog of confusion in the public mind over color. Did Sarnoff really have a workable system? Could CBS get incompatible color sets on the market quickly? Should the family hold off purchasing a black-and-white set, as CBS protagonists were suggesting; or should they buy one immediately and then wait for electronic color, as other manufacturers urged? Congress seemed to share in the confusion and calls for hearings to reexamine the color problem began echoing through the capital.

The efforts of both sides to influence official Washington took on almost ludicrous cloak-and-dagger overtones. As described by Goldmark, he and his associates attempted to shroud their meetings at the capital in total secrecy. "To conceal our relations with Washington," he said, "we never took the Pennsylvania Railroad from New York because the press and RCA spies might wonder why. Instead, we took a circuitous route over the Baltimore and Ohio. When we arrived in the capital, we registered incognito in a small hotel and held meetings with various influential senators. I might add that these undercover precautions made little difference. The next day we read about our meetings in the paper." Similarly, RCA agents led by the ubiquitous Scoop Russell were busily at work patrolling the halls of the nation's capital, buttonholing legislators they thought might have influence with the FCC.

The Chicago District Court first granted a temporary injunction against CBS color, but then refused to block the FCC ruling. So Sarnoff appealed to the U.S. Supreme Court in March 1951. Within three months, the High Court affirmed the FCC's action as a proper exercise of regulatory authority, although it did not pass judgment on the relative merit of the two systems. Only Justice Felix Frankfurter questioned the wisdom of the FCC action in a separate dubitante, or expression of doubt. He had been a friend of Sarnoff's for many years, introduced to him by Baruch, and during his tenure as a visiting professor at Oxford before his court appointment, the two men frequently corresponded on the implications of wireless technology in modern life and the need for progress through obsolescence. Perhaps this stimulated Frankfurter's doubts about approving a previously discarded body of technology, but he was not able to persuade his fellow justices. The last legal restraint on CBS color was thus removed. The victory seemed final, and Goldmark exulted: "We had taken on the great Sarnoff, the king of Radio City, and we won."

Yet it was a victory still not sealed, because not even the nation's highest tribunal could force manufacturing conformity on the industry. "The Supreme Court can't order me to make color sets for CBS," Sarnoff commented grimly, and he didn't. Nor did other manufacturers, whose production lines were loaded with monochrome merchandise. Faced with this tacit boycott, CBS's management decided on a series of bold expansionist steps that would carry the network far beyond broadcasting. First, it determined to manufacture its own color sets and color converters and adapters for monochrome sets. In exchange for shares of CBS stock then valued at $18 million, the network purchased the Hytron Radio and Electronics Corporation, the fourth largest maker of TV tubes, and its wholly owned subsidiary, Air King, one of the fifteen largest set manufacturers. The Coffin brothers, owners of Hytron, joined the CBS Board of Directors. A manufacturing subsidiary, CBS Columbia, was established; a license to manufacture semiconductor devices was obtained at substantial cost from Philco; plans were drawn up for the nationwide marketing of CBS brand-name sets; and the network's leading stars, like Arthur Godfrey, were enlisted as spokesmen for CBS color.

The junior broadcasting organization thus geared up to move with giant RCA pari passu, or so it appeared. But far from appearing concerned, Sarnoff told associates he welcomed the broad scope of the CBS challenge. From long experience he knew the cost in time and resources of building an effective national distribution system for a new consumer product. The complex processes involved in the manufacture of a color set would tax the know-how of the most experienced companies in the business, even RCA. New production line techniques would have to be invented. Sarnoff saw CBS stepping into an electronic quagmire, and he felt this might make it easier for RCA to regain the initiative in color.

Even though the last legal avenue had closed, RCA still possessed the FCC-granted authority to field-test color developments, and this was the principal means Sarnoff chose to mount his counterattack. He would schedule a series of carefully spaced demonstrations in New York for press and opinion leaders, billing them as progress reports on compatible color.

But first he had to have progress to report, and that hinged on the massive scientific effort under way at the Princeton laboratories, where all color research had been concentrated. Sarnoff was there frequently, prodding, encouraging, demanding. While he was not part of the creative process, his presence had extraordinary impact on the technical staff. "It wasn't the normal boss-employee relationship," Charles Jolliffe later recalled. "It was as if Sarnoff became one of the group, he acted that way. He was probing all the time. It was a way of working with a top man you don't usually experience." Merril Trainer was a junior engineer when he was first exposed to the Sarnoff hands-on style. "He would stand under those terrifically hot lights, perspiration pouring from him, and say, 'Boys, it's remarkable what you've accomplished.' Sometimes we had and sometimes we hadn't, but you have no idea what that did for our morale; for somebody of his importance to come down and suffer that torture just to see for himself really impressed us."

Later, Engstrom would tell a Washington hearing that hundreds of scientists and engineers were involved in the effort, specialists in electron tube design, in broadcasting, in receiving sets, in fluorescent materials and electron guns. Behind them all, according to Engstrom, was the drive and determination of Sarnoff. "He saw what was needed and, applying wartime techniques, directed us at forced draft." Such tactics, Engstrom admitted, "are not always productive of speed in achievement when applied to creative effort dependent on new knowledge and new scientific principles." But Sarnoff, he said, "taught us the word impossible had no place in our vocabulary."

Out of this forced draft, which was perhaps unique in industrial annals ("invention on demand," one engineer called it), emerged a new version of a high-definition tricolor tube. Six months of round the clock effort had gone into its development, and it provided the breakthrough Sarnoff had been seeking. The tube possessed three electron guns that bombarded and excited hundreds of thousands of tiny phosphors of the three primary colors etched on the viewing screen. Through the addition of an ingenious shadow-mask screening device, van Gogh's brush was steadied. Excellent color was achieved and Sarnoff exulted: "The mechanical scanning disc now belongs to the ages."

When first demonstrated in NBC's Washington studios and then at the RCA Exhibition Hall in New York, the new tube proved conclusively that monkeys and bananas and pretty girls could indeed be faithfully portrayed in electronic color. Actress Nanette Fabray pirouetted and sang show tunes, and the color registry never wavered. More than two hundred reporters witnessed the New York demonstration in July 1951, and most did an abrupt reversal from their earlier negative evaluations. "Much improved," commented the *Wall Street Journal;* "No one could ask for better color," said *Broadcasting Magazine;* "All electronic color is now an actuality," said the Baltimore *News Post.* Jack Gould, radio-television editor of the *New York Times,* wrote that the success of the demonstration "changes the whole outlook on the dispute over video in natural hues." Beyond being a feather in Sarnoff's cap, he said, it put the FCC "on a spot which is certain to become controversial and embarrassing. Technically, it ultimately may be proved that the FCC committed a classic 'boner.' "

Because of the additional information transmitted by the color camera, the picture received on black-and-white sets was adjudged by the press to be of even better definition than in standard commercial telecasts. Some eight thousand viewers in the metropolitan area who saw the test on monochrome receivers wrote RCA to praise its quality.

The first demonstration of the new tricolor tube followed closely the official premiere, on June 25, 1951, of the FCC-approved CBS system. Sarnoff timed it that way in order to achieve dramatic contrast between the compatible and incompatible systems. The first hour-long CBS color telecast featured Chairman Coy praising the CBS leaders in "this hour of triumph" for their vision and faith in fighting "the long uphill battle" to secure adoption of "the only system authorized." Senator Edwin Johnson telegraphed his congratulations "on this historic day in the progress of man." But while small studio parties witnessed the colorcast in Washington, Baltimore, Boston, and Philadelphia, the public could not. Any of the twelve million monochrome-set owners tuned to the CBS channel stared at a blank screen. This was incompatibility. In Sarnoff's caustic phrase, it was the premiere of horse-and-buggy era mechanical color. Had it been telecast in compatible color by RCA, he pointed out, every set owner in the nation could have joined the party in black and white.

In October 1951, as CBS struggled to exploit its FCC-mandated victory, another war intruded on America. With little warning, troops of Communist North Korea swarmed across the Thirty-eighth Parallel in an effort to engulf the southern half of that divided nation. President Truman rallied America and the United Nations behind South Korea. A massive military buildup began, and the nation found itself on a partial war footing, only six years after the end of the last world conflict.

In Sarnoff's view, Truman's action was indisputably correct. Stern measures were required to thwart Russia's ruthless domino strategy in the Far East. "If Korea falls, they'll be knocking on the door of the Philippines. The time to stop them is now," Sarnoff said. Quickly, he wired Truman pledging full support by RCA, and he ordered the company's operating heads to be prepared for a quick shift to military production. He had not the slightest doubt that America's military forces, supported by their UN partners, would achieve quick unification of Korea under democratic rule. Like most Americans, he did not foresee the stalemated conclusion of that remote war—nor did he foresee that the Korean war would lead to a swift conclusion of the first phase of the color television war.

The reason Korea impinged on color was that materials deemed critical to the war effort were involved in the production of color sets. Truman's newly appointed defense mobilizer, Charles E. Wilson, former head of General Electric, placed color phosphors in this category, and he therefore requested CBS to halt set production. At the time, only a few hundred hand-tooled sets had trickled into homes, and CBS promptly complied. It also did not build its schedule of color broadcasts as Stanton had promised. In effect, CBS color went on hold for the duration of the conflict. In the view of the *New York Times,* this was a "decided break" for RCA since, for "an indefinite period," it could continue to perfect its color system without losing further ground.

In Sarnoff's view, the reverse was true. He told his staff that Wilson's order in reality might save CBS from debilitating financial losses for years ahead. He contended that CBS was just beginning to incur the heavy start-up costs involved in any new product cycle. He derided their ability to manufacture quality color sets, and he insisted that no one in the industry, not even Zenith, was about to come to their rescue. Long after the issue had been settled, Sarnoff recalled that his initial evaluation had been correct. "Look at how bad they turned out to be in manufacturing. They produced second-rate stuff, and Paley knew it. He'd have known it a lot sooner except for Charley Wilson's order."

However, in a different sense than the *Times* suggested, Korea did provide Sarnoff with a decided break. No critical materials were involved in black-and-white production. While RCA's defense business increased substantially, the company was not required to convert its plants to total war production, as it had a decade earlier. Thus it continued to turn out monochrome sets up to its productive capacity, and so did other manufacturers. As the Korean conflict neared its stalemated conclusion in 1952, with that nation still bifurcated, an additional six million sets that could not receive CBS color were in the marketplace. As CBS's principal spokesman for color, Stanton continued to make determined statements about developmental work on improved tubes and adapters. But the perception was spreading throughout the industry and its trade press that the network's color stance was increasingly untenable. The lack of compatibility with the now huge black-and-white set population loomed as an almost insurmountable barrier for CBS color. No one recognized the CBS dilemma more acutely than Sarnoff, and he was not above baiting his rival. When the National Production Authority called hearings in 1952 to consider revocation of the color production ban, Sarnoff implied that CBS and Stanton were duplicitous, that they wanted the ban continued because it took them "off the hook" with a product of dubious salability. Stanton lashed back that Sarnoff was "abusing the processes" of the government defense program in order to "carry on his bitter and desperate campaign to frustrate color." He meant, probably, that the RCA leader was enjoying seeing CBS twist and turn in the wind, and Sarnoff didn't deny it.

The lifting of the ban confirmed that CBS was having serious second thoughts about color. The network made no discernible effort to recapture its color momentum, as it had after the end of World War II. Conversely, with Sarnoff's concurrence, the National Television Standards Committee was reconstituted, with Dr. Baker of GE again at its head and with RCA, represented by Engstrom, as its most influential member. After further demonstrations in August 1952, the press reported that superb results were being obtained, with the NTSC technicians registering important advances in both transmission and reception. To Sarnoff, the committee was enacting a charade, but he was willing to play along since he recognized the political advantages of an industry system—a "face-saving" device for the FCC, he privately called it. Within the company and among friends he assured all that it was the RCA system coated with an industry veneer, a repetition of the black-and-white experience.

On March 26, 1953, just two years after FCC approval of CBS color, a *Times* page one headline read: CBS JETTISONS MONOPOLY ON COLOR VIDEO PRODUCTION. Testifying before a House committee investigating the status of color, Stanton signaled the surrender of the incompatible system. By then, 23 million black-and-white sets were in American homes and this, he admitted, made it "economically foolish" to broadcast color programs that could not be received in either color or black and white.

"I do not think that the problem of incompatibility is necessarily fatal," he testified, "but I do think [it] has now grown to such proportions that, in combination with other factors, it becomes quixotic and economically foolish for us single-handedly at this time to resume a large scale broadcasting and manufacturing program."

CBS's capitulation left the FCC with no choice but to reconsider color standards. The commission found itself under heavy pressure from every quarter—government, press, the industry, the public (through irate letters)—to adopt the system that the Baker committee and RCA continued to demonstrate. Representative Charles A. Wolverton, chairman of the House Interstate and Foreign Commerce Committee, witnessed a demonstration at Princeton as Sarnoff's guest and professed himself to be "astounded" by the color quality. "The public should have its benefits immediately," he said. Even CBS joined the industry committee in field-testing the system it had predicted would never emerge from the laboratory.

On December 17, 1953, the FCC voted to reverse itself and accept the NTSC standards patterned after those proposed years earlier by RCA. It was a total reversal, unprecedented in regulatory annals, and Coy, as much as Goldmark, wore the goat horns of miscalculation. The reversal was made to seem particularly odious by the press, which conveniently forgot its prior adoration of CBS color. Editorialists flayed the FCC. A group of nontechnical, politically appointed commissioners had, in the collective judgment of the press, resisted for years the best technical advice of the industry it regulated. "The history of television is a history of official procrastination," the *New York Times* summed up, "a history that brings out the danger in bureaucratic rule."

Behind the CBS decision to withdraw was the growing disillusionment of its founder and chief executive officer. For months Paley had remained backstage while Stanton and Goldmark were fighting the public battle, watching with growing unease the millions of dollars being poured into color, the flood of black-and-white sets flowing across America, and the unsuccessful effort to turn out competitive, top-quality electronic products by his subsidiaries, Hytron and Air King—"a persistent headache," Paley complained in a rather stinging memorandum to Stanton. As recounted in Paley's memoirs, Goldmark in particular was becoming a "thorn in my side," promising among other things a resolution of the CBS compatibility problem that he never achieved.

The conflict between the two CBS executives came to a head in March 1955, two years after Stanton's announcement of withdrawal. Goldmark, who was nothing if not persistent, had continued to expend corporate research funds in the development of a new color camera that could be used with the approved NTSC-RCA system. Known as the Chromacoder, the camera could, Goldmark insisted, deliver superior quality color, and he importuned CBS's management to stay in the color race by manufacturing it. Finally, Paley rented a small Manhattan theater and ordered a side-by-side comparative demonstration of the RCA and CBS color cameras. Twelve executives attended the command performance, including Goldmark, who watched silently, according to Paley, while "beads of perspiration dribbled down his face."

"We observed a CBS live audition on two television receivers set upon the stage," Paley wrote. "We watched in tense silence for fifteen minutes. When the program ended, there was a deadly pause before anyone would venture an opinion. I knew exactly what I thought. I stood up and said, 'Gentlemen, I'll be glad to speak first. I think the RCA camera has us beat. It has better quality.' I looked around and saw a general nodding of heads. No one spoke. So I walked out and that was the end . . ."

The ramifications of CBS's doomed color venture were many. When the network was seeking to leapfrog black and white with color in 1946, it did not apply for four additional station licenses (to which it was entitled by FCC allocation) under the existing monochrome standards—a gesture to show its faith in color. It had also advised its affiliates against applying for monochrome licenses. The purchase of stations in four major markets later in the 1950s cost CBS $30 million. This was in addition to the millions spent in color research and the excessive price in CBS stock paid to acquire manufacturing facilities that never turned out competitive products and which were ultimately jettisoned through a write-off. Collectively, it added up to the biggest business mistake of Paley's career.

The years spent attempting to challenge Sarnoff in his own backyard of technology cost CBS more than $60 million—an expensive lesson for what was rapidly becoming the world's most successful broadcast organization.

As set forth in his biography, the only solace the CBS founder could realize from this exercise in "poor judgment" was that CBS had goaded Sarnoff into a crash program that Paley insisted brought America color television earlier than it would normally have arrived.

In Sarnoff's judgment, CBS failed in color because its executives and its principal scientist, Dr. Goldmark, failed to grasp the essential role of the electron in modern technology. Had they understood the lesson of the twenties, when experimenters discarded the mechanical spinning disc as "a crude and impractical device for monochrome television," they would never have attempted to impose the same theory of transmission and reception on color. Goldmark's system, he insisted, was merely an alluring expedient. "It gave laboratory technicians something to play with, while the tricolor tube was being perfected." Years later at a staff luncheon, Sarnoff harked back to the color struggle: "They [CBS] were seduced by a spurious technology. Mechanical parts and electronics won't mix. They're like oil and water. I warned Bill but he wouldn't listen."

Goldmark, of course, never reconciled himself to that view. Until his death in an automobile crash on a Westchester, New York, highway nearly twenty years later, he continued to insist that his color system could have become the world standard had the Denny-led FCC approved it in 1947, before the monochrome flood crested. The CBS system did, in fact, find certain later applications, such as in space satellite color transmissions, where the small size and relative simplicity of the camera was an advantage and the lack of compatibility with broadcast standards not a factor. But the scientific and industrial worlds never accepted the Goldmark rationale, and properly so. Had America early on embraced CBS color, Sarnoff would not have been deterred in his pursuit of an electronic substitute. Those who knew him well were certain that would have been contrary to his nature. He was too prideful, too stubborn, too intransigent in his perception of the right path for electronics, to admit defeat. Even *Time* magazine came to concede "driving through obstacles is his habit, his joy, his bitter necessity." Sooner or later, whether a year or a decade, the tricolor tube would have emerged, with all its manifest advantages. Then the probable dislocations— the shift of broadcast standards, the obsolescence of transmitting and receiving apparatus—would have been incalculably more costly, in time and money, than in color's all-electronic gestation, difficult as that would prove to be.

Nearly three decades after the FCC decision, at a 1981 lunch in his dining room at CBS headquarters in New York, Paley recalled for an RCA executive of the Sarnoff era the trauma of CBS's color withdrawal. By then his old rival had been dead ten years, but their strangely close relationship had never ruptured over color. They were friends until the end. The color inventions of RCA had been licensed from Japan to Germany, forming the technical interstices of a global color television industry. Paley himself was a silver-haired octogenarian, universally recognized as the preeminent broadcaster in America, but his memories of the color struggle were still acute. How did he appraise Sarnoff's role?

"The way he refused to accept defeat . . . the way he kept coming back to Washington and rallying his people . . . the way he drove those scientists to perfect his system. No doubt about it, he was magnificent in color."

As much as the FCC was faulted for poor judgment, Sarnoff was praised for the courage and tenacity of his leadership of the compatible forces. Frederick Kappel, chairman of giant AT&T, against which Sarnoff had waged bitter war in the radio networking conflict of the twenties, wrote him that he deserved the gratitude of the American people for the "beautiful and pure" color system he had developed. Bob Hope was asked on his network television program how color TV worked. "General Sarnoff stands behind the set with color crayons," he quipped—and the RCA leader would often reprise this comment of his favorite NBC comedian.

Even his manufacturing rivals, his ancient enemies from the radio era, applauded. The fear of what incompatible color might do to their flourishing monochrome sales and profits was erased. They reasoned that Sarnoff might try to trample them in the future, as he had in the past, but at least for the present the greatest peril had been removed. R. J. Sherwood, sales vice-president of Hallicrafters, announced that "anybody who doesn't like compatible color needs their head examined." To James Carmine, executive vice-president of Philco, the tricolor tube was "nothing short of phenomenal," and Dr. Allen B. Dumont, head of Dumont Laboratories, an early skeptic, now suggested that the quality of compatible color "was good enough to start commercial operations immediately."

A far more personal conflict, one that ended in tragedy and that troubled Sarnoff more profoundly than any of his career, reached its peak in this period to mar his color victory. It was with Edwin H. Armstrong, whom many considered radio's premier inventor and whose relationship with Sarnoff dated back to 1914. At that time Armstrong had invited the young Marconi executive to his physics laboratory at Columbia University to demonstrate his invention of a regenerative feedback circuit that vastly amplified the ability of vacuum tubes to pick up wireless signals over great distances. Over earphones, Sarnoff heard coded transmissions from as far away as Ireland and Honolulu, and he reported to his Marconi superiors that Armstrong had invented "the most remarkable receiving system in existence."

Out of this first encounter, a staunch friendship developed. They were approximately the same age. Although physically dissimilar—Armstrong was tall, fair, slope-shouldered, and balding—they shared a passionate belief in radio's future. During the period when Sarnoff and his young family lived in Mount Vernon, New York, Armstrong, who lived nearby, would drop by his friend's home for a cup of morning coffee and a discussion of technical developments. To Sarnoff's children, he became known as "the coffee man." The inventor would also frequently visit Sarnoff at his office, and he soon fell in love with his friend's attractive blond secretary, Marion MacInnis, who after a courtship of several years left her job to become Mrs. Armstrong.

In 1922, when radio set sales were vaulting, Armstrong demonstrated to his friend an improved regenerative circuit. A year later, he came forth with a superheterodyne circuit that permitted reception in home receivers without an external antenna. Sarnoff was so impressed that he persuaded the RCA board to buy both inventions for the then staggering price of $200,000 in cash and eighty thousand shares of RCA common stock. Overnight, the inventor became a millionaire and the largest individual holder of RCA securities—far more than his benefactor and friend possessed. The superheterodyne set became a national best-seller when RCA introduced it in 1924.

The cause of the rupture between the two men was Armstrong's subsequent development of an FM (frequency modulated) radio, which virtually eliminated the static inherent in reception over the standard AM (amplitude modulated) sets. Armstrong saw his invention as a revolutionary new communications service that would make AM obsolete. Sarnoff saw it as an important advance in sound technique, but not a new core technology like television. He, in fact, wanted FM as the sound supplement for television. The space in the radio spectrum that Armstrong sought for FM Sarnoff coveted for the video service. The difference soon became irreconcilable. On Sarnoff's orders, Armstrong and his staff were evicted from the RCA transmitter site at the Empire State Building, where they had initially been given space for FM testing. Now, Sarnoff contended, the space was needed for television tests. So Armstrong built his own 400-foot FM transmitter tower on New Jersey's Palisades, across the Hudson from Manhattan and Westchester, and began operating on test frequencies, transmitting mostly classical music. When RCA engineers soon countered with their own version of an FM system, Armstrong sued in U.S. District Court in Delaware, alleging patent infringement and a conspiracy to undercut and confuse the development of the FM service. When Sarnoff offered to settle the litigation by purchasing Armstrong's patents for $1 million, the inventor spurned the amount as insultingly inadequate.

For five years after World War II, the litigation dragged on, the two old friends hopelessly alienated. But Sarnoff was victorious in securing from the FCC the channels he sought for television, and the new visual service dwarfed FM in its impact on the nation. The embittered Armstrong refused to settle, depleting his fortune by continuing to push FM and in court costs and legal expenditures. Finally in 1954, overburdened and exhausted, the high-strung inventor penned a note to his wife asking that "God keep you and may the

Lord have mercy on my soul"—and plunged to his death from a window of his Manhattan apartment.

Sarnoff was stunned by the tragedy. He quickly settled the litigation by paying Armstrong's estate $1 million, the same amount he had offered years earlier. Sorrowfully, he led an RCA delegation to the inventor's funeral. Soon after, he encountered Carl Dreher, the RCA engineer who was a close friend and biographer of Armstrong. According to Dreher, Sarnoff looked him in the eyes and said: "I did not kill Armstrong." And of course he didn't. Armstrong fell victim to a lifetime of frustration and struggle, not only against RCA, but others in the industry and other inventors who challenged the validity of his patents. Unfortunately, he lacked the Sarnoff stomach for prolonged battle.

The color victory projected Sarnoff into the national limelight to a degree that even he had never experienced. One admiring journalist referred to him as the General MacArthur of American industry, a description to which Sarnoff took no exception. Demands for interviews engulfed him. More and more the press began to probe beyond the laudatory stereotypes that poured from the mimeograph machines of his suddenly overburdened public relations department. What made this formidable man tick? What was his personal life like? His relations with his family? How did he deal with his subordinates? What was his managerial style? What was he like as a human being? What kind of dent would he make in history?

The answers, the press found, were not always easy to come by. For despite his unorthodoxy as an industrial innovator, Sarnoff was essentially a disciplined organization man who did not enjoy having members of his staff sound off to the press about his private life. Rigid controls were enforced within RCA about who would speak to reporters and what they would say. "There can be only one voice for this company," Sarnoff would say, as so many industrial leaders before and after him have. While he was not averse to giving interviews to those he considered "responsible" journalists, he shrank from the tabloid limelight. "I don't want to be treated like a movie star or a television comedian," he told his press staff.

By the time of his color victory, of course, the dominant traits of his personality and character were clearly limned. As commander in chief of RCA, he headed up the largest single radio communications empire in the world—nearing $1 billion in annual sales—and his bearing reflected it. Thomas Whiteside, a seasoned magazine journalist who interviewed Sarnoff several times after the color triumph, wrote of his "baronial charm" and his "commanding air," and his tough, ruddy face with "sharp blue eyes that can fairly transfix subordinates," leaving them somewhere between mesmerization and paralysis. When Whiteside interviewed RCA executives seeking anecdotal material about their boss, he found it hard to come by. "Approached for the little personal reminiscences that most people around important men are usually eager to retail," Whiteside wrote in *Collier's,* "RCA executives either develop a sudden amnesia or take flight in highly generalized eulogy." To the writer, Sarnoff seemed a figure "far remote from the clatter of everyday affairs within his sprawling dominions." He was impatient of waste motion or trivial matters, explaining "I don't want to do what someone else can do." He was fastidious about his dress (conservative blue and brown suits) and he expected his subordinates to be. "If I see someone come in here with a disheveled look and wearing sloppy clothes, I don't want any part of him. If a fellow has sloppy clothes, the chances are he has a sloppy mind," he told Whiteside, who concluded that Einstein might never have made the grade at RCA.

Whiteside observed that everything in Sarnoff's life was done by plan, everything in its proper sequence. "A meticulously synchronized reception greets whoever has an appointment with him," he wrote. "When a visitor to the 53rd floor has gone through the ritual of being marched under escort from the outer reaches of the general's suite through deeply carpeted corridors and an impressive succession of inner offices—even the antechambers of Sarnoff's office have their antechambers—he is ushered in to see Sarnoff at almost the very second that the interview was arranged to begin. The general is all attention; when he has heard and said what he wants to, he closes the interview with firm and unmistakable finality and then, in the manner of a man tearing off a page of a desk calendar, he turns to the next piece of business."

The professional style Sarnoff cultivated was one of total discipline, and in this he was reinforced to an extraordinary degree by his elderly spinster secretary, Ella Helbig, whose passion for order matched his own. She had come to him on the recommendation of her former boss, Edward McGrady, a labor relations specialist who was an RCA board member. Tall, spare, gray-haired, and blue-eyed, Miss Helbig had two passions in life—her Catholic faith and her position as RCA's secretarial queen. She lived alone in an apartment only a few blocks removed from the two edifices around which her world orbited—RCA's headquarters and St. Patrick's Cathedral across Fifth Avenue, where she regularly attended mass. Most of the remainder of her waking hours, often seven days a week, were spent at her fifty-third-floor desk, maintaining meticulous files of Sarnoff's correspondence, watching over his bank account, preparing his income tax returns, responding to multitudinous requests from his immediate family, other relatives, and acquaintances. Her desk was positioned immediately outside the entrance to Sarnoff's inner sanctum, which she guarded like Horatio at the bridge. When a new staff member breezed past her desk once in response to a summons from Sarnoff, she shouted at him to come back. "I'll tell you when you can go in," she erupted.

Ella, as she was known to the organization, was the custodian of Sarnoff's daily calendar, which she treated as a sacred rota. If meetings were running beyond schedule, she would not hesitate to interrupt them. If a subordinate was a few minutes late for a meeting, he would be greeted by two icy stares, first Ella's and then Sarnoff's. She selected menus for his office luncheons, arranged place cards for the guests, ensured that the cooks and butlers adhered precisely to the luncheon schedule. For his trips, she prepared looseleaf notebooks that were logistical masterpieces, detailing not only times of departures and arrivals, modes of transportation, hotel accommodations, but the names of those who would greet him, down to chauffeurs, and brief biographies of his hosts and others of importance he would meet. Beyond being a consummate scheduler, she was also a pipeline to the organization on his moods. If he came in edgy or irate, she would tip off those who might be seeing him later in the day. If an executive fell into disfavor, she was the warning conduit to his associates. When Sarnoff induced Orrin Dunlop, RCA's veteran head of advertising and publicity, to accept early retirement in 1960, Ella spread the explanation around: "His brains dried up." To those whom she felt did not pay her proper deference, even senior executives, she could be haughty and disdainful ("the Virgin Queen," they would call her) and even troublesome in curbing their access to the boss or in dropping deprecatory remarks concerning them. But she was a perfectionist in her job, so much so that an IRS agent once wrote Sarnoff a letter of congratulations on the accuracy and precise documentation of his income tax return. And she created an environment of orderliness around his business day, even in the most turbulent periods, that responded to his own ethos of disciplined work. Ella was the only RCA employee, apart from family members, that Sarnoff remembered in his will, with a bequest of $10,000.

In a typical working day, Ella would precede her boss to the office by at least an hour, sometimes arriving as early as 7 A.M. When he appeared, she would greet him with an appointment schedule, a list of telephone calls to be made or responded to, and a summation of incoming documents which he would then dispose of one at a time. Like Winston Churchill, he insisted that memos from his staff be limited to a single page. For those requiring action from him, he would scrawl across the top in heavy black pencil his approval or disapproval. Those he wanted to discuss went back with the notation "PSM [please see me]—DS." It never ceased to astonish RCA's longtime general counsel, Robert Werner, that the response time to his memos to Sarnoff was briefer than for those to any other member of the organization.

Sarnoff believed his passion for discipline was inculcated in his boyhood rabbinical training at Korme. The number of pages he must memorize daily was precisely defined by his rabbinical elders, as were the hours he must devote to study. Thus, in later life, the popular concept of a chief executive barking out orders to minions streaming in and out of his office, issuing instructions over a bank of telephones, shuffling through mounds of paper heaped on his desk, dictating simultaneously to two or more secretaries—this, to him, was simply a movie caricature of a tycoon's role, and it affronted his sense of order. "If I saw one of my executives doing that, I'd fire him," he said. Only one telephone rested on his desk. Only one paper was there at a time, and it was dealt with before Ella brought the next. "My mind isn't a wastebasket. Why should my desk be?" he once asked an interviewer.

The one area of Sarnoff's life where the discipline ethic occasionally failed was with his family. In the early rearing of his three sons, he was, he admitted, too often the absent father. His work took priority over coping with the problems of growing up, and Lizette often played a dual parental role. This was a mistake, he conceded, and it later led to periods of conflict and misunderstanding, particularly with his oldest son, Bob, who would follow him at RCA but who would never completely bend to his disciplinary injunctions.

Sarnoff was extraordinarily frank to close associates in conceding his failures as a father. In part, he attributed them to the vastly different cultures in which he and his sons grew up; in part, he said, because he expected too much maturity of them too early. His boyhood milieu was one of work for survival, of being forced into mature decisions while still immature. "I didn't have the time to play," he often explained, and therefore he never learned how. Thus, "I just couldn't meet my boys on their own level on the playground. When I went to baseball games with them, they knew so much more about what was going on that I made very little impression on them." Beyond that, he conceded he was incapable of enacting a conventional father's role—hikes in the mountains, camping trips, touch football. He didn't know how to throw a ball. He'd never tried. "I was always physically lazy," he admitted. "I never liked to do things with my hands."

When he came home, Sarnoff tended to bring his office with him, and this caused generational problems. His youngest son, Tom, whom he considered most like him in temperament and intellect, had a favorite dog that the father once found nesting on a sofa in his study when he walked in with a briefcase full of homework. Unceremoniously, he shooed the dog out while his son watched. "I'll bet you wouldn't mind the dog if you could talk television to him," Tom said. Years later, when the boy was a man, the memory of that incident remained fresh with both son and father. It seemed to symbolize the problems of growing up as David Sarnoff's son, the existence of a generational and cultural dichotomy not easily overcome by either side.

Later, Sarnoff sought to atone for his early failures as a parent by intruding in the careers and affairs of his sons to a degree that was not always welcome, even a cause of resentment. It was rumored within RCA that he had been heavy-handed in seeking to inject himself into Bob's divorce from his first wife, thus provoking interfamilial clashes. There was an irony in this late-blooming solicitude that he himself recognized on occasion. As a boy he had missed the strong tiller of fatherly guidance and he sought to compensate by a search for father figures, first Marconi, then Young, and later to a lesser degree his "Boss" Eisenhower. It perplexed him, even frustrated him, that when he sought to play a similar role with his offspring, the reaction was not always positive. Once, after a clash with Bob over a business matter at RCA, he told an aide that "nobody at RCA has ever talked to me like that. I won't tolerate it." But he did. Like other fathers, he discovered that sons as business subordinates do not always respond to discipline like other subordinates.

Sarnoff's management style was often described as relentless, intimidating, hardheaded, and demanding. Alex McKenzie, senior editor of the engineering publication *Spectrum,* was close to many RCA technical employees, and he once wrote that "the fear of bringing down Sarnoff's wrath—which could strike like a thunderbolt at some non-function—was strong in all RCA employees." Yet his underlings were also aware that, if Sarnoff demanded much of them, he demanded even more of himself. Carl Dreher, an early engineering colleague of Sarnoff's, observed that "if Sarnoff had been a severe taskmaster but had indulged himself, he would have provoked resentment, perhaps even rebellion. But we knew—the evidence was always before us—that he worked harder and thought and planned more assiduously than any of us did or could do. That did not make us love him; nor did he care about our love. It did make us feel obliged to exert ourselves as he did, or come as close as possible. When we failed him, we feared not only his contempt, but our own toward ourselves." For several years, as the color battle waged, Sarnoff employed David Lilienthal, former director of the Tennessee Valley Authority, as a consultant in organizational matters. The two became close, and for a time Sarnoff considered him a potential future president of RCA. But Lilienthal was not interested in becoming part of the organization, perhaps because while he found the RCA leader "a strong and very human man, a fighter, a pioneer," he was still not "an easy man to understand—too complex."

In the climactic months of the color struggle, Sarnoff was a driven man, often working in eighteen-hour stretches. His day in that period often began with an office breakfast, perhaps with his investment bankers or directors, then a morning-long strategy session with his senior staff and technical advisers, then the race for a train to Washington, then dinner at his suite in the Carleton with Scoop Russell to be briefed on the political eddies, then past midnight studying his briefing books in preparation for the marathon testimony he would give the next day at an FCC hearing on color standards. Up early, a quick breakfast in the suite, a call to the indefatigable Ella for an update on developments at the command post, then onto the witness stand for eight hours of grueling interrogation by the FCC staff and CBS lawyers. Then the race for a late train to New York, accompanied by staff members. Clouds of cigar smoke would seep from a compartment of the Congressional as he postmortemed his testimony and devised follow-up strategy. As midnight approached, his limousine would deposit him at the Manhattan town house where his wife awaited. Typically, Lizette told friends, the greeting was, "Well, I guess I'll go upstairs to the office and get some work done."

For a sixty-two-year-old, which was Sarnoff's age when the FCC reversal sealed his victory, his schedule required depths of stamina that few even much younger men possessed. But now the struggle was ended and he could relax. A world of color, compatible color, lay beckoning, and he would preside over its frictionless, triumphant introduction to the American marketplace. Or so it appeared at that euphoric moment.

9 / *Color Victory*

The long Cadillac limousine halted at the canopied entrance of 30 Rockefeller Plaza and the uniformed doorman hurried to open its rear door. First emerged the long cigar, tilted at a jaunty angle, and following it in a wreath of smoke came the stocky figure of the building's principal tenant. A waiting elevator operator, alerted to his coming, whisked him to the fifty-third floor. With measured strides, he moved past RCA's receptionist, nodding good morning, through the carpeted anteroom of his office suite, pausing briefly to discuss the day's schedule with the omnipresent Ella, through a concealed white-oak paneled door into his private barbershop, where Mario, his barber, waited to minister a shave and facial massage, complete with hot towels, and a manicurist stood by to buff and trim his nails.

As this ritual was being enacted in late December 1953, a member of Sarnoff's staff sat on a stool facing the barber's chair. While Mario's fingers kneaded his jowls, Sarnoff listened intently to a verbal report on late breaking developments in color: both NBC and CBS were preparing to start nightly commercial color telecasts; more than a dozen local stations around the country had placed orders with RCA for broadcast equipment that would permit local origination of color programs; all the major manufacturers, except Zenith, were signing patent licensing agreements for RCA's color technology; and the trade press was full of reports that the leading brand names, GE, Philco, Westinghouse, were tooling up color production lines to tap into the rainbow of television's new mother lode. Again, as he had predicted, the followers were latching onto the coattails of the pioneer.

Indeed, it was difficult at that time for Sarnoff to discern any clouds on his, or RCA's, horizon. Fortune's pendulum was clearly arcing in his direction. Coy, the obstreperous, pro-CBS chairman of the FCC, had left his position, replaced by the more moderate Roswell Hyde, with whom Sarnoff was confident he could work. His "Boss" Eisenhower was in the White House, and Sarnoff wore the symbol of their wartime comradeship—a gold ring embossed with SHAEF's flaming sword insignia. The Korean conflict had been concluded, removing all critical material restraints on color production. The threat of a business recession had given way to a new boom, fueled by consumer spending. Under its benevolent, father-figure president, the nation was anticipating an era of prosperity that it had not known since the Coolidge years. A *Time* reporter who interviewed him captured the Sarnoff of that era: "Modesty, false or otherwise, does not disguise his power and success.

His chill blue eyes shine with impatient energy, his boyish, scrubbed pink face radiates cockiness. All 5 feet 5 inches [not true, insisted Sarnoff, who claimed five feet eight inches] of his bull-necked, bull-chested figure bristles with authority and assurance. He dresses with conservative, expensive elegance, even carries a gold frame to hold matchbooks . . . He says there are three drives that rule most men: money, sex, and power. Nobody doubts that Sarnoff's ruling drive is power. Says a deputy: 'There is no question about it, he is the god over here.' "

Whatever Sarnoff's godlike attributes, they did not include infallibility. In the emergence of radio and black-and-white television he had often misgauged the degree of industry support he could muster and the depths of animus that existed toward him in his fellow manufacturers. His contemptuous assessments of his competitors—that they were ruled by their pocketbooks rather than the long-range welfare of their industry—had created a widespread yearning among them to "cut him down to size," as Goldmark expressed it. Even the color victory, the most dramatic and seemingly conclusive of his career, could not, as events soon proved, obliterate that yearning.

In good measure, Sarnoff himself was responsible for its renewed expression. With the industry more united on color than it had been on any new product for thirty years, he could, simply by remaining silent, have permitted the momentum of newfound unity to build. But it was alien to his nature to share with others that to which he did not feel they were entitled. In his judgment, the NTSC color standards had been a convenient camouflage in the battle against CBS, but now Sarnoff felt the time was ripe to acquaint the world with the real facts behind the development of electronic color. As in monochrome's introductory phase, he simply couldn't resist the desire to focus all credit on himself and RCA. Within days of the FCC's reversal, full-page advertisements blossomed again in leading newspapers. Alongside a picture of Sarnoff, the text proclaimed another "great victory." Recalling the World's Fair of '39, it said, "At that time we added sight to sound. Now we add color to sight." The closing peroration nettled every RCA competitor: "The opportunity to enrich the lives of people everywhere is a privilege of leadership." An irate Philco responded with full-page ads contending the color standards were the product of the industry's leading scientists, "not the work of any one company." McDonald of Zenith wrote the FCC demanding that Sarnoff and RCA be censured for misleading advertising, but the chastened commission ignored him. Yet Sarnoff wouldn't let it lie. "We know of no significant contribution to color by Zenith," he wrote his old foe in reply. So, in typical fashion, the industry began to fragment. At the time, Sarnoff said, it didn't particularly concern him because he assumed that color sales would follow the soaring trajectory of black and white in its introductory years, and that industry dissonance would be drowned in a new wave of profitability. Even skeptical Wall Street responded to this logic by shoring up the laggard price-earnings ratio of consumer electronic stocks, in particular RCA, which moved from a depressed 16 to 23.

In March 1954, RCA announced that it had begun production of color receivers at its new Bloomington, Indiana, plant. The first set had a 12½-inch viewing tube and was priced at $1,000, compared to a 21-inch black and white selling for less than $300. This single introductory model, costing the equivalent of $3,500 in 1985 dollars, was aimed at the upper end of the buying spectrum. The rich, it was assumed, would preempt the first offering as a status symbol. Then prices could gradually lower as production increased. Both NBC and CBS announced stepped-up nighttime color programming, including musical and dramatic specials. Several manufacturers revealed their model plans and Westinghouse actually outpaced RCA by invading the market with the first commercial color set. Sarnoff announced his sales projections: 1954—75,000 units; 1955—350,000; 1956—1,780,000; 1957—3,000,000; 1958—5,000,000. No one else ventured such extravagant and precise predictions, but again no one risked contradicting him. He had too often been right in the past. In Sarnoff's view, the most promising growth industry in the century's second half was being launched, and he asserted that it would lead America to an era of unprecedented prosperity, providing up to a half million new jobs and billions in retail sales.

As 1954 reached midpoint, a series of developments, separate yet interrelated, began to cloud Sarnoff's euphoric projections. His morning barbershop briefings began containing disconcerting hints that all was not well on the color production lines. Color technology was proving far more difficult to master in mass production than it had been in carefully controlled field demonstrations. Daily production figures on his cherished tricolor tubes showed that only one out of three tested well enough to escape factory rejection. They were the seminal invention of his color system, but they were also the most complex consumer device ever mass produced. Beyond the tube problem, a high incidence of circuit failures was reported in the first sets installed in homes. RCA service men were receiving calls for repairs at twice the per set frequency of monochrome models, and they were also reporting back considerable customer grumbling over difficulty in tuning the colors into precise alignment. Perhaps most alarming of all, Folsom's field merchandising staff was encountering stiff price resistance. The $700–$800 differential between a small-screen color unit and a large-screen black and white was apparently too great for the public to swallow, even the affluent style setters.

With surprising suddenness, the prospects for color seemed to turn from rainbow hued to Gothic gray. Only five thousand sets were in homes by early 1955, and thousands were stacked in inventory. Those manufacturers who had spoken pridefully of their contributions to the NTSC standards suddenly reversed course. The old coalition of anti-Sarnoff forces was back in business. Almost gleefully, Zenith announced it would make no color sets until the technology was improved. It dismissed the RCA color model with that favorite industry phrase of derision, "a Rube Goldberg contraption." Philco, GE, and Westinghouse stopped production because the public wasn't buying. Perhaps the single most damaging blow came from the respected head of GE, Ralph Cordiner, who complained, "If you have a color set, you've almost got to have an engineer living in the house." Broadcasters other than NBC shrank from the heavy costs of converting their facilities for colorcasts. CBS, no longer the gracious loser of an epic battle, quickly dried up plans for extensive colorcasts, saying it would wait until there was an audience for color. Advertisers also refused to pay a premium for color sponsorship until circulation justified it.

Quite unexpectedly, RCA found itself virtually alone in color and Sarnoff found himself personally in "the toughest battle of my life." By 1955 he had spent $65 million in color developmental and manufacturing costs, plus additional millions for NBC's incremental color costs. Occasionally, there would be an uptick in sales, as with a World Series colorcast or Mary Martin's *Peter Pan* spectacular on NBC, which emptied the nation's streets of traffic, but the persistent sluggishness in public response caused rising concern within RCA and in financial circles.

"We were being deserted in droves," Sarnoff would later recall. "Everybody in the business was walking away from us. And it wasn't just indifference. It was hostility. Dealers were being warned by our competitors, 'Keep RCA color off your floors. Otherwise you'll wreck your black-and-white sales. Wait until they get a bigger picture tube and get the price down.' "

But for RCA to turn back was unthinkable. As Engstrom put it, "We had our arms around color, and we couldn't let go as the others could." Beyond that, Sarnoff's personal reputation was at stake, including his credentials as the industry's seer. No other major product introduced in postwar America had encountered such rocky beginnings, so much hope and ballyhooed expectations, so little performance. Where had Sarnoff gone wrong? Was age creeping up on him, dimming his capacity to foresee the future and to inspire the industry to march with him?

In Wall Street the view was surfacing that RCA should cut its losses by putting color in a commercial deep freeze until it had improved the quality and reliability of its sets. Even along the corridors of RCA's executive offices, whispered doubts about the future of color were being exchanged. "Maybe we jumped the gun on this one," the senior corporate marketing executive, Marin Bennett, confided to a younger colleague. "Maybe we should have waited until more of the bugs were shaken out." No one, of course, challenged Sarnoff openly with such concerns, any more than they would have raised the subject of his advancing years with him. The fact was he gave little thought to birthdays, which were simply workdays like any others. More likely, he measured time in terms of his career anniversaries—the fortieth, the forty-fifth, the fiftieth—which he used as festive occasions to look to the future, not as signposts of the past, of a career that sometime must terminate. He never discussed with his associates the subject of sometime stepping down. Probably he never allowed himself to think of it, and particularly not when the color battle was in peril of being lost.

In its issue of October 27, 1956, *Time* magazine infuriated Sarnoff by describing color TV as "the most resounding industrial flop of 1956." It quoted Zenith's McDonald as saying RCA had engaged in "premature tub thumping" to force its competitors into color so it could "collect millions of dollars a year in royalties from its color patents." According to McDonald, "color had been slow taking hold for the simple reason that our industry has not yet produced a good enough color picture to make people want to pay the extra price." In the judgment of the *Time* writer, "the trouble goes deeper than the quality of the color. The black and white programs that make up the vast bulk of TV fare often seem wan and whiskery on color sets. Color reception takes such keen tuning that many a would-be customer loses heart while the salesman fumbles. Moreover, color reception must be live to be good. In the west, where nightly network color shows are often kinescoped to meet the time differential, viewers complain that all the hues come out blue."

Again, in Sarnoff's judgment, *Time,* by its sneering headline reference to the "Faded Rainbow," had exposed its bias toward him. Yet even he had to concede that public apathy toward his new product existed. A viewer of a color set in Rich's department store in Atlanta summed up the problem. "I know the grass is green in Ebbets Field," he said. "It isn't worth $600 more to find out how green." Or there was the complaint of a San Francisco dealer who said, "The less I sell the better. There's a shortage of proper technicians to repair them, and I don't think the buyer is always happy with what he gets."

Sarnoff was frankly perplexed by the size of his miscalculation. There had been other highly regarded new products introduced with great fanfare, such as the Pierce Arrow automobile, that had failed to win public acceptance because of radical design changes. At a later date, the Edsel would encounter the same fate. But his was no Pierce Arrow or Edsel. Color was not a gadget. It was a new dimension. It represented the next great cycle in electronics. The world needed it ("What is a rose without color?" he would rather plaintively ask) and the times were ripe for it. America was flush, Europe was reviving under the stimulus of America's Marshall Plan beneficence, the "American Century" was at its midpoint, total employment of 52 million was an all-time high. Even the wages of factory workers had achieved a record $81 per week. The rich and the middle classes were buying luxury items—fur coats, jewelry, Cadillac cars—in greater profusion than ever. If Cadillac could sell 178,000 cars in 1956, why couldn't Sarnoff sell at least that many color sets?

That was the grim year in which Sarnoff observed his sixty-fifth birthday. Fifteen years had elapsed since CBS's first color application to the FCC, and now he was at the upper reaches of middle age, the normal retirement time for industrial executives, including RCA's. A half century had gone by since he started at Marconi as an office boy. But to Sarnoff, the thought of phasing out at this crucial juncture was preposterous. Until electronic color crested, his rendezvous with history would be unfulfilled. Retirement was simply not on his agenda. He told a friend the idea of lolling on a Florida beach, observing the pastels of an evening sky with his fellow sexagenarians or playing in the sand with grandchildren, appalled him, as did the luxury liner cruises that Lizette frequently proposed to ease the pressures on him. Apart from a high blood sugar count, which forced him to curb his appetite for sweets and starches, and such a relatively minor affliction as hemorrhoids, his health was excellent. He remained overweight—180 pounds packed on a rather small-boned frame, with most of the surplus concentrated around his middle—and the pressures of color had taken some toll. His hair had whitened and become wispier on top. The furrows between nose and mouth were more sharply etched, and small brownish skin blotches had cropped up around his temple and on his hands. While he still resisted his personal doctor, Cornelius Traeger's, urgings to undertake a regimen of physical exercise, he insisted to his staff he had never felt better, been more alert mentally, or more attuned to the task at hand, which was the implantation of RCA color sets in every American home that could afford one.

Given these circumstances, it was not enough for Sarnoff merely to have his employment extended by RCA's board of directors. There must be dramatic affirmation of his indispensability. The McDonalds and others who opposed him must not be encouraged to continue the struggle against color through hope for his disappearance from the scene. The thirteen-member RCA board, each selected by him, four of them company executives whose careers had flourished under his hegemony, eight outsiders who were old business associates and personal friends, quickly sensed what his desires were. It responded with the offer of an employment contract of unprecedented duration, longer than any ever offered a company executive. For ten years, to age seventy-five, he would continue as RCA's chairman and chief executive officer, with his salary pegged at $200,000 annually, plus new stock options. If he survived the full period, his tenure promised to surpass that of any other chief executive of a major corporation who was not a founding owner or controlling shareholder. At a time when most men looked to the sunset, he was still the absolute prince. He had won job security rivaling that of his rabbinical forebears, and the pay was better.

With the retirement problem out of the way, Sarnoff threw all his energies, and most of RCA's resources, into another bet-the-company struggle that would stretch out another five years. A task force of senior executives, staff and operating, was brought together under his command, with the mission of making America color TV conscious. The corporate advertising budget was tripled. Color sets with service contracts flowed out as gifts from Sarnoff to America's opinion leaders, to financiers and editors, broadcast sponsors and advertising agency heads, congressional leaders and the White House. Even Blair House was color equipped for the indoctrination of state guests. Sets were installed in the editorial anterooms of major newspapers. RCA's field marketing staff arranged neighborhood viewing parties across the nation, keyed to major NBC colorcasts. Advertising time on NBC was bartered for color spreads in major magazines, such as *Life*. The recurrent theme: Be the first on your block to own one. Sarnoff's goal was to make RCA color sets the nation's status symbol.

Characteristically, he carried his color proselytizing to the White House in a personal meeting with President Eisenhower. Accompanied to the Oval Office by NBC White House correspondent Ray Scherer, Sarnoff was greeted by "What can I do for you, Dave?" from his wartime boss. In a burst of overoptimism, he assured the president that color had arrived as the next great product on the American scene. He offered a graphic depiction of how color would enhance Ike's appeal over television. The presumption was that the famous Ike smile would now be conveyed in a new dimension of reality. While Eisenhower offered no formal endorsement of RCA color, he did later appear before NBC's color cameras in dedicating the new all-color studios of station WRC, the network's Washington outlet.

In a further effort to overcome industry opposition, Sarnoff had Folsom invite seventy manufacturers' representatives to the new Bloomington color plant and offer them RCA's color know-how, just as he had with black and white in 1947. Its latest receiver blueprints, production details, bill of materials, even tours of the manufacturing facilities, were proffered. "We stripped ourselves to the buff for them," Sarnoff said grimly, but it did little good. The industry he had upbraided so often seemed to wallow in his discomfiture. In *Fortune*'s words, the others "just sat back and jeered."

That same magazine later summed up the dilemma: "For five years after it marketed its first set in 1954, RCA found itself the solitary tenant of the new world." After the first year's meager sales of 5,000 units, RCA dropped the price to $700 and advertised an improved model in '55. The public, still content with its monochrome toy, yawned in response; only 30,000 units, a tiny fraction of Sarnoff's original estimate, cleared dealer showrooms. So he determined to accept even greater losses by dropping the price of a new table model to $500. A new 21-inch tube with improved color contrast and reliability was announced, and offered, almost pleadingly, to an industry that wouldn't buy it. In 1956, RCA claimed sales of 120,000 units, but those were factory sales and RCA refused to reveal the number that clogged the distribution pipeline. *Time* estimated only 75,000 sets were in the public's hands two years after market entry. By 1957, the color investment had reached $100 million.

Increasingly angered by the industry boycott, Sarnoff erupted publicly at a Miami, Florida, gathering of NBC affiliates. Talking extemporaneously, he described in acid tones the "Johnny Come Latelies" who coast on the tail of the pioneer.

"Remember when black and white television arrived? They called us televisionaries. They [meaning Zenith primarily] said they would never produce black and white sets because television broadcasting could never be self-sustaining. They said revenues from advertisers would be insufficient to maintain it. But when the wagon was pushed uphill and began to roll, they jumped on the wagon. Plenty of them will jump on the color wagon when the going gets easier."

Sarnoff's dissatisfaction at color's congealed pace began extending to his own organization. The merchandising verve that his president, Folsom, had demonstrated in monochrome's introductory phase was not so evident in color. Very much a family man, the RCA president had been devastated by the recent death of his wife. The enthusiasm seemed to drain out of him. "Frank has lost his drive," Sarnoff remarked, almost sadly, to a friend. The problem was compounded by a slippage in black-and-white sales, a perhaps inevitable result of the organization's preoccupation with color. Zenith took over sales leadership and McDonald gleefully advertised that his "hand crafted" set (put together with the same loving care as a Stradivarius violin, the ads implied) had now become America's leading monochrome brand. A draft of wormwood would have been easier for Sarnoff to take. He had lost leadership to the man and the company that had fought him every step of the way in television's introductory years. The parasite was engulfing its host.

So Sarnoff decided to make a change at the top. He liked Folsom personally, sympathized with his bereavement, and did not want to embarrass him. He made Folsom chairman of the executive committee of the board, a previously nonexistent position that entailed no organizational responsibilities but provided him with the senior executive perquisites of an office, secretarial help, a company limousine, and a nominal salary of $25,000 annually.

As his new president, Sarnoff went outside the organization for the first time to select John L. Burns, vice-chairman of the leading management consulting firm of Booz, Allen & Hamilton, Inc. For nearly a decade Burns had served as a consultant to RCA and NBC on organizational matters. Like Sarnoff, he had started at the bottom, working his way through Northeastern University in Boston and winding up with a doctoral degree from Harvard.

After production line experience as a steel worker, he had moved up rapidly in the consulting field, numbering among his clients Tom Watson of IBM, when he was preparing his thrust into computers. Like Folsom, Burns possessed a genial personality and a love of golf, which he played regularly at clubs near his Greenwich, Connecticut, home. Sarnoff admired his grasp of modern management techniques, his ability to streamline an organization, and in particular his toughness in cost-cutting techniques—a paramount consideration in view of the continuing hemorrhage of color dollars. Along with a ten-year contract and an option on fifty thousand shares of stock, Burns was given much latitude, as chief operating officer, to overhaul the executive structure and revitalize the color drive. When he began addressing the chairman as "Dave," everyone knew his clout was considerable.

In 1957, coincident with the change of presidents, Sarnoff's color problems were compounded by a $150-million treble damage antitrust suit filed by Philco, which charged RCA with monopolistic practices in the operation of its patent pool in radio and television. GE, Westinghouse, and AT&T were named codefendants because of their original involvement in the pool, but no one doubted that the target was RCA, and Sarnoff in particular. Among its charges, Philco advanced the novel claim that its monochrome set sales had suffered because of RCA's "persistence in offering its color television sets for sale despite the fact they are not perfected, and persistence in advertising that RCA has pioneered and developed the compatible color television system." By charging "unreasonably low" prices for color, Philco added, RCA was trying to eliminate its competitors. To Sarnoff, this was the supreme irony. He had been pleading for years for Philco and the others to join him.

Although RCA countersued, accusing Philco of attempting to block color and ridiculing its claim of technical contributions to it, Sarnoff could not take lightly the fact that the Justice Department had earlier initiated a civil antitrust action aimed at the patent pool and patent policies of RCA, with strong implications of possible criminal charges to follow. The department's antitrust division had concluded that the consent decree of '32, freeing RCA from its electrical company ownership, had not gone sufficiently far in curing the monopoly inherent in the original patent pool, which, by 1957, with the addition of major color inventions, had grown to ten thousand patents. The government and Philco actions had been foreshadowed by an antitrust suit filed against RCA years earlier by its old rival Zenith, which announced concurrently that it would no longer pay royalties to the patent pool. RCA had previously sued Zenith, alleging patent infringement, and those actions still dragged on in the courts.

To Sarnoff, these attacks seriatim were becoming intolerable. He and his senior executives found their color drive deflected by quotidian legal demands—hearings, depositions, file searches—that consumed, by one lawyer's estimate, 40 percent of their working hours. More than once Sarnoff grumbled that "the one thing I won't do for this company is go to jail for it." Ultimately, at the urging of Burns and his legal advisers, he decided to settle all the litigation, and the price, in effect, was abandonment of the original domestic patent pool and its related package licensing, which he had structured with Owen D. Young in RCA's founding years. The royalties from the pool, Sarnoff claimed, had underwritten most of the basic research for the entire industry. But he was weary of defending the pool principle, and privately he recognized its dubious legality under the Sherman Act.

In approaching his legal problems, Sarnoff demonstrated increasing caution, a late-developing trait for him, and one in marked contrast to the boldness of his technological thrusts. He had come to realize that in an age when electronic mass communications had become among the most powerful forces shaping society it was not always prudent to be out front in matters of public controversy, and this was where the antitrust actions had thrust him. And now, in particular, with the outcome of his color battle still uncertain, he wanted to rid himself permanently of competitive cries of "monopoly." While he publicly treated them contemptuously—"we've got more competitors than a dog has fleas"—he recognized the potential for further trouble, perhaps a new congressional investigation of monopolistic practices in the industry, if RCA continued in the antitrust limelight. The fact of his company's size alone had given him, in the words of a retired RCA executive, "a quite realistic sense of the limitations of his power," and of the need for steering cautiously away from trouble. In the words of a *Collier's* article, he had become "as cautious as a Cardinal where matters of public controversy are concerned." He took no public position on Senator McCarthy's communist hunt. Increasingly, he turned to a small group of New York power brokers for advice when ticklish external questions arose. Among them were Bernard Baruch, Herbert Bayard Swope, the banker Andre Meyer (an RCA board member), and Francis Cardinal Spellman. Within RCA they became known as Sarnoff's "kitchen cabinet," and generally their recommended course of action was to play it safe.

On October 29, 1958, RCA accepted a consent decree that ended the federal civil suit. It also pleaded nolo contendere, or no defense, to criminal charges and paid a $100,000 fine—perhaps the most humiliating incident of Sarnoff's career, even though he was not named personally, as he had feared. A story whispered in RCA's legal department held that Sarnoff's name was on a criminal indictment drawn up in the Justice Department by an eager young antitrust staff that vowed to put the RCA leader behind bars for his alleged years of monopolistic patent practices. Only when the indictment reached the steps of the White House, the story went, was it finally quashed by Sarnoff's old comrade in arms President Eisenhower.

Under the terms of the consent decree, RCA was compelled to place its one hundred principal color patents in a separate pool, along with other color patents from a half dozen companies. Any competitor without color patents could draw on the pool royalty-free. Once the shock of the settlement had passed, Sarnoff typically attempted to put a best-face construction on it, employing again his favored metaphor of the lemon. "We'll make lemonade out of this lemon. This will encourage others to finally come into color," he said with as much cheer as he could muster.

Sarnoff shed his other legal encumbrances through settlements with Philco and Zenith that, while involving payments of several million dollars over a period of years, did no material damage to RCA, although in each case Sarnoff's pride suffered. Then he did his best to bury the litigation, even the memory of it. He seldom spoke of it within the company. He refused to cooperate when various business magazines sought to probe unrevealed aspects of the Zenith settlement. His official press biography glossed over the long royalty battle. Later, he turned abroad, with considerable success in Japan and Europe, to recoup lost domestic patent income. But more important, he was again free to concentrate all his energies on color.

"In the uphill struggle to popularize color television," Gould of the *Times* wrote on June 14, 1959, "the Radio Corporation of America has been a lonely corporate figure. Without significant support from other segments of the broadcasting and manufacturing industries, RCA and its subsidiary, the National Broadcasting Company, have poured almost $130,000,000 into the project."

For that then formidable sum, the largest single product investment in electronic history, RCA could count a color set population of less than half a million, with each sold at a loss. It was only a pale shadow of Sarnoff's sales projections of five years earlier, and it was dwarfed by forty-five million black-and-white sets in use.

But there were positive signs cropping up, among them the generic popularity of color. In many new forms, color was spreading pervasively across the canvas of American life in the fifties. Henry Ford's dictum that his cars would be available in any color so long as it was black had long since been outmoded by the varied hues of competitive models from General Motors and Chrysler. The somber decades of war and depression had given way to a new thrust toward the good life, which America seemed to want to celebrate in color. The clothing and hats of fashionably dressed women reflected the raiment of the peacock. Gaudy ties and sports clothes came into vogue for men. Homes, outside and in, were drenched in the varied colors of the spectrum; magazines blossomed with color photography, and the advertisements adjoining their texts were soon multihued as businesses found their products sold better in color. With motion pictures, color had eclipsed monochrome film almost as completely as talkies had silent fare.

Sarnoff was convinced a syllogism existed in the advance of color. If color enhanced the selling value of cars and magazines and movies, so too must it with television. In his effort to colorize the new medium, he felt he was responding to a basic American appetite that sooner or later must be appeased. And as the decade of the sixties unfolded, events began to validate his thesis.

In the summer of 1960, after prolonged secret negotiations, an announcement was made that the popular Walt Disney television program, which had been broadcast over ABC for several years in black and white, would shift to NBC that fall and be broadcast entirely in color. For weeks in Hollywood and in a midtown Manhattan hotel suite, senior RCA and NBC executives met with Walt's top business executives, his brother Roy and his assistant, Cardon Walker, to hammer out the multimillion-dollar deal that would unlock to television many of the animated color films that had captivated the moviegoing world, plus new color shows that Disney would create. There was endless squabbling over costs—for the Disneys always drove a hard bargain—but the controlling consideration was that Walt Disney, the master cartoonist who pioneered color in motion pictures, wanted to repeat in television. The program's cosponsor with RCA was Eastman Kodak, also a color pioneer, which wanted to test its commercials in color. Retitled "Walt Disney's Wonderful World of Color," the new series became an instant, and long-running, hit on NBC's Sunday evening schedule, providing a powerful impetus to color set sales.

Another development that Sarnoff had factored into his color strategy became increasingly valid. The black-and-white market was nearing saturation, with replacement or second set purchases mainly in low-profit table models. Price-cutting infested the industry, and color seemed less a threat and more an opportunity. And the massive RCA engineering effort in color was translating into real achievement: less bulky sets, larger screen sizes, simpler tuning, greater picture stability. Perhaps not surprisingly, the caustic anticolor comments of competitors were suddenly muted.

Sarnoff capped these pluses by announcing in 1960 that RCA had made a profit from color set sales for the first time. The amount was not released, and Sarnoff conceded internally, with a grin, that it was closer to one digit than seven. But he felt it broke an important psychological barrier and he was right. One of the smaller set manufacturers, Admiral, announced plans to enter the color market, its sets equipped with picture tubes from RCA, and Packard Bell followed. By 1961 industry color sales reached the $100 million level and RCA announced a $1 million profit.

The construction of a color industry, Sarnoff often said, was based upon a tripod of research, manufacturing, and broadcasting—and broadcasting now became the crucial leg. "If we hadn't owned NBC," Sarnoff later reminisced, "I don't know if color would ever have taken off. The other networks just sat back on their hands. Until there was set circulation out there they wouldn't touch it. Of course, the only way we could get that circulation was through NBC programs. It was our chicken and our egg, nobody else's."

The initial cost of colorizing a program was 25 percent greater than black and white, a burden that advertisers initially refused to bear. So NBC absorbed up to $6 million annually in gradually building up colorcasts to 95 percent of its entire nighttime schedule. This meant that any night of the week, and also through much of the day, the color set owner could view programs in color, always alerted to their coming by the introductory logotype of NBC's increasingly famous color peacock. When audience research established that color set owners watched color programs 50 percent more than black and white, ABC began to stir. It placed orders with RCA for studio equipment and cameras and announced it was considering occasional shows in color.

If one single incident spelled victory for Sarnoff, it occurred on February 22, 1961, when Joseph Wright, president of Zenith, the successor to Sarnoff's most implacable foe, McDonald, phoned John Burns and placed an order for fifty thousand 21-inch RCA color tubes. Despite its leadership in monochrome sales, Zenith had concluded it could no longer ignore color. This was the break in the dike. Sarnoff's favorite example of a parasite company had, as he predicted, finally boarded the bandwagon. After years as the leading color boycotter, Zenith announced to its distributors that it would bring out in the fall a "completely new and unique" line of color receivers.

This time the elated Sarnoff did not rise to the claim. He had no desire to reignite the controversy that his advertising provoked in 1953. A dignified RCA statement welcomed Zenith's entry as a "further indication of the rapidly mounting interest" in a color industry at last beginning to march. There were no caustic comments, at least externally, about Rube Goldberg RCA picture tubes in Zenith sets. Even though GE and Philco continued their truculent stance, Sarnoff knew that with the brand names of the two biggest producers in the marketplace together industry opposition would soon melt.

At a luncheon following Zenith's symbiotic action, a mellow Sarnoff fondled his king-size cigar and said, "I never thought I'd see the day. RCA and Zenith in bed together. It won't last long, but the fact is by doing themselves a favor they did us one." He predicted all the rest of the "sheep" would soon fall in line, and he was right. Eight years after the first RCA color set came off the Bloomington production line, the fledgling industry developed a growth pulse of its own. By 1965, twenty companies were manufacturing color sets in response to a "crushing consumer demand," as the *Herald Tribune* described it. Set sales had vaulted to the 5 million level and color was a billion-dollar industry, the fastest growing in the nation's consumer sector.

During the first five years of the sixties, RCA's profits grew at a rate triple the average of all American manufacturing enterprises. Per share earnings went from $.72 to $1.70. The color orphan became a major contributor to company profits, and the ratio of corporate profits to sales more than doubled, from 2.3 to 5 percent. Wall Street's pariah of earlier decades became as blue chip as the blue in its phosphor dots, recapturing the luster of Radio's halcyon days of the late twenties. RCA common stock soared toward the 100 mark, and Sarnoff's board embraced his proposal for a three-to-one stock split, to be followed in subsequent years by a 10 percent and three 2 percent stock dividends. By 1965, RCA's stockholders numbered 257,187, making it the eighth most widely held American company. Its sales had passed the $2 billion level, making it the twenty-sixth largest corporate enterprise, and net profit for the first time surpassed $100 million. And color TV was outearning all RCA's other consumer products combined.

It was a time when seemingly nothing could go wrong for the company and its seventy-four-year-old leader. "This is the year of fulfillment for our long struggle," he told RCA's 1965 stockholder gathering in Chicago. GE, the most stubborn holdout, had just come on stream in manufacturing, with color tubes and components purchased from RCA, and Sarnoff couldn't resist rubbing a little salt in "Cordiner's wounds." (GE had recently been involved in a major price-fixing scandal.)

"Those [meaning GE] who only a few years ago advanced the specious argument that an engineer is needed for each color receiver are now manufacturing and selling these receivers themselves," he told the applauding RCA shareholders. "Any child can tune a color set, and, in fact, this has been the case for years." So much for the followers who latch on the coattail of the pioneer.

Sarnoff particularly relished the dilemma of CBS, the failed protagonist of the horse and buggy. While NBC had aggressively liquidated its color start-up costs, and ABC and hundreds of independent stations were beginning to embrace the new medium, CBS remained the lone major holdout, insisting the added cost of colorizing programs—by then reduced to between 10 percent and 20 percent—was not justified by the color set population. But it was an increasingly unpersuasive argument to CBS affiliates, who wanted to share in the excitement that color's introduction generated locally, and to influential segments of the press, which began to question whether CBS was fulfilling its public licensee responsibility by ignoring the dominant development in broadcasting.

"CBS seems to be saying," the *Times* complained on November 29, 1964, "that when Sarnoff makes color TV sufficiently profitable then CBS will enter the color field." And the *Times* added ominously: "The time may be at hand when the Federal Communications Commission should move into the color situation. . . . The controversy over color no longer is the parochial trade matter it was for so many years; the public's stake is now paramount."

Bolstered by a now supportive press, Sarnoff elected to remain silent. He knew CBS had suffered through a manufacturing disaster, that Paley's apparent goal of creating a rival electronics empire had crumbled, and he wisely refrained from any of his earlier Zenith-type castigations. Within months, quietly, through the back door, CBS moved into color. Its commitment to a schedule of nightly colorcasts provided the epitaph to one of the century's bitterest industrial conflicts. To Peter Goldmark, the maverick inventor whose spinning disc triggered the color war, defeat was total. His repeated assertion that RCA compatible color was technically unachievable made his clouded crystal ball famous in engineering circles. "I couldn't wait until he [Goldmark] reached sixty-five so I could retire him," a disillusioned Paley said years later.

With the major manufacturers and networks in color, and four hundred TV stations in the process of equipping for color, mostly with RCA transmitters, Sarnoff now faced a different challenge. No other manufacturer had tooled up to produce tricolor tubes, and RCA became a sole source supplier. Sarnoff found himself in the Solomon-like posture of allocating picture tubes among his competitors until they could ready their own production facilities. He ordered a crash $50 million plant expansion program. The industry that had resisted him so long was now pleading for help, and he gave it on terms advantageous to RCA. Each tricolor tube sold to a competitor returned a $35 profit. RCA was soon back-ordered in all its color plants—from cameras and studio equipment to receiving tubes and components.

From the mid-sixties vantage point, Sarnoff saw a bottomless color cornucopia, a 55-million-set American market to replace the current monochrome population, followed by smaller second and third table-model and portable sets to equip bedrooms, kitchens, and dens as well as living rooms. From an initial $1,000, the price of sets had declined to an average of $500, with the lowest model at $380.

Americans were pouncing on their new toy with undisguised glee. The Viet Nam conflict had not yet reached its grim stage, with the colleges in revolt. Color was a status symbol, but it was also fun. "I Love Lucy" seemed funnier in color, and so did Jack Paar and Bob Hope. Even prizefight addicts were enthusiastic. "You can tell it's really gore now," one wrote NBC. And the thirst for color seemed to feed on itself. Investment banker Robert Lehman, one of America's wealthiest art collectors, telephoned an RCA executive to complain that his color set wasn't working. Could a replacement be rushed over to 625 Park Avenue? He didn't want to face his guests that night without a color set to view an NBC special on the Louvre. The obstacle of price seemed to wash away, with luxury furniture models moving as swiftly as the cheapest table model. If prosperous America could afford guns and butter, as President Johnson promised, it could assuredly afford color.

Color also began catching on abroad, and Sarnoff eyed the world markets, not as a source for export of RCA brand name sets, but for licensing income from its formidable array of patented technology. With the altered configuration of the domestic pool, Sarnoff had determined to replace his lost licensing income by foreign licensing, which was legal under antitrust doctrine, rather than the sale of RCA consumer products. He did not feel it advisable to compete by brand name in foreign markets with those who were paying RCA a royalty for each consumer product they sold.

This was a decision of enduring significance to RCA's future. In effect, it confined the company, whose advertising slogan then was "World Leader in Radio, First in Television," to the North American market for brand name consumer goods. The sole exception was Victor Records, which were manufactured and distributed in Europe, Canada, South America, and the Far East under the RCA label, but this represented only a small percentage of total sales. Component plants, commercial electronics and television tube plants, would be built over several decades in Europe, South America, Malaysia, and Taiwan, but they did not produce finished consumer products. Occasionally there were joint ventures with foreign enterprises, in which RCA tubes and components would go into the brand name set of the foreign company. Indeed, RCA color tubes manufactured in the United States and Canada would flow anywhere, but with isolated and brief exceptions, the symbol of RCA did not mingle with the neon-lit signs of other leading companies in the merchandise marts of the world.

Other manufacturers in America, leaders like RCA of their domestic industries, charted a different path. The logotypes of IBM, Ford, General Electric, and General Motors, among many others, became almost as familiar abroad as at home. They built foreign manufacturing plants and sold their brand name products wherever a hospitable environment could be found. Long after the Sarnoff era, other companies, principally Japanese, rushed in to fill the international consumer electronics vacuum which RCA, during its dominant years, chose not to address. In the early eighties a single Japanese company, Matsushita, had consumer electronics sales four times as great as RCA's. Its marketplace was the world, but RCA addressed only a third of that market in North America.

To a greater degree than any other American company, RCA reverenced the patent. It was the company's building block, even if originally tainted with illegality, providing the royalty income that in several depressed years during the thirties spelled the difference between profit and loss, a stream of bottom-line dollars that flowed into the research laboratories and nourished new technologies like color. Over the years a corporate culture emerged that held the licensing activity of RCA sacrosanct, and its principal disciple was Sarnoff. The slogan "world leader" was soon abandoned. The decision had been made to license the world rather than sell RCA products to its consumers.

In the pursuit of foreign licensing income, Sarnoff focused first on Japan. Emerging from years of postwar military occupation under MacArthur, the Japanese saw technology as their salvation. Like Sarnoff, they hitched their wagon to the electron, and the strategy they adopted was remarkably similar to his—the long-term view of the future, the refusal to be discouraged by setbacks, the almost mystical faith in the problem-solving ability of the technician. During the fifties, teams of Japanese scientists and engineers had paid frequent visits to America, inspecting RCA's television plants and interviewing Sarnoff on his management philosophy. To them he became a role model of enlightened industrial leadership.

The 525-line American transmission was adopted for black-and-white TV in Japan, and in color the NTSC standards, or the Sarnoff standards as many Japanese viewed them, were also accepted. The entire Japanese electronics industry signed licensing agreements with RCA, renewable every five years. Japan became the largest single foreign contributor to RCA income.

In October 1960, Sarnoff accepted an invitation to address the Japanese Federation of Economic Organizations in Tokyo. Accompanied by Lizette and an RCA director, Lehman Brothers partner Paul Mazur and his wife, Dolph, he made a triumphal tour of the island nation which was rebuilding its shattered industrial plant with phenomenal speed and beginning to eye world markets for its electronic exports. He was feted by industrialists and government leaders, eulogized in the *Japan Times* as the hero of color, and received in private audience by Emperor Hirohito, who bestowed upon him the Order of the Rising Sun, Japan's highest decoration for foreigners. Addressing the Japanese Federation, he noted that black-and-white sets in 91.2 percent of Japanese homes rivaled the density in the United States. "To me," he said, "Japan's progress in electronics is best symbolized by its growth in television. Almost alone, television initiated the upsurge in Japanese consumer sales. One of every five TV sets installed throughout the world last year was in Japan." Then he turned to his absorbing interest: "I am delighted that Japan is pioneering in color on a national basis. I am told that eight stations on three networks have been authorized to begin colorcasting, and that many manufacturers have started production of color receivers. To me there can be no finer opportunity than color television for a fusion of Japanese artistry and technical progress."

Sarnoff found that TV had become as vital a cultural element in Japan as in America. The crowded, pressured island populace found it a comparable form of escapism. In his hotel suite, he watched televised tales of the samurai and ronin, and he coined a phrase for them; "Eastern Westerns." Understandably, Japan became Sarnoff's favorite foreign nation, down to the chopsticks he enjoyed wrestling with, seated straddle-legged on the floor, surrounded by his Japanese hosts, a chunky little buddha whose blue eyes gleamed with pleasure as geisha girls pampered him. He responded to Japanese hospitality with the most significant gift he could imagine—the establishment of a small RCA technical center in Tokyo's outskirts as an offshoot of his Princeton laboratories.

Sarnoff also sought to impose American color standards on the Western world. He dispatched his top scientists to Vienna in April 1965 to urge the adoption of American color—i.e., RCA color—over rival French (Secant) and German (PAL) systems, both of which employed all-electronic technology, but differing broadcast and reception standards. An RCA color caravan toured the capitals of Europe and then followed Napoleon's invasion route to Moscow, where it conducted numerous demonstrations for the Soviet broadcast and technical hierarchy. When Russia later opted for France's 625-line Secant system and brought along its eastern European satellites, Sarnoff was persuaded the reasons were nontechnical. The Cold War continued unabated, and Sarnoff persevered as spokesman of the anti-Communist right, scathing in his denunciation of the Marxist government of his homeland. An article he wrote in *Life* magazine in 1960 on how to "Turn the Cold War tide in America's favor" by foreswearing appeasement and accommodation drew an unusually long and vituperative response in *Pravda*. So now he was being repaid. "The Russians saw an opportunity to slap the United States and me at the same time," Sarnoff explained to a staff member.

Most of Europe, plus England, later chose the PAL system, but this was of lesser concern to American aspirations because PAL was considered a close variant of this nation's color system. Regardless of the system, however, RCA patents were essential to technical implementation. Even the French demonstrations of Secant in Vienna employed RCA tricolor tubes in the receiving sets. And Sarnoff's patent licensing staff achieved remarkable success in forging contracts with technologically advanced nations around the world. As much as $80 million annually in patent licensing revenues flowed into RCA's coffers, and most of it dropped to the bottom line. Color technology was the principal lure.

The tricolor tube, simplified through the development of a single electron gun instead of three, became a worldwide symbol of America's mass producing skills. Tens of millions were poured out, either in RCA plants or under license to others, and repeated efforts over the years by the best technical brains of America, Europe, and the Orient failed to obsolete the core concept. Among the thousands of products and services generated by RCA's scientists and engineers, the tricolor tube was Sarnoff's favorite. He described it in marbled prose: "Never before have I witnessed compressed into a single device so much ingenuity, so much brain power, so much development, and such phenomenal results."

With the worldwide sweep of color, Sarnoff became more than ever the electronics industry's supreme dialectician of will and purpose. He saw himself in the role of elder statesman, not unlike his friend Bernard Baruch, although he never adopted the conceit of a bench in Central Park from which to dispense homilies on the public issues of the era. At lunches in his executive dining room, he held forth with representatives of the international press, Reuters and the *Times* of London, *Le Figaro* of Paris, telling and retelling the story of color. Increasingly in such interviews, he tended toward orphic pronouncements on progress: "Whatever the mind of man visualizes, the genius of modern science can turn into functioning fact." Increasingly, he broadened the scope of the future he loved to predict: "Atomic batteries will be commonplace long before 1980 . . . a box no bigger than a suitcase and containing 'atomic garbage'—the waste products of commercial atomic energy plants—may, when safely buried in an average householder's cellar, provide enough power to run all his householder equipment, including heat for his home, over a period of twenty years." Within the same time frame he foresaw cancer conquered and "fresh waters purified from the briny seas, making deserts flourish and opening to human habitation immense surfaces of the globe now sterile or inaccessible." As always he genuflected toward the future: "The challenge of tomorrow fascinates me much more than the achievements of yesterday."

Sarnoff's personality changed little as he aged. Unlike many older men, he did not become more crotchety, and his outbursts of temper were less frequent. Color's success had a mellowing influence, and humor surfaced more frequently in his conversation. His wife became the "policeman" who monitored his diet with iron rigidity. While he never discussed what might happen to him after RCA—he simply couldn't visualize such a time—he could joke about senility. "If you ever see any signs of it in me, let me know," he told an aide. The younger man gulped and said, of course. A friend once mentioned that it was remarkable he had never incurred ulcers, given the pressures and intensities of his life. "I don't get ulcers," he said. "I give them."

His philosophy of life was that of a twentieth-century rationalist. Science and reason, he believed, would map human progress, not divine intervention. On rare occasions, he would address himself to the meaning of being a Jew, and the cause of conflict between Jews and non-Jews. In an interview with a reporter from the *Jewish Journal* of New York, on March 24, 1960, he expressed a pragmatic view, saying it was pointless to question whether Jews were a race or a group of coreligionists. Their identity, he asserted, came through a common experience shared in the course of a long history. Then he added:

"The essential Jewish identity is worth preserving because it is an influence that conditions the formation of a better type of human being. Jewish ethics, morality, and wisdom are constructive influences. This does not mean that all Jews are angels, or that they are generally better than other peoples. As we know ourselves, there are bad Jews, just as there are bad non-Jews.

The trouble is, however, that whenever they encounter a corrupt Jew, most non-Jews tend to draw general conclusions and accuse all Jews of corruption. Of course, this is a grave injustice, but it is a fact. And we must reckon with existing facts. Every individual Jew must therefore assume responsibility for the honor of the entire Jewish people, and realize clearly that improper conduct on his part may be damaging to all Jews by encouraging anti-Semitism.

"As a Jew whose lot it has fallen to be in the public eye in America, I always remember this responsibility, this additional obligation imposed upon me by existing conditions. Let us hope that further progress, further enlightenment, and a broader humanism will abolish these conditions and bring about a time when non-Jews will cease to make distinctions in their minds between Jews and non-Jews."

Before he became ill late in the decade, the sixties were Sarnoff's golden years, and color made them so. The recognition he had always so avidly sought came in fuller measure than ever. Problems within RCA, such as mounting computer losses and neglect of the solid-state technology of the future, were submerged by the flood tide of color dollars. The press, which had pricked him in the past for his vanities, was fulsome in chronicling how he had snatched victory from defeat. The paper that over the years had roused his ire more than any other was the *Times*. In particular, his resentment stemmed from the *Times*'s frequent references to him as Mr. Sarnoff rather than General Sarnoff, the form other papers used. When his public relations department complained, the answer came back that this was a stylistic rule. Only career officers in the regular army were accorded their rank in print. To which Sarnoff irately responded that the *Times*'s own general manager, Julius Ochs Adler, was frequently referred to in its columns as Major General Adler, even though he was a national guard officer, not a careerist. To Sarnoff, the injustice was manifest. But now the *Times* headlined, SARNOFF TRIUMPHANT. He was portrayed as a Napoleonic figure, storming grim-lipped down to Princeton in the early days of color, reading the riot act to his scientists, demanding they "get something off the breadboard" so he could march on Washington under the banner of compatible color.

Even his competitors became strangely respectful, no longer challenging the legitimacy of his color leadership claims, and seemingly almost eager to do penance for their earlier hostility. This attitudinal sea change was best exemplified by a sixtieth anniversary in electronics banquet given him in 1966, by major industry organizations at the Waldorf-Astoria grand ballroom. Its hosts were many of the men who had spent a lifetime fighting him. Apart from the usual encomiums expected at such an affair, a deep strain of affection was evident. Robert Galvin, head of Motorola, described him as "our industry's most distinguished citizen" and then became poetic: "By his wisdom he has stirred us, by his perseverance he has profited us, by his success he has garnered success for all." Even his prime color adversary, Bill Paley, provided, with a grin, a rueful postscript: "He never relaxes his efforts, and I've got the scars to prove it." One of those who attended the banquet, seated at a front table with several members of the Sarnoff family and frequently rising to his feet to applaud, was the head of the company that had fought him longer than any other, Joe Wright of Zenith. Another present was his old antagonist Peter Goldmark.

The thirteen-year color struggle was the last major product introduction of Sarnoff's career. Reminiscing later from his bed at Lenox Hill Hospital in New York, he said, "Color was the toughest one, no doubt about it. It stretched us more financially. It was harder to manufacture. It took longer to perfect. And it drew more competitive bad blood than I'd ever seen."

Would color television have swept across American within the same time frame without a David Sarnoff? The answer is almost surely no. Only his type of authoritative leadership could have prevailed so decisively over opposing forces unusual for their breadth and intensity. Not one company of the scores in the electronics industry chose to march abreast of him until the issue was no longer in doubt—nor a major broadcaster except NBC, which he controlled. Even within his own company, had the checks and balances of modern management prevailed, it is probable that the bloated proportion of total corporate resources lavished on color would have been questioned seriously by financial management and an independent board. Years of subpar earnings were the price Sarnoff paid, but he was never seriously challenged. The shareholders who heaped denunciations upon his successor managements at RCA seemed awed by the nimbus of his leadership.

A further question is whether American-made sets, without Sarnoff's relentless persistence, would initially have dominated the domestic color market. A resourceful Japanese electronics industry waited in the offshore wings, its collective characteristics remarkably Sarnoffian. The Japanese development of video recorders, a thirteen-year effort marred by repeated failure before it led to world dominance, bore many similarities to RCA's color effort. Japan's later incursion in the American color market, with small screen sets of unusual clarity and stability, featuring such advanced technology as the Sony Trinitron tube, reached serious proportions only after Sarnoff abdicated to age and illness. Perhaps the timing was coincidental, although old-time Sarnoff associates, like the inventor Zworykin, were never persuaded.

In his own introspective assessment of the qualities of character that produced his color triumph, Sarnoff placed courage, tenacity, and self-confidence on the highest rungs. "I was never fearful of the outcome. I never got butterflies," he said in an interview with *Fortune,* and that summed it up.

More even than in the creation of radio and monochrome television, color certified the validity of the management credo which he had first outlined in 1928 to students of the Harvard Business School. There he had emphasized the need for a new type of executive "trained in a manner not always associated with the requirements of business management." From its classic entrepreneurial function, he suggested, business was entering a new phase, in which success would hinge upon correct interpretation of the direction in which technical developments could lead. This would require the manager to involve himself in the gestatory phase of the inventive cycle, discussing with the scientists directly the technical implications of their embryos, dreaming up possible product applications a decade hence, encouraging further avenues of exploratory work. In effect, the modern manager must achieve a psychic kinship with his technical staff. "I always told my scientists I believed in them more than they believed in themselves," he said.

Although Sarnoff was not an inventor, he was the most successful innovator of his era, with the ability to pinpoint the need for an invention and then flog it through developmental stages to the marketplace. In the words of the renowned Columbia Nobel-laureate physicist Michael Pupin, a Sarnoff friend, that type of innovation represented 50 percent of the invention itself.

Unlike most of his management contemporaries, who were specialists in law, finance, or marketing, Sarnoff possessed an inbred understanding of the language of technology. His years of engineering self-training, his night courses at the Pratt Institute, his continuing apprenticeship under Marconi (through exchanges of letters and visits here and abroad) until the inventor's death in 1937, the path he wore to the RCA laboratories, the extolling of science in his public statements, the lofty positions he bestowed upon scientists and engineers in the RCA executive hierarchy—all these combined to forge an almost mythic bond between him and the technical community. Even his lack of formal training perhaps redounded to his advantage. "He would ask us for things that seemed beyond our technical reach," Engstrom once said. "A degree-bearing engineer might have been hooted down. But Sarnoff could get away with it."

When he first viewed the rudimentary beginnings of electronic color, some of his senior scientists urged him not to divulge their work. It was too primitive. It might never emerge as a commercial system. Qualified scientists like Goldmark of CBS would later say the system was fatally flawed. But Sarnoff, stubbornly, would not listen, and finally his ugly duckling of color, his Rube Goldberg contraption, would emerge as the most graceful swan of twentieth-century technology.

Sarnoff's personal peccadilloes were, of course, not unnoticed by his scientists. Privately, they joked about his voracious appetite for publicity. One of his top scientists, Dr. George Brown, dismissed Sarnoff, in his memoirs, as a publicity seeker. It became conventional wisdom at Princeton that any time news of a development there filtered up to 30 Rockefeller Plaza, Sarnoff would turn it into a headline. Some of them, like an experimental solar battery that powered a radio receiver, faded as quickly as yesterday's headline, more technical gimmickry at the time than scientific substance. His demands for specific inventions as future birthday presents to him were ridiculed by his Ph.D.'s as the ultimate in personal glorification. Yet these fanciful adjurations never obscured to most of RCA's technical people the underlying strength of their relationship to Sarnoff. "We always knew someone up there understood us," Jolliffe, RCA's longtime technical chief, once reminisced. "We knew we were important to him. We knew the value of our work was recognized. I've never been more stimulated than through those long years of television's development. We felt we were doing the most important job in the world. That's how Sarnoff made us feel."

No chief executive of his era placed science on the pedestal that Sarnoff did. None drew more from the wellsprings of research. None telescoped time more effectively between invention and the marketplace. A scientific leader who grasped the transforming import of his work was Dr. Jerome Weisner, president of the Massachusetts Institute of Technology and chief scientific adviser to President Kennedy. After observing from the sidelines the long years of the color struggle, Weisner summed up the qualities that he felt set Sarnoff apart from other industrial titans: "It was his combination of a visionary and determined builder and hardheaded industrial leader. He was among the first to recognize the role that science could play in modern industry and to stake his future entirely on that promise."

10 / Losing Battles

Fifty years after he had begun sweeping floors and polishing spittoons in the American Marconi Company office in 1906, Sarnoff indulged in a bit of reminiscence: "Teddy Roosevelt was president then. Horsecars plied the streets of New York. You could get a schooner of beer for a nickel, and a free lunch at the bar. Gaslight was used in most homes. The horseless carriage was a novelty. Radio broadcasting was unheard and television was unseen.

"I was only fifteen years old and life for me was a blank page—challenging and a bit frightening in its clean white emptiness. Well, I have done a good deal of scrawling over it in half a century. I'd gladly make some erasures and edit out some errors if I could. Yet on the whole I am content. For they have been endlessly fascinating years for me and for the world of science, business, and industry where fate has placed me."

This, for him, rare exercise in nostalgia was inserted in his golden anniversary speech in 1956 at the Waldorf-Astoria and it was as significant for what it omitted as for what it revealed. For more than half those fifty years, he had been overseer of one of America's two most powerful broadcasting networks. The very concept of networking had been his. The flush of profits from NBC had helped underpin the technologies he created. Yet he did not mention broadcasting in his world of science, business, and industry because he never really considered himself a broadcaster. Quite probably, he was thinking of NBC when he spoke of erasing and editing out the errors of his career. It was there that his most serious mistakes of judgment occurred, and loss of leadership in network competition was the price he and RCA paid. He had defeated CBS in color, but just as conclusively CBS had toppled NBC from network leadership, first in radio and then in television.

In the mid-sixties, as color sets were flooding across America and as the liturgy of praise for him mounted ("Fulfillment of the great American dream—the office boy who became head of a tremendous and powerful corporation," a typical editorial in the New York *World-Telegram* read), Sarnoff considered getting rid of NBC. "Maybe this is the time to sell it," he muttered to a startled staff associate at lunch one day in his private dining room. He had recently gone through the tension-filled dismissal of an NBC president, which had created open dissension within the RCA board for the first and only time in his career. The price of television stations was skyrocketing and NBC owned five of them in major markets from New York to Los Angeles. Between the television and radio networks, the studio facilities and the owned stations,

NBC might be worth somewhere between three-quarters of a billion and a billion dollars, or so he speculated while staring into the thick spirals of a freshly lit Monte Cristo cigar. "We could use the money. Data processing eats it up," he said, referring to RCA's newest venture, in which this time it was not the pioneer but a relatively small challenger to mighty IBM. Beyond that, he suggested provocatively, the price NBC could fetch might never be as high as it was right then. He speculated that within the next twenty years the sweep of new technology would undercut the network service, with direct broadcasts from communications satellites bypassing affiliated stations and with such threatening ancillary services as cable television, video tape recorders, and video disc players chipping away the mass audiences that the networks controlled.

Again, at age seventy-five, he was playing his favorite game, conjecturing about the future, thinking thoughts that would explode into headlines if they seeped beyond his dining room sanctuary. Physically, he had slowed perceptibly. His gait had stiffened, become slower, and at times halting. His hair was white and sparser around the pate. Recently, he had undergone an operation for removal of his gall bladder and, while successful, it seemed to drain him of his reserves. He would come later to the office, take occasional naps in the afternoon, and even turn down minor new honors if the price was another speech at another late night banquet.

Perhaps it was the growing perception of his mortality that led him to drop the thought of disposing of the network he had been instrumental in founding forty years earlier. He knew it would cause fierce debate within the company and the industry. There would be endless hearings in Washington, since whoever controlled NBC controlled one of the nation's major resources for news and information. It would be difficult replacing NBC's annual profit contribution on the corporate ledger—sometimes as much as 40 percent of the whole—because it would be years before the computer division could hope to move firmly into the black. If color sales ever tapered off, the financial effects could be serious. But that was a problem future generations of RCA management would have to wrestle with. Looking out the window of his dining room, he saw the dark, fluted columns of CBS's new headquarters skyscraper—"Black Rock," it was called—at 52nd Street and the Avenue of the Americas, only a few blocks removed from his own command post at 30 Rockefeller Plaza. It towered there, in its sleek austerity, an elegant, but to Sarnoff irritating, symbol of leadership in American broadcasting—leadership that he had held for two decades and then allowed to slip away. . . .

From its creation in 1926 on the foundations of AT&T's aborted toll broadcasting network, NBC won public acceptance with a speed and enthusiasm unrivaled in media history. In the words of broadcast historian Erik Barnouw, NBC was "born with a silver spoon . . . It entered the world at a moment of business affluence. Godfather sponsors stood ready with rich gifts." There were then 5 million radio sets in American homes, and the sale of set and studio apparatus had passed the half-billion-dollar mark annually. Stations scrambled to affiliate with NBC's Red and Blue networks, whose programs originated out of New York stations WEAF and WJZ. Many of the early offerings were musical—"The Maxwell House Hour," "The Cities Service Orchestra," "The General Motors Family Party," "The Cliquot Club Eskimos," and "The Ipana Troubadours"—with each carrying the sponsor's name because there was only one sponsor per program. Monthly dramas, carefully scripted and extensively rehearsed, were presented on "The Eveready Hour," and the principal actors were paid up to $125 per performance. The commercials were modest in tone, widely spaced, and usually delivered in an unobtrusive manner by a male announcer.

The return of Charles A. Lindbergh from his solo crossing of the Atlantic affirmed the capacity of the network operation to provide continuing live coverage of special events. On June 11, 1927, the Lone Eagle moved up the canyons of Wall Street and Lower Broadway, drenched in ticker tape and buffeted by the screaming adulation of vast sidewalk throngs. A relay team of NBC announcers maintained a running commentary as Lindbergh's cortege moved northward, bringing to fifty affiliated stations and an audience estimated at 15 million the greatest welcome ever accorded an American hero.

The spread of networking was accompanied by an almost frantic buildup of facilities. NBC spent a half million dollars for new studios at 711 Fifth Avenue, complete with modern soundproofing equipment and the largest air-conditioning system ever installed in an American building. New staff members were added, among them Frank A. Arnold as "director of development," a euphemism for advertising manager. A model shop was created to devise studio and control room equipment. Everything about the new network operation was geared to the development of a quality service being operated in the public interest.

In March 1927 there were 732 broadcasting stations in the United States, the vast majority not network affiliated. Nearly a hundred were educational stations, operated by universities and local boards of education, some offering courses for college credits. There were religious stations providing hours of sermons and liturgical music. Others were owned by newspapers and department stores and used mainly to publicize their services and products. In New York, Mayor John Hylan employed the city-owned station to attack his political enemies until a court injunction stopped him. In this welter of disparate sounds, the NBC network service began swiftly to emerge as the one distinctive national voice of radio. In addition to its musical programs and dramas, news and sports events became increasingly prominent on the schedule. The Iowa farmer could listen to a live broadcast of the Kentucky Derby, or to announcer Graham McNamee's coverage of a New York Yankee baseball game, including an interview with the famed Sultan of Swat, Babe Ruth.

Only 10 percent of its shows in that introductory year were sponsored, and to each station that carried them NBC paid $50 per hour. But for sustaining, or nonsponsored, shows the Red and Blue networks charged each station $45 per hour. With the preponderance of network shows in the latter category, NBC wound up its first year of operations $400,000 dollars in the red. Yet the loss was not troubling to NBC's first overseer, RCA Chairman Owen D. Young. He wanted NBC to achieve self-sufficiency—in other words, to break even—but its real purpose, he told the first meeting of his NBC Advisory Council of eminent Americans on February 18, 1927, was to sell sets. At the time only one out of twenty-two people possessed a radio set, compared with one automobile for every five and one-half persons. "It seems quite clear," he told the council, "that the key that will unlock that market is high-class broadcasting widely distributed. This is the reason for the organization of the National Broadcasting Company."

There was a lofty, self-congratulatory tone at the first meeting of the Advisory Council, over which Young presided. One of its seventeen eminent members, the Reverend Charles F. MacFarland, general secretary of the Federal Council of Churches of Christ in America, said the world of education was "dazed over the vast possibilities of radio as an instrument of education." Walter Damrosch, conductor of the New York Symphony, predicted that music brought to the little red schoolhouses of the nation via NBC would be "the crowning arch of our building." Elihu Root, eighty-two-year-old secretary of state under Teddy Roosevelt, suggested scientific research might be conducted by the network to determine whether its audience was primarily ear-oriented or sight-oriented. There was learned discussion, in which Charles Evans Hughes participated, over whether Socrates' students were ear-minded or eye-minded. Radio was indeed, as NBC's first president, Merlin "Deac" Aylesworth, proclaimed, "a matter for the consideration of statesmen." The Advisory Council was to be NBC's public guardian, an ombudsman ensuring that its programs responded to the nation's highest cultural aspirations. The mere fact of its existence prompted NBC executives initially to delay acceptance of a toothpaste commercial while they debated whether a subject of such personal intimacy as brushing the teeth was suitable for the airwaves.

In the beginning, Young and his council unquestionably influenced the network schedule. A "Farm and Home Hour" was originated out of Chicago, bringing America's isolated rural families the latest information on crop planting techniques and news of general interest to the farmer and his wife. Conductor Damrosch presided over a "Music Appreciation Hour" that became part of the curriculum in 125,000 little red schoolhouse classrooms. Politicians of all persuasions were offered free air time to debate issues of national importance, such as the wisdom of high tariffs. Across the broadcast day, the initial program offerings of the Red and Blue networks provided a rich and varied content of cultural, educational, and informational programs. Great opera stars—Schumann-Heink, Martinelli, Jeritza, Rosa Ponselle; eminent conductors—Serge Koussevitsky and the Boston Symphony, Arturo Toscanini and the New York Philharmonic; the best of the grand opera—*Faust, Lohengrin, Rigoletto;* Shakespeare's classics—*Hamlet, Romeo and Juliet, Othello;* sermons by leading clergymen—Dr. S. Parkes Cadman, Dr. Harry Emerson Fosdick, Rabbi Steven Wise; lectures on government and current events by prominent journalists—Walter Lippmann, David Lawrence, Elmer Davis—all were presented in 1927 before NBC microphones that reached audiences of up to fifteen million people. And they were not confined to broadcasting's later so-called ghetto hours of late night and early morning, but were often scheduled at peak listening hours in the evening.

By 1928 Young's emphasis on cultural content seemed to be paying off. Expenditures on radio sets and components jumped more than $200 million to a record level of $650 million, a faster rate of growth than automobiles or electrical equipment were experiencing. A potent sales stimulus proved to be NBC's extensive live coverage of the Republican convention, which nominated Herbert Hoover for president, and the Democratic convention, whose nominee after prolonged balloting was New York's Catholic governor, Alfred E. Smith. Both candidates relied extensively in 1928 on NBC's microphones in the first national election in which radio played a significant role. Hoover would doubtless have won without it because of the religious issue and because the nation was suffused with Coolidge prosperity. But Smith's East Side twang, borne to the midwest and south by the airwaves (he pronounced radio "raddio"), probably contributed to the landslide proportion of Hoover's victory. The combination of prosperity, increased set circulation, and mounting advertiser interest made it impossible for NBC to hold at Young's break-even goal. In 1928, its second full year, the network reported a $400,000 profit, and subsequent years provided quantum increases.

Three developments occurring in rapid succession converged to move NBC off the lofty pinnacle to which Young had consigned it. A rival network, the United Independent Broadcasters, which was soon to evolve into the Columbia Broadcasting System, began operations on a financial shoestring in 1927. A pair of white comedians, skilled in Negro dialect and known as Amos 'n' Andy, went on NBC in the summer of 1929 and demonstrated for the first time the ability of light entertainment radio programs to rivet the nation. The depression that followed left the country yearning for escape from the grim realities of breadlines and bankruptcies, and radio provided it. Increasingly, sponsors turned away from cultural programming to the comedy and romance that attracted audiences—and moved products.

The rise of CBS accentuated that trend. A year after its formation by

Arthur Judson, a concert hall impresario who favored classical musical programs, the new network had affiliations with only sixteen stations in eleven states and it had run out of money. Enter Paley, the millionaire son of a Philadelphia cigar maker. Then twenty-seven years old, a University of Pennsylvania–Wharton School of Finance graduate, Paley had dabbled in local radio as the advertising manager of the family's Congress Cigar Company and had become intrigued with its commercial possibilities by the response to advertisements of La Palina cigars over Philadelphia station WCAU. With support from his father, he purchased a controlling interest in the struggling network for $500,000. Within months of his assumption of the presidency in September 1928, he had tripled the number of CBS affiliates, had purchased a New York station for program originations to the network, and had begun to attract a formidable roster of popular entertainers, including the jazz band leader Paul Whiteman, a young comedian named Eddie Cantor, and the nation's favorite humorist and raconteur, Will Rogers. It was Paley's theory that "those who put on the most appealing shows won the widest audiences, which in turn attracted the most advertisers, and that led to the greatest revenues, profits, and success." It proved to be an enduringly correct analysis of commercial broadcasting's mission, and Young and the eminent statesmen of his Advisory Council were powerless to counter it. This did not mean that cultural programming was suddenly washed off the network schedules. Both the Red and Blue chains and CBS continued to offer classical music, and educational forums continued to be broadcast, mostly on a sustaining basis but sometimes commercially sponsored. Grigsby-Grunow, RCA's largest competitor in radio set manufacturing and therefore an ardent CBS supporter, sponsored "The American School of the Air" five times weekly on the junior network. Yet the trend was unmistakably toward light entertainment for mass audiences, and the greatest impetus was provided by the two young comedians in blackface, Freeman Gosden and Charles Correll.

Amos 'n' Andy brought the comic strip formula to radio. Gosden was born in Richmond, Virginia, and reared by a black mammy. Touring with minstrel shows as a young man, he played the banjo and did Negro dialect jokes. He teamed up with a fellow performer on the minstrel circuit, Correll, a piano player from Peoria, Illinois, to create blackface routines which were originally broadcast from a Chicago radio station. Their radio characters were two simpleminded blacks from Atlanta who had come to Chicago to start the "Fresh Air Taxicab Company of America, Incorpulated," whose principal asset was one broken-down, topless automobile. The unsophisticated Amos—"Ain't dat sumpin'?"—and the conniving Andy, who was always "workin' on the books," soon attracted a large local following over station WMAQ. Gosden and Correll hit upon the idea of recording the program, which they did live in the studio, and offering it to other stations. By 1928 they had thirty outlets for their pioneering syndicate, and the trials and tribulations of Amos 'n' Andy became a national conversation piece. One of their biggest fans was President Coolidge, who reportedly always set aside matters of state during their fifteen-minute program.

In the summer of 1929, NBC paid Amos 'n' Andy $100,000 annually, an unheard-of price, to go on the national network. Telephone surveys soon established that more than half of all radio set owners were tuned to the program when it was broadcast from 7:00 to 7:15 P.M. Sales of radio sets in 1929 soared to $842 million. More than any other program, Amos 'n' Andy established the national character of radio and sealed its entertainment imprimatur. Gosden and Correll became front-rank celebrities, invited to the White House in 1929 by new President Hoover, who allegedly swapped jokes with them for an hour.

By 1931 the profits of both NBC and CBS exceeded $2 million annually. They were among the nation's few depression-proof businesses. The Red and Blue networks were supplemented by an Orange network on the West Coast, and the affiliate total reached eighty-seven. By the time Sarnoff assumed full control of NBC in 1932, when RCA achieved independent status, NBC was an oasis of prosperity in a nation with 12 million unemployed, its terrain dotted with thousands of failed banks and boarded-up business properties. Despite his aversion to advertising, Sarnoff made no effort to limit commercials, which were becoming increasingly strident in tone. Advertisers wanted maximum results for their financially strained clients, and the era of the hard sell in broadcasting waxed as the depression intensified. Prizes were offered over the air to those who sent in box tops of products advertised. More than 400,000 inserts in Ovaltine cans were mailed to the sponsor in order to get pictures of Little Orphan Annie, heroine of one of the most popular radio serials.

Only a third of NBC's, and a fifth of CBS's, full broadcast schedules were commercially sponsored in 1932, but they were concentrated in the heaviest listening hours of the evening, and the impact of radio pitchmen began to grate on the ears of some intellectuals and politicians. Across the Atlantic, Britain's government-operated BBC was pure of commercialism. When its chief, Sir John Reith, was visited by an American broadcasting delegation, he asked perplexedly, "How can you Americans successfully worship God and Mammon at the same time?" Somewhat similar questions were beginning to be asked in the U.S. Congress. Senator Burton K. Wheeler of Montana complained that the airwaves had become "a pawnshop." A liberal social commentator of the era, James Rorty, described the American apparatus of advertising as unique in history—"a grotesque, smirking gargoyle" whose mouth was a loudspeaker that "is never silent, it drowns out all other voices, and it suffers no rebuke, for is it not the voice of America?" To Rorty, the American culture was becoming permeated with "jabberwocky," poured out ceaselessly by countless thousands of loudspeakers. Is it any wonder, he asked, that the population "tends increasingly to speak, think, feel in terms of this jabberwocky?"

But it was too late, even in the restless New Deal atmosphere in which most institutions of the capitalist order were under scrutiny, to tamper with the structure of radio. To the people, it was akin to a savior. There was a hunger for easy and mindless entertainment, a compelling need for a companion to share lonely, jobless hours with. The price of listening to hard-sell commercials was a small one to pay for the only free entertainment available. While numerous measures were introduced in the Congress to restrict radio's commercialism, none emerged into legislation. Perhaps the fact that leaders of both political parties had ready access to the network microphones influenced their attitudes.

Sarnoff never directly involved himself in the day-to-day operations of NBC, and the swing away from the public-service, restricted-commercial type of radio so long espoused by Young was not particularly to his liking. Unlike Paley, he had no attachment to, or feel for, popular entertainment programming. While the youthful CBS head made frequent trips to Hollywood to mingle and socialize with the moguls and stars of the entertainment world, Sarnoff centered his trips far more on his technical laboratories to check on the progress of television. It was clearly more his emerging management style to focus on the future of technology than to wrestle with the quality of radio programming or the intrusiveness of commercials. Besides, NBC seemed to operate on a momentum of its own. As the first network, it had most of the leading stations across the nation as its affiliates. Its new, soundproofed studios on the lower floors of the Rockefeller Plaza headquarters, to which it moved in 1933, were the envy of the industry. By that year it had eighteen hundred employees, more than double CBS's total. With the upsurge of commercialism, advertising agencies became increasingly influential in the creation of programs, and their first choice in placing them was usually NBC, the most prestigious network. Under agency sponsorship, a young singer named Rudy Vallee began crooning into NBC microphones and almost overnight became a national idol, rivaling Amos 'n' Andy in popularity. Similarly the Lucky Strike Dance Orchestra was agency-created and placed on NBC. It soon ranked in the top five most-listened-to programs, according to a Crosley telephone sampling of radio homes in the first regular national audience rating service.

The swing to pop music and comedy in the thirties was accompanied by the emergence of mystery thrillers, such as "Gangbusters" and "The Shadow," and by the introduction of a new genre of daytime programs, known as soap operas. These were daily serials with a regular cast and a running plot theme, usually turgidly romantic. With such colorful titles as "Our Gal Sunday," "Just Plain Bill," and "Ma Perkins," the daily soaps attracted an audience of fanatically loyal housewives who could listen while washing the dishes or performing other househould drudgeries. The ladies responded to this weepy, low-budget fare by purchasing the products of sponsors in vast amounts, and the daytime soaps soon became one of the most profitable segments of the broadcast schedule to the networks. They also became the most enduring program format in broadcasting, an American phenomenon.

The fiction that commercials were not a form of direct advertising was maintained by the networks for a few years, since they prohibited mention of product prices in sales pitches. They also prohibited certain product categories, such as deodorants and sanitary napkins, along with any descriptive language that might be considered offensive to family listeners. But even these taboos began to evanesce as network competition intensified. First CBS and then NBC caved in on price mentions and more lurid phrases began creeping into commercials. The hard-sell school of advertisers was led by George Washington Hill of American Tobacco, who believed commercials had to shock and irritate in order to sell. Through his agency, Lord and Thomas, Hill began switching shows from NBC to CBS because the junior network would allow his commercials to say Cremo cigars were rolled by workmen without using spit as a binder. "There is no spit in Cremo" came bellowing into the nation's homes, followed by the assurance that the cigar still cost only five cents. Hill's fame as the high priest of commercialism spread when he became the model for the broadcast sponsor in Frederick Wakeman's best-selling novel *The Hucksters,* which was later made into a motion picture with Hill portrayed by the sinister Sydney Greenstreet. His most famous line in the novel: "All you professional advertising men are scared to death of raping the public. I say the public likes it."

From the elder statesmen of the NBC Advisory Council, control of network radio's schedule was clearly shifting to commercial interests—soap and cat food manufacturers, toothpaste peddlers, tobacco tycoons like Hill. Owen Young's vision of radio as "the greatest potential educator and spreader of culture ever dreamed of" was being eclipsed by the cacophonous rhythms of the sponsor's message. Slogans became the literature of radio: "Reach for a Lucky instead of a sweet." One of radio's primary inventors, Dr. Lee De Forest, would soon cry out in anguish, "what have you gentlemen done with my child?"

By the mid-thirties, light entertainment programs represented more than half of NBC's total schedule, with a virtual monopoly on the evening hours when viewing was heaviest. The trend toward what Sarnoff had begun privately describing as "mindless entertainment" seemed irreversible.

He was not happy about it, yet he felt there were limits on what he could do. NBC's annual profits had passed the $4 million level and he needed them desperately in those depression-pinched years to offset the developmental costs of monochrome television. If he attempted to redress the scheduling imbalance by imposing shows of his own taste, he risked losing network leadership to an aggressive CBS. But psychologically he could not attune himself to popular tastes. At home, when Lizette was glued to the latest episode of Amos 'n' Andy, he would disappear into his study. Year later, he would discuss his feelings with an associate, George Marek, head of the RCA Records Division. "His outlook on life was simply too serious to accommodate to popular tastes," Marek would recall. "He did not understand the hunger for easy entertainment. He didn't understand people's loneliness. He saw broadcasting as a means of bridging cultural differences, bringing people together in greater understanding of one another. He thought it should uplift society, should be an instrument for peace."

On occasion, Sarnoff would swim against the mass tide with bold programming innovations designed to uplift. In the early thirties he initiated regular Metropolitan Opera weekend broadcasts over NBC and, as a supportive gesture, served on the Met's board for seventeen years. In 1937, he brought Dr. James Rowland Angell, president of Yale University, to NBC to design and counsel on educational programs. This proved more a gesture than an achievement, for Angell was clearly adrift in the commercial waters of broadcasting.

In that same year, however, Sarnoff did pull off the greatest cultural coup in broadcasting history. It had its origin in a chance meeting between him and Samuel Chotzinoff, music critic of the New York *Post*, who was a close friend of the foremost conductor of the era, Arturo Toscanini. "We talked about music," Chotzinoff later wrote, "and discovered in each other an admiration for the great voices of the past, a brash addiction to melody, and a reverence for the art of Arturo Toscanini. 'What a pity,' I said, 'that America will never hear and see the Maestro again.' He agreed it was a pity and something should be done about it."

From 1925 until 1936, Toscanini had conducted the New York Philharmonic Symphony at Carnegie Hall. Then, because of an obscure disagreement over orchestral matters, the Maestro had quit abruptly and returned in anger to his native Italy, vowing never again to set foot in America. Countless importunings to reconsider had not swayed him.

Three weeks after their first meeting, Sarnoff encountered Chotzinoff at a New York theater. He offered the critic a ride home in his limousine. Without any explanatory preamble, he asked Chotzinoff to come to NBC as a musical consultant at a substantially greater salary than the *Post* paid. The bemused Chotzinoff accepted, but it was not for several weeks after he reported to work at NBC, with no assigned duties, that the reason for his hiring emerged. Called to Sarnoff's office, he was told: "I want you to get Toscanini."

Since the first meeting of the two men, Sarnoff had come to the conclusion that the best answer to the growing legion of radio's commercial critics would be to sign up the greatest living musician and showcase him in prime time on NBC with no commercial intrusions. He induced Chotzinoff to send a cabled invitation to the Maestro in Milan, but the answer came back promptly, THANK YOU DEAR FRIEND NO.

Sarnoff was not deterred. If it would take something exceptional to change Toscanini's mind, he would provide it. "Why not create an orchestra for him? A radio orchestra. The best musicians in America brought together under his baton. An NBC Symphony. Would he go for that?" Even the doubting Chotzinoff was impressed. The concept of creating an elite orchestra for a conductor, tailored exclusively to his specifications, was so radically different that it just might appeal to Toscanini's formidable ego.

But this time, Sarnoff said, no cables. "You, Chotzie, get on a boat and go to Milan. Confront him directly," In January 1937, at a time when Edgar Bergen and his puppet Charlie McCarthy were the talk of radio, Chotzinoff set forth on a different type of radio mission, accompanied by his wife, Pauline, the sister of violinist Jascha Heifetz. Greeted warmly by Toscanini and his wife, Carla, the Chotzinoffs spent two weeks wining and dining the Maestro before the reason for the trip emerged. As related in his memoirs, Chotzinoff, following an evening of tippling fine Italian wines, showed the mellowed Maestro an American newspaper clipping which told how canaries in Cincinnati, listening to a Toscanini recording of Beethoven, had begun to warble the Ninth Symphony. Just think, Sarnoff's emissary said, if the Maestro could so mesmerize canaries what his impact on millions and millions of Americans would be through radio. He spelled out the details of the Sarnoff proposal, the absolute artistic control the Maestro would possess over the finest musical ensemble unlimited funds could procure, the availability of the greatest American network to spread his music instantaneously to audiences of a size that no conductor had ever reached. Fascinated by the story of the canaries— "*Meraviglia*," he exclaimed—Toscanini agreed to return to America for a season of ten concerts, with a fee to him of $40,000, exclusive of taxes and living expenses. Then seventy years old, he accepted Chotzinoff's persuasive argument that this could provide a grand and different finale to his illustrious career.

A telephone call from Milan to New York informed the elated Sarnoff of the Maestro's decision. He offered to come to Milan for a contract signing, but Chotzinoff assured him he would return with Toscanini's signature. So now Sarnoff had his answer to radio's carpers. Into the network schedule of soap operas, cloak-and-dagger thrillers, and dialect comedians, he would inject luminous music that would stir the soul of America and restore radio to the lofty pedestal he and Young had originally envisaged.

Immediately on Chotzinoff's return, the work of putting together radio's first symphonic orchestra began. Sarnoff devoted as much attention to it as he had to Zworykin's television inventions. Artur Rodzinski, conductor of the Cleveland Symphony, was hired as assistant director, and he and Chotzinoff began assembling the ninety-two artists that Toscanini had set forth as his requirement in a handwritten letter to Sarnoff. Studio 8-H at NBC's 30 Rockefeller Plaza headquarters was enlarged and acoustically upgraded, with space provided for an audience of fourteen hundred. Shortwave links were set up between the studio and Toscanini's Milan villa, so that he could listen to Rodzinski's rehearsals of the carefully selected instrumentalists. True to his promise to the Maestro, Sarnoff had spared no expense in their selection. He had gone to the RCA board for a quarter-million-dollar grant, the equivalent of nearly 3 million in current dollars. Everything would be paid for by RCA. There would be no taint of commercialism in this majestic endeavor, no spitless Cremos in tandem with Wagner and Bach.

Sarnoff personally wrote the press announcement of Toscanini's impending return, couching it in the flowery phrases that had become his hallmark. The "incomparable genius" of the twentieth century's preeminent musical figure would soon reach out to all Americans, thus stimulating and enriching musical appreciation on an unprecedented scale. The first concert would be broadcast on Christmas night, 1937, thus providing the nation the richest of holiday gifts.

The response overjoyed Sarnoff. The musical world applauded. Mayor Fiorello La Guardia told him, "The city is grateful to you." To the *New York Times,* "David Sarnoff, who began life in America as a messenger boy, has again glorified his office." Invitations to the inaugural concert in Studio 8-H became the most sought after of all prizes for the city's social and financial elite.

When Toscanini arrived in early December, Sarnoff and Chotzinoff were at the gangplank to greet him. The gray-haired conductor's first words assured them of the seriousness with which he addressed his new assignment. "NBC orchestra very good . . . first clarinetist not so good." His uncanny ear had picked out a flaw listening to Rodzinski's rehearsals from 3,000 miles away. But he shrugged aside Chotzinoff's offer to replace the first clarinetist. He would remedy the flaw.

Through December, the volatile Toscanini rehearsed his new orchestra, pleading, cajoling, fuming, striving for musical perfection with a tirelessness and intensity that amazed Sarnoff, who was twenty-four years his junior. Often, the RCA leader would slip away from his office and sit in a rear row of Studio 8-H to listen to a rehearsal. Sometimes he would take friends with him, among them Joe and Rose Kennedy and their daughters. He also had a line strung from the studio to his office so that he could "pipe in" to rehearsals during free moments on his calendar.

In the remembrance of Sarnoff's old associates, this was one of the happiest periods of his career. "He was like a kid with a new toy," Alfred Goldsmith recalled. Yet his orchestra was more than a plaything to him. The love of music had been bred into him as a child, when he listened to cantorial

phonograph. The idea is to bring music into the home by wireless." In 1922, directors of Radio Corp. of America, which had absorbed Marconi, skeptically put Sarnoff's "radio music boxes" on the market; in the first three years sales came to $83 million, exceeding even Sarnoff's estimate of $75 million.

TV: But Sarnoff already was peering into the future. In 1923 he wrote: "I believe that television, which is the technical name for seeing as well as hearing by radio, will come to pass in due course." So strong was that belief that all through the precarious Depression years, Sarnoff, who by then was RCA's president, sank huge sums into TV research. An RCA scientist, Dr. Vladimir Zworykin, recalled later that when Sarnoff first asked him how much the project would cost, "I pulled a figure out of the air—$100,000. When he had spent $20 million on television and we were still experimenting away, he said he was just beginning to realize what a good salesman I was." But Sarnoff's vision was proved again in darkened living rooms across the country after World War II, when a new generation of Americans huddled transfixed around their new television sets.

By that time, however, Sarnoff was spreading the gospel of color television, which turned out to be one of his greatest challenges. First, the feisty pioneer had to get the Federal Communications

was the natural enemy of radio, they said—Sarnoff showed them a unique opportunity: "We'll combine radio and the phonograph in the same set." And though he was a foe of "cheap entertainment" in the early days, he accepted the bland fare on which broadcasting thrived. Said Sarnoff, who watched little TV himself: "We have a certain responsibility for creating programs, but basically we're the delivery boys."

Yes, Sir! Sarnoff, however, was anything but a delivery boy. He ruled RCA with an iron hand until he turned over the chief executive's role to his oldest son, Robert, in 1966. From the time he was a brigadier general on Gen. Dwight D. Eisenhower's staff in World War II, no one at RCA called him anything but "General." Though the title obviously played on his vanity, it also suited the man: for despite his lack of imposing physical stature and formal education, Sarnoff cut a figure of uncommon authority and confidence. His fearless combat-

...on the first TV broadcast...

...and as ruler of RCA

rious side: listening to music, reading history and biographies and adding to his exhaustive collection of the memorabilia of electronics history. It was typical of the man that up to his death last week—though an illness of more than three years impaired both his sight and hearing—he was as concerned as ever about the problems facing RCA.

But for all his toughmindedness, Sarnoff also had a warmth that made for enduring friendships. Last week 10 fewer than 700 mourners jammed Manhattan's Temple Emanu-El for his funeral service; the outpouring prompted police to close Fifth Avenue to other traffic. The cantor was the Met's Richard Tucker, and the eulogist, New York Gov. Nelson Rockefeller, who delivered this tribute: "Others looked at radio and saw a gadget; his genius lay in his capacity to look at the same things... but to see far more. In David Sarnoff, the word "visionary" meant a capacity to see into tomorrow and make it work."

David Sarnoff
1891-1971

On the night of April 14, 1912, a 21-year-old operator on duty at the wireless station atop the old John Wanamaker store in New York picked up a message that shook the world: "SS Titanic ran into iceberg. Sinking fast." For the next 72 hours, during which President William Howard Taft forbade all other wireless transmissions, David Sarnoff stayed at his post, receiving names of survivors from the rescue ship Carpathia.

The Titanic tragedy proved to be a milestone for both radio and young Sarnoff, whose family had come to New York from Russia in 1900. In fact, Sarnoff and broadcasting became so inextricably entwined that it was difficult to say if the new industry made the man or vice versa. Sarnoff himself once said, "I happened to be born about the time radio was born and I happen to have gone along with it." But it was Sarnoff above all others who foresaw the profound effect that the electron would have on the world. "I have learned to have more faith in the scientist," he said, "than he does in himself."

Indeed he did. In 1916, when radio's progenitors thought of it primarily as a rescue device, Sarnoff wrote a now famous memo to his superiors at the Marconi Wireless Telegraph Co. of America: "I have in mind a plan of development

Commission to reverse itself and approve RCA's color system over one developed by the rival Columbia Broadcasting System. Then Sarnoff and RCA virtually had to go it alone for almost a decade before an initially indifferent public finally took to color. He invested $130 million before earning a dime.

Unlike many visionaries, Sarnoff was the consummate businessman. To make sure that people who bought radios would have a steady stream of programs to listen to, he formed the National Broadcasting Co. in 1926. Similarly, he promoted the sale of color-TV sets by pushing NBC into all-color broadcasting long before the rival networks took the plunge. When other RCA executives objected to his 1929 purchase of Victor Talking Machine Co.—the phonograph

iveness made him a tough adversary for anyone, and his intolerance of bumbling subordinates was legend.

Above everything, Sarnoff's fetish was hard work. As a youngster on Manhattan's Lower East Side, he had to quit school to support his family when his father died, and Sarnoff later said that an honorary diploma from Stuyvesant High School in his old neighborhood was among his most cherished awards. Bent on getting a job as a copy boy with the old New York Herald, he walked through the wrong door and ended up as a $5-a-week messenger boy with the Commercial Cable Co. But the wrong door had led to the right place; soon Sarnoff had taught himself the Morse code and was working as a Marconi operator. Even Sarnoff's hobbies were on the se-

Sarnoff: As a Marconi operator . . .

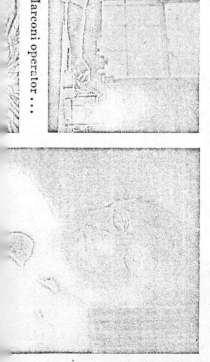

chants at Sabbath services and later in America when he sang as a boy soprano in synagogue choirs. In the Russia of his youth, musical ability was prized nearly as much as spirituality. Those who demonstrated early gifts as instrumentalists or vocalists—even Jews—could hope to be exempt from later compulsory military service in the czarist armies. In Marek's view, Sarnoff's response to classical music was not that of the expert technician, attuned to the nuances of each musical phrase. Rather, it was "like a warm bath flowing over him," relaxing, comforting, washing away the tensions involved in guiding his empire.

Christmas night, 1937: the world threatened by war, and America still in the grip of depression. As Toscanini lifted his baton, Studio 8-H was crowded to overflowing. The pellucid strains of Vivaldi's Concerto Grosso in D Minor filled the NBC microphones, and millions in American and Canadian homes listened, an aggregate audience estimated to rival that of the big entertainment shows. To the New York *Herald Tribune,* it proved that "the popular appetite for the greatest things that music has to offer is neither a delusion nor a dream. It is an actuality." In the ensuing week, thousands of letters flowed into NBC, expressing gratitude in extravagant terms for this supreme offering of symphonic art.

While subsequent Toscanini concerts did not hold to the high audience level of the emotion-filled premiere, millions continued to listen, and the critics continued with unanimity to applaud the Maestro, that "most fanatically uncompromising of musical idealists." As the ten-concert series concluded in March 1938, Sarnoff strode to the microphone at intermission to announce that he had signed a new three-year pact for Toscanini to return, and the Studio 8-H audience responded with an ovation. Sarnoff was determined to continue the orchestra on a sustaining basis, and he explained his reasons to the network audience: "The National Broadcasting Company is an American business organization. It has employees and stockholders. It serves their interests best when it serves the public best."

These were lofty words, with which not everyone agreed. George Washington Hill of Cremo fame was the largest NBC sponsor in total dollars, and he requested a meeting with the RCA chairman through Albert Lasker, a Sarnoff friend who headed the agency that then handled the tobacco account. The encounter took place in Sarnoff's office, and Hill came quickly to the point: "If I were one of your shareholders, I'd vote to fire you. Symphonic music has no place in a mass medium." Against this, Sarnoff could counter with a letter he had received from the inventor Lee De Forest. The Toscanini symphonies, he wrote, "constitute the capstone to the structure of broadcasting, the realized perfection of my life's dream." Together, De Forest and Hill—the music-loving inventor and the tobacco huckster—came to symbolize in Sarnoff's mind the dichotomy of mass broadcasting with which he would struggle for the remainder of his life, and which persists to this day.

In 1939, Sarnoff nearly lost his prized Maestro. Returning to Milan after another acclaimed NBC season, Toscanini spoke out vehemently against Mussolini and fascism, which he detested. The Axis pact had been signed, war was imminent, and only Toscanini's international renown saved him from imprisonment for treason. When he sought to return to America that fall, no exit visa was forthcoming, and Il Duce's foreign office would give no reason. Frantically, Toscanini cabled Sarnoff for aid. Perhaps the State Department would intervene. But Sarnoff had a better thought. His friend Joe Kennedy was then America's ambassador to England, an outspoken critic of American involvement in the European conflict and, many suspected, sympathetic because of his Irish heritage to the aspirations of the Axis powers. It had been rumored in the press that he had close connections to ruling circles in Berlin and Rome. Beyond that, Sarnoff knew of his reverence for classical music and for Toscanini. Together they had attended rehearsals of the NBC Symphony. When Kennedy went to London, he requested Sarnoff to ship him albums of classical recordings, which he never tired of playing at his embassy quarters. So Sarnoff called London, over an unused NBC circuit, and explained his dilemma to the ambassador. Toscanini's first concert of the season was within three weeks, so time was of the essence. Kennedy agreed to look into it.

A week later, Sarnoff received wireless confirmation that Toscanini and Carla had slipped across the frontier into Switzerland and were en route to America. In Sarnoff's mind, there was no question what had happened. "I don't know how Joe did it," he later recalled. "I never heard from him. But I never doubted that he was responsible. Without him, Toscanini would have been a casualty of the war." A quarter century later, Senator Ted Kennedy wrote Sarnoff asking him to compose a reminiscent chapter on his long relationship with the senior Kennedy. It was to be incorporated in a privately printed book about their grandfather for the Kennedy grandchildren. Sarnoff chose to relate the story of the Toscanini escape, although of course omitting any suggestion of Axis ties.

Through the war years, the Maestro remained in America, continuing to conduct the NBC Symphony in broadcast concerts that were deemed too important to morale to cancel. After the war and Mussolini's demise, he returned to his homeland for occasional concerts, but always he would come back to New York for "just one more year." Ultimately, his engagement stretched to seventeen years. From 1948 to 1954, his concerts were simulcast on both radio and television and in the final years they originated from other major American cities to which Toscanini and his orchestra were transported by an NBC special train. When he was eighty-seven, he decided to lay down his baton, writing Sarnoff that "I must reluctantly say good-bye to my orchestra." This time it was final. Three years later he died in New York, by general consensus of the obituary writers history's greatest conductor. He was buried in Milan.

The cost of Toscanini to NBC and RCA over seventeen years was never precisely measured because Sarnoff didn't want it to be. He didn't want a price tag, which would have been in the millions, bandied about for the spiritual heirs of the Cremo king to shoot at. There had, of course, been some tangible rewards. Recordings of the broadcasts were issued under the RCA Victor label and sales, by classical standards, were enormous. Even today, the collected albums of Toscanini and the NBC Symphony represent an important part of the nation's musical heritage and are occasionally reissued. Many of the gifted musicians in the orchestra had played in commercial musical programs on NBC during the Maestro's off seasons. But the greatest gain that Sarnoff measured was the intangible of goodwill and prestige that Toscanini had brought to broadcasting and NBC. In a perhaps overenthused evaluation, he told friends the reason congressional investigations of radio's commercial content never progressed beyond the talking stage was because of the towering rebuttal provided by *his* orchestra. He also often expressed regret that his broadcast competitors had not made comparable financial sacrifices to shore up radio's public service image. It seemed to him another example of his pioneering, with others standing by and sharing in the benefits.

A personal plus to him out of the Toscanini experience was the relationship he developed with Chotzinoff. They became the closest of personal friends, the slender, courtly Chotzie, with his vast fund of musical knowledge, a frequent visitor at the Sarnoff town house, as much loved by Lizette as David. Beyond his Toscanini contributions, Chotzie displayed a quite rare capacity to fuse musical culture with the popular idiom of broadcasting. With Sarnoff's encouragement and financial backing, Chotzinoff created, after the Toscanini era had ended, an NBC opera company for television. Among the operas he commissioned was Gian-Carlo Menotti's poignant Christmas parable *Amahl and the Night Visitors,* which became a television classic, repeat broadcast for several years during the holiday season. It was the NBC opera company which launched the illustrious career of soprano Leontyne Price. Chotzie's death in 1963 left a painful gap in Sarnoff's life, and his enthusiasm for creating new cultural forms for broadcasting waned.

Toward the mass entertainment programs that continued increasingly to constitute the backbone of the network schedule, Sarnoff maintained an aloofness that mirrored his lack of rapport with them. In 1934, after Young's departure, he took the additional title of chairman of the board of NBC and maintained a large, elegantly furnished office next to the boardroom on the sixth floor. Yet he was seldom there, seemingly more comfortable in his fifty-third-floor eyrie guiding RCA's technologies. To NBC's presidents, beginning with Young's choice of the electrical utility executive Merlin

Aylesworth, he deputized the day-to-day details of running the network.

And NBC continued to flourish, generating a momentum that seemed almost impossible to arrest. As new stars flashed in the nation's entertainment firmament, their agents and sponsors sought the secure lodgment of a time slot with the premier network. Fred Allen, the dry-witted overseer of Allen's Alley; a young, parsimonious comedian from Waukegan, Illinois, named Jack Benny; the husband and wife team of George Burns and the fey Gracie Allen; a dimpled, carrot-topped comedian named Red Skelton—all gravitated to NBC in the late thirties and forties, joining Amos 'n' Andy and Bergen and McCarthy at the top of the Hooper ratings. Even the FCC-forced divestiture of the Blue network in 1941 did not alter the network power balance. Out of the commission's decision that no radio station could affiliate with a broadcast company owning more than one network, Sarnoff was forced to shear off the junior Blue network. He grumbled privately at the FCC action but he was unwilling to risk further antitrust exposure by a court challenge. So he sold the Blue chain, which broadcast NBC's least popular programs, for $8 million to Edward Noble, the Life Saver magnate. Thus was born the independent American Broadcasting Company, which struggled for years in third place, competitive with neither NBC nor CBS in program popularity, station lineup, or profits. The comedians stayed with NBC Red, whose clutch on the nation's funnybone seemed unshakable.

Yet Sarnoff found himself on the defensive in network radio's growth years. He could not ignore the growing criticism of commercial blatancy, nor the voices of intellectuals, some his friends, raised against what they called programming for the lowest common denominator. It was not enough to throw Toscanini at them. They wanted "good" programs available when they wanted them. Why, they asked, when they had an occasional free evening and flipped on the dial could they find nothing but raucous comedians or "the Shadow knows," interspersed with pitches for patent medicines or spitless Cremos? Why were there no programs suited to their tastes? It was the beginning of the argument of "mass versus class" in the public domain of the airwaves and it continues unresolved.

One of Sarnoff's questioning friends was Felix Frankfurter, Harvard law professor, a philosopher of Roosevelt's New Deal, later to become a Supreme Court justice. In 1934, while a visiting professor at Oxford, Frankfurter sought in a letter to draw out Sarnoff's personal philosophy of broadcasting's responsibility. Where did he stand on the growing issue of culture versus commercialism?

In his response, Sarnoff attempted to define the dilemma facing him and other broadcasters. In the "mass versus class" argument, he came down on the side of "catering to both tastes"—the "uncultured" tastes of the masses and the "discriminating" taste of the educated elite. Yet the difficulty of achieving it, he implied, was at least in part the responsibility of the intellectual. In words that would be echoed by countless broadcasters over the years when under attack, he explained to Frankfurter:

"I have often tried the experiment, in talking with well intentioned critics of broadcast programs, of asking them how many of the outstanding broadcasts of the week they have heard. Almost invariably they have heard none of them and did not know they were on the air although their existence was advertised in the daily press. What these people want is, at the moment when it suits their fancy to turn on the radio, to have the loudspeaker pour forth the particular kind of music or information in which they happen to be interested. They would not expect this in a theatre or an opera house because they would have to select the date, pay for a ticket, and take their person to the place of entertainment. In radio, however, entertainment comes to the place where the person is, and there being no work to do and no payment to make, it is natural and understandable that the listener should be even more demanding."

Sarnoff insisted to his friend that there were "cultural programs of high artistic value heard over the air time and time again." And it was the commercial revenues from mass appeal shows that made them possible on a sustaining basis. Still, Sarnoff was defensive. He conceded to Frankfurter his reasoning might sound like "an apologia for the bad pipes of my plumbing trade," and he admitted there were inadequacies in the network service. He wound up the letter with a rather plaintive appeal to Frankfurter and other "creators of thought and artistry" to help "the mechanic and the plumber."

The coupling of radio to plumbing was an ill-chosen symbolism that would plague Sarnoff for years after. Early in his RCA career, his mother, Leah, whose command of English was halting, expressed bafflement at the language of his new profession. Frequencies, the ether, the spectrum, all the esoterica of technology: How could she explain it to her friends? "Just tell them I'm in the plumbing business," he said. "Just say we build our pipes in the air, not in the ground." It had been an off-the-cuff response, but the humor of it appealed to him. Also, it conveyed a modest, rather self-deprecatory image of a young man on the rise, one not overwhelmed by the awesome complexities of wireless. So he began employing the plumbing metaphor periodically in interviews or informal communications, as to Frankfurter. But to those unsympathetic to programming trends in radio, and later in television, it began to acquire a less innocuous connotation. To syndicated columnist John Crosby of the *Herald Tribune,* it suggested more concern with the technology of radio, its "pipes," than with what flowed through those pipes to the public. In angry rebuttal to Crosby and other critics, Sarnoff would reprise his cultural contributions to the medium— Damrosch and the school of the air, Toscanini and the symphony, Menotti and the opera.

Yet with those luminous exceptions, Sarnoff made little pretense of influencing program decisions at his network. It was not until after World War II that an unexpected competitive thrust forced him to pay serious attention to the entertainment side of his enterprise.

During the war years, the fever chart of radio's Hooper ratings was eclipsed by the demands of the nation's defense. Radio became the fount and the voice of patriotism. War bond rallies were broadcast, and massive patriotic extravaganzas exhorting the population to buy bonds, work harder on war production lines, and seal its lips against Axis spies. Spit disappeared from the airwaves. Now it was "Lucky Strike Green Has Gone to War." The networks labored round the clock providing entertainment, through the Armed Forces Network, for the fighting men abroad. The villains of radio dramas became Huns and Japs. The music of radio became martial, soaring off into the wild blue yonder.

The most competitive wartime arena for the networks was in news, and here CBS excelled in the quality and depth of its foreign coverage. From London, Edward R. Murrow's stirring reports of a Britain under siege won him and CBS acclaim on both sides of the Atlantic. Eric Sevareid, William L. Shirer, Charles Collingwood, and Winston Burdette formed, with Murrow, the nucleus of a foreign staff that made CBS news programs the most listened to in broadcasting.

Like Sarnoff, Paley served in uniform during the conflict. He was a colonel in the psychological warfare branch of Eisenhower's headquarters staff in London. But where Sarnoff returned from the conflict obsessed with the idea of introducing television, Paley returned with a determination to build on the leadership of CBS News and seize the high ground of entertainment programming, the ultimate determinant of radio success. For twenty years, without interruption, NBC had held that ground in radio.

Paley's strategy was neither complicated nor devious. The maximum tax bracket during and immediately after the war was 77 percent for incomes above $70,000. To top entertainers, whose careers could be suddenly truncated by a shift of public whim, the burden seemed particulary onerous. Paley consulted his tax lawyers and came up with the idea of buying the programs of entertainers as a property or a "package." Thus the star, instead of receiving straight income for his services, could sell his program package to the network and pay only 25 percent tax as a capital gain, thus providing an immediate estate for himself and his family. Paley first worked on the idea with Lew Wasserman, president of the Music Corporation of America, the major West Coast talent agency which represented most of radio's stars. The initial targets were Amos 'n' Andy.

"Wasserman and I entered into long and intense negotiations," Paley later wrote. "We realized there were tremendous advantages for both sides if we could make a deal. Freeman Gosden (Amos) and Charles Correll (Andy) would build up an immediate estate for their families, MCA would collect its agent's commission, and CBS would score a positive coup in the broadcasting industry."

If Sarnoff was aware of the negotiations, he gave no indication. Monochrome television sets were finally surging off RCA's production lines and into American homes, and the color television standards battle was heating up. He was preoccupied with the "pipes" of broadcasting, not with what went through them.

In September 1948, Paley was able to announce publicly that CBS had made a package purchase of the "Amos 'n' Andy" property. After nineteen years on NBC, the program would switch to CBS's Sunday evening prime time schedule. "It created quite a splash," Paley said laconically.

But, strangely, Sarnoff did not respond to his competitor's provocation. Some in the industry speculated that NBC's depth in comedians was so great that the loss of one team could not alter the network balance. It was further rumored that Amos 'n' Andy were in the waning phase of their popularity cycle. For several years, their Hooper ratings had plateaued. So perhaps Sarnoff was simply being shrewd in anticipating a shift in the public's volatile appetite for entertainment, thereby saving RCA a costly investment while dumping a fading comedy team on his competitor.

If such was his reasoning, it was quickly invalidated by Paley's next thrust, which was directed at Jack Benny, the king of the Hooper ratings and the linchpin of NBC's dominating Sunday night comedy schedule. Paley judged that with Benny at 7 P.M. Sunday on his radio network, followed by Amos 'n' Andy at 7:30, CBS would receive "the kind of lift, thrust and public image I thought it needed." Again negotiating through MCA, Benny's agent, he offered a package buyout of the comedian's corporation on a capital gains basis. The price was $2,260,000, independent of the generous salaries to be paid Benny and his co-stars for performing. It was a deal that foreshadowed the $30–40 million packages configured for today's stellar athletes and rock stars.

However, this time Paley encountered a stumbling block other than RCA. The American Tobacco Company, Benny's longtime sponsor, heard of the proposed network shift and became alarmed. Would Benny's vast audience, accustomed over sixteen years to tuning him in on NBC, follow him to a different station? Through the tobacco company's advertising agency, Batten Barton Durstine & Osborn, NBC and Sarnoff were warned of the impending deal and prodded to make a counteroffer of the same dimension to retain Benny's services. NBC and BBD&O executives flocked to the West Coast and converged on the MCA offices just as the CBS offer was about to be consummated. When Paley was apprised of this development, he felt personally betrayed. On impulse, he picked up a phone and called Benny directly, offering to come to the West Coast and discuss with him personally this "unfair" turn of events. The comedian agreed, apparently flattered that one of broadcasting's two most eminent leaders would court him directly.

Sarnoff was soon made aware of Paley's personal intervention, but he did not follow him to the West Coast. Had the services of an electronics scientist been in contention, he would have been on the first plane out. But for an entertainment star? A comedian? No, that would demean his stature as an industrial tycoon. That was a job for lawyers and agency and network executives. Beyond that, he was troubled by the terms of the proposed contract, which had been sent to him at 30 Rockefeller Plaza. Should a comedian be able to amass a vast fortune through a legal contrivance aimed at avoiding tax payments? The more Sarnoff studied it, the more he became convinced that it was legally and ethically wrong. So he ordered his emissaries back to New York for further study of the "tax question." This was perhaps the single most fateful error of his career.

To the on-the-scene Paley, Sarnoff's decision provided the opening he needed. Both Benny and MCA were annoyed at Sarnoff's temporizing, and when the CBS leader assured them, "I'm prepared to sign the contract," they swiftly acceded. To American Tobacco, which held for several more years a personal contract for Benny's services, including the right to name the network on which he appeared, Paley made an unprecedented offer: if Benny lost any rating points as a result of the network shift, CBS would compensate American Tobacco under an agreed-upon formula for the duration of the contract. In effect, it was a daring guarantee that CBS would underwrite the switch with no financial risk to the sponsor. It was sufficiently persuasive for Vincent Riggio, who had succeeded Hill as president of the tobacco company, and he ordered BBD&O to effect the change.

Even more than the Amos 'n' Andy defection, the Benny announcement sent tremors through the broadcasting world. More than any single development since the start of radio networking in 1926, it signaled to the industry a shift in the pattern of broadcast leadership. Within a period of months, most of NBC's top entertainers followed Benny to the junior network, entranced by the lure of capital gains. In January 1949, Red Skelton defected. In the same month, Paley grabbed Bing Crosby from ABC, followed a month later by Edgar Bergen and Charlie McCarthy from NBC. In March, it was Burns and Allen, and soon after Ed Wynn, Fred Waring, Al Jolson, Groucho Marx. Even Frank Sinatra, who had left CBS, returned to the fold. The stars who had underpinned NBC leadership for more than two decades followed the pied piper of instant wealth into the enemy camp, and the vast American radio audience followed them.

By 1949 twelve of the top fifteen shows according to the Hooper ratings and sixteen of the top twenty according to the newer Nielsen measuring service were with CBS. In total audience, the junior network was 14 percent higher than NBC. The idea in some broadcasting circles that listener loyalty was vested in a network rather than individual programs was washed away in the tidal wave of audience support that propelled CBS to ascendancy. Benny's rating on CBS, stimulated by the vast publicity attending the switch, improved over his NBC performance, and no rebate was ever necessary. The "Paley raids," as they were soon known, became part of the lore of broadcast history—perhaps the single most decisive competitive development. From 1949 onward, carrying into the television era and through the remaining years of Sarnoff's life, CBS was number one in commercial broadcasting.

Almost as astonishing as the audacity of Paley's raids was Sarnoff's lethargy in responding to them. Nothing could have been less in keeping with the pattern of his life—his fierce competitiveness, his Dionysian belief in the leverage strength gave against those who were weaker, his determination to rebuff those who followed the pioneer, attempting to usurp his leadership. With the resources available to him at RCA, then more than five times as large as CBS, he could have blunted Paley's talent forays simply by meeting the capital gains offers. To the comedians, keeping money was the paramount consideration, not network affiliation. But to Sarnoff another factor was involved, a factor rooted deep in the psyche of his immigrant youth. It was loyalty, the virtue he prized almost above all others. He was personally affronted that the comedians would even consider a network change. It was his concept of networking, his development of the technology—the pipes of broadcasting—that had made their fame and fortune possible. He had made them part of his family. Now they were betraying the stern Old Testament code under which he had been reared. Beyond that, it troubled him that entertainment stars could so dominate a technology he had created. He would not listen to NBC executives who pleaded that the additional cost of the package deals was a small price to pay for continued network leadership. He disliked the whole star system because he felt it gave the entertainers a whip hand over those who had created the industry. Strolling up Fifth Avenue with an associate soon after the mass defection had occurred, Sarnoff commented almost contemptuously: "A business built on a few comedians isn't a business worth being in."

At the annual meeting of RCA shareholders following the debacle, Sarnoff responded to grumbles by elaborating on his theme: "Leadership built over the years on a foundation of solid service cannot be snatched overnight by buying a few high-priced comedians. Leadership is not a laughing matter." But events proved him wrong. The star system continued to flourish in every branch of the entertainment world, and the price for those entertainers adored by the public continued to escalate.

He realized, of course, that something had to be done to placate his shareholders and his shaken NBC organization. So he mounted a crash effort to create new programs and develop new talent. In his mind, it would be a comparable effort to his triumphant come-from-behind battles in the technological arena. Just as he had thwarted Zenith and Philco in the television standards battle, now he would retaliate against CBS in broadcasting. A million and a half dollars was earmarked to refurbish the NBC schedule. Lavish new programs, such as "The Big Show," starring Tallulah Bankhead on Sunday night, were mounted in prime time to undercut the audiences of the defectors. Nationwide talent searches were launched. But the cumulative effect was niggardly. His programmers were simply unable to respond with fresh concepts and faces, as his scientists had done with new technology. Tallulah proved no antidote for the loss of Benny.

The disaster might have been of greater magnitude, perhaps even bringing Sarnoff's rule of RCA into question, had it not been for the great sweep of postwar prosperity that produced a bonanza of sponsor dollars for radio and the television service that was soon to follow. Even from its chronic runner-up position, NBC managed to generate substantial profits. It continued, even after the Paley raids, to provide about 20 percent of RCA's annual sales volume and sometimes more in after-tax profits. And Sarnoff's spectacular success in the introduction of monochrome television tended to eclipse the embarrassment of the defected stars. But the loss of prestige that network leadership provided soon became a major irritant to him, and particularly when CBS print ads began proclaiming that it was the world's number one advertising medium, watched by more people than any other network.

Once Sarnoff had won his battle of television standards, and the nation raced to embrace the new medium, it became apparent that radio's days as the major source of information and entertainment were numbered. As quickly as television stations went on the air, audiences switched from the audio to the visual service. Supported by RCA's leadership in the new technology, including the production of television transmitters and antennae, NBC moved swiftly into the pole position in the video race in the late forties and early fifties. It had the first owned stations on the air; it established the first and most extensive interconnected network, and it came forth with the first authentic television star, a baggy-pants former burlesque comedian named Milton Berle. The zany skits and leering humor of "Uncle Miltie" captivated the nation as Amos 'n' Andy had a generation earlier. Each Tuesday night the indefatigable Berle performed live on the "Texaco Star Theater," and people jammed bars, clubs, restaurants—any place with a television set—to guffaw at his pratfalls and his antic humor. In the press he became known as Mr. Television, its premier salesman. Even Sarnoff was so impressed by his command of the medium that he sanctioned a renewal contract with Berle of unprecedented size and duration. It bound the comedian to NBC for forty years, guaranteeing him a minimum of $100,000 annually whether he performed or not. It eclipsed anything Paley had offered the radio stars, and it suggested to the industry that Sarnoff had learned a lesson from the talent raids—that he was not prepared, despite his feelings about the disloyalty of performers, to abdicate entertainment in television as he had in radio.

But Berle alone was not enough. CBS countered with its vast depth of comedy stars, most of whom made a successful transfer from radio to television. Benny made it, and made it big. So did Skelton. So did Burns and Allen, and others. The momentum CBS generated through the radio talent raids carried into television. Its reputation as the most hospitable home for entertainers grew, and promising new talent gravitated toward it. As Berle's grip on the national audience lessened in the mid-fifties, CBS launched or acquired such fresh new stars as Lucille Ball and Desi Arnaz, Arthur Godfrey and Jackie Gleason. By 1958 the weekly Nielsen popularity poll often reported CBS television programs occupying every position in the Top Ten, which was considered the industry's barometer of success.

At NBC, the impact of Sarnoff's historic miscalculation radiated inward. The internal organization had known only broadcasting leadership and found it difficult to adjust to a follower's role. Executive shuffling became commonplace, and tensions built. Harry Bannister, NBC's veteran head of affiliate relations, observed that life in NBC's executive suite in the years after the Paley raids was comparable to that in a pressure cooker. No one proved it more than Frank White, an experienced broadcaster who had headed the smaller Mutual Broadcasting System for several years and who was brought in by Sarnoff as NBC's president at the end of 1952. Within seven months, he was an emotionally unhinged man who tearfully resigned and left for a lengthy convalescence abroad.

On nine different occasions during his long RCA tenure, Sarnoff shuffled chairmen and presidents of his subsidiary. Conversely, at CBS there was continuing stability at the top. Unlike Sarnoff, Paley involved himself directly in the program selection process, which he considered the heart of broadcasting, and in the nurturing of talent. He left the administration of the network to his longtime president, Dr. Frank Stanton. For more than a quarter of a century, during the years of radio's maturation and television's emergence, the Paley-Stanton team provided a continuity of leadership and strategic direction that NBC was unable to match. Above all, both men were broadcasters, and when they stuck to broadcasting they succeeded. When they attempted to invade the Sarnoff domain of electronic technology, as with color television, they failed.

In Paley's judgment, Sarnoff's inability to select qualified leaders for NBC contributed almost as much to the network's problems as his lack of rapport with the star system. "The General sometimes demonstrated almost a genius for picking the wrong people to run a network business," Paley commented reflectively during a 1981 luncheon.

In the beginning, in 1926, there was Deac Aylesworth, whom Sarnoff inherited when he took command of RCA in 1932. Aylesworth, the electrical industry spokesman, had been chosen by Owen Young, who valued his public relations skills. But Sarnoff was never completely comfortable with him, too much a creature of the Young era and suspect in his loyalty because he had initially balked at reporting to Sarnoff. In 1935, Aylesworth was replaced by Lenox R. Lohr, an outsider with no broadcast experience who had headed the Chicago Museum of Industry and Commerce. Rather than dipping into the entertainment or broadcasting fields to find an executive knowledgeable in programming and talent relations, Sarnoff elected to go the same route Young had. It was a mistake. Lohr survived for four and a half lackluster years during which he created few waves but did little to fortify NBC's leadership posture for the challenges ahead. His replacement was Niles Trammell, and this time Sarnoff did select a professional broadcaster who proved to be, in Paley's view, NBC's most effective president of the Sarnoff era. Ironically, it was in Trammell's regime that the famous talent raids occurred. Trammell sought courageously to prevent them but was overruled.

Born, reared, and educated in the south, Trammell possessed the courtly mannerisms of a plantation aristocrat, but he also exuded a great deal of personal warmth and an engaging sense of humor. His close personal friendships ranged the worlds of broadcasting, business, and finance. Like Paley, he enjoyed the company of entertainers and advertising executives, and he became a golfing companion of many of NBC's leading sponsors. Thoroughly schooled in broadcast station management in Chicago, whence Sarnoff brought him to NBC, he quickly displayed a grasp of all facets of the network operations. Unlike Sarnoff, he considered himself a broadcaster and he genuinely liked the business, his competitors as well as his associates.

Above all, Trammell was fiercely loyal to his RCA boss, who was fond of him personally. When the Benny defection was announced, it was Trammell, who had sought fruitlessly to block it, who attempted to shield his boss from the devastating consequences of his decision. "Until the United States Treasury Department says that such transactions are lawful," Trammell announced in a press statement, "the National Broadcasting Company will continue to refuse to purchase stock in so-called production corporations where the artists who control such corporations are performing on the NBC network. Such arrangements are bound to lead to charges of discrimination between artists who are paying income taxes at the higher regular rates and those who are paying at the lower rate of 25 percent based on so-called capital gains."

But it was a fruitless gesture. Although a few congressmen grumbled at the practice of entertainers selling their services as "a business," the Internal Revenue Service made no effort to challenge the legality of the package deals. And CBS pounced on Trammell's statement, describing it as "unwarranted," and accusing him, not Sarnoff, of "reflecting unfairly on many creative artists who have done no more than abide by our tax law like any business man or corporation."

The frustration of seeing his program schedule gutted by CBS raids eventually took its toll on Trammell. He remained personally loyal to Sarnoff but increasingly, as the CBS comedy juggernaut gathered momentum, he took refuge in golfing outings with cronies at the Indian Harbor Club in Miami and the Lake Placid Club in New York's Adirondack mountains. In 1952, he elected to leave NBC to run a television station in Miami in which he shared an ownership interest with the Knight and Cox newspapers. Presumably as a reward for more than a decade's service as NBC's titular leader, longer than any of his predecessors had survived, Trammell received an NBC affiliation for his station. It was reminiscent of the practice in the automotive industry, where retiring—or shunted aside—executives were rewarded with a dealership in a lucrative market.

In his final two years, Trammell served as the chairman of the NBC board with the mission of training the new president Sarnoff had picked. He was Joseph McConnell, another southerner, schooled as a lawyer, who had made his mark as head of the legal division of RCA Victor, then the company's manufacturing arm. McConnell was bright, personable, and articulate, but whether he could have surmounted his lack of broadcast experience was never conclusively ascertained because he opted after two years to leave NBC for the presidency of the Colgate company. Within RCA there was speculation that McConnell sought a safer haven in the soap and toothpaste business than the turbulent environment of NBC promised. To the frustrated Sarnoff, McConnell's defection represented another breach of family loyalty, and he was as unforgiving toward him as toward the departed entertainment stars.

Next came the brief tenure of the unfortunate White. When he departed, emotionally spent, incapable of reaching decisions, Sarnoff decided, for the first and only time, to assume direct control of NBC's affairs. Since 1934 he had been chairman of the network, except for Trammell's brief tenure, maintaining an office on NBC's sixth floor. But always there had been the intermediary of a president between him and the executive staff. Now he would make his own judgment of the capabilities of the senior executives and determine which, if any, possessed the leadership qualities necessary to mount a new challenge to CBS. No longer would he detour outside the organization. There were a half dozen NBC executives in programming, sales, and station administration, all with substantial network experience, to be scrutinized and tested. And one of them was his eldest son, Robert William Sarnoff.

After graduation from Harvard and World War II service as a naval communications officer in the Pacific, the younger Sarnoff began his career in Des Moines, Iowa, as a special assistant to Gardner Cowles, a leading newspaper and magazine publisher who also owned broadcasting properties affiliated with NBC. Years later, Cowles would assert that "my arm was really twisted" by Niles Trammell to hire Bob Sarnoff. There was no doubt in Cowles's mind that he had been selected by the General to provide the entering wedge for his son in the communications field. But by 1948, after a brief stint in magazine advertising, Bob had shifted to NBC, hired by its then executive vice-president, Frank Mullen, as a time salesman, allegedly without the knowledge of his father, although few in the industry believed it. Bob's progression upward was rapid, from manager of television program sales to head of program production and then, in 1952, to vice-president in charge of the NBC film division. One of his major early achievements was as executive producer of television's first important documentary series, "Victory at Sea," which in twenty-six episodes portrayed the dramatic saga of Allied naval victory in World War II. For this, he was given the Navy's Distinguished Public Service Award, and his reputation as a broadcasting executive began to emerge from the shadow of his father.

Parallelling the younger Sarnoff's swift ascent was the emergence of Sylvester L. Pat Weaver as the head of NBC programming. A former advertising agency executive who bristled with unorthodox ideas about how the new television service should be shaped, Weaver was primarily a programmer. Bob Sarnoff was primarily a businessman. So David Sarnoff decided, after an executive analysis of several months, to couple them as a team and place NBC's destiny in their hands, with Weaver as president and Bob executive vice-president. THE PAT AND BOB TEAM, a *Variety* headline proclaimed when they took over in December 1953. With David continuing as chairman and with his son in a top executive position, both flanking Weaver, the trade press speculated that the game of musical chairs in the NBC executive suite had ended. At last there would be stability at the top, and a new challenge to CBS in the television era could be mounted.

The "Pat and Bob" team promptly began generating considerable excitement in the entertainment industry through a series of bold and innovative programming concepts fathered by Weaver. He opened up early morning to network television with the "Today" program, which was initially ridiculed by newspaper critics because of Weaver's grandiose claims that it would reshape the nation's living patterns. Originally ignored by sponsors because of low ratings, the program gradually built a solid and loyal audience base for its varied menu of news, topical interviews, book reviews, and other service features. It became a national conversation piece when its host, Dave Garroway, introduced as a regular performer a chimpanzee named J. Fred Muggs, whose engaging antics soon had millions of Americans setting their alarm clocks early. Advertisers began flocking in, and the "Today" format became an enduring and profitable part of American television, as hardy as the soap opera and later aped by the other networks.

At the opposite end of the broadcast day, Weaver introduced the "Tonight" show, which promoted insomnia on a national basis. From Steve Allen to Jack Paar to the durable Johnny Carson, the comedians who were master of ceremonies kept millions titillated late at night with their celebrity interviews and humorous skits. Again Weaver hit a sponsor jackpot in a fringe area of television viewing, and the fortunes of NBC seemed clearly on the rise. While his other program innovations lacked the staying power of "Today" and "Tonight," they helped create a sense of vibrancy about NBC that had been lacking since the Paley raids. On Sunday afternoon, Weaver introduced "Wide, Wide World," the first live attempt to capture vignettes of American life on coast-to-coast television. "Matinee Theatre" brought hour-long live dramas to afternoon television in a highly praised but ultimately unsuccessful effort to break the viewing stranglehold of soap operas. The "Home" show, which had a service orientation for women, offered a similar alternative to the soaps, and it was also highly praised but short-lived.

Perhaps Weaver's most publicized innovation was his prime-time "spectacular," a high-budget cultural or entertainment special of ninety minutes or more which preempted regular nighttime series with the aim of giving America something to talk about the morning after. The spectaculars were a daunting effort to unsettle normal viewing patterns, and Weaver hoped through them to keep television in a state of creative flux. In some instances, such as Mary Martin's live performance in "Peter Pan," the spectaculars lived up to their name, enthralling the nation, thinning traffic on its roads for a night of family togetherness. But with others, such as a beautifully performed Sadler's Wells ballet, they failed to erode the vast and committed audiences of "I Love Lucy" and other situation comedies, and were deemed by their sponsors to be commercial failures.

But whether he succeeded or failed, the magnetic Weaver attracted attention. Tall and boyishly handsome, a Phi Beta Kappa graduate of Dartmouth College, where he was a classmate and close friend of Nelson Rockefeller's, he was a voluble freethinker who disdained the mores of corporate life. In his office he kept a bongo board on which he would sometimes jump during meetings, rocking back and forth to strengthen his leg muscles for skiing, which rivaled programming as a primary passion. He also loved to compose long, convoluted memos in which he set forth his programming ideas and his aspiration for elevating American culture through television. In every mass appeal program, he insisted that some form of cultural snippet be injected, so that even the most uneducated viewer would benefit.

Weaver's unorthodoxy fascinated the press, and soon the Pat of NBC's management team began to eclipse the Bob. The Pat became a media figure of star quality, profiled at length in *The New Yorker,* featured on the cover of *Newsweek,* captured in his Long Island home with his wife, Liz, in a lengthy *Life* photo-text essay. Even rival CBS seemed to recognize his stature when Edward R. Murrow invited the Weavers to be guests on his highly rated "Person to Person" program. Within months of achieving NBC's presidency, Weaver had become television's mover and shaker, its Don Quixote tilting against entrenched mediocrity. And more and more it was Pat who flared in the limelight and less and less Bob.

To David Sarnoff, this was not a welcome development. Suddenly there were two stars in the RCA firmament, where there had long been only one. And the other star seemed increasingly to Sarnoff to be more like the entertainers he disdained than a corporate executive cut to the traditional cloth. To other RCA executives, Sarnoff complained of Weaver's "insatiable appetite for publicity." Caustic DS memos began arriving at Weaver's office, questioning why CBS programs continued to dominate the Nielsen ratings despite Pat's program innovations, and why CBS profits continued to exceed those of NBC. And the irreverent Weaver did little to heal the widening breach. To cronies, he began to describe the elder Sarnoff as "General Fangs." In a crowded elevator once, he informed a friend that he was en route to "a meeting with Fangs." There were RCA executives on the elevator, and Sarnoff soon learned of his new nickname. It did not amuse him.

Rather than summarily dismissing the highly visible Weaver, and thus risking another round of stories about executive turmoil at NBC, Sarnoff decided to strip him of his authority under the guise of promoting him. In 1955, an NBC press release announced the promotion of Weaver to chairman of the board, the position David Sarnoff had held, with one brief interruption, since 1934. Bob Sarnoff was promoted to president, and ostensibly the Pat and Bob team remained intact. In reality, Weaver's new title was meaningless since a change in the bylaws made Bob the chief executive officer. Within a year, with the Sarnoffs firmly in control, the frustrated Weaver was eased out of NBC. Through a personal visit to Paley, he probed the possibility of joining CBS. But his reputation as a free-spirited maverick discouraged CBS, as well as other broadcast organizations from hiring him. While he never again served as a network executive, he continued to make significant contributions to the broadcasting industry in a variety of roles.

Within the RCA organization, David Sarnoff professed relief at Weaver's departure. "Pat got too much publicity, and he just couldn't handle it," was the explanation. Now there would be no one between him and his son in policy determination. Now NBC would be run like a business, with a stable executive structure.

For a decade, beginning in 1955 when the younger Sarnoff became chief executive, this expectation was born out. NBC profits continued steadily to rise despite the heavy costs of color programming and facilitation. Although CBS continued to lead in the audience polls, the gap between the two networks narrowed, and NBC entrenched itself in a strong number two position, ahead of the trailing American Broadcasting Company in all the indices of broadcasting success. And Bob Sarnoff's reputation as a serious, profit-oriented business executive continued to grow.

A year after taking over, Bob made an executive move that was widely regarded as astute in the industry. The president of third-ranked ABC, Robert E. Kintner, was dismissed by that network's chairman, Leonard Goldenson. No reason was given, although it was rumored in broadcasting circles that Kintner's drinking was a factor. Sarnoff had heard the rumors, but he nonetheless decided to bring Kintner, who was regarded as an effective operator, to NBC as executive vice-president in charge of the color television development program. He gambled that he could control any aberrant tendency of Kintner's and capitalize on his great administrative strengths.

Bob Kintner first made his reputation as a journalist. With Joseph Alsop, he wrote a widely syndicated Washington political column, and the two coauthored books on political developments that achieved best-seller status. Brought to ABC by its first owner, Edward Noble, Kintner had quickly emerged as a hard-driving, cost-conscious executive who could wring maximum results out of a shoestring budget. Overweight and short, a chain-smoker with a Buddha-like face partially obscured by thick-lensed glasses, he resembled David Sarnoff in his dislike of physical exercise and his passion for work. Fourteen-hour days were his norm, and Bob Sarnoff soon discovered, to his delight, that he had acquired an executive dynamo. On July 11, 1958, Kintner was made NBC's president and chief operating officer, the junior partner in what *Variety* now headlined as the "Bob and Bob" team, with the younger Sarnoff becoming chairman of the board.

Where Pat Weaver had generated excitement with his entertainment innovations, Bob Kintner generated a new sense of the importance of broadcast news. The fulcrum of the vastly expanded domestic and foreign news staff that he built was the anchor team of Chet Huntley and David Brinkley. Beginning in 1956, when their coverage of the national political conventions vaulted NBC past CBS news in audience popularity for the first time since the war, the Huntley-Brinkley team became the hottest property in broadcast journalism, eclipsing even CBS's newest young star, Walter Cronkite. In the key evening news segment, which introduced the nighttime network schedule, NBC's Huntley-Brinkley team became number one, and its success radiated across the full spectrum of broadcast journalism. When the three networks covered a special event simultaneously, such as a presidential speech or a congressional hearing, the largest portion of the viewing audience would tune in NBC. Similarly, NBC's news documentaries, of which Kintner ordered increasing numbers, pulled larger audiences than competitive efforts.

Leadership in this important segment of the network service created an aura of success that turned a negative press, critical of Weaver's firing, into supporters of the Bob and Bob team, and particularly of the newly arrived Bob. Kintner's rapport with the press, rooted in his own journalistic background, became somewhat akin to Pat Weaver's. He assiduously cultivated reporters who covered the broadcasting beat, and he was rewarded by admiring features in such publications as *Business Week* and the Sunday *New York Times*. Within RCA and NBC speculation arose that Kintner was treading a dangerous path by threatening to outshine the senior Bob and even challenging the General on his own turf of public recognition.

Contrary to these internal suppositions, the elder Sarnoff did not begrudge the new man's laudatory coverage. Kintner, he explained to an associate, never "let it get out of hand," as Weaver did, and Kintner was always respectful of the RCA chairman, at times almost obsequiously so. Further, Sarnoff admired Kintner's dedication to his job, his passion for work, and his loyalty to Bob Sarnoff, who in effect had rehabilitated his career after the ABC firing.

Still, the General never felt completely easy toward Kintner. He had heard the stories of his tippling at ABC, and later rumors had reached him from the West Coast that Kintner, on visits there as NBC's president, had indulged in drinking binges at the Beverly Hills Hotel. These were confirmed in the General's mind when he personally encountered Kintner during a visit to NBC's Burbank headquarters. "He looked awful, disheveled and unsteady," Sarnoff disgustedly told an associate. So once again David Sarnoff decided to effectuate a change in NBC's top management, less than four years after the ouster of Weaver.

He ordered his son and RCA president John Burns to join him and hear at first hand the evidence of Kintner's condition from those who had observed it. The meeting, according to one NBC participant, had all the trappings of a court-martial, with the elder Sarnoff the implacable prosecutor. But there proved to be an equally obdurate counselor for the defense, and he was the younger Sarnoff, who did not share his father's abhorrence of alcohol. To Bob, a Kintner hangover did not outweigh his value as the operating head of NBC. He was as stubborn as his father. According to a rumor within the organization, if Kintner went, the implication was that so might he. The son prevailed. No word of the encounter ever leaked to the press.

Apparently shaken by his close call, Kintner quickly mended his ways. The Bob and Bob team continued to operate NBC harmoniously, profits continued to rise, and the network's dominance in news, under Kintner's watchful eye, remained secure. Even though CBS held to its leadership in the cash-rich entertainment area, and consequently in profits, NBC through the late fifties and early sixties enjoyed a degree of management stability and continuity that it had not known since the Paley talent raids.

In 1961, David Sarnoff decided to make a change in the RCA presidency. To the RCA staff, he professed a growing disenchantment with the performance of John Burns, whom he had brought from Booz, Allen, Hamilton five years earlier. He accused Burns of failing to structure an effective management succession, of alienating outside directors, and of attempting to usurp authority beyond his operating responsibilities. He informed the RCA board, all Sarnoff loyalists, that he wanted to replace Burns with Elmer Engstrom, his senior scientist and his longtime right hand in developing RCA's technologies. According to Burns, the cause of his ouster was entirely different. He insisted to friends that the General was reneging on an earlier commitment to turn the company over to him, and specifically not to bring Bob Sarnoff to RCA as his eventual successor. Since he was younger than Engstrom, Burns maintained that he was being sacrificed to pave the way for the ultimate coronation of a second generation of Sarnoffs at RCA.

Four years later, the scenario that Burns had sketched began to take place. In 1965, Bob Sarnoff moved up to RCA as president and chief operating officer. According to the RCA press release, the appointment was made at the suggestion of Engstrom, who became chairman of the executive committee and chief executive officer. David Sarnoff, then approaching seventy-four, remained as chairman, and no one doubted that the team of Sarnoff, Engstrom, and Sarnoff was his creation, and that his son would be his ultimate successor.

To a certain extent, the timing of the change was probably conditioned by the continuing strong performance of Bob Kintner at NBC. Since the Burbank encounter, his personal behavior appeared to be exemplary. Even the elder Sarnoff was persuaded that NBC would be secure in his hands, and he was given the dual titles of chairman and president. He was also elected to the RCA Board of Directors, as was customary for NBC chief executives. For ten stable years, Bob Sarnoff had been NBC's overseer, and now his handpicked successor, in his mid-fifties, could look forward to comparable tenure.

In reality, Kintner lasted three months. In circumstances more bizarre than a television soap opera script, Kintner was summarily fired by his most steadfast supporter, Bob Sarnoff. Again the problem was drinking, but this time of such duration and intensity that the younger Sarnoff decided he could not excuse it. It had begun at an NBC affiliate gathering in Mexico, where Kintner's inebriated condition soon became the main source of conversation. Senior NBC executives were increasingly appalled because Kintner's heavy drinking continued when he returned to his New York office. Reluctantly, they concluded that Kintner was not in condition to run the network, and so reported to Bob Sarnoff. At first, the new RCA president temporized, announcing at a meeting of the company's executive council that Kintner's absence was due to a cold. Later, he concluded that Kintner's aberrant behavior could not be excused. With his father's full concurrence, Bob confronted his old associate after he had sobered up and, in a personal encounter of marked brevity, told Kintner he was fired because of his drinking.

The press release announcing to a stunned industry Kintner's departure made no reference to the reason, other than Kintner's desire to pursue other interests. It was at his insistence that no reference was made to health problems. On the surface, it seemed an amicable parting of ways, but in fact Kintner and his wife, Jean, were deeply affronted by what they considered to be Bob Sarnoff's callous and peremptory manner in handling his dismissal. Jean told the story in indignant and tearful fashion to their friend Andre Meyer, a senior outside RCA board member and managing partner of Lazard Frères. Meyer was an investment adviser to the Kintners, as he was to David Sarnoff, who was also one of his closest personal friends. Normally, Meyer sided faithfully with Sarnoff in any matters relating to RCA, but in this instance Jean Kintner stirred his sympathy and his wrath, and he decided to make an issue of the Kintner firing before the RCA board. Thus, in 1965, just after his seventy-fourth birthday, Sarnoff faced the first challenge to his authority by a board member in the thirty-five years he had guided RCA.

The special meeting, held in RCA's fifty-third-floor boardroom, was the most tense, most emotion filled, of the Sarnoff era. In his heavily accented English, the French-born Meyer said he intended to resign from the board because he did not wish to continue his association with a company that was so brutally indifferent to the sensitivities of its employees. Regardless of the offense, Kintner's years of distinguished service to NBC, including his leadership of the news division and his effective stewardship of network operations, entitled him, in Meyer's view, to special consideration if the company wished to dispense with his services. Not even a janitor should be fired so callously, the irate banker said, and his accusing glare was fixed on Bob Sarnoff. "I couldn't believe such language would ever be directed against a Sarnoff in an RCA boardroom," an RCA executive who was present would later recall.

With his son's conduct under question, Sarnoff became the injured parent more than the conciliating board chairman. He defended the wisdom of the dismissal, the manner in which it was handled, and he suggested, his anger flaring, that if board members disagreed, perhaps they should resign. This was an action within the purview of management, he insisted, and the board's only other recourse was to remove the Sarnoff management, since it did not intend to reverse itself on the firing. His challenging tone nettled another old friend on the board, Paul Mazur, senior partner of the investment banking firm of Lehman Brothers, who said that "others of us" might also "walk out the door" if management adopted such a truculent attitude.

Robert Sarnoff moved into the developing breach with a detailed and highly personal account of why he had found it painfully necessary to dismiss the man he had hand-picked to succeed him at NBC. He discussed the disruptive effect on NBC affiliate relations of Kintner's suddenly intensified drinking bouts, and the uncertainties they created in the network's decision-making process. Sarnoff's conciliatory analysis was supported by David Adams, NBC's senior executive vice-president and a longtime Kintner crony, who had been called into the board meeting, and their joint accounts served to defuse the emotionally charged atmosphere. A generous severance settlement was proposed and, in deference to Kintner's wishes, it was agreed there would be no public airing of the reasons for his departure, nor would the dispute within the boardroom go beyond it. The minutes of the meeting made no reference to it.

As a further conciliatory gesture to Meyer and Mazur, RCA's general counsel recommended that consideration of any resignations from the board be tabled until some unspecified future date. With tempers calmer, all involved, including the chairman, agreed. As the furore over the announcement of the NBC chief's departure subsided, the resignation question faded away. The rift between Sarnoff, Mazur, and Meyer was soon patched up through personal meetings, lunches, and dinners, and they remained close friends until Sarnoff's death. Surprisingly, considering the spotlight in which RCA and NBC operated and the number of people present at the board meeting— at least twenty—no word of the short-lived rebellion ever leaked to the press. Kintner, apparently sobered by his second firing, soon joined the White House staff as secretary of the cabinet, and served as an influential adviser to his friend Lyndon Johnson.

Sarnoff's defense of his son was his last direct involvement with NBC. He left the question of Kintner's successors to Bob, who chose as chairman and president two longtime NBC executives, Walter Scott, president of the television network, and Julian Goodman, a Kintner protégé and head of the news division. From 1965 until his departure from RCA a decade later, Bob was NBC's overseer, involving himself through weekly meetings in every aspect of its operations. He understood, and liked, the broadcasting business better than his father, and during most of that decade NBC ran a competitive second to CBS in entertainment program popularity and continued as an important profit center to its parent.

Despite the years of continuing profitability and such formidable contributions to the nation's cultural heritage as the Toscanini series, Sarnoff privately placed broadcasting on the debit side in the ledger of his life's work. More than any other operation, he fretted over NBC. He found its problems more intractable than the most complex technological challenge. His original concept of a public service network had never materialized. He had failed to block the intrusion of advertising. He had failed to contain the star system and entertainer dominance of the medium. Years of management turbulence and loss of the network leadership that had been NBC's birthright were the price he paid—that plus constant press allusions in his later years, which he could not escape, to CBS as the most prestigious, the most profitable of broadcast organizations, the Tiffany of networks.

By his own admission, he could never comfortably fit NBC into his family of RCA technologies. He felt that pay scales at NBC created an economic warp within RCA. It disturbed him that broadcasting executives, whose salaries mirrored entertainment industry scales, made more than manufacturing executives on the same organizational rung. He could never reconcile in his own mind how a comedian could reap a hundredfold the financial rewards of a Vladimir Zworykin, whose inventions made the medium of television possible. Discussing this imbalance once at a small staff meeting, he labeled it "an indictment of the economic values in our society."

In a related field of entertainment—recorded music—Sarnoff also suffered a losing battle, and a causal relationship probably existed between it and his broadcasting defeat. The RCA Records Division was, like NBC, an early leader in its industry, and the principal competitor to evolve over the years was CBS Records, another offshoot of Paley's growing entertainment empire. As in broadcasting, CBS was aggressive in its pursuit of recording artists, and it also concentrated in its laboratories, under the ubiquitous Peter Goldmark, on the development of new recording technology.

In 1948, just before Benny's landmark defection from NBC, CBS announced the development by Goldmark of a new LP (long-playing) audio record. For many years the record industry had standardized on 78 rpm discs. But the new CBS disc revolved more slowly, at 33⅓ rpm, thus permitting more than twice as much music to be stored in the same record space, and with a superior quality of sound. In CBS's view, it promised a revolution in the recording industry, and Paley decided, as Sarnoff had in the television standards battle, that the support of more than one company was needed to swing the industry behind it.

So Paley turned to Sarnoff, whose lineage in the record business traced back to 1929, when he acquired Victor in exchange for RCA stock. Victor had long been the premier classical record company, with contractual ties to the greatest musical stars of the era, from Caruso to Jeritza. Its Red Seal recordings symbolized the best in musical quality, and Paley hoped Sarnoff would convert them to 33⅓ rpm. He arranged a special demonstration of his LP for Sarnoff and later repeated it for two dozen RCA executives and engineers. The RCA contingent was obviously impressed, but Sarnoff confided to Paley that his scientists also had developed a new system that recorded at 45 rpm and featured a remarkably fast record changer. A product of ten years of research, the small 45 rpm disc had less playing time than the LP but promised, in RCA's assessment, substantial economies in production and distribution.

It was while weighing the pros and cons of the two recording systems that Sarnoff learned from Niles Trammell of Paley's campaign to win Benny. Sarnoff was so deeply affronted, at both Benny and the man who was attempting to induce his departure, that he sent word to Paley he would not accept the CBS LP as the new industry standard.

In Paley's judgment, this was the primary reason—pique over Benny—

that a new industry war erupted, a view also held by George Marek, longtime general manager of the RCA Records Division. In effect, Sarnoff was going to teach a smaller rival a don't-tread-on-me lesson. Paley had already gone to market with the LP system when RCA suddenly announced the commercial introduction of the 45 rpm in January 1949.

The war of the record speeds, as it became known, continued through a bitter and raucous year. Millions of dollars were spent in promoting the rival systems. With the old 78 rpm players and discs still in plentiful supply at music stores, a confused public didn't know which way to pick among three available speeds. Dealers had to carry a triple inventory. In Marek's recollection, the war "came within an inch of killing off the record industry."

From the beginning Sarnoff lacked allies. The influential National Association of Music Dealers came out in favor of the LP. The three largest independents—Decca, Mercury, and London—opted for CBS. More worrisome, numerous RCA artists expressed interest in the longer recording time and the sound quality of the LP. The eminent conductor Bruno Walter led an increasing artistic defection to Columbia Records.

With defeat becoming more apparent daily, Marek called the RCA chairman and requested an urgent meeting. "The afternoon is yours," Sarnoff told him and Marek used his allotted hours to set forth to a hastily assembled group of senior RCA executives the company's deteriorating competitive position, including the very real danger of a further talent hemorrhage. Marek's plea was, "Let's sell music, not speeds."

Reluctantly, Sarnoff came around. He agreed to let Victor license from CBS and invade the LP market. But he would not sanction total abandonment of the 45 rpm, nor did Marek seek it. Later developments proved this a sound decision. The emergence of jukeboxes provided an ideal home for the doughnutlike 45s because of their quick-change capability. In virtually all other recording sectors, however, the LP established itself over the 78 rpm and the 45 rpm as the industry standard.

Unlike the loss of comedians, the record war produced a Sarnoff defeat in technology, which was made the more perplexing by his earlier abandonment of the LP approach. In the recollection of both Marek and Meade Brunet, former head of RCA's international business, the company's scientists put together a demonstration model $33\frac{1}{3}$ rpm record player years before CBS unveiled one. Marek recalls escorting the conductor Leopold Stokowski to an LP demonstration at RCA's laboratories in 1932, and Brunet remembered inspecting a pilot player with Sarnoff. Apparently, it was the judgment of RCA's technical staff that the costs of manufacture would rule out a commercially competitive LP record player and disc. It was also assumed that no artist would want to record over such extended time as the LP offered, and that the public would have no appetite for records of such length. Sarnoff accepted that judgment, which was wrong on every count, and supported the decade-long effort that produced the 45 rpm. But it was not a priority item on his agenda, not a new core technology like television, and that perhaps explains why RCA was late in the marketplace with a competitively disadvantaged product.

The LP defeat was compounded by CBS's subsequent success in creating a multilabel record club, one of the first among scores of mail-order clubs that changed the distribution pattern of American business. The key, according to Paley, was the development of lightweight but durable shipping cartons that permitted record albums to be mailed safely and economically. Again RCA was slow in responding, but not for technical or marketing reasons. With various antitrust issues still in contention, Sarnoff's legal staff expressed concern that a grouping of competing labels within a club might provoke a fresh government challenge. He accepted that precautionary view, and RCA record executives fumed on the sidelines as CBS ran off with another important segment of the record market, with no serious constraints ever imposed by the government.

RCA's decline in records was even more precipitous than NBC's in broadcasting. Pop stars became the principal source of industry profits, eclipsing the symphonic and operatic performers who had provided Victor's historic luster. With the spectacular exception of Elvis Presley, whose recording career on the RCA label initially arrested the downward slide, RCA failed to achieve a strong pop-artist roster. The experienced Marek retired, and successor managements lacked his rapport with recording artists and the ability to discern fresh talent. Not only CBS but Warner Records and a host of new independent labels eclipsed RCA, whose percentage of the total market shrank to a one-digit figure. On several occasions, the RCA Records Division contributed red ink to the parent company's annual balance sheet, and it suffered the same management turmoil as NBC.

Sarnoff's role in the records decline was not as direct as in the decline in broadcasting, and much of it occurred after his departure. Still his personal tastes in music were well-known to the Victor management and possibly had an indirect influence in the selection of artists. He was a classicist to the core, and he admired the great artists of his era, above all Toscanini. The Maestro and his family became personal friends and were frequent guests in his home, as were Chotzinoff, Jascha Heifetz, and the tenor Richard Tucker. Within the RCA organization, few had as close personal ties with him as George Marek.

In the view of Pat Weaver, Sarnoff was an "elitist" in his personal preferences and thus out of step with any medium involved in mass entertainment. Years after his dismissal from NBC, Weaver remembered his former boss as somewhat condescending in his attitude toward popular entertainers and the programmers and advertising agency executives who put them on the air. Sarnoff was shocked at the dollars involved in a proposed contract for a rising young comedian whom Weaver wished to put on NBC television in its early years. So Jackie Gleason instead went to CBS, where he became one of the medium's most durable stars. The loss of Gleason, as much as the earlier Paley talent raids and the precipitate decline in the fortunes of records, came to symbolize Sarnoff's unsure hand whenever he touched enterprises encompassing elements of show business or based on a fragile coalition of entertainment stars. In essence, he could never resolve the dichotomy between that world and the world he preferred, of science, business, and industry.

Yet, from a contemporary perspective, it can be persuasively argued that Sarnoff, despite his failures in RCA's entertainment ventures, did more to change this nation's living pattern and cultural values than anyone of his generation. There can be little argument that he was the conceptualizer of wireless as an instrument of mass communications, or that he was the architect of the network broadcasting structure that exists today. If he was indeed the "Father of American Television," as the industry's leading trade organization ordained him in TV's developmental years, then he sired an offspring of awesome dimensions—the ultimate electronic communications system. In the mid-eighties, more than a decade after Sarnoff's death, broadcast television and its ancillary cable delivery services had matured into the most influential and pervasive instrument of entertainment and information in existence. The average American, according to a congressional study corroborated by numerous private polls, devoted more than a quarter of his or her waking hours to watching its around-the-clock transmissions, far more than any other leisure activity. Its most popular entertainment and sports shows reached national audiences in excess of a hundred million, and often additional tens of millions abroad through satellite relay. It provided the most formidable marketing force available to American finance, business, and industry—far more heavily endowed with advertising dollars than competitive print media. It had become the principal forum of political campaigning, nationally and locally, and the principal communicating channel for American presidents to their constituents. Indeed, the all-inclusiveness of its reach stirred media observers like David Halberstam to hyperbolic extremes. In both overt and subliminal ways, Halberstam wrote, television was "more important and dominant in our lives than newspapers, radio, church, and often, in the rootless America of the seventies, more important than family and more influential and powerful than the government itself."

Such extreme interpretations, of course, did not imply endorsement of the television service. Many of the features that Sarnoff attempted initially, without success, to arrest had become dominant—the overwhelming advertising presence, the surge of programming he privately called mindless, and the diminution of offerings for discriminating viewers. Over the years, he had heard all the charges levied against his offspring—its high-decibel jabberwocky, its lowest common denominator programming; the pablum of the masses, it was called, increasingly voyeuristic and violent. Even the technological marvel he had placed in the American home was being disparaged as the "boob tube." In the early years of his RCA stewardship, he often wrote or spoke in defense of the network service, as he did with Felix Frankfurter and in letters to various critical editors. But in his latter phase, he left that job to others, distancing himself from such controversies as the rigging of quiz shows in 1959 and television coverage of Joe McCarthy's anti-Communist crusade in the Eisenhower years. When Newton Minow, chairman of the Federal Communications Commission during the Kennedy presidency, shocked and infuriated the broadcasting establishment by describing the total television schedule as a "vast wasteland," Sarnoff decided not to place the weight of his personal prestige behind an industry rebuttal. "I rather admire the young man [Minow]," Sarnoff told a close aide. "He has the courage of his convictions."

In London at the beginning of a European tour in 1967, Sarnoff watched television briefly one evening in his suite at the Savoy Hotel. As a documentary of European political trends concluded, he commented to a friend who accompanied him that the overall BBC service was probably closer to what he had originally envisaged for television than the commercial schedules of the American networks. Of course, it was financed with public funds and operated under royal charter, which he opposed originally and still did. And it had arid patches in its overall schedule. But it seemed to him to address more effectively those cultural and educational areas that he and Owen Young and the long-defunct NBC Advisory Council had originally targeted for their network. Indeed, if he had succeeded in shaping the financial and programming structure as he had the technology and transmission standards of American broadcasting, things, he seemed to be implying, might well have been different.

might visualize them plotted along the elliptical path of an orbiting communications satellite. At its apogee would be color television technology; at its perigee, network broadcasting.

11 / *The Final Years*

The year 1967, when he turned seventy-six, was the forty-eighth and final full year of Sarnoff's RCA service. For most of those years, he had been the company's president or chairman, the shaper and controller of its destiny. Yet at no time did he own as much as one half of one percent of its common stock. His peak holding in 1967, acquired through market purchases and the exercise of stock options, was 204,527 shares. There were 62.7 million shares outstanding, with a trading range in the first quarter of that year between $42 and $51 per share, which meant that the value of his RCA stock at the time was between eight and ten million dollars. His salary then was $290,000, which, with dividend income of $1 per share, brought his RCA earnings to approximately a half million dollars annually.

In that preinflationary year, when the salaries of baseball superstars like Mickey Mantle topped out at $100,000, Sarnoff was demonstrably among America's financial elite. Yet he did not consider himself a wealthy man by the standards of the burgeoning industry he had done so much to create. True, it was a far cry from the $2 to $3 weekly he had earned as an immigrant newsboy, but it was also a far cry from the fortunes of men who had followed him into the industries he pioneered. Bill Paley of CBS and Leonard Goldenson of ABC were dominant shareholders of their enterprises, who would reap fortunes twentyfold his if they cashed in their vast blocks of stock. Eugene McDonald of Zenith, who fought him relentlessly over three decades, left an estate that would dwarf Sarnoff's. So did Robert Galvin, Sr., of Motorola. Edward Noble, to whom he sold ABC for $8 million, pyramided radio onto Life Savers to build one of America's great fortunes. Even station owners who had heeded his pleas to acquire government licenses in the early days of radio and later in television far outdistanced him in the accumulation of wealth. "I've made more millionaires than any man in America," he told an associate at lunch one day in 1967. As he tolled out a half dozen names, there was an edge of resentment in his voice, the implication being that he had taken the risks and they had reaped the rewards.

Yet the source of his resentment was not the fact that his competitors had more money than he. It was that they never properly recognized him as the fount of their wealth and never acknowledged their indebtedness to him. "I saw Ed Noble on an elevator," he recalled, "just after I sold him ABC. He never even thanked me. I gave him ABC on a platter." The hunger for appreciation, for recognition of the profound impact of his trailblazing on

American society, grew as he aged, and indeed became the motive force that drove him in his final years.

Had great wealth been a Sarnoff goal, he could easily have chosen other paths to attain it. At an early age, he was offered partnerships in Lehman Brothers and J. P. Morgan, with the glittering promise of quick millions in investment banking. In the depressed thirties, he said he was offered a million dollars annually, far more than the highest salary of any industrialist at the time, to join his friend Albert Lasker in guiding the leading advertising agency of Lord and Thomas. But he was not tempted. There were scores of investment bankers and advertising executives, but there was only one RCA and only one man equipped to implant it in the pages of history.

On January 1, 1965, when Sarnoff turned over the chief executive reins to Engstrom, and his son, Bob, became RCA's president, a spate of newspaper and magazine articles and editorials greeted the transition. Some had the end-of-an-era theme, almost obituarylike in tone, but others, more astutely, assumed that as long as his health held, the elder Sarnoff's hand would be at or near RCA's tiller. "I'm not dead yet," he told an associate with a grin. Nor did he disagree with the summation of a eulogistic *Fortune* editorial: "Sarnoff *Is* RCA." And indeed little changed physically. He still occupied the same imposing office suite, still the same barber came, and the manicurist. Ella continued to preside as queen of the secretarial corps. At meetings of the RCA executive council, he continued to preside at the head of the board-room table, beneath a portrait of himself, flanked by Engstrom on his right and Bob on his left. As the titular chairman, he continued to preside over board meetings, and this was a function he would never abdicate. The board was the locus of his power. For most of RCA's life, he had handpicked its members, and personal fealty to him had become the sine qua non of membership. So what difference whether he maintained the chief executive title? What difference whether he owned one share or ten million shares of RCA stock? He had the board, his board.

Sarnoff also continued to enjoy all the emoluments of corporate power. Two chauffeured company limousines attended him and his wife daily. A yacht was chartered for him by RCA for summer cruises off Long Island and Cape Cod. On a final European tour of RCA facilities in 1967, he and Lizette occupied the largest cabin on the *Ile de France*. They toured Europe in the longest stretch limousine Mercedes ever built, its previous renter the Shah of Iran. At the Ritz in Paris, they occupied the royal suite. Paley and Goldenson and McDonald might have had larger bank accounts, but they probably didn't live better or possess more of the trappings of corporate princedom.

In subtle ways, nonetheless, his position at RCA was changing. The triumph of color left him for the first time without the challenge of creating a new core technology. The company was heavily involved in data processing, but here the challenge was to carve out a profitable niche, at best a runner-up position to dominant IBM. The resolution of that struggle would require several years at least, and he accepted the fact that his son, Bob, would be the principal player for RCA. Day-to-day dealings with operating and staff executives he left to Engstrom and his son, who appeared to him to function well as a team. From the involved leader he had traditionally been, he was becoming more the patriarch, his wisdom available to those in the organization who sought it and to those outside in the media and government who sought his views on such subjects as the proper structuring of America's satellite communications system.

Increasingly, he turned to his own affairs. He became absorbed in planning his estate. He decided to give each of his three sons ten thousand shares of his RCA stock. He began paying attention to the modest stock portfolio that accompanied his RCA holdings, even complaining on occasion to intimates that his friend Andre Meyer was doing a "lousy job" of handling it. He began the planning of a David Sarnoff Library, which would be an adjunct of the Princeton laboratories, the repository for his papers and awards. He undertook to raise a half million dollars from several members of his family for the reconstruction of a building at the Educational Alliance on the Lower East Side of New York, where he had received his early education and which would now be named after him.

The man who had built his reputation on peering into the future was shifting his gaze to the past, his past, to consolidate the permanence of his contributions. For many years, various New York publishers had approached him about a book on his life, but he had turned them aside—too busy. But now he concluded the time was ripe, and in 1965 he invited an old friend, Cass Canfield, publisher of Harper & Row, to luncheon in his private dining room to discuss a biography. Also present was Sarnoff's cousin Eugene Lyons, a *Reader's Digest* editor who was also on the RCA payroll as a public relations consultant. For more than a decade, Lyons, a former Soviet sympathizer who had turned stridently anti-Communist, had drafted Sarnoff speeches on the Cold War. He had also researched his cousin's career extensively. Sarnoff told Canfield he was prepared to contract for a biography, provided it was authored by Lyons, with RCA having full editorial control, and provided it was supported by a massive promotional effort from Harper & Row. The elderly publisher obviously hungered to have the story of the Lion of Color in his catalog, and he agreed on all counts.

In the ensuing months, Sarnoff devoted hours to interviews with Lyons, occasionally in his office, often in the study of his town house in sessions that ran late into the night. In addition to being relatives they were personal friends, politically coupled by their antipathy to Soviet Russia. Sarnoff had admired an earlier Lyons biography of Herbert Hoover, and he felt more comfortable confiding in him than in any other journalist. Any request from the slight, bespectacled Lyons for information on his subject's life was treated as a priority item by the RCA public relations department, which had been told that this would be the definitive opus on their boss's legendary life. Lyons drove himself hard, confident this would be the most lucrative and the most attention-getting project of his career.

Within a year, the author had completed the first draft of his manuscript, and it was delivered to Sarnoff's office late one afternoon. "I'll read it tonight at home," he told an aide, obviously in a highly anticipatory mood. But the next morning when Sarnoff returned to the office, his mood had altered. He was disturbed and angered, his eyes red-flecked, his face lined with fatigue. "Well, I stayed up all night reading it," he told the aide, "and I didn't like it." In explicit, earthy language, he suggested that his cousin had committed a public nuisance on his leg.

To the handful of others within RCA who secured copies of the draft, the cause of Sarnoff's dudgeon was soon apparent. While the text was fulsomely laudatory of his vast achievements, Lyons had sought to strike a degree of biographical balance by alluding to a few blemishes. He touched on Sarnoff's often rumored propensity for liaisons with prominent women in the theatrical and publishing worlds. He highlighted some of his business setbacks, the harsh nature of his feuds, and the occasional excesses of personal vanity that some in the press had played upon. But except for these pinpricks, the staff members felt, the draft was far more press-release positive than critical in overall tone, almost more hagiography than biography.

But the subject of the draft felt he had been dealt a disservice by a member of his family. Again, it translated in his mind into disloyalty, and his friendship with Lyons withered. Quickly, he began expurgating the draft, devoting the entire following weekend to it. He asked for suggestions from several outside directors and senior RCA executives, none of whom attempted to defend the author's transgressions. Laboriously, page by page, he weighed each word and phrase, checked company and personal files to strengthen his memory of an event, excised passages that he considered unwarranted, patched in suggestions of his colleagues that he liked, and rewrote portions of the text where his view differed from the author's. Within a month, a sanitized version was returned to the chastened Lyons, who hazarded no rebuttal. On Sarnoff's orders, all copies of the first draft were shredded.

The biography, titled simply *David Sarnoff*, was published on his seventy-fifth birthday, with heavy print and television promotional support. Lyons, for example, was interviewed on NBC's "Today" program, which was then considered the surest route to best-sellerdom. Full-page ads appeared in the Sunday book review sections of leading newspapers. Several thousand copies were purchased by RCA at a discount price and sent to congressmen and senators, the White House, leading editors, NBC affiliates, clergymen, state governors, and RCA distributors. Yet the biography never achieved significant best-seller status because most of the leading book critics found its adulatory tone distasteful. *Newsweek*'s reviewer, for example, wrote that it did a disservice to its subject's deserved reputation for greatness and suggested that his true biography had yet to be written.

Seeing his dreams of a smash best-seller beginning to erode, Lyons wrote Sarnoff urging RCA to take additional full-page ads. Sarnoff sent the letter to his advertising department with a scrawled notation: "If Gene wants more ads, let him pay for them." He was not particularly perturbed by the book's sales or its negative critical reception, which was directed more against Lyons than himself. The fact was it provided an accounting of his life as he wished it presented. "I want it for my grandchildren," he explained. To friends, he often described it as "my legacy," and he had copies bound in red leather, along with other biographical material, to be presented to his children and grandchildren as a personal memorial from him.

Soon after the Harper & Row publication, Sarnoff contracted with McGraw-Hill to publish a hard-cover volume, underwritten by RCA, of his important memoranda and extracts of speeches in which he forecast the future. Titled *Looking Ahead,* its 305 pages ranged from his famous radio music box memorandum to his percipient forecast of television's impending birth to his vision of the ultimate configuration of satellite communications. More than the Lyons biography, it was intended for internal distribution, and thousands of copies were sent to RCA executives, RCA's distributor family, and those in the industry with whom Sarnoff felt a kinship. Sarnoff wanted it studied in particular by younger executives as a means of stirring their enthusiasm for peering into the future. Little critical attention was paid to the volume—its outside sales numbered fewer than five thousand copies—but again he was content. It added to the legacy. It provided more foundational cement on which historians of the future could build the statuary of his life.

As part of the legacy-strengthening process, his pursuit of honors and awards intensified in the patriarchal years. In particular Sarnoff sought honorary degrees, since he felt they dramatized his lack of formal education and even compensated for it. In all, he collected twenty-seven, many from major institutions such as Notre Dame and Columbia, where he had participated in early electronics experiments in the laboratories of Michael Pupin and Armstrong. Despite intense lobbying by Ivy League associates, he did not receive doctoral awards from Harvard, Yale, or Princeton. This was a disappointment—particularly Princeton, since his scientific laboratories virtually adjoined the university—but it was somewhat offset by the shower of awards that fell on him from electronic, broadcasting, educational, civic, and patriotic organizations. The final edition of his RCA press biography listed 105, probably more than any other business and industrial leader ever collected before or after him. In the citations accompanying the awards, he graduated from the early "Father of American Television" to "Pioneer of Electronics" and then to "Creative Genius of Communications."

Like his biography, the language of award citations could be controlled, which he considered a plus. Sarnoff, in fact, never made an awards acceptance speech without knowing in advance precisely what the citation would say. With things he could not control, such as critical press stories, he was always faced with the problem of setting the record straight—either through a letter to the editor, a corrective follow-up story, or a conference with the editor so that errors regarding him would not be repeated or left in the files. He disliked the thought that, buried in newspaper or magazine morgues, there were yellowed clippings that could lead research historians up false paths in tracking his career. Just as the first draft of his biography was shredded, unfavorable press stories were expunged from the RCA files.

Because of his obsessive concern for what existed in print about him, much of one of his last years was devoted to warring with a little-known West Coast publisher—one of the school known as vanity publishers—who sought to profit from an unauthorized Sarnoff biography. In terms of Sarnoff's full career, it was a trifling episode, but more than any other it served to dramatize Sarnoff's implacable determination to fend off what he considered a distortion of his achievements. Ironically, in this singular instance, it was excessive puffery that roused him.

Nearly a decade before, in 1957, Sarnoff had been approached by Leon Gutterman of Los Angeles, editor and publisher of a magazine titled *Wisdom*. Gutterman offered to devote a complete issue to "The Wisdom of Sarnoff and the World of RCA." This was in accordance with the magazine's attractive *Fortune*-size format, in which each issue was devoted solely to indepth pictorial and text treatment of a single individual, living or dead, of world or national prominence. Albert Schweitzer, Albert Einstein, and Jesus Christ were among prior subjects. To Sarnoff they were congenial company, and he agreed to cooperate, subject to final approval of all copy.

Gutterman pressed him to commit in advance to purchase a large number of the magazines, but Sarnoff held off until the final dummy reached New York. What he saw pleased him—his favorite Karsh photos, intimate family groupings, copy that extolled his achievements in language similar to RCA press releases—and the public relations department, at his direction, ordered fifty thousand copies at $1 each. A massive mailing followed—from the upper to the median executive tiers in RCA, to Congress, the White House, university presidents, public libraries, newspaper editors, and NBC affiliates. The company mailing far exceeded *Wisdom*'s own subscriber list, which was never divulged but reportedly numbered about twenty thousand names.

Gutterman did not forget the ensuing bonanza of free circulation, free publicity, and dollars. A live corporate head was obviously more profitable than a dead scientist or an African medical missionary. In 1966, Gutterman notified Sarnoff of his plan to launch a *Wisdom* encyclopedia, with the RCA head prominently featured. He requested pictures and biographical material, which the RCA press department routinely provided.

But what emerged was not an encyclopedia but a *Wisdom* book, in hardcover and paperback editions, entitled, again, *The Wisdom of Sarnoff and the World of RCA*. The first copies were forwarded to Sarnoff in Baden-Baden, Germany, where he was taking the baths, with a note from Gutterman, who clearly expected another massive RCA underwriting, saying he awaited the subject's blessing before commencing distribution. But this time the puffery was too transparent. The volume was replete with long, obviously fabricated quotes on Sarnoff's greatness from famous people, like the late Ernest Hemingway, whom Sarnoff had never met. A sketch of him with a crown on his brow suggested a monarch or a deity. In a signed frontispiece, Gutterman nominated him for a Nobel Prize.

Sarnoff was appalled. He ordered an aide to fly to New York, contact Gutterman on the West Coast, and demand that publication be stopped until "major revisions" were effected. Gutterman agreed verbally, but then proceeded to launch a direct mail-selling campaign for the hardcover edition to a broad cross-section of American leadership, apparently assuming their favorable response would change Sarnoff's mind. Copies of the book, with a sales invoice of $10, were accompanied by a covering letter from Gutterman implying RCA's cooperation in preparing the book.

On his return from Europe, Sarnoff soon heard from friends and associates who had received copies—and this time he was in no mood to compromise. All the implacable determination and the steely will that made color television a household product were now concentrated on blocking, or at least discrediting, the *Wisdom* book. First Sarnoff wrote Gutterman directly, demanding that he halt distribution of "this transparent and unappealing attempt at deification." Next, he dispatched his lawyer, Judge Simon Rifkind, former solicitor general of the United States, then the managing partner of a major New York law firm, to the West Coast to confront Gutterman and threaten legal action. But the elusive Gutterman could not be located; his Wisdom Society address, as listed on his stationery, turned out to be a mail drop in downtown Los Angeles.

So Sarnoff began a national canvass to locate every individual or institution who might have received a copy. RCA field representatives checked public libraries, universities, banks, legislative offices, brokerage offices, and law firms. As their reports filtered in, colored pins were placed on a map at RCA headquarters in an effort to chart distribution patterns, both geographically and by profession. If the head of one bank in Chicago received a book, then the heads of all midwestern banks were sent letters from RCA or Judge Rikind, explaining why the volume offended, disowning any RCA endorsement, and suggesting it be returned without payment if received.

A report from the West Coast indicated Gutterman had printed up to fifty thousand hardcover copies, with those not distributed being held in an unknown warehouse, probably in the forlorn hope of an RCA purchase order. Apprised of this, Sarnoff said if it took fifty thousand letters to invalidate fifty thousand books, RCA would send them. The letters flowed out to Congress, to the White House, to ex-President Eisenhower (who had received a copy at his Gettysburg, Pennsylvania, farm), and Gutterman soon became aware, through mounting book returns, of the RCA counterattack. He wrote Sarnoff from the West Coast threatening legal action, accusing RCA of attempting to undermine freedom of the press and of abridging his First Amendment rights. This was followed later by a plaintive appeal to get together, just the two of them, "and work things out." It was ignored, and Gutterman finally abandoned the mailings. Along with his *Wisdom* enterprises, he faded into obscurity.

The toll on Sarnoff in time and effort had been heavy, but he was satisfied that he had succeeded in discrediting this "monument of puffery." The press never became aware of the story, for which he was grateful since he recognized the possibilities of satirical coverage or even ridicule. Within the RCA organization, there was wonderment among those aware of the months-long struggle that their aging chairman would squander so much of his remaining resources on such a lightweight opponent. After all, Gutterman was no Cordiner or McDonald.

Perhaps it was because there were no new major competitive challenges to energize him that small things loomed larger. Perhaps this explained why a serious confrontation developed between him and his son over such a relatively minor consideration as how the name of the company was to be displayed in its annual report.

When the younger Sarnoff became RCA president in 1965, he felt that the RCA of Owen Young and his father needed to be brought into the modern world, not only in terms of broadening its product lines—he began a campaign of nonelectronic acquisitions, starting with Hertz rental cars in 1965, that fundamentally transformed RCA's business mix—but in the image that it presented. His personal orientation was far more sophisticated than his father's. Harvard was the antipode of Uzlian, as was the world of modern art and sculpture—which Bob avidly collected—from the rabbinical environment of his father's early years. Both Sarnoffs recognized the generational and cultural chasm, and that differences of management style and viewpoint were perhaps inevitable and would have to be tolerated—up to a point.

To speed RCA's modernization, and to place his own stamp on the company, Bob decided, with his father's reluctant approval, to develop a new graphic dress for products and facilities wherever RCA did business. He retained the industrial design firm of Lippincott and Margulies to revamp, modernize, and systematize the use of all the company's symbols and designs, from corporate logotype to dealer displays, product cartons, truck signs, and stationery, and from office interiors to the display of artworks.

Out of a year-long study came far-ranging recommendations for abandonment of the most hallowed symbols of the David Sarnoff era. The famed old logotype—the encircled letters RCA undergirded by a lightning bolt—was to be replaced by the letters RCA standing alone in arresting and modern acrylic dress. The little dog Nipper listening to His Master's Voice, a household symbol to generations of Americans, was to be kenneled, except for limited use on Red Seal classical records. Even the name Radio Corporation of America was to become RCA Corporation, since radio no longer played a significant role in the company's business, and since RCA's operations, in Bob Sarnoff's view, must become increasingly international.

At the final Lippincott and Margulies presentation, the elder Sarnoff was in attendance. Stolidly, he witnessed all the proposals for graphic change, reminding one onlooker of an old war-horse seeing his cherished epaulets sacrificed to more modern battle garb. He was "suffering a little inside," he later confessed to an aide, but he would not undercut one of his son's first major programs as president. So the complete revamping was accepted—with one exception. On the proposed name change, the father would not yield. He had been there at the birth of the Radio Corporation of America, in 1919, and he was not going to see a name that was almost synonymous with his own entombed during his lifetime. So Bob decided to wait, rather than mount a challenge on this sensitive point. Verbal orders were circulated for the full name to be quietly phased out of company written materials, with the legal change to be effectuated later—presumably after the father had gone.

The transition into the "new" RCA proceeded smoothly until the next annual report was in preparation. At lunch one day with the head of corporate publications, the General inquired casually how the company's name would be featured in the report, which he considered the most important publication of the year and which was traditionally mailed to shareholders on his birthday. Told that the full name wouldn't be in the report, that at Bob's direction only the letters RCA would be used in the text and on the cover, his jaw dropped and his face began reddening. "You tell Engstrom and Bob that I want to see the full name in that report," he said, pushing away from his half-finished lunch and standing up. "I want their assurance on it before we leave the office today. Otherwise, I'll call a special meeting of the board and demand that the annual report be rejected." Then he stormed out of the dining room.

A series of crisis meetings ensued that afternoon, with Engstrom, Bob, and several senior staff members participating. The elder Sarnoff sat alone in his office, grimly puffing a cigar while awaiting their response. He knew that the board was his board, and thus his hole card in this tense game of managerial poker. Engstrom and Bob must have sensed it too. After several hours of discussion and study of the text, they decided to insert in small type the words "For Radio Corporation of America" at the conclusion of management's letter to shareholders at the beginning of the report. Five small words, hardly noticeable to any but the most discerning reader, but they satisfied Sarnoff, and the crisis receded. He had made his point. The name was still Radio Corporation of America, and he was still its final authority.

However, the problem of the name cropped up again a year later when the chairman was returning from a visit to Australia. As part of the graphic revamp, new stationery forms had been prepared for all the company's executives. Only the letters RCA in the new logotype were displayed at the top, above the name and title of the executive. When the new forms reached David Sarnoff's office, Ella Helbig viewed them with distaste. Like her boss, she was of the old school and she knew what his reaction would be. Rather than await his return, she airmailed copies of the stationery to his hotel in Honolulu. A day later, he was on the long-distance telephone fuming, ordering the new stationery removed from his office. He would continue to use the old letter forms, with the company's name spelled out and with the old circle and lightning bolt logotype. Further, he warned that if there were any attempt to couple the new logotype with his name—such as at the David Sarnoff Laboratories in Princeton—he would call a special board meeting and block it.

By then Bob Sarnoff had succeeded Engstrom, who was preparing to retire, as chief executive officer. But again he elected not to challenge his father in an area of such personal sensitivity. So for the remainder of the elder Sarnoff's chairmanship, RCA operated with two names and two logotypes—the old for his office and the Princeton laboratories, the new for all other RCA facilities and its 128,000 employees. In this instance, the "man of the future," as Henry Luce and many others had called him, would not abandon his past.

Apart from such intermittent squabbles with his son, which never reached the point of rupturing their relationship, Sarnoff in his final years found broader and more profound reasons to be unhappy about the forces of change that were playing on his industry and his company. The vacuum tube on which RCA had been built—it had sold more around the world than any other company—was becoming virtually obsolete, replaced by a miracle of compressed ingenuity known as the transistor. But it was a product of the Bell Laboratories, not another seminal invention of his scientists. And other companies, such as Texas Instruments and Motorola, were achieving dominant positions in transistor manufacture, with RCA a late also-ran. Much of the scientific effort that had produced the color victory was focused now on an increasingly tenuous challenge to IBM in computers. The core businesses on which his and RCA's reputations had been established were becoming dispensable. The original radiomarine business, which had manufactured and serviced wireless equipment for oceangoing vessels, had been sold off. The full range of audio products—radios, phonographs, tape player and stereophonic components—was in the process of elimination, a victim of lower-priced competition from the Far East. Monochrome television had become a marginal product line, and there were indications that the domestic color market, unsettled by a surge of Japanese imports, was leveling off.

The answer of RCA's new management to the twin threats of foreign competition and market maturity was, like that of many other American corporations, diversification into nonrelated business areas. A new word, "conglomerate," was coined. Whether or not it applied to the new RCA Bob Sarnoff was beginning to construct—he always disputed it—the company moved through acquisitions into such disparate areas as book publishing, car rentals, frozen foods, carpets for the home and office, commercial real estate, Alaskan telephone service, and later, after both Sarnoffs had departed, into commercial finance and factoring, insurance and greeting cards.

A disabling illness that struck him in 1968 removed the elder Sarnoff from involvement in most of the acquisition program, which stretched out over fifteen years. He had endorsed the purchase of Random House on the theory that book publishing and electronic information-gathering techniques could be married. Originally, he told an aide, he had opposed the purchase of Hertz but had bowed to his son's persistence. After that, as his involvement lessened, the acquisition pace quickened. Whether he would have halted or reversed it, had his health permitted, can only be conjectured. Yet diffusion of the type that was then occurring at RCA was contrary to everything his career stood for. He had constructed an electronic monolith by sticking to electronics. He believed that growth should come through the creation of new technology. In his management formula, you induced technology, you molded it, and you guided it as it emerged in the marketplace. Would the purchase of a carpet company or a frozen prepared food company, which owned and plucked millions of chickens, have fit within that formula? Unlikely.

Essentially, Sarnoff believed in the efficiency of bigness. He was an oligopolist. He believed in big companies dominating big industries, like GE in electricity, General Motors in automobiles, AT&T in wired telephony, and RCA in radio and television. With each, it was the responsibility of the leader to guide the industry, strengthening its product lines, innovating, but always sticking to its own. His career had, in effect, begun in the protected environment of a patent pool and international wireless monopoly. He had devoted years to beating down infringing competitors seeking to sap RCA's patent strength. From the scientific research he had succored, great technologies, such as color television, had resulted. As competition emerged in RCA's first core business of international wireless, he had urged the Congress and various administrations over four decades to permit the merger of the international carriers into one company that would give the nation a unified voice in dealing with government-protected foreign wireless monopolies. That he failed to achieve enabling legislation—his last attempt being made in the mid-sixties—was further evidence to him of a powerful trend toward fragmentation of the nation's communications, and he forecast, correctly, that not even giant AT&T could withstand it. It ran counter to his philosophical concept of the correct path for his technology, but he became resigned to it.

In one of his last informal meetings with RCA senior managers, in the summer of 1968, Sarnoff admitted that change was occurring in electronics at a rate and in a direction that he could no longer influence. "The whole communications business is being chopped into pieces," he said in a somber voice. "It will no longer be what it was before. It's no longer one big organization controlling everything." While he assured the younger managers present that the "bits and pieces" then emerging would provide great opportunities for the innovators of the future to provide a multitude of new communications services, he also seemed to be conceding that his era was over. In tolling the bell for communications oligarchies, he was also tolling it for David Sarnoff. His ambition to dominate had always extended far beyond his own company. His personal grail was electronic industry leadership, which in turn was available only through control of a large, dominating organization. He, of course, succeeded in possessing that leadership to a greater degree and for a longer period than anyone of his generation. But now, he was conceding, the splintered future would no longer permit it, not even if one with his vision and entrepreneurial skills were to surface anew.

In that same summer of '68, when he was seventy-seven, illness struck and his active career at RCA ended. During a leisurely weekend luncheon with his wife at the Century country club in Westchester, some nerves in his cheek snapped and his face suddenly twisted out of shape and his speech became slightly slurred. Rushed by limousine to his Manhattan town house, he was examined by several doctors, who diagnosed his affliction as shingles, a painful disease of the nerve ends which required rest and medication. He was ordered to bed, and he would never again set foot in his RCA office.

Yet as he rested, enduring considerable pain and shielded from telephone calls and visitors by the vigilant Lizette, Sarnoff determined there was one engagement on his calendar that must be kept, whatever the cost to him physically. On July 1, 1968, RCA's principal executives were gathering for luncheon in the Hunt Room of Twenty-One. The occasion was an informal celebration of Bob Sarnoff's impending fiftieth birthday, and the father seemed to sense that this "intimate little luncheon party" might provide his last opportunity to place the weight of his immense prestige behind his son. So he made it there, his balance unsteady, supported at either arm as he shuffled into the room, his face contorted as he began his brief valedictory.

First, he acknowledged the problems of the generation gap, admitting "there always was and there always will be a difference between the generations, and there is no formula to meet it." But he also spoke, in words no RCA executive had ever heard him use before, of his love for his son and his great pride in his "success" at NBC and RCA.

"I know it's sometimes claimed that it's a cinch to be the boss's son," he continued. "All you have to do is be born and the rest is made for you. Well, neither the father nor the son would agree to that formula. It isn't easy for either one, but it's probably more difficult for the son than the father. The father has caught the trolley car, but the son still feels that he has to run after it and sometimes the shadow of the father obscures the son—never intentionally, but sometimes unwittingly."

Every executive present was aware of the intermittent clashes between the two Sarnoffs over the years, and of their differing philosophies. Undoubtedly, the ailing father had that in mind when he said in an emotional tone: "I cannot separate RCA and Bob and David Sarnoff. The fortunes of one are the fortunes of all of us. Any hurt to one is a hurt to all."

After this final salute, the father returned to his home and the commencement of the final chapter of his life—three and a half bedridden years which involved three mastoid operations as infection spread from his ears through all the sensory organs of his head, ultimately robbing him of most of his speech, sight, and hearing, wasting him physically into a skeletal frame kept alive by tube-injected liquid foods.

Yet they were remarkable years, not only for the tenacity with which he clung to life but for his stubborn refusal to accept the fact that he was no longer a vital factor in the affairs of RCA. Months before the shingles attack he had lunched in his dining room with his old adversary and friend Bill Paley, and had asked him what his retirement plans were. "Bill told me they would have to carry him out with his boots on," he later recounted with a chuckle. "I told him I could understand that." And now he was about to prove it.

On the eve of his first mastoid operation, on August 29, 1968, which was to be performed at Lenox Hill Hospital on Manhattan's Upper East Side, he called one of his closest RCA associates to his town house for a brief farewell. Garbed in pajamas and dressing gown, he stood up to greet his younger friend. Impulsively, he embraced him and kissed him on each cheek, something he had never done before. "I don't know if I'm going to make it," he said haltingly, his face still warped by shingles, his eyes moist. "But if I do, I'm counting on you. As soon as the doctors will permit it, I want you to come to the hospital and brief me on everything that's happening at RCA."

The operation, which extended over nearly four hours, did not clean out all the infection, and the convalescing Sarnoff was confined for months in a corner suite at Lenox Hill. As he partially regained strength between operations, senior RCA staffers began receiving calls from nurses at the hospital: "The General wants you here at two thirty. Bring any papers you think he should see." And memos written in a shaky but still familiar hand began arriving at the 30 Rockefeller offices, often peremptory inquiries on the status of color sales, computer leases, the profit outlook. "Maybe he's forgotten since the operation that he made his son chief executive," one staffer mused half seriously to another.

Another preoccupation was with his library, which he intended to be his most enduring memorial. To house his voluminous collection of business documents—nearly a thousand volumes covering technical and commercial developments in which he had been involved, letters, speeches, and public statements—plus award citations, cases of trophies, and autographed pictures of world leaders, a wing had been constructed at the Princeton research center. In the months before his illness, he had gone there on an almost weekly basis to oversee the unpacking of crates, the precise placement of each piece of memorabilia, and the filing of every document. Many of the major ceremonies in which he had been involved had been filmed by NBC television crews, and audio tapes had been made into phonograph records by the RCA Records Division. Under his supervision, they had been carefully cataloged and placed in files in temperature-controlled rooms of the library. As curator, he had selected Cary King, an administrator of the Princeton laboratories, and dispatched him on idea-gathering trips to the Roosevelt Library at Hyde Park, New York, the Eisenhower Library at Abilene, Kansas, and the Truman Library at Independence, Missouri. He wanted his Princeton pantheon to be of comparable caliber.

Now, from Lenox Hill, he barraged his curator with instructional memoranda and inquiries. He sketched the precise position where a bust of him sculpted by Jo Davidson should be placed on its pedestal. He called for figures on how many school students were visiting the library in guided tours. How many professors from Princeton and adjacent universities were engaged in research projects? Had any press tours been arranged? In each of his inquiries, there was a sense of urgency, as though time were running out on him.

As the library's documentary centerpiece, he ordered the installation of a thirty-volume history of his career, bound in hard covers, which had been compiled over nearly three decades by one of his early RCA associates, an engineer named Elmer Bucher, who devoted his retirement years to the massive project—more than ten thousand typewritten pages. Sarnoff had personally reviewed and edited each one of them. He hoped the Bucher volumes would provide definitive source material for scholars, an elongation of the Lyons biography. He had discussed with the Library of Congress placing a set there and had been informed it would be welcomed. But when, from his bedside, he ordered it done, the RCA legal department reluctantly concluded that it would not be wise to comply. The volumes were so biased, it was felt, in their recounting of complex and controversial events, and so repetitively eulogistic in tone, that circulation outside the company might cause public embarrassment and, in the long run, do disservice to his memory. Sarnoff, of course, was never told of this rare instance in which one of his orders to subordinates was not fulfilled.

His principal support during the long months at Lenox Hill was Lizette, who, in her seventies and in somewhat precarious health herself, ministered to him with such unflagging daily devotion that the hospital staff was moved and a little astonished. Earlier, she had suffered heart problems and undergone a mastectomy. But now she was his tower of strength, spending long hours at his bedside, arranging visits from those he wished to see, responding to many of the hundreds of get-well letters that poured into the hospital and RCA, importuning other members of the family to write and call often, and in the early months when he could still ingest food orally bringing home-cooked dishes to supplement the rather monotonous hospital menu. His dependence upon her had always been far greater than he ever admitted publicly, but now it was total. On occasion in years past he had complained to intimates that she tended to smother him with attention, but no more. On November 30, 1968, her birthday, he wrote her what she described to a friend as "the most wonderful letter I ever received." Written in a hand that still retained some of its strength and addressed to "My dearest Lizette," it spoke of his deep sorrow at being unable to join her and their family at home for the birthday observance. "My fondest wish and hope," he wrote, "is that we may be spared for the few years ahead so that we can celebrate our birthdays together in good health and make up some lost time. I'm doing my best to survive and your help and devotion makes it possible." The note bore the traditional Sarnoff interfamily sign-off, "LAMK"—meaning love and many kisses.

Ultimately, his wish to be home again with his family was realized, but only when the mastoid operations had run their course and his doctors had concluded that his afflictions were incurable. A steady erosion of his strength occurred through 1969. The prominent paunch that he had sought fruitlessly for many years to reduce through dieting had wasted away. He still struggled to compose handwritten memos to the RCA staff, with a nurse or Lizette holding the pad and positioning a pencil in his hand. But he was nearly blind and the words were indecipherable, trailing off the bottom of the pad.

Sarnoff still retained the title of chairman of the board, and for many months, out of deference to his sensibilities, RCA maintained to its share-holders and others who inquired that he was continuing to convalesce and anticipating a return to his office. Finally, the board, which was still composed of such old friends as Mazur, Meyer, and Lewis Strauss, felt compelled to act on the basis of medical advice. As of December 31, 1969, his half century of employment at RCA was terminated, and he was accorded the title of honorary chairman of the board.

To his son Bob, who succeeded him as chairman, fell the task of informing the father. Two senior staff executives were designated to accompany him, and there was a sense of apprehension as the three entered the hospital suite accompanied by Lizette. True, he was half dead, but would he construe this as being borne out with his boots on? The legacy of his power clung so strongly that one of the staff members visualized him sitting up in bed and countermanding the board's action. Yet he gave no outward sign of distress as his son, speaking in a forceful voice close to his ear, explained the decision. The father listened motionless and then muttered something almost inaudible which seemed to indicate his acceptance, perhaps even his approval, since a Sarnoff would continue at the helm.

In 1970, he was moved by ambulance to his town house, where the solarium on the top floor had been converted into a medical center, with emergency equipment installed and with nurses in attendance around the clock. A hospital bed was placed in its center, and Sarnoff was too weakened to leave it, even to perform bodily functions. Yet still the calls went forth for staff members to come and "brief" him. As his speech continued to deteriorate, only his nurses and Lizette could understand the sounds he uttered through the tube in his throat, and they served as interpreters for visitors. At his insistence, newspapers were read to him and a radio was placed beside his bed, its volume tuned up when he wanted to catch snatches of NBC broadcasts. To occupy him further, Lizette had a Morse code telegraph key placed near the bed, and attached by wire to the RCA Communications transmission center in downtown Manhattan. Arrangements were made for other old-timers with trained fists to be available to exchange coded messages with him and thus stir memories of his youth. But after one or two efforts, he forgot the key, either too enfeebled or too bored to pursue it.

As in many others approaching death, Sarnoff's interest in the religion of his childhood was rekindled. Despite his extreme sensitivity about his Jewishness, religion had been of secondary concern during most of his professional career. For many years, he was an official of Temple Emanu-El in New York, but he attended services only on infrequent occasions. On Yom Kippur, that holiest of holy days, Sarnoff occasionally went to the office after a stop at his synagogue. Within RCA, the vast majority of executives were Christian, and he had been scrupulous in enforcing a policy of promotion without regard to race or creed. His successor as chief executive and his chief scientist for many years, Elmer Engstrom, was a Christian fundamentalist who in the early sixties organized and directed a Billy Graham crusade at

New York's Madison Square Garden, using RCA public relations support services with Sarnoff's approval. Only once had they ever gotten involved in a theological dispute, and the outcome amused Sarnoff as much as it irritated him. As a fundamentalist, Engstrom argued that the only route to salvation for Christian and non-Christian alike lay in acceptance of the divinity of Jesus Christ. In other words, failure to accept that path, either as an act of omission or commission, was a conclusive bar to heaven. "Elmer was telling me he was going to make it," Sarnoff later recounted, "but that I couldn't unless I changed my ways. I didn't buy it." But it caused no problem in their relationship.

In 1965, on an airliner en route to Chicago to pick up an honorary degree from Mundelein College, a Catholic institution, Sarnoff espoused to his traveling companion his own views on religion. He said he did not believe in a personal God nor in the infallibility and dogmatic rectitude of any religion. Had he felt that way about the Jewish faith, he explained, he would have pursued a life-style in conformity with the edicts of the ancient teachings, such as the kosher dietary laws. But he consciously decided as a young man not to, in part because they made little sense to him in the modern world, in part because he simply didn't believe in their divinity. He likened his religious convictions to those he attributed to Albert Einstein—acknowledgment of the existence of a superior power in the universe, a creative and governing force of unknown dimensions, but not a personal God passing judgment on the daily acts of individuals, keeping a scorecard of pluses and minuses to determine their admissibility to his ethereal realm. But now, six years later and at death's threshold, he asked Lizette to arrange visits by rabbis of Temple Emanu-El. He seemed to find solace in their reading of Talmudic passages which stirred memories of boyhood days in Uzlian and Korme. He also accepted the performance of bedside rituals of the Jewish faith by the visiting rabbis.

Similarly, he sought solace in visits from relatives and old associates. Engstrom, who had offended him by siding with his son in some of their disagreements, came from his retirement home in Princeton. Gene Lyons, the partially estranged biographer, came to visit. Through Andre Meyer, Sarnoff asked that Bill Paley see him. As the CBS leader sat at his bedside, Sarnoff reached out and clutched his hand, holding onto it, and the two giants of modern mass communications reminisced, through a nurse interpreter, and said their farewells.

Sarnoff was still alive in September 1971, when RCA elected to withdraw from the mainframe computer field, accepting a huge write-off, and every effort was made to spare him the unsettling news. Inadvertently, a nurse who had overheard a radio announcement told him of the withdrawal. "A terrible tragedy," he whispered, and later he asked a visitor what would happen to his son Bob. Nothing at all, he was assured.

But there was also good news to lighten his last days. Wall Street generally applauded the younger Sarnoff's decision to staunch the mounting computer losses, and RCA's stock took a sharp upswing. The invalid was also informed by a visiting staffer that he had learned the *New York Times* had prepared an obituary of him that covered nearly a full page of pictures and type. "Wonderful," he whispered. He would have been even more pleased could he have known that the *Times* obituary summed up his career in these words: "His knowledge and ambition were the driving force behind the development of the electronic media and their profound effect on American life."

Sarnoff died in his sleep, of cardiac arrest, the morning of December 12, 1971. His death was announced that afternoon, a Sunday, on the NBC television network, with a bulletin interrupting "Meet the Press," one of the few programs he enjoyed and often watched. Later, a special half-hour film program was aired, highlighting his life, and a great outpouring of print reportage followed. Most of it hewed to the conventional rags-to-riches theme, reciting the boiler plate of an extraordinary life, and, predictably, with emphasis on the *Titanic* heroics. But among journalists who knew him personally, like Jack Gould, radio-television editor of the *New York Times,* other insights crept through.

"To Mr. Sarnoff," Gould wrote in a brief appraisal of his career, "life was always a challenge and, whatever his intensely human faults, he had an overriding virtue. In a world beset by committees and enervating blandness, he was an individualist to the core. . . . There was never any shortage of reasons either to like or dislike Mr. Sarnoff. But only a bore could ever call him dull."

The funeral service three days later at Temple Emanu-El drew a vast outpouring of leaders in the worlds of business, finance, the arts, and government. The principal eulogist was Governor Nelson Rockefeller of New York, whose family's life had been entwined with that of the Sarnoffs for two generations. Standing beside the coffin draped in an American flag, he capsulized a "life of greatness":

"His genius lay in his capacity to look at the same things others were looking at—but to see far more. Others looked at radio and saw a gadget. David Sarnoff looked at radio and saw a household possession capable of enriching the lives of millions. In others, the word visionary might mean a tendency to see a mirage. In David Sarnoff, the word 'visionary' meant a capacity to see into tomorrow and to make it work."

The brief Temple Emanu-El service, which concluded with Hebrew prayers for the dead, was transmitted in its entirety to the David Sarnoff Research Center, approximately ninety miles away at Princeton. There the scientists—his scientists, he would have said—gathered beneath a portrait of him in the auditorium adjoining his library. Dr. William Webster, a young

Princeton University physicist who later became head of the RCA Laboratories, was among those present in the hushed assemblage. Years later, he still remembered the sense of loss and sadness that permeated the auditorium. "More than a few were wiping their eyes," he recalled. It was as if they suddenly realized that the man who had placed their profession on the loftiest pedestal in the world of industry was no longer there to rally them under the banner of the electron.

Lizette Sarnoff decided, after consultation with her sons and some of her husband's RCA colleagues, that he should not be buried in an exclusively Jewish cemetery. He had lived and worked with people of two monotheistic faiths and he should therefore rest among them. A 10,000-square-foot plot was acquired at Kensico, a Judeo-Christian cemetery in Valhalla, Westchester County, New York, and an imposing mausoleum was constructed of white marble brought from Vermont. Gabriel Loire of Lyons, France, crafted the stained-glass windows, which were etched with symbolic depictions of Sarnoff's life work—from Morse code wireless to space satellites. Many of the surrounding mausoleums were adorned with a Christian cross or a Jewish Star of David, but not his. The front door bore an elliptical design of the path of the electron, that tiny particle of matter to which, as he often said, he had hitched his wagon. It was his religion.

12 / *An Appraisal*

In 1964, as acknowledgment of Sarnoff's color achievement was cresting, an RCA-commissioned study of the company's reputation among Wall Street financial analysts was undertaken by the Opinion Research Corporation of Princeton, New Jersey. The results were distinctly mixed. The company won praise for its scientific strengths, its technological leadership, and its willingness to gamble on new products. But the observations on its top management were mostly negative: "too dictatorial," "not profit oriented," "controlled too much by one man." Through pages of comments, the same refrain pulsed on: RCA's one-man rule had become anachronistic, the time for change had arrived.

The reaction of RCA staff members involved in the study was one of stunned surprise and indignation, probably akin to the reaction of Winston Churchill's staff when he was unceremoniously dumped by the British electorate after World War II. But unlike Churchill, Sarnoff was never aware of the Wall Street plebiscite on his rule. At the suggestion of the cautious Engstrom, then president, who was concerned for the sensibilities of his prideful chairman and also perhaps a little fearful of his reaction, the staff suppressed the report before it reached Sarnoff.

Had he read it, and however angered it might have made him, the seventy-three-year old leader most certainly would not have altered his views or changed his managerial approach. He had always been contemptuous of Wall Street, and particularly of financial analysts. "The trouble with analysts," he often said, "is that they don't analyze." In his judgment they could not see beyond the bottom line. They could not comprehend the need to penalize profits on occasion in order to achieve long-range goals. Where they were seduced by quick returns, he was wedded to the long view.

In one sense Wall Street probably had a point. To a unique degree among publicly held companies, RCA's management under Sarnoff fused the old and the new. A company perched on the cutting edge of technology had been guided for thirty-five years by one man, not its founder or owner, whose visceral judgments and perceptions of the future served as its principal corporate planning mechanism. Without question it was not the type of management coming into vogue in the sixties as the diversification mania intensified, fueled by investment bankers like RCA board member Andre Meyer, whose Lazard Frères firm harvested millions by initiating and managing corporate acquisitions and divestitures. A new generation of business leaders responsive to that trend had begun to move into America's corporate suites. They were skilled in the management of large hordes of cash, devoted to quarter-by-quarter profit increases, adept at sophisticated financial controls and at juggling a portfolio of nonrelated acquired companies. Their exemplar was Harold Geneen, chairman of International Telephone and Telegraph, whose pyramiding growth through acquisitions here and abroad had dazzled Wall Street for two decades.

But granted its somewhat hoary approach, had the Sarnoff managerial style in fact become outmoded? Nearly a decade after his death, business scholars began examining the rise of the new managerial breed and found disturbing implications for the nation's industrial future. They noted the substantial increase in company presidents with financial and legal backgrounds who tended to slight developmental technology in favor of the quicker, more visible returns that acquisitions seemed to provide. In the *Harvard Business Review* of July 1980, Professors Robert H. Hayes and William J. Abernathy disagreed with this trend:

"The key to long term success—even survival—in business is what it has always been: to invest, to innovate, to lead, to create value where none existed before. Such determination, such striving to excel, requires leaders—not just controllers, market analysts and portfolio managers."

No description of business leadership could have been tailored more precisely to Sarnoff. His cardinal leadership principle was growth through innovation. Core businesses must be germinated through in-house creation of technology. How often he had said: "The heart of RCA is its scientific laboratories." Through the worst of the depression years, the last thing he would permit to be cut was his research budget. Without hesitation he would, and often did, sacrifice profits to the creation of technological values where none existed before.

From a different perspective in 1981, MIT's Jerome Weisner wondered aloud to a visitor at his Cambridge campus whether Japan's formidable encroachment into the American electronics market reflected the fact that no David Sarnoffs were any longer around to guide the domestic industry in the type of struggle for leadership in technology that he so often mounted. Perhaps, Weisner suggested, the Japanese drive for dominance in the video tape recorder market would have been met in the Sarnoff era with a crash program to develop a superior competitive system—just as happened against CBS in color.

In a study of the dramatic rise of the Japanese video recorder industry, Professor Richard S. Rosenbloom of the Harvard Business School noted the capacity of Japanese electronics companies "to maintain a strategic commitment that kept development going in the face of disappointment and failure. . . . Their managements perceived potential consumer applications of video recording fifteen years before the market actually could be tapped.

They persisted in their commitment to develop the technology, even when prematurely commercialized consumer products failed in the market."

How extraordinarily similar to the Sarnoff approach a generation before—persistence in the face of disappointment and failure, an unyielding commitment to technology, a clear perception of potential consumer applications of the devices and systems invented by his scientists. True, he was not a skilled financial manager—and certainly he was no portfolio juggler or trained market analyst. His intuitive judgment was the lodestar that guided RCA, and in pursuing it he gave new meaning to the word "resolute" in the business vocabulary. More than any others, the Japanese seemed to understand this.

In other significant ways, Sarnoff deviated from the new style of business leader. By nature, he was fiercely competitive—indeed, he was never known to weep when lesser enterprises were driven to the wall—but in his last years he could be surprisingly protective of competitors if he felt the reputation of his industry would otherwise be harmed. In the early sixties, as color was beginning its sweep, he received a complaint from Henry Luce about the quality of color reception on the set at his summer home on the Hotel Biltmore grounds in Phoenix, Arizona. At luncheon with a group of *Time* editors, the publisher told Sarnoff, rather deprecatingly: "Of course, I never watch it, but Clare [Mrs. Luce] and the servants sometimes do. They tell me the picture on your RCA set is terrible, very blurry. I guess the people who say color isn't ready might have a point."

Sarnoff promised to look into the problem, and he did the minute the lunch ended. He instructed the head of RCA service operations to get a service man "immediately" to the Luces' home. Informed that no RCA color service branch had yet been opened in Phoenix, he arranged to have a chartered plane flown to Phoenix from Los Angeles with the best West Coast technician available and a full kit of repair equipment, including a new outdoor receiving antenna.

The next day Sarnoff received a direct report from the Luce household in Phoenix, and it was surprising. The Luce set was a Zenith, not an RCA. And it was linked to an outmoded antenna array, along with several black-and-white sets scattered through the house. The serviceman said the sets had been in such heavy use that various tubes and circuits had worn out. Sarnoff instructed his emissary to fix up all the sets and install the new, more powerful antenna. If he needed help with the color set, Sarnoff said, call the nearest Zenith dealer and "send the bill to my office." Later, describing the incident to a staff man, Sarnoff said, "Harry must have been watching television all the time. I wonder how he found time to read his magazines."

RCA publicists were overjoyed by the story. For years they had sought to counter Gene McDonald's contemptuous description of RCA color sets as Rube Goldberg contraptions. The press would pounce on a leaked story about the case of mistaken brand identity, and Zenith's misadventures with America's most eminent magazine publisher. But Sarnoff muzzled them, and the story never surfaced. "Sure it would embarrass Zenith," he explained. "But it would hurt the color industry more. I just don't want to do that." Later, without mentioning what had happened, he sent the Luces a new RCA color set as a gift. The serviceman who installed it had instructions to make certain the quality of the color picture was superior and continued that way.

In this instance, which was not atypical of his final decade, Sarnoff perceived himself functioning as the industry leader, sacrificing a temporary competitive advantage for his company to the broader good. And, as usual, he had acted intuitively and swiftly, never doubting that his judgment was correct, nor being concerned that anyone in his company might question it. His view on management authority was simple and direct: "You don't need to assert it unless it's challenged." The reality of RCA during his long stewardship was that no serious challenge was ever mounted. If Wall Street construed this as autocratic one-man rule, so be it.

Among Sarnoff's contemporaries in industrial leadership, perhaps the one who most rivaled him in public awareness was Alfred Pritchard Sloan, who guided the vast growth of the General Motors Corporation and whose name became synonymous with managerial skill. Sloan became GM's president in 1923, when Sarnoff was RCA's general manager, and chairman in 1937, when Sarnoff was in his fifth year as RCA's president. In their belief in the economies of bigness, the two men were similar. Yet in their approaches to management, they were as different as were their personal qualifications for leadership.

Where Sarnoff started life in the Old Testament world of the Russian pale, Sloan emerged in the comfortable middle-class environment of New Haven, Connecticut, in 1875, sixteen years Sarnoff's senior, the oldest of five children of a moderately successful wholesaler of tea and coffee, and the grandson of a Methodist minister. Graduated in electrical engineering from Massachusetts Institute of Technology, he began work for the Hyatt Roller Bearing Company of Newark, New Jersey, a tiny enterprise struggling to produce an antifriction bearing. With the financial support of his father, Sloan took over Hyatt and made it profitable by becoming a component supplier to the emerging automotive industry.

By 1916, as Sarnoff was erasing the slums of Manhattan from his life, Sloan was selling Hyatt to General Motors for $15 million and becoming president of United Motors Corporation, a newly formed GM sales and service subsidiary. As his genius for orderly management in the traditionally freewheeling automotive industry became recognized, he moved up to vice-president of the parent company and then, with strong support from GM's Dupont shareholders, head of the nation's largest industrial enterprise.

Tall and slender, patrician in bearing, Sloan believed passionately in collective, or consensus, management. His life was devoted to its achievement through a decentralized executive structure in which independent operating heads were counseled by numerous specialized committees. He believed the chief function of corporate management was to "dig out" scientific facts for the operations to act upon. "I never give orders," Sloan said in 1924 in explaining the rule of "We" rather than "I." Policy could originate from anywhere within GM, but it had to be appraised and approved by committees before being acted upon. In the constitution of the board of directors and its committees, Sloan insisted upon strong shareholder representation, with any personal ties to him secondary, if existent at all.

Sloan wrote the classic textbook of American business management, and in many essentials it was the antithesis of Sarnoff's personalized hegemony. Sloan designed complex management charts, with the flow of authority delineated in minute detail. Sarnoff often affirmed that he ran a company of men, not charts, with one man the ultimate decision maker.

Sloan's management style was attuned to a relatively stable one-product technology, with the annual model changeover normally more cosmetic than fundamental. Sarnoff managed an emerging technology noted for its volatility and the swiftness of product obsolescence. In his early executive experience, he grew to resent the committee structure imposed on RCA by the electrical companies. He watched in frustration as RCA's radio set sales eroded because smaller, more agile competitors introduced new features that committees of GE and Westinghouse engineers debated at length before adopting. To Sarnoff, committees came to mean bureaucratic delay; to Sloan, committees guarded against hasty mistakes.

"It's easier not to do it at all than to do it haphazardly or without due consideration," Sloan wrote his organization in 1931. "Even if we lose an opportunity, it will come up again sooner or later and in the long run we will gain by more thoroughly dealing with our problems."

Sarnoff innovated, Sloan organized—and two more disparate corporate leaders could not be found on the American scene. Had Sloan run RCA and Sarnoff General Motors, both conceivably would have failed as managers. Both succeeded brilliantly because their strengths were those needed in the industries and the time periods in which they functioned.

In 1975, *Fortune* magazine launched a Business Hall of Fame. Among the first fifteen inductees, reaching back to the republic's beginning, were Sarnoff and Sloan, the two opposites who had pioneered different management techniques to give America a then dominant position in the automobile and electronics fields. The citation accompanying his induction described Sarnoff as "this intense, opinionated, farsighted, driving man," and he would not have disagreed with it. He alone represented the electronics industry, and he would have been pleased at the roster of those who joined him in the first Hall of Fame group, among them Andrew Carnegie, Eli Whitney, Cyrus McCormack, Thomas A. Edison, John D. Rockefeller, and Henry Ford. All were creators or leaders of businesses that gave the nation new industrial resources, and this was how he liked to view himself.

In any attempt to assess Sarnoff's role in industrial history, two yardsticks seem to be required: the first, to gauge the success of his company against other technologically based enterprises that emerged contemporaneously, or at least overlapped, in his era; the second, to measure his broader and more enduring impact as a conceptualizer and creator of new technologies, as a shaper of the future.

In the first assessment, employing the conventional gauges of business success, Sarnoff does not tower above his contemporaries. Over the thirty-six years of his stewardship as chairman and president, other major enterprises often outperformed RCA as a business. Between 1932 and 1968, for example, RCA's founding parent, GE, grew more than twice as rapidly in sales and from four to six times in profits. In 1950, IBM, then a relatively small business-machine company, had sales of $215 million and net profits of $33.3 million, versus RCA's $586 million in sales and $46 million in profits. But as IBM seized the high ground of computer technology, the competition soon became no contest. By 1960, the two were comparable in sales but IBM was more than four times as profitable. A decade later IBM reached $7.5 billion in sales and more than $1 billion in profit, compared with RCA's $1.7 billion in sales and $92 million in profit.

In a sense the comparison is inexact, since the technological thrust of the two companies differed substantially. But the early perception of RCA was comparable to IBM's a half century later. No security traded in Wall Street in the late twenties had more appeal than RCA as leader of the most promising technology in the business horoscope. When Sarnoff needed large amounts for acquisitions, such as the Victor Talking Machine Company in 1929, he did not have to borrow or issue additional stock in order to raise cash. RCA's high-priced, gilt-edged common stock was the currency of purchase. RCA was a growth company when the word was new. Yet, and this is where it differed from GE and IBM, it never delivered profitable growth on a comparable sustained basis, never completely fulfilled the original prospectus.

Even among smaller competitors, RCA's performance often compared unfavorably. By 1956, fledgling Texas Instruments was realizing a 21 percent return on equity, versus RCA's 8 percent. Another newcomer in component electronics, Hewlett-Packard, achieved a 19 percent return in the same year and 7 percent net income as a percent of sales, more than twice RCA's level. And among older competitors, such as Philco and Zenith, for varying periods RCA surrendered marketing leadership of the radio and TV products it pioneered.

Sarnoff's RCA was inherently a cyclical company, its consumer orientation making it sensitive to pocketbook economics and business recessions. But it was also cyclical because of Sarnoff's management style. To him the cycle of technology was the dominant consideration in achieving growth, dictating more than did the economy or the bottom line, or even the corporate debt structure, where his company was headed, and at what speed. There were the long valleys when research costs and prolonged field tests and costly product introductions depressed earnings. But then there were the soaring peaks: new technologies bursting on the American scene, inspirational in character, changing life-styles and living patterns, enhancing profits, winning plaudits from friend and foe alike.

Increasingly in the modern era, American business has been oriented toward the elimination of surprises. Steady profit growth, steady sales growth, steady improvement in margins—all to be achieved through integrated long-range planning at the upper corporate level. Viewed within this perspective, Sarnoff cannot be considered a role model for today's MBA student. The perception that he lacked financial acumen was widespread, extending beyond Wall Street. And he contributed to this perception by scorning or ignoring new management tools. The science of econometrics, or the construction of elaborate economic planning models, was too late to capture his interest, for his was a company of men, not charts.

But measured on the broader canvas of leadership of an emergent technology, Sarnoff assumes enduring, even heroic, proportions. His forecasts of the potential of wireless communications for commerce, information, and entertainment were prophetic and influential. The creation of twentieth-century communications technology has expanded a millionfold the capacity of human beings to experience the world about them, and Sarnoff was at center stage in the conceptualization and implementation of that revolution.

He did not create it—any more than William the Conqueror created the stirrup that changed the throne of England through his victory in 1066 at the Battle of Hastings. The stirrup emerged from the mists of history, perhaps in primitive form from second-century India, but William was the first to conceptualize and employ it as a decisive tool of battle. The stirrup provided his mounted knights with a platform that permitted them to thrust their lances with maximum impact and accuracy. His cavalry shock troops decimated the foot soldiers of Harold of Saxony.

"New technology," the historian Lynn White, Jr., wrote, "creates new possibilities but they remain just that—possibilities—until someone, in some society, perceives and acts on them."

Whether a stirrup or a wireless signal moving at the speed of light, conceptualization of use was as significant as the discovery itself. Marconi discovered wireless, but his concept of its usage did not extend beyond conventional communications practices. All prior forms of electric communications—cable, the telegraph, the telephone—went from one point to another point, personal in nature, prized for their confidentiality. So, Marconi assumed, would wireless evolve in the same pattern.

Sarnoff removed such blinders and that was one of his surpassing achievements. Years before others, he described with great prescience how point-to-mass communications would evolve. His radio music box was a key conceptualization in the use of Marconi's "stirrup" to transform the modern world.

Almost as important as Sarnoff's vision was his implacable determination to fulfill it. To supporters it was courage, to opponents it was stubbornness. Either or both, the effect was profound, and never more so than in the color TV battle. Had he capitulated, as many urged him to do, an inherently inferior mechanical system of color TV might well have spread around the world. Ultimately, it would have been rendered obsolete by the superior electronic system Sarnoff espoused. But the cost to society in wasted years and resources could have been immense.

To a degree that few of his contemporaries could match, Sarnoff was a risk taker. This was perhaps because his life itself had been a series of high-risk encounters, beginning with his battles over news routes in the ghetto, his struggles with electrical company executives, his confrontation with giant AT&T over the future of radio networking, his endless duels with competitors and the FCC over television standards, his lonely fight against his government and his industry to win acceptance of his color system. To him, risk taking became a normal part of living; indeed, it was the most exhilarating part. Success in overcoming risks fueled his ego, strengthening his perception of himself as a superior individual, endowed with qualities of character and intellect that few, if any, of his peers could match. When he said he never knew fear, he said it not boastfully but more as a statement of fact. "All of life is a risk," he would say, "and I learned it earlier than most."

Had Sarnoff not insisted in his later years on excessive glorification of his life's story, draping it in such biographical adulation that many could not separate the reality from the hyperbole, a different, more enduring picture might well have emerged for future generations, including those Harvard Business School students who asked, only a decade after his death: "Who is David Sarnoff?" Those contemporaries who worked with or against him could answer that question because they were able to penetrate the obfuscatory tinsel and measure the substance of his achievements. To them, men like Paley and Weisner, he was one of the giants of industrial history, a leader of perception and courage.

Another who recognized this was the principal architect of the electronics industry of another nation that would soon challenge, and sometimes surpass,

America in the technology to which Sarnoff devoted his life. Japan's venerable Konosuki Matsushita, founder of a world-girdling electronics empire, had viewed the decades of creation and conflict from a half world away. He wrote to Sarnoff in 1966 when the RCA leader relinquished his chief executive position.

"You are," Matsushita said, "the bravest man of our generation."

13 / *Postscript: RCA*

Several years after Sarnoff's death, the RCA Corporation, as it had been legally renamed, experienced management turmoil and internal stress to such a degree that *Business Week* described the sequential developments as "a tumultuous passage, unprecedented in corporate annals." It was a period that might well be examined by future business scholars interested in the genesis of corporate upheavals, probing the complex interplay of events and personalities that left the company by 1981 in a straitened financial position, burdened by debt in excess of $1 billion, its continuity threatened by soaring interest rates in a recessionary economy. Within six years the chief executive officer would be changed four times. A 1982 poll of business leaders undertaken by *Fortune* singled out RCA as one of America's least admired companies—only seven years after the board of editors of that magazine had chosen David Sarnoff, posthumously, as one of the first fifteen business immortals in its Hall of Fame.

In brief summation, the turmoil at the top started in November 1975, when RCA's board of directors voted unanimously not to renew the expiring five-year contract of Robert Sarnoff, then fifty-seven, as chairman and chief executive officer. Among the fifteen outside and inside members, only one was a holdover from the last David Sarnoff board, but not one came to the defense of his son—even though he had personally selected, or approved the election of, each board member. They professed disenchantment with a lackluster earnings record and with internal executive conflicts. To the stunned second-generation Sarnoff, who had guided RCA for nearly a decade, the charges were unfair and without foundation. But he was unable to rally any support, and his family's forty-four-year rule of RCA came to a headline-making end.

As his successor, the board chose Anthony L. "Andy" Conrad, a career RCA employee who had risen through service company ranks to the company's presidency in 1971, and who was one of the leaders in what the *New York Times* described as a "palace revolt" against the younger Sarnoff. But Andy Conrad, a genial, low-key manager, lasted only ten months and eleven days. In the most bizarre episode in the company's history, Conrad, under pressure from the Internal Revenue Service, revealed that he had failed to file income tax returns for the preceding five years, even though he had paid most of his taxes through payroll deductions. On the advice of his attorney, he refused to explain why, and the board summarily fired him. Headlines blazed, many with suggestions of crime in the corporate suite.

As Conrad's successor, the board turned to Edgar H. Griffiths, another career employee who had risen through financial ranks to oversee most of the company's operating divisions. More than any of his predecessors, Griffiths moved to distance himself from the David Sarnoff era, of which he was openly disdainful. He became known as "Bottom Line Ed," an experienced financial executive, adept at imposing strict control over costs, a devotee of quarter-by-quarter profit improvements—all the things David Sarnoff was not. For a time in the late seventies, Griffiths's decisive and confident leadership produced positive results. He stilled the clamor over Conrad's tax problem, convincing the press that the company was not involved. He reorganized the consumer products division and strengthened leadership in color sales. The profit line began a steady ascension, reaching new record levels, and Griffiths won press approbation as the apotheosis of the "hands on" manager who never allowed his gaze to be deflected from the balance sheet. A new era of steady progress, unmarred by cyclical downturns, by the "surprises" that had so often discomfitted Wall Street in the David Sarnoff era, appeared to be at hand.

Within the company during Griffiths' regime, which extended from September 1976 to June 1981, the picture of the elder Sarnoff in the eyes of company executives was subtly changing. The long years under his leadership of fluctuating and indifferent profit performance, burdened by the developmental costs of monochrome and color, were being reassessed as the "bad" years. Now, at last, it was being said, RCA had real professional stewardship. In a 1978 cover story on Griffiths, *Fortune* wrote glowingly of the "reformation" at RCA, of the careful monitoring of operational performance by corporate management, of its willingness to face up to hard choices to achieve its transcendent goal of improved profits.

Yet Griffiths ultimately failed as a manager, failed dramatically in a flow of harsh and unforgiving headlines that destroyed any lingering perception of RCA as the leader of its industry and its technology. The seeds of destruction were perhaps planted in his early successes, which seemed to be matched by an increasingly contemptuous attitude toward outside board members who, he told his staff, "don't understand the business." When he attempted to impose additional directors of his choice, the outside members refused to accept most of them, inferring that he was attempting to "stack" the board. Shouting matches began erupting in tense boardroom encounters. Griffiths seemed unable to accept, as David Sarnoff did, the fact that the board was the indispensable wellspring of his power, its "care and feeding" his responsibility.

Inevitably, as the economy worsened under the impress of inflation, soaring interest rates, and declining production—stagflation, it was called—

Griffiths did encounter negative surprises. In 1979, a severe recession struck the record industry, causing massive returns of singles and albums by distributors, and a projected RCA Record Division profit for that year turned into a $20 million loss. Griffiths' response was first to demote, and then to fire, the executive overseeing the division, who happened to be a protégé of his.

Firing, as a solution to problems, was to become a hallmark of the Griffiths management, and often in the later stages was accompanied by a burst of negative publicity. Early on, he dismissed the head of the company's communications businesses and forced RCA's chief scientist into early retirement. Soon after, he fired the head of Hertz, accusing him of disloyalty. In his running dispute with the board, he sought to force the resignation of an outside director who frequently opposed him, but had to retract when the entire outside board threatened to resign, which would have ensured another management crisis.

Of all RCA's operations, NBC proved most intractable in responding to Griffiths' hands-on supervision. It remained mired in third place in audience ratings and profits. He removed one chief executive officer and installed a new team at the head of the network, but then in short order he fired the new chairman of the board. Under pressure from the RCA board to designate a successor, Griffiths chose, after a lengthy search, an outsider to be RCA's president and chief operating officer. Within four months he was disillusioned with his hand-picked successor and within six months had fired him, telling staff members the new president was a "hipshooter" and incapable of winning the respect of senior operating executives.

Of RCA's twenty-five officers when Griffiths took over, only fourteen remained when he departed less than five years later. Five board members had left. By 1980 the havoc he generated at the top had disillusioned the business press—he was described as a "bully" in *Business Week,* a "corporate Robespierre" in the *Wall Street Journal*—as well as the RCA board. When Griffiths offered to take early retirement in mid-1981, the board eagerly acquiesced. Its outside members felt RCA's public image had been severely damaged. Profits were on a downward toboggan, declining by $55 million in the year's first half; corporate debt was at a record level, and RCA's commercial paper had been downgraded by Standard & Poor's and Moody's rating services. The company's management, as the *Fortune* poll suggested, was being viewed in the business community with perplexed disdain, almost as though it had lost its moorings.

Why was the company that had been guided longer by one executive than any other in the public domain unsettled so quickly? Was it because the decades of so-called one-man rule had precluded the development of an orderly management succession? Was Sarnoff's insistence on a dynastic succession at fault? Had fate, which had smiled so benificently on RCA in its glory years, suddenly turned on it? How else explain the mystery of Conrad's failure to file income tax returns—a simple requirement for one surrounded by accountants, lawyers, and secretaries.

Perhaps nothing in the pattern of post-Sarnoff tumult was more puzzling, not even Conrad's inexplicable act, than the behavior of Griffiths as adversity intensified. Surely nothing in his rise through the ranks would have suggested it. Over thirty years he had forged a reputation within the company as a sound executive and a dependable, goal-oriented manager. Nothing in his private life seemed to offer a clue. He was considered an intensely moral man, devoted to his wife and fiercely protective of their private lives. Could the answer to the enigma of Griffiths be found in a view expressed by Professor Abraham Zaleznik of the Harvard Business School, a psychoanalyst and a specialist in executive behavior under stress? Writing in 1980 in *The Executive,* a magazine published by Cornell University, he offered the observation, unrelated to any individual, that "when an executive detaches himself emotionally from subordinates and higher authority, he also tends to overvalue himself. Operating out of an inflated ego—a sense of grandiosity with little regard for other people—produces a tyrant who typically throws caution to the wind."

Was there a link betweeen Professor Zaleznik's observation and a comment Griffiths himself made to *Fortune* in 1976, soon after his tenure began? "My decisions will be made with the head, not the heart," he told the magazine's interviewer. Could the head, divorced from the heart, succeed in guiding an institution whose heritage included its long-time leader's perception that "this is a company of men, not charts"? Surely, it was a comment that David Sarnoff, who practiced leadership by inspiration, who charted the company's future through his visceral judgements, would never have made.

As Griffiths' successor, the RCA board sought an executive of national stature, one seasoned in administering a large business organization and capable of imparting a new sense of purpose and direction to RCA's rather bewildered executive staff. The choice was Thornton F. "Brad" Bradshaw, president of the Atlantic Ritchfield Company. As an outside director of RCA for nine years, Bradshaw had witnessed the turbulence of the transitional era at first hand. Now nearing his sixty-fourth birthday, he saw the massive job of rebuilding the company and its morale as the ultimate managerial challenge in a career that had started as a teacher at Harvard Business School.

Originally, Bradshaw assumed he had a year of grace in which to settle the organization down and develop a long-term strategy for growth. But events quickly overrode him. A joint color-picture-tube venture with a French company to supply the European market began hemorrhaging losses under the dual onslaught of Japanese imports and a growing European recession. At NBC an inventory of unsalable programs overhung the efforts of a new management team to dig out of the ratings basement. Even Hertz, still the number-one car-rental company, presented Bradshaw with an ominous plunge into the red in its truck division.

Within weeks of his arrival, the new chairman decided to accept a write-off in the three troubled areas, throwing RCA into a third-quarter loss of $109 million. Again the business press headlined disaster at RCA. Questions were raised about whether Bradshaw was too old, too lacking in leadership drive, to salvage a company so burdened by debt and operating deficiencies. Why, one writer mused, had he abandoned the sunny climes of California, where Atlantic Ritchfield was headquartered, for the storms of New York—and RCA?

In his years with the oil company, Bradshaw had built a reputation as a team player and as a humanist on social issues affecting the environment in which his company and industry operated. He was a believer in structured management development programs. Since his graduation at the top of his class at Harvard Business School, he had been an adherent of long-range planning. In a sense, Bradshaw's management style was as different from David Sarnoff's as was Edgar Griffiths'. Yet he respected the elder Sarnoff and understood the unique nature of his long stewardship over RCA—the "genius" of his leadership had shaped the company, in Bradshaw's view, giving it purpose and vitality.

As an initial step in turning RCA around, Bradshaw retained outside consultants to analyze the emerging new communications technologies and to determine where RCA's strengths should be concentrated. In parallel, he created internal task forces of senior operating and staff officers to pinpoint specific growth targets for the remainder of the century, and to determine the best allocation of limited corporate resources.

Out of these coordinated studies, Bradshaw arrived at the central decision of his management. "We've got to get back to the basics," he concluded. "We've got to go back to our roots"—the roots planted a half century earlier by David Sarnoff. The years of wandering into businesses unrelated to electronics and communications must end. To Bradshaw, the earlier acquisition of Banquet frozen prepared foods symbolized how RCA had gone off the track. "We became the biggest chicken pluckers in America," he said. "The problem was our technically trained managers didn't know how to manage chicken plucking."

There were three areas they did know, and Bradshaw determined to focus the company on them: electronics, communications, and entertainment, primarily NBC, all synergistically linked to the burgeoning new technologies of information transmission. The success of such a far-ranging change of corporate direction, Bradshaw conceded, would take years to consummate. In 1942 RCA's scientists accounted for approximately a quarter of all basic electronics research in the United States; in the eighties it was less than

3 percent, even though the company employed more than 5,000 scientists, engineers, and technical support staff in its laboratories and operating divisions and even though the patents issued to RCA inventors in 1980 exceeded those of the giant Bell Laboratories.

So the technical sinews were still available. But the environment in which to flex them was vastly different from that of the Sarnoff era. The components he had watched being produced by American workers at Camden for radio and television sets were now being created and put in subassemblies by cheaper foreign workers—23,000 all told—in Taiwan and Malaysia and Juarez, Mexico. A new generational electronic development that the elder Sarnoff had prophesied in 1953—the home video tape recorder—had been realized, but not by his company. Only the RCA trademark went on the Japanese-made video recorders that RCA marketed by the millions in the United States during the eighties. In a sense, the company had come full circle. It began as the marketing arm for radios produced by General Electric and Westinghouse; a half century later, it performed that function in America for video recorders made by Matsushita and Hitachi.

In implementing his long-range goals, Bradshaw also managed to settle the organization down. Working long hours and with an intensity that belied his years, he succeeded in eliminating factionalism and forging a stronger team spirit. He created a management council of senior executives that met weekly to review operations and shape policy. He realigned the board to make outsiders dominant, and he recruited leaders from the military, educational, and scientific worlds to broaden its range of advisory skills. In 1981, in close consultation with the board, he selected a new president who would later succeed him as chief executive. He was Robert Frederick, executive vice president, sector executive, and thirty-two-year veteran of General Electric, the company with which the RCA odyssey began.

Within four years, Bradshaw achieved a reversal of RCA's fortune that, while not as spectacular as Sarnoff's color victory, was perhaps as significant in terms of the company's well-being. In 1984, sales passed the $10 billion mark, and profits of $341 million were at the highest level in sixty-five years. Corporate debt had shrunk and the credit rating of commercial paper had been upgraded. The market value of its common stock had appreciated by more than 130 percent. And a new *Fortune* poll of the business community had voted RCA's management among the most improved in American industry.

David Sarnoff always professed that luck played an important part in his career. So too had it with Brad Bradshaw. As he took over RCA, the prime interest rate was cresting at 20.5 percent and inflation was peaking. The strong rebound of the economy in the early eighties, accompanied by sharply reduced interest and inflation rates, eliminated a threatened liquidity crunch that had originally confronted Bradshaw, forcing him to slash dividends and to seek to sell assets in an unfavorable environment. The renewed pulsations of growth in 1982 spread to most of his core businesses, nudging profits upward and permitting him greater maneuverability in implementing long-range plans. As the financial markets strengthened, he began a search for buyers of the nonelectronic businesses. A greeting-card company was sold off, providing cash reserves when they were most acutely needed. Three years later, he achieved his most significant divestiture. The C.I.T. Financial Corporation was sold to Manufacturers Hanover for $1.51 billion, providing RCA with a massive infusion of capital to support its core electronic businesses, such as the new generation of space satellites it was pioneering. A year later the Hertz rental car concern was sold to United Aircraft, and the healthy glow of the company's balance sheet resembled that of the peak color years.

In one of his core areas, broadcasting, Bradshaw achieved the goal that had eluded David Sarnoff for so many frustrating years. His first act as head of RCA, on July 1, 1981, had been to appoint Grant A. Tinker as chairman and chief executive of NBC, which was then running a distant third to CBS and ABC in most areas where the networks competed. As Bradshaw did at RCA, Tinker moved swiftly to stabilize an organization that was in disarray, shaken by years of internecine feuding and executive firings. And like the young Paley at CBS in broadcasting's formative years, he began to forge new bonds of trust and understanding between NBC and the West Coast creative community that was the source of most of television's entertainment programming. Before accepting Bradshaw's offer, Tinker had been head of MTM productions, one of the most successful television producing companies. Before that, he had been an NBC program executive, known and respected throughout the industry. Like Paley, he was first and foremost a broadcaster, discerning of audience tastes and sensitive to the aspirations of those who created and produced programs and those who acted in them. His urbane, nonpressurized management style, almost collegial in the environment it created, opened doors in the creative community that had long been closed to NBC. With increasing frequency, the Tinker network became the first port of call, not the third, for fresh program ideas and pilot productions of proposed new series.

Tinker did not dig out of the ratings basement overnight. However, by late 1984 he had succeeded in positioning NBC as a strong second, ahead of ABC, in the network prime-time viewing hours, where success in broadcasting had traditionally been gauged. NBC's profits improved from $48 million in 1981 to $218 million three years later—still the lowest among the three networks but improving rapidly and, once again, the largest single contributor to RCA's balance sheet.

In the fall of 1985, as the new broadcast season commenced, NBC's evening schedule attracted the largest national audience of any network.

Finally, the pioneer company that Young, Harbord, and Sarnoff launched in 1926 was leading the pack in the entertainment race. As the Tinker management sustained its prime-time momentum into the summer of '86, NBC became first for a full season—first for the first time since the Paley talent raids of 1948. Nearly four decades after Sarnoff failed to respond to the competitive challenge of the junior network, the pendulum of NBC-CBS rivalry appeared to be reversing decisively.

The stage thus seemed set for years of corporate renewal. Struggle had been RCA's leitmotif since its founding, and that had not changed. Under Bradshaw, efforts by the Bendix Corporation to acquire RCA had been fought off in a bitter clash of words and legal maneuver. The video disc had fought a losing battle in the commercial marketplace. One of the oldest manufacturing businesses, in broadcast equipment, was phased out and written off, another casualty of the Japanese invasion.

But the internal tumult had been stilled, a new management was in place, a new captain on the bridge, and the course being charted responded to, and drew sustenance from, the company's technological heritage. The RCA of David Sarnoff was back on track. As Bradshaw and Frederick reported in a letter to shareholders on February 14, 1985, the company they owned had been "set firmly on the path of long-term growth." A prosperous, independent future appeared to beckon—until the night of December 11, 1985, when a corporate announcement shook the company to its roots. The world of RCA was, in fact, upended. A vision flashed before the eyes of more than one company veteran—a vision of David Sarnoff in a sepulchral spin.

14 / End of the Journey

Few pronouncements have descended on corporate America with greater impact than the one issued that December night. It was fifty-three years since Sarnoff, with government help, had won his long battle to free RCA from G.E.'s corporate embrace. Now, a joint release by the two companies turned back the clock of industrial history. A banner headline on page one of the *New York Post* proclaimed that GE was acquiring RCA, the company it had founded in 1919. At the time, it had paid $3.5 million for a controlling block of the stock of American Marconi, later to become the Radio Corporation of America. Now, it was offering $6.28 billion, the equivalent of $66.50 per outstanding share of RCA stock, to effect the largest non-oil merger in industrial annals. Out of this union, scheduled for consummation in 1986, would emerge a technological behemoth that dwarfed the most grandiose of David Sarnoff's visions—its sales approaching $40 billion annually, with net profits exceeding $2.5 billion, with total assets of $33 billion, and with 400,000 employees worldwide. It would become America's seventh-largest industrial enterprise, rivaling IBM in size, and capable, in the words of the GE and RCA executives who crafted the merger, of successfully competing "with anyone, anywhere, in every market we serve." Again, as in RCA's founding, the ensign of patriotism was unfurled. America was promised a formidable new corporate dreadnought capable of countering Japanese commercial forays across all the seven seas.

Yet, had Sarnoff been alive, there is little doubt that the merger, despite its oligarchial dimensions and the Dionysian appeal of its strength and power, would have devastated him. The RCA he had built over five decades, which had arced with cometlike brilliance across the industrial skies of the early and mid-twentieth century, would no longer survive as an independent corporate entity. It would be subsumed within GE. His scientific laboratories, "the lifeblood of RCA," would probably become part of the vastly greater research apparatus of the parent company. The defense, communications, service, and electronic tube and component businesses he had founded would probably be fused with their GE counterparts. Even in consumer electronics, in which RCA was two and a half times larger than GE, there was no guarantee the RCA logo would continue in perpetuity.

To stunned RCA veterans who had lived through the color wars, it seemed as though Sarnoff's old foe, the late GE chairman Ralph Cordiner, was having the last laugh on him in the Elysian fields. It was Cordiner who had nearly destroyed his early thrust in color by publicly complaining that an engineer was needed in the home with every color set. Now Cordiner's heirs would dictate the future of his seminal creation.

Even Sarnoff's old command post on the fifty-third floor of 30 Rockefeller Plaza, still New York's most attractive office building, faced an uncertain future, perhaps rental to another tenant, possibly the Manhattan lodgement for a GE staff executive or the operating head of one of its far-flung satrapies. The nerve center of the merged entity would be GE's corporate headquarters at Fairfield, Connecticut. Ironically, only NBC, of all the electronic offspring he had reared—NBC, which had thwarted and frustrated him at almost every turn—seemed assured of remaining intact, with its own board of directors and with promised sovereignty for news, programming, and station operations. To the second-generation RCA Sarnoff, the ousted Bob, the meaning was clear: "One of America's greatest and best-known international companies, whose pioneering efforts in communications and electronics over six decades have contributed so much to our country and world, will cease to exist. . . . I think it's a tragedy." His father would have agreed.

But this view was not shared by the men responsible for managing RCA. To Bradshaw and Frederick and the RCA Board of Directors, the merger represented a "bold and creative step to generate the critical mass essential to continued market leadership in a rapidly evolving global economy." Implicit in their statement was the concession that the $10 billion in revenue and $343 million in net profits RCA generated in 1984 no longer constituted a critical mass. Their RCA was more than four times the size of the company David Sarnoff left behind, but that apparently was not enough. As a company "standing alone," Bradshaw explained to the *Wall Street Journal,* "I just don't know whether we could compete fully on the fronts we would like to compete on." Not only the Japanese but other players on the world scene, like Phillips of Holland and Siemens of Germany, had far outgrown RCA in their global market reach and in their capacity to muster technological resources behind new advances.

Perhaps RCA's willingness to surrender its independence had been foreshadowed a year earlier by the commercial failure of the last major invention to emerge from the David Sarnoff Laboratories in Princeton. It was the video disc machine, a home instrument capable of playing back video records of movies and other features. RCA had gambled during the Griffiths regime that it could repeat Sarnoff's success in color, and the disc was introduced to the domestic marketplace on March 22, 1981 with the most lavish product introduction the company had ever attempted. But despite the disc player's low price and simplicity of operation, sales lagged far behind initial projections. More sophisticated and more expensive Japanese video tape machines were already being sold in the American market, and they permitted not only the playback of prerecorded features but also the taping of programs off the air. To the public, the price differential seemed not enough to offset the technological advantages of the Japanese product.

Soon after Bradshaw took over that "hotbed of dissension"—as *Time* described the prior management—the disc player was contributing to the unrest by funneling millions of dollars of losses into a balance sheet already burdened by excessive debt from nonelectronic acquisitions. Where Sarnoff accepted continuing losses in color because he knew his technology was right, Bradshaw soon discerned in the disc-tape competition that the technological edge rested with his competitors. Years earlier, RCA scientists had rejected videotape machines as too complex and too costly for employment in home instruments, thus abandoning the field to the Japanese. So Bradshaw was faced with the consequences of that miscalculation, and he took the difficult, but undoubtedly correct, decision to phase out the disc player, accepting cumulative losses that exceeded $300 million. Perhaps with that decision came the realization of how high the stakes were in the modern game of technology. No longer could RCA alone force on the nation, as Sarnoff had done, its own mousetrap—and particularly when it was a flawed mousetrap.

But the problems facing Bradshaw as he nursed RCA back to health extended beyond technology into the changing environment that affected all of American business. Encouraged by relaxed antitrust enforcement and the development of innovative methods of margin financing, a new genre of takeover artists, leveraged buyout specialists, arbitragers, and specialists in the flotation of high-risk junk bonds were changing the contours of corporate America. The early '80s became a time of merger mania. With Wall Street encouragement, the business community began a frenzied mating dance, a celebrate-now, pay-later party of unprecedented abandon. The dollar values of mergers in 1985 approached $150 billion. Companies were acquiring, or being acquired, wholly or in part, at the rate of eleven daily. American companies were expending their stock for takeovers or in defense against them—nearly $200 billion worth in just two years—and incurring a total corporate debt that approached $1.5 trillion. The era of megadeals was underway. "Rather than planning new products or considering new markets," *Time* observed on December 23, 1985, "many executives are spending their time looking around at whom they might takeover, or who might takeover them. In a less frenetic period RCA might not have been so eager to find a merger partner. The motto of these executives could be borrowed from the legendary baseball pitcher, Satchel Paige: 'Don't look back. Something might be gaining on you.' "

Ironically, Bradshaw's dramatic success in reviving RCA placed the company in jeopardy. Its profit upsurge, and the turnaround of its crown jewel, NBC, caused many in Wall Street to view it as a tempting prize. Its defense, service, and broadcasting businesses were insulated from foreign competition. Despite Japanese incursions, RCA color sets were the nation's largest seller, with a 19 percent market share. Only a few months before the GE merger agreement was signed, a leveraged buyout of RCA, which would have taken the company private, was informally proposed by the investment firm of Kohlberg, Kravis, Roberts & Co., but quickly rejected by management because of the mountainous residue of debt that would ensue. A merger with the West Coast entertainment empire of MCA, in which RCA would have been the survivor, came close to fruition but collapsed in a final negotiating session.

All around RCA's core businesses, merger activities were swirling in 1985. Capital Cities Broadcasting was acquiring ABC for $3.5 billion. CBS was fending off the Turner Broadcasting System's takeover attempt, and piling up a burdensome debt for repurchased shares in order to preserve its independence. New communications satellite and cable TV companies were cropping up and merging or disappearing. Only RCA and Zenith remained among the forty American brands that once manufactured television sets in this country. Motion picture titans of an early era, like MGM and Twentieth Century–Fox, were being acquired, sold, and reacquired like baseball cards or antique cars.

In this volatile, don't-look-back climate, only thirty-five days were required to cement the union of GE and RCA. The initiative apparently came from GE's intense, nail-biting, fifty-year-old chairman, John F. Welch, Jr., a self-made, Sarnoff-style leader, work-obsessed, whose electric-blue gaze could also pinion subordinates, moistening palms and beading brows. For five years, Welch, a chemical engineer from a working-class family in Massachusetts, had been planning and executing a massive transformation in the electrical giant's business mix—away from his predecessors' concentration on household appliance manufacturing and more into service and high technology. On November 6, 1985, Welch arranged a get-acquainted meeting with Bradshaw at the Upper East Side Manhattan apartment of Felix Rohatyn, investment banker and senior partner of Lazard Frères & Company, financial adviser to RCA. Together over a drink, with only Rohatyn and his cat present, the two industrialists exchanged views on world markets, Japanese competition, and the future of broadcasting. "I discovered we thought almost alike," Welch later told a business reporter, "and when you meet people with the same philosophical bent and you both see global markets and you can both agree, you move." Later, when the merger discussions began, Welch expressed the view, with which Bradshaw agreed, that there would be "an excellent strategic fit for both companies." Thus from the beginning a harmony, both intellectual and pragmatic, developed between the two men— a rather novel circumstance in the often acrimonious arena of merger making.

For many months before the meeting at Rohatyn's apartment, a GE staff team assembled by Welch had been examining potential acquisition candidates. Now, he focused the team's attention on RCA. "We tore the numbers apart," he said. "We knew everything about that company by the time we were through." He quickly concluded that RCA, alone among the incredible total of three thousand companies he said his team had studied, possessed the unique complementary strengths required to propel GE to new plateaus of global leadership. It was almost as though he had been exposed, like Saul of Tarsus on the road to Damascus, to a flash of revelatory light.

On December 6, having mulled over his strategy during a Thanksgiving holiday with his family in Florida, Welch met again with Bradshaw at the latter's company apartment in Manhattan's Dorset Hotel. Welch submitted what, the RCA chairman later said, "I could only construe as a binding offer." Bradshaw promptly notified the RCA directors and asked authorization to proceed with negotiations. Initially, he was opposed by Frederick, the former GE'er who was now RCA's chief executive officer. Frederick argued that the company should continue to pursue its strategic plan for growth as an independent entity, but the board overrode him and Bradshaw won his authorization.

A week of feverish meetings ensued, involving outside merger counsel for both companies, investment bankers, and financial and legal officers for GE and RCA. Welch upped his initial offer of $61 per share to the final $66.50. In the early evening of December 11, both company boards, at special meetings held in great secrecy, unanimously endorsed the definitive merger agreement, subject to RCA shareholder and government regulatory approval.

It was imperative to move swiftly, because rumors of a merger involving RCA were sluicing like an open fire hydrant onto Wall Street. For three days before the definitive agreement was signed, RCA stock had gyrated upward in massive block trading on the New York Stock Exchange. Not since the 1929 market boom, when the "Radio" beloved by Scott and Zelda Fitzgerald was at its peak, had there been so much frenzied activity in RCA equities. Between Monday and Wednesday, the per share price jumped almost $16, an increase of 33 percent, which added $1.5 billion to the company's market valuation. On the Chicago Board Options Exchange, the futures price of one hundred RCA shares went from $100 on Monday to $1,100 on Wednesday. More than 8.7 million shares exchanged ownership in those three hectic days on the New York Exchange, and it became apparent that speculators were shearing millions in profits from the unwary or uninformed.

Suspicions of irregularities came to a head when *Newsweek* in its issue of December 23 posed the headline question: "Foul Play on a Megamerger?" The accompanying article suggested darkly that traders with advance knowledge had fattened on the deal, in violation of strict rules governing insider trading. The New York Stock Exchange, the Securities and Exchange Commission, and the Chicago Options Exchanges promptly announced investigations to ferret out the guilty if they could be found. *Newsweek* predicted that "the deal may end up as one of the most controversial in years."

The GE and RCA executives with advance knowledge could argue, as they did, that the negotiations had been conducted in absolute secrecy. Yet the fact remained that in piecing together a deal of such magnitude and complexity, many outsiders remote from corporate restraints had to be involved. There were investment bankers representing both companies and outside legal firms specializing in merger law. Backing them up were secretaries, paralegals, and clerks who prepared and delivered the prospectuses and contracts that had to be exchanged, discussed, and revised. A single individual, perhaps far removed from the locus of corporate authority, could have confided in a friend and that friend in a broker, and the hydrant thus could have begun to spew. "The thing about Wall Street is they all talk," observed analyst William Relyear of Eberstadt Fleming, Inc. "Everybody has a friend." Even GE's Welch, according to *Newsweek,* admitted that the talks were being compromised by "a pouring leak." An irate RCA shareholder filed a class-action suit in Federal District Court, alleging that his company & GE had failed to make timely disclosure of merger negotiations.

Yet legal action, whether by individuals or government agencies, seemed unlikely to unsettle the merger, which Welch estimated would require about nine months to complete. Tolerance of big mergers had become a hallmark of the Reagan administration, and repeated efforts to legislate restraints on size in the Congress had gone no further than committee. The climate was indeed far different than that of 1930, when another conservative Republican administration, that of Herbert Hoover, had set about to rip RCA and GE apart, and had succeeded, in a flare of approving press headlines.

Before he became president in 1928, Hoover had served as Secretary of Commerce in the Coolidge administration, and he had oversight responsibility for the emergent radio industry. As described in his memoirs, Hoover believed that one of his responsibilities was to maintain an independent radio structure by supporting "the lovers of liberty fighting off those who would have government ownership and monopoly on the one hand, and preventing private enterprise from creating monopoly on the other." The price of liberty, he suggested cryptically, "was not only a matter of eternal vigilance, but of a good attorney general."

In Hoover's view, the principal threat to radio's future well-being was the consortium of competitors in set manufacturing—GE, Westinghouse and RCA—and he decided to seek the dissolution of this "radio manufacturing trust."

"I suggested to Mr. Mitchell [the Attorney General] that we place former Judge Olney of California in charge of the case," Hoover wrote in 1952 in his memoirs. "I directed the Attorney General to let them have both barrels."

Strong words indeed for the head of an administration fighting to overcome a searing depression through its alliance with big business. But to the Quaker president, the antitrust laws were unambiguous in their intent, and

GE and RCA were violating them. "It took Mr. Mitchell and Judge Olney a year," he wrote, "but within that time they made the concerns willing to accept a 'consent decree' which, translated from legal terminology into plain English, was a complete admission of violation of the law."

The same laws governing monopolies and illegal restraints of trade that Hoover employed to free RCA from its electrical company owners remained in effect a half century later. But the competitive environment they were designed to protect had altered radically. "Under the benign gaze of the Reagan White House," *Time* observed in December, 1985, "bigger most often means better. Charles Rule, Deputy Assistant Attorney General in the antitrust division notes that recent years have brought 'a sea change in public opinion regarding the costs and benefits of regulation,' including the antitrust laws. Says Rule: 'After years of experience with The Great Society, we discovered that more government doesn't make society all that great. Indeed, it often makes it worse.' "

Not everyone agreed, however, that in the GE-RCA reunion bigger necessarily meant better. The first flush of approving headlines and stories soon gave way to second thoughts. In an editorial a week following the merger announcement, *Business Week* expressed a "pang of disappointment." While conceding the validity of some mergers in terms of healthy corporate restructuring and a more productive deployment of assets, the editorial said the GE-RCA deal suggested a "distressing failure of imagination that besets many of today's major corporate players. Its principal effect is simply to bring together two world-famous corporate giants. The acquisition, at least at the outset, creates no new products, no new jobs. It remains to be seen to what extent it will produce more than a sterile transfer of assets. In any case, managing the new corporate behemoth will be a more formidable job than running the two companies separately." Further, lamenting that "GE—a company famed for proclaiming its commitment to creativity and innovation—could find no better way to spend $6 billion than to buy a major rival," *Business Week* suggested, "sadly," that the deal was simply a "jumbo version" of commonplace mergers.

To Welch, such stories were simply "missing the point." In his view, it was not just another big merger but a watershed development in business history. Where Sarnoff a half century earlier had postulated at the Harvard Business School a coming revolution in the management of technology, Welch was now projecting a new concept of American corporate power, fueled by the new breed of "dynamite company" he was fashioning, a "breakthrough" company, with the profits from its insulated domestic operations providing the financial sinews to battle low-cost foreign competitors on their own terms and wherever market opportunities emerged. "It's a fundamental concept of strength," he told the *Wall Street Journal*. "You take a powerful broadcasting network, a strong defense business and a billion dollar service company, all relatively invulnerable to imports, and they strengthen your domestic base to make you a stronger, more viable exporter." It was a concept somewhat akin to that of the Japanese, who shielded their domestic markets from external competition, with the financial power thus generated supporting their exploitation of foreign markets. Addressing the Japanese challenge directly, Welch said, "Every day we're meeting the Toshibas of the world, the Hitachis of the world. We have to get larger and more powerful to compete or just give up and let imports take over."

Generally, Wall Street accepted Welch's evaluation of his new dynamite enterprise. In a bull market, GE's stock rose nearly six points after the merger announcement. Analysts speculated that NBC, supported by GE's greater financial resources, could accelerate its drive for leadership in all parts of the broadcast day and flesh out its owned station line-up through additional purchases in major markets. In other parts of RCA, analysts suggested major economies could be effected. Much of the large corporate staff at 30 Rockefeller Plaza would become redundant. Millions could be saved in corporate advertising and promotion costs, since the corporate identity would disappear.

Yet as analysts and institutions holding RCA stock pondered the financial terms, some began suggesting the company had sold itself too cheaply. "GE may have picked up a bargain," *Fortune* commented in its January 6, 1986, issue. "Wall Street estimates of RCA's real worth range anywhere from $70 to $90 a share." The *Wall Street Journal* quoted other offended shareholders as saying, "it's a steal by GE," and suggesting that RCA had been "out-negotiated in sweetheart negotiations" by the formidable Welch. Within a month, sixteen lawsuits were filed by shareholders, many challenging the terms on which RCA was willing to surrender its independence.

In his five years as GE's chief executive, Welch had developed a reputation as a nonpareil cost cutter and economizer, selling off 120 businesses, eliminating aging factories, reducing total employment nearly 20 percent. Between 1980 and 1984, GE's profits rose 50 percent on a sales increase of 12 percent. Welch's reputation as one of America's strongest, and toughest, entrepreneurs grew in proportion to his earnings record, and that fact was not lost on fearful RCA employees. With trepidation, they read in *USA Today* the comment of a former GE executive, Nicholas Heymann, who had become a security analyst at Drexel Burnham: "I can guarantee you there's not going to be life as normal at RCA. If he [Welch] could do it to his own troops, he'll do it to the new troops. A lot of fat and overhead will go by the wayside."

Even before such warnings began to surface, the merger announcement had echoed through RCA's corporate headquarters like a toll of doom. To staff members who had lived through the tension and turmoil of the later Griffiths years, Bradshaw's success in restoring profitability and stability had revived their careers and made them, once again, proud to say they worked for RCA. But now, without warning, the leader they had come to respect had acceded in their sale to a powerful competitor. Lower-echelon corporate staffers were informed by their department heads that they could count on an additional nine months of employment, the time estimated to be necessary to fuse the two organizations. After that, nothing could be guaranteed. "I've never seen morale as bad around here as it is now," observed Vincent Borello, manager of RCA's editorial services, a thirty-four year veteran who started as a messenger boy but still considered himself too young to retire. "Nobody knows what to do or where to turn." The *Wall Street Journal* questioned employees and concluded that "many of RCA's white-collar and blue-collar workers . . . are far from certain that they will benefit much when the merger is completed. . . . The charged atmosphere that pervades RCA illustrates the upheaval and uncertainty caused by an unexpected, if friendly, takeover." Even the genial, people-oriented architect of the merger conceded the human toll involved in RCA's loss of identity. "It's an emotional shock to all of us," Bradshaw said.

Among career employees, a different view emerged of why the merger went through with such dramatic suddenness. "It was because outsiders were running RCA," in the opinion of George Fuchs, a former executive vice-president for industrial relations who had retired two years earlier. "Most of the key people had been with the company only three or four years. They didn't have a sense of our heritage, of the way we had fought to win our independence and hold it. Those of us who spent our business lives here wouldn't have given it up so quickly. RCA was bred into us."

Even those at or near RCA's top were uncertain what the future held. Bob Frederick had left his GE executive vice-presidency after losing out to Welch in the race for chief executive. He had just taken over as RCA's chief executive from Bradshaw who, approaching sixty-nine, would retire on the merger's completion with a three-year consultancy contract to GE at $500,000 annually. Frederick knew both companies well and would play a key interim role in blending their two cultures. But after that, he conceded at a postannouncement press conference, "it's up to Jack." Sixty other principal executives were awarded new contracts, from three to five years' duration, that would provide varying degrees of financial independence if their responsibilities, like their company, evanesced. No longer would the "care and feeding" of RCA's board of directors—a favorite David Sarnoff chore— be the responsibility of his heirs. The board, too, would evanesce.

Perhaps most unsettled as a group was RCA's middle management— men and women between forty-five and fifty-five who had worked up to responsible and well-paying jobs and who considered themselves, in the words of one, "too young to retire, too old to change careers." Many were pillars of the suburban communities in which they lived, city councilmen, United Fund organizers, church leaders, school board members. RCA had always encouraged their participation in civic affairs, and now their family roots were deeply planted. They had read press stories quoting the dynamic Welch as promising, "We're going to kick ass" when he assumed the stewardship of GE. Would his kicks now be aimed at their posteriors? They had seen him described in print as "Neutron Jack"—when he went through plants the buildings remained but the people were gone. Would their workers be swept away? Would they be uprooted? Not even Bradshaw's calm reasoning that the alliance with a financial powerhouse might lead to more jobs, not less, could completely reassure them.

The emotional intensity of many career employees and elderly Sarnoff-era shareholders found dramatic vent on February 13, 1986, when a special meeting of nearly a thousand owners of RCA stock convened in the grand ballroom of Manhattan's Marriot Marquis to vote on the merger. During the prior month, RCA management had solicited proxies from large institutional holders who controlled most of the 91 millon shares outstanding. When chairman Bradshaw called the 11 A.M. meeting to order, he possessed proxies in favor of the merger that accounted for 61 percent of total shares. So the issue was not in doubt as he set forth in explicit terms why management favored the surrender of RCA's independence:

"GE has a greater capacity to ride out business cycles and endure fundamental shifts in the economy. Over the past five years, GE has substantially outperformed companies of similar size and comparable business in sales, earnings, dividends and stock prices—all the while investing $10 billion in plant and equipment and $10 billion in research and development. The combined company will have the resources and staying power to face the challenges and reap the benefits of the new international marketplace."

But for three hours, a choreography of rancorous dissent flowed across the grand ballrom. Angered shareholders seized floor microphones to protest "selling us out." They accused RCA's management of "just looking out for yourselves," of bartering the company's independence for $33 million in "golden parachute contracts" designed to provide financial security for sixty senior officers. "You people have killed this company," one shareholder asserted. Another charged: "You have raped us." Another asked: "Why are you obliterating the name RCA? I am terribly opposed to this giveaway. What you are doing is a disgrace." Even those who conceded the merger's inevitability were irate at management's failure to negotiate a tax-free exchange of their stock for GE common, rather than a straight cash purchase that would require substantial capital-gains tax payments. The fact that shareholders would receive nearly four and a half times the market value of their holdings when Bradshaw took over RCA's management in 1981, that the purchase price was sixteen times earnings and twice book value, was brushed aside. "Your interest in the shareholders," one elderly holder told the imperturbable Bradshaw, "is a farce." Assurances from Bob Frederick that GE had no intention to "lose the value of the RCA name" elicited no response. A charge that Lazard Frères was guilty of a conflict of interest in proselytizing for the merger, and then reaping large fees from it, won widespread applause. Motions were made to adjourn the meeting without acting on the merger, only to be voted down by management's proxies.

As the chronology of protest unfolded, an undercurrent of frustrated sadness could also be sensed. The votes of shareholders present could not alter the outcome, and most realized it. The older ones, in particular, seemed to be there as David Sarnoff's proxies, opposing what, in the words of one, he would never have agreed to. To an RCA veteran observing from the balcony, they recalled Greek sentinels at the Acropolis, fighting a delaying action against the Macedonians. They were defending their dead leader's citadel of technology, which they feared GE would dismember. But it was to no avail. The final tabulation showed 56.1 million shares in favor of merger, or 92.7 percent of the votes cast. One of the ironies of this final historic assemblage of RCA's owners, although they were unaware of it, was that the government's antitrust division, acting on a long-standing submission of RCA's legal department, had only months earlier abrogated the provisions on the 1932 consent decree, which sundered RCA from GE. Otherwise, the legal barrier to reunification would have remained intact.

Of the principals in the merger drama, none symbolized its many ironies more than Felix Rohatyn, the brilliant, ubiquitous Lazard investment banker who had played matchmaker between Welch and Bradshaw. When the RCA board deliberated the merger offer, Bradshaw called Rohatyn before it to certify the fairness of GE's proposal and the values implicit in the union. Even though two of the older members were reported to be deeply disturbed at the loss of RCA's independence, Rohatyn's persuasiveness, coupled with that of Bradshaw, carried the day. Rohatyn, alone of the principals, possessed the cachet of a link to David Sarnoff's RCA, and he had nurtured that link through successor managements. As the protégé of André Meyer, the powerful postwar head of Lazard's American office and close friend of Sarnoff, Rohatyn had been a leading participant in the creation of conglomerates in the sixties and seventies, particularly Harold Geneen's ITT, of which he was a director. He had so impressed the elder Sarnoff in the early sixties with his grasp of modern finance that the General sought to bring him to RCA as chief financial officer, only to be gently dissuaded by Meyer, who pointed out that the youthful Rohatyn was already making more than five times the salary of RCA's highest-paid staff officer.

Together, Meyer and Rohatyn played a central role in the shift of RCA away from its core technologies. As the elder Sarnoff's rule phased out, the Lazard partners, working with RCA's other investment bankers, Lehman Brothers, became increasingly active with successor managements in producing new candidates for acquisition—a randomly selected grab bag of carpets, frozen foods, real estate, office furniture, rental cars and trucks, financial services, insurance companies, and greeting cards. Always the rationale of both bankers and management was the achievement of greater balance in products and services, the hedge that would be erected against cyclical downturns in RCA's traditional business. For many years, it seemed an exciting game—identifying the target company, flushing it out, and then bagging it. It was only later that the problems would crop up—the indigestible nature of some of the unrelated businesses, the debt that grew more burdensome in a high-interest economy, the "chilling effect" (as *Business Week* phrased it) on RCA's scientific community as it watched corporate resources go for nonelectronic purposes. Perhaps it was only coincidence, but RCA's abandonment of video tape to the Japanese—a technology which it and another American firm, Ampex, had pioneered—occurred during the years when it was preoccupied, in Bradshaw's later words, with "chicken plucking."

To senior staffers who bridged the years of fluctuating priorities, the influence of investment bankers on RCA's corporate culture had become a source of continuing conjecture and, often, dismay. Was there not, they would often ask at luncheon meetings or other informal gatherings, a blatant conflict of interest when investment bankers serving as directors of companies—as Lehman and Lazard had for years at RCA—earned millions in fees for acquisitions sanctioned by their fellow directors? Was the fact that banker members would not vote on mergers they managed anything less than a charade? When acquired companies were divested several years later, as with Hertz, Banquet Foods, and C.I.T., why should the same bankers harvest additional millions? The practice became known among staff members as "the double dip." A corridor catechism emerged: "They get it coming and they get it going." A thirty-year veteran seeking to penetrate the shroud of gloom that followed the merger disclosure commented to some younger associates: "Well, at least you won't see Lazard and Lehman stalking the fifty-third floor any more."

For their role in this largest of non-oil marriages, Rohatyn and Lazard, according to a *Wall Street Journal* report, would reap an estimated $16 million in fees on consummation of the transaction. "In the world of high finance," *Time* observed, "where an elite group of Wall Street dealmakers command million-dollar fees for putting together megadollar agreements, Felix Rohatyn is the first among equals," and the GE-RCA deal seemed to confirm it. For nearly two decades, he had helped devise the financial tools that made the supermerger a staple of corporate life. On Wall Street, he became known as "Felix the Fixer," the cleverest of merger manipulators. Yet to many RCA executives, he was seen through a different prism—as an outside force of incredible authority, a mesmerizer of management, an influential course setter in charting the company's future, more powerful than any outside director (although never a member of the RCA board), and perhaps the key player in the ultimate drama of merger, and possibly of dismemberment.

At the time of his involvement in GE-RCA negotiations, Rohatyn was also speaking out forcefully against the dangers to America's financial structure of the orgy of mergerism—and this, to the RCA'ers, seemed a further supreme irony. In *Time*'s words, he was becoming "like the sorcerer whose apprentices have run amok." In the same issue of that magazine featuring the proposed GE-RCA merger on its cover, Rohatyn was quoted as telling a group of its editors, "Today things are getting badly out of hand." His concern was the huge load of debt, primarily high-risk junk bonds, being piled up in mergers and thus eroding the "climate of confidence required of our financial institutions." No such speculative financing, of course, would be required if his newest merger finalized, not with GE's gilt-edged balance sheet. But GE would nevertheless, according to Welch, borrow between $4 billion and $5 billion from banks to finance the RCA purchase, thus adding to the corporate debt load that Rohatyn described as "crippling."

Speaking with all the fervor of the penitent, Rohatyn told *Time:* "The way we are going will destroy all of us in this business. Someday, there is going to be a major recession, major scandals. All of us may be sitting in front of congressional committees trying to explain what we were doing." There was little likelihood, of course, that the GE-RCA merger would provide a flash point for Congressional action, even though Senator Howard Metzenbaum of Ohio, former chairman of the Senate Antitrust Subcommittee, contended that "the deal raises serious antitrust questions." And the soundness of the financial structures of both enterprises, plus their vital importance to the nation's hope of sustaining technological leadership, made it even less likely that Rohatyn would be called on the Congressional carpet to explain how and why he had brought Welch and Bradshaw together.

The merger made its way safely through the regulatory shoals on June 9, 1986, just as this book was going to press, and the answer to the question of its enduring value to America should not be long forthcoming. In Welch's projection, only a year would be required to overcome the small dilutive effect of the purchase price on GE's total corporate earnings. After that, the positive impact of growing profits from RCA's insulated domestic operations would be felt. At RCA's Princeton laboratories, a new generation of television devices for the home had been in the developmental stage for several years. Would this intense scientific effort be supported by GE funding and brought to fruition, giving America once again leadership in the field David Sarnoff had pioneered? Would his early concept of an interactive information center for the home, capable like the telephone of sending as well as receiving intelligence, be high on GE's list for future attainment? Or would the Welch management decide that low profit margins in consumer electronics were not worth the effort, and perhaps abandon the field entirely? A few years should provide the answer to whether the merged company would succeed in coalescing two different, yet often complementary, cultures into a single, harmonious unit, providing America with another IBM of technology. Or whether it would lapse into simply another big, unwieldy conglomerate. Would it be, in *Electronic* magazine's phrase, "a new powerhouse or a stodgy behemoth?" That was the question Jack Welch would have to answer.

Had David Sarnoff been confronted with the fait accompli of GE and RCA together again, and had he achieved control of the merged entity, he would quite probably have shaped a different company than the one that will soon emerge. Its focus would have been purely on the electron. The household durables, the light bulbs, the airplane engines, would be sold off. The GE Corporate Research and Development Center in Schenectady, New York, would derive its guidance from his laboratories in Princeton. The recapture from the Japanese of leadership in consumer electronics would be a primary goal. The GE committee structure that had always irritated him would, if it still existed, be wiped out. A small corporate staff beholden to him alone would guide the empire from 30 Rockefeller Plaza, which he considered the epicenter of the industrial world. Like Agamemnon sailing against Troy in the Hellenic wars, he would offer any sacrifice to ensure the sempiternity of RCA. Never, one can hear him confide with steely inflection, would he capitulate to the heirs of the arch foe, Cordiner. The surviving company must be RCA—*the* RCA, as he always labeled it—the golden Radio of his youth, the RCA of monochrome and color, the RCA that cohered the nation with broadcast sound, the RCA that pursued the electron wherever it led. And, as always, the mission would be to innovate, to inspire, to create new wealth and new values where none existed before.

Selected Bibliography

Archer, Gleason L. *Big Business and Radio*. New York: American Historical Society, 1939.

Barnouw, Erik. *A Tower in Babel: A History of Broadcasting in the United States*, vol. 1. New York: Oxford University Press, 1966.

———. *Tube of Plenty: The Evolution of American Television*. New York: Oxford University Press, 1970.

Beard, Charles. *The Rise of American Civilization*. New York: Macmillan, 1927.

Bergmann, Carl. *History of Reparations*. Boston: Houghton Mifflin, 1927.

Bitting, Robert C., Jr. "Creating an Industry: A Case Study in the Management of Television Innovation." Master's thesis, MIT, Cambridge, Mass., 1963.

Boorstin, Daniel. *The American Experience*. New York: Random House, 1965.

Bucher, Elmer E. "History of Radio and Television Development in the U.S.A." David Sarnoff Library, Princeton, N.J., 1952.

———. "Short Wave Radio and David Sarnoff," vols. 1 and 2. David Sarnoff Library, Princeton, N.J., 1952–53.

———. "Radio and David Sarnoff," vols. 1–3. David Sarnoff Library, Princeton, N.J., 1953–54.

———. "Broadcasting and David Sarnoff," vols. 1–5. David Sarnoff Library, Princeton, N.J., 1956–57.

Campbell, Robert. *The Golden Years of Broadcasting: A Celebration of the First Fifty Years of Radio and TV on NBC*. New York: Scribner's, 1976.

Case, Josephine, and Everett, Owen D. *Young and American Enterprise*. Boston: Godine, 1982.

Chandler, Alfred D., Jr. *The Visible Hand: The Managerial Revolution in American Business*. Cambridge, Mass.: Harvard University Press, 1977.

Daniels, Josephus. *Annual Report of the Secretary of the Navy*. Washington: Navy Department, 1919.

Dreher, Carl. *Sarnoff: An American Success*. New York: Quadrangle/The New York Times, 1977.

Dunlop, Orrin E., Jr. *Radio's One Hundred Men of Science*. New York: Harper & Row, 1944.

Edel, Leon. *Writing Lives: Principia Biographica*. New York: Norton, 1984.

Federal Communications Commission. *Petition of Radio Corporation of America and National Broadcasting Company, Inc., for Approval of Color Standards for the RCA Color Television System*. Washington, D.C., 1953.

Federal Trade Commission. *Report on the Radio Industry*. Washington: Government Printing Office, 1923.

Goldmark, Peter, C. *Maverick Inventor: My Turbulent Years at CBS*. New York: Saturday Review Press/Dutton, 1973.

Halberstam, David. *The Powers That Be*. New York: Knopf, 1979.

Hoover, Herbert. *Memoirs*. New York: Macmillian, 1952.

Johnson, Paul. *Modern Times: The World from the Twenties to the Eighties.* New York: Harper & Row, 1983.

Kahn, E. J. *The World of Swope.* New York: Simon & Schuster, 1965.

Kilbon, Kenyon. "History of the RCA Laboratories," vols. 1 and 2. David Sarnoff Library, Princeton, N.J., 1965.

Kornitzer, Dr. Bela. *American Fathers and Sons.* New York, Harper & Row, 1952.

Lamont, Thomas W. Lamont Papers, Baker Library, Harvard Business School, Boston.

Lilienthal, David E. *The Journals of David E. Lilienthal.* vol. 7: *Unfinished Business, 1968–1971.* New York: Harper & Row, 1983.

Lyons, Eugene. *David Sarnoff: A Biography.* New York, Harper & Row, 1966.

Marek, George R. *Toscanini: A Biography.* New York: Atheneum, 1975.

Naval Department. *History of Communications: Electronics in the United States Navy.* Washington: Government Printing Office, 1963.

National Broadcasting Company. *A History.* New York: NBC Reference Library, 1966.

Paley, William S. *As It Happened: A Memoir.* New York: Doubleday, 1979.

Radio Corporation of America and RCA Corporation. Annual Reports, 1919–1984. New York: RCA Department of Information.

Reich, L. S. "Research Patents and the Struggle to Control Radio." *Business History Review,* 1977.

Sarnoff, David. *Looking Ahead: The Papers of David Sarnoff.* New York: McGraw-Hill Book Company, 1968.

Schacht, Hjalmar. *Confessions of the Old Wizard.* Boston: Houghton Mifflin, 1956.

Schairer, Otto S. "Patent Policies of the Radio Corporation of America." David Sarnoff Library, Princeton, N.J.

Sennett, Richard. *Authority.* New York: Vintage Books/Random House, 1981.

Sloan, Alfred P., Jr. *My Years with General Motors.* New York: Doubleday, 1964.

Tebbel, John. *David Sarnoff: Putting Electrons to Work.* New York: Encyclopaedia Press, 1963.

Udelson, Joseph H. *The Great Television Race: A History of the American Television Industry 1925–1941,* University, Ala.: University of Alabama Press, 1982.

Wakeman, Frederic. *The Hucksters.* New York & Toronto: Rinehart, 1946.

Waller, Judith C. *Radio: The Fifth Estate.* 2d ed. Cambridge, Mass.: Riverside Press, 1946.

Zaleznik, Abraham. "Why Authority Fails." *The Executive,* Cornell University, 1980.

White, Lynn. T. *Medieval Technology and Social Change.* Oxford: Clarendon Press, 1962.

Index